SHAPE

SHAPE

Talking about Seeing and Doing

George Stiny

The MIT Press
Cambridge, Massachusetts
London, England

MIT Press books may be purchased at special quantity discounts for business or sales promotional use. For information, please email special_sales@mitpress.mit.edu or write to Special Sales Department, The MIT Press, 55 Hayward Street, Cambridge, MA 02142.

This book was set in Stone Serif and Stone Sans by Asco Typesetters, Hong Kong.
Printed and bound in the United States of America.

Library of Congress Cataloguing-in-Publication Data

Stiny, George.
Shape : talking about seeing and doing / George Stiny.
    p.   cm.
Includes bibliographical references and index.
ISBN 0-262-19531-3 (alk. paper)
1. Shapes—Design—Art. 2. Geometrical models—Design—Art. 3. Creation (Literary, artistic, etc.)—Mathematics. I. Title.

QA445.S764   2006
745.4—dc22   2005043899

10 9 8 7 6 5 4 3 2 1

To Alexandra and Catherine

Contents

Acknowledgments

This book is about drawing shapes and calculating by seeing. This takes a lot of doing, and I've had plenty of help to make it happen. A number of people have commented on parts of this book with fresh and useful insights—alphabetically, Chris Earl, Jim Gips, Iestyn Jowers, Terry Knight, Lionel March, Bill Mitchell, Mine Ozkar, and Sherry Turkle. But in many other ways, the following pages show the results of the conversation Lionel March and I have had on design over the past twenty-five years. My real hope is that this book is just a preface to more seeing and doing, and talking about it in new ways. And then there are the figures, at least 1,126 of them by one count and more it seems by others. These computer drawings are almost entirely the work of Mine Ozkar—with the exception of a handful of scanned images, and Jacquelyn Martino's "tadpole" in part I and "no ambiguity" sign in part II and part III. With heroic intelligence and skill, Mine took my original pencil sketches and verbal descriptions through my continual changes to what's printed on the page. At times the process must have seemed interminable, but she kept at it with enthusiasm and an undiminished sense that drawings are as important as words. And in fact, that's another way to approach this book. Drawing then looking meld seeing and doing—there are shapes and words calculating together in an open-ended process in which you're always free to go on in your own way.

I would also like to thank The MIT Press for its patience, and especially Doug Sery for pushing softly but never doubting that it would all get done. A book like mine where drawings are used like words is a huge commitment, and I'm truly grateful that The MIT Press was willing to take it on with a full measure of its resources.

INTRODUCTION: TELL ME ALL ABOUT IT

Inasmuch as philosophers only are able to grasp the eternal and unchangeable, and those who wander in the region of the many and variable are not philosophers, I must ask you which of the two classes should be the rulers of our State?

—Plato

Looking at Shapes and Talking About It

I'm often asked to explain what I do, so that everyone understands. I used to take this seriously and try for a definite answer. Then I learned how hard the question is to get right. It's nearly impossible to satisfy yourself and others in the same way, especially when what you do can change. Some people work in recognized professions with time-honored names. It's OK to be an accountant, architect, artist, chemist, composer, doctor, engineer, lawyer, linguist, mathematician, philosopher, physicist, teacher, etc.—the list is endless, and if that's not enough, it's easy to add a few technical details to personalize the name of what you do. But this doesn't help—I can't tell you I'm a shape grammarist. That's no better than idly glancing around or just wandering away. Names don't always work—especially novel ones—and what a shape grammarist does may sound pretty confusing when it's described only in words. I'm really lost. I don't know how to answer the question to make you understand. Sooner or later, it's time to give up on a set reply. It means more to try whatever you can as you go on. I have two replies that I've used before, and they're a good start. First I have an answer that explains what I do using words and shapes—it's verbal and visual. I enjoy seeing things in new ways and saying why I think it's worthwhile, so I usually try this right away. My other answer is more autobiographical—it's a story I tell about how I got interested in looking at shapes and using them to design. There's no reason my answers shouldn't show what I do. Having two is already a lot like seeing shapes in alternative ways—shapes have parts that change as I go along. And it's the same for my answers—I can flip back and forth from one to the other whenever I want in a kind of gestalt switch. In fact, exposition and autobiography mix in my answers as they unfold. They're both personal and subjective—wandering freely from here to there with no end in sight is a good way to talk about shapes that also shows how they work, and it's probably the same for design. Neither what parts shapes have nor what's exposition and what's autobiography can be settled permanently. Making up your mind is a process that's always open-ended—what counts can be seen in many ways. It all adds up as I change my point of view and what I say about what I see.

Making sense of shapes concerns me most, and this motivates my answers. Shapes are things like these

that I can draw on a page with points, lines, and planes. They're the first three kinds of basic elements of dimensions zero, one, and two. Shapes made up of basic elements have parts that can be seen in many ways. That's what rules are for—to make sense of shapes and to change what I see. Showing how rules work is something I do a lot—it's all about seeing and doing. Then, there are also shapes made up of solids. These are another kind of basic element of dimension three. They extend beyond this page or any other surface. Solids go together to make the shapes of everyday experience—the shapes of things that are easy to hold and bump into—for example, the shape of this book at different times. And there are other shapes that extend farther than this page—shapes that include points, lines, and planes that are located in space.

After I introduce shapes in the following section, I use them in the story I tell about design. Both of my answers converge around similar ideas. If you want, you can try them in reverse order. I've already said this is easy to do. I like to read books by sampling them haphazardly. Usually, I read many at once, shuffling through them in this random fashion until I've finished everything. It's the same looking at shapes—you do it one way now and another way later. With shapes, there's always something new to see.

Answer Number One—What Do You See Now?

I'm obsessed with shapes. They're almost everywhere I look, and once they're in view I can't take my eyes off of them. I always wonder what I'm going to see next. Nothing looks the same for very long, but this needn't be as strange and confusing as it sounds. I know what to do with the ambiguity. Shapes change—I can see them in alternative ways anytime I choose—and I can use the novelty to design. It's an inexhaustible source of creative ideas.

The crux of what fascinates me is evident whenever I draw lines with pencil and paper. Suppose I draw the following shape the way an experienced draftsman would, drawing only the longest lines, perhaps in this counting sequence

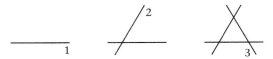

without thinking how the shape looks or worrying about what it means, and then see the equilateral triangle

You probably see the same triangle I do. It's obvious. And this seems perfectly natural. Only there's a big discrepancy between the actual lines I've drawn and what's potentially there to see. I didn't draw the sides of the triangle on purpose. They're all defined as I draw the last line

one side a little before the other two. The three sides of the triangle are shorter than my lines. They're formed when my lines intersect. No one intentionally put the triangle where it is. Yet it's there anyway, patiently waiting to be seen. I'm sure because I can trace over its sides—they're embedded in the lines I've drawn. And in the same way, other shapes are eventually parts of my shape, as well. There are a myriad of them that I've neither drawn nor thought of beforehand, and most of them have lines that aren't determined in intersections. There are plenty of other ways to embed lines in my lines, so that these segments interact meaningfully.

　　Consider a few examples. I can see abutting bits of hexagons

that change the way my shape looks. And then there are a lot of A's in three different orientations

that appear to shrink

But when I look rapidly again and again, A's flip back and forth with X's. They're also in three different orientations

and come in many sizes

It's animation—A's and X's move, yet the lines I've drawn don't. Is this a new kind of paradox? Shapes are supposed to be static, but mine is unstable. What I see holds still only if I fix it. I'm free to see anything I choose, as long as I stay within the lines. Parts are everywhere. And most of them—in fact, all of them I can see—are a complete surprise.

No matter how I draw the shape

it's going to be ambiguous. Whatever I do, lines fuse. I can't tell you what I've done simply looking at the result. There isn't any record either of what I do or of what I see in my drawing, and try as I might, I can't see how to use it to store (conserve) the details of anything that's happened before. Let me show you what I mean.

If I draw a line

———————

pick up my pencil, and then go on from where I left off

——— ———

it doesn't show that I've drawn two lines. I see only a single unbroken line

———————

In the same way, if I have two collinear lines

———   ———

and fill in the gap between them—connecting either end of one line with either end of the other—I'm left with a single line again

_____

not three. If I do this every way I can—there are four distinct possibilities that I can show schematically like this

_____ _____ _____

═══════════ _____ _____

_____ _____ ═══════════

═══════════ _____ ═══════════

—and then shuffle the results, I can't tell them apart by what I've done. They're all ex-actly the same. And once lines fuse, I can divide them as I please to see whatever there is. The line I have now may break in half

_____ _____

or anywhere many times, whether the pieces were originally drawn or not.

Fusing lines and dividing them are the flip sides of embedding. The ambiguity is inevitable, but this isn't a problem. I've learned to go on from what I've done with-out hesitating every time I see something new. I never have any doubts. I trust my eyes. In fact, changes can be so rapid and smooth that I don't notice them. Then if I want to check what's happening, I have to stop what I'm doing in midcourse. I have to remember everything that's transpired. But I may forget, with no one to remind me. It's lucky—what's lost in my head can't bother me. Memory just gets in the way, limiting the things I'm able to see here and now. That's how it is with definition and circumstance—getting it right or taking a chance on something new. The one fore-closes the other, offering the same old things in return. Whatever I see is new, even if I've seen it before. I guess shapes aren't for the constructionist. Adherence to original intent or prior use is senseless. And it's easy to see why.

There's no obvious change when you look at the shape in my original drawing

not knowing what I've done. What is there to notice? Nothing keeps you from seeing anything you want to see or doing as you like independent of anything that's hap-pened before. We can both use the drawing profitably without saying what parts it has. We don't need to agree on what we see. You never have to ask me how the drawing got there, or which of its lines were actually drawn. Remember, it's possible to forget. And even if I know, I can be wrong. For example, I may inadvertently rotate the drawing. Its history is as irrelevant as it is invisible. You're free to start over, or to change your mind. It's completely up to you. Whatever you see is right. There are no prior results to guide you. And it's no good trying to cheat. Analysis won't buy you anything. There's nothing to figure out in advance—parts aren't definite. Shapes are always ambiguous. It's no use asking me what I've done—I can't do your seeing for you. It's always the same. What you see is what you get.

This is like relaxed conversation with friends. Talking can be aimless—fluid, funny, full of irony, irreverent, illogical, lacking any definitions, frustrating, enjoyable, and so much more—and even so, very useful. You don't know what you're going to hear until you've heard it, and this goes for what you say. You just go on talking. And in the same way, you don't know what you're going to see until you've seen it, and this goes for what you draw. You just go on looking with your eyes. You've got the knack. But don't be complacent. It's never absolutely sure. An automatic process can be stopped. Then everything can go horribly wrong. It all falls apart. And when shapes are in pieces, their changes are in the past with nothing new in sight. Analysis decides what there is before I look. There's no more to see, only arrangements of pieces combined in alternative ways. These are easy to count, and the results are always the same. Analysis settles everything before it begins. Nothing is ever really new.

What can I do to stop you from using your eyes? Are there neat examples of this? Are they something to worry about? How do you go on seeing anyway? What does it mean when you've got the knack? These are some of the questions I'm going to answer. But like many good questions, their importance is established only as their answers unfold. Everything depends on shapes and their properties. I want to take advantage of these properties to get something new—to use shapes in a continuous process that doesn't check my ability to see in another way as I go on. Look at it like this. I want to have the ability to act on what I see, whatever it is and whenever I see it. Much more, I want to try and explain how all of this works. I want to figure out what's going on as shapes change.

Another one of my big questions is how to be creative in design. My guess is that shapes—drawing them and seeing them—have a lot to do with the answer. If designers use shapes in their work as sketches, drawings, models, and the like, then they can't do anything more than shapes allow. This is a lot for both hand and eye. Still, there are telling implications for creative activity. Understanding shapes is a useful place to start and outline the limits of design. First, there are experiments to run with pencil and paper, and other devices to get the facts right, so that seeing is never lost. This is like physics. There are phenomena—shapes and the lines, etc., that go to make them—and observation. Everyone can see what's happening and talk about it in his or her own way, while shapes ground the discussion in concrete experience. Shapes are there to see and to see again. Then, there's the mathematics to describe the many and varied results of these experiments, and to tie them together in a meaningful way that enhances rather than diminishes what's possible in drawing and making things. It doesn't work to say you understand design unless this explains what you can see and do with pencil and paper. These are the flip sides of what I want to show. There's a lot to see and a lot to say. And there's more.

Designers tell me they're special. It's evident that what they do when they're being creative—that is to say, designing in practice—distinguishes them from everyone else. When I first heard this, I wasn't really sure. I wondered how anyone could tell. Luckily, Donald Schon had a reason why—"reframing" and "back talk" make the difference. This is the ability to interact with your work in the same unstructured way you argue about something new in vague and shifting terms that haven't been defined—to reconfigure what you're doing before and after you act, to react freely as you see things in different ways, and to try new ideas in an ongoing process as you like. Designers work in this way. And in fact, everything about drawing confirms it. Shapes are the reason why—embedding and the consequent ambiguity make reframing and back talk inevitable. That's how they work. But Schon went on to say that designers aren't alone in their use of reframing and back talk. Reframing and back talk are hallmarks of all professional activity. Good doctors, lawyers, and planners use them, too. However, shapes still make a difference that may make designers right. There are devices for visual expression—shapes—and devices for verbal expression—symbols—that aren't the same. Designers may be special because they use the former before the latter. Only the difference isn't categorical, even if shapes and symbols classify professions, the mainly visual ones and the mainly verbal ones. There are some decisive relationships, and an unexpected kind of equivalence. Shapes are full of ambiguity—this explains reframing and back talk in design and may show something about how they work elsewhere. It's still a question of ambiguity and how to use it.

I'm going to develop a unified scheme that includes both visual and verbal expression with shapes and symbols, respectively. My scheme has two aspects. First, whenever I use symbols, it's a special case of using shapes. Embedding is restricted, so that it's identity. This may seem like a minor change—it's merely a question of whether the things you're dealing with have dimension zero or more, whether they behave like points or not—but the implications are huge. It makes all the difference. Take the shape

and assume that its three longest lines—the lines that I drew—are individual symbols. Then the triangle is no longer part of the shape—it simply isn't there to see—because its sides aren't embedded in these lines. There's no identity. (The elements in sets work in this way.) And for the same reason, A's and X's and bits of hexagons aren't parts of the shape either. The lines and their combinations are parts of the shape. That's all there is, and that's all there is to see

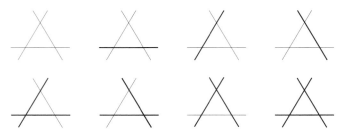

And second, my scheme implies a kind of inverse relationship. Anything I can do with shapes visually I can do just as well with given symbols, at least if shapes are described in certain ways that I'm going to specify. For example, symbols are all I need for shapes like these

made up of points, lines, and planes that I can draw on paper with a pencil and a ruler. This is really important—it means that computers can deal with shapes and ambiguity exactly as I do. A machine can see what I see no matter how it's drawn. What's there for me is there for the machine, and vice versa.

The way different kinds of expressive devices connect up in my scheme—whether they're visual and use shapes or verbal and use symbols—puts design with other kinds of professional practice. Design belongs with business, education, engineering, government, law, medicine, and planning, and with history, literary criticism, logic, mathematics, philosophy, science, and anything else you care to name. Designers may be as creative as you like—geniuses, in fact—but their reliance on visual devices doesn't exclude them from the ambit of expression fixed by everyone else in the course of their everyday activities. The scheme I have in mind makes it difficult if not impossible to believe in two cultures—one visual and the other verbal, separate and equal—that have nothing in common. Whatever people are doing—within professions and across them—they can always communicate. The expressive devices they use make their activities commensurable. And it's good to talk. But it's easy to be lazy when it's time to show someone else what you're up to in a straightforward way, or not to make the effort to see what the other guy is working on in his or her terms. Designing is a practical way of thinking (reasoning) in which seeing is key—that's its chief difference with many professions—but it's thinking all the same. Designing is what some people do. It goes with everything else people try.

Answer Number Two—Three More Ways to Look at It That Tell a Story

Getting Started—What I Wanted to Know That No One Could Tell Me

Let me begin early on. I've been interested in shapes for a long time. It all started when I was a child. Miss H—— was one of my teachers. She was the daughter of a renowned American painter, so I thought she would know the answer. I asked Miss H—— how to put lines on a blank sheet of paper. Everyone in my grade was good at drawing the usual stuff—cats, dogs, flowers, horses, houses, insects, lakes, mountains, people, rivers, trees, etc.—so my question wasn't about that. No, my question was about creative design, and pictorial composition and expression. Miss H—— understood this perfectly, and her answer was swift and sure.

If you don't know that, you'll never be an artist.

This surprised me then—I guess she wanted to be certain I wouldn't ask again—and it surprises me today.

Miss H—— was intelligent and educated. She had good ideas about verbal and symbolic material in basic subjects like reading, writing, and arithmetic, and also in geography, history, language, and science—in subjects with rigorous standards and tests to measure your strengths and weaknesses. You could always depend on the results. There were answers that were right or wrong and true or false. But when it came to the use of visual and spatial material in design—to seeing and drawing—I was supposed to know already, or not to worry too much that I didn't. Miss H—— was happy to let me figure out lines for myself, maybe even a little embarrassed that one of her pupils was worried about design. There wasn't anything to teach. Why didn't I see that? It was clear to everyone else. The standards were missing—what tests could you take to tell how well you were doing? There were no answers. It was all up to you.

Even so, Miss H—— wanted to help—that's what dedicated teachers do. So she tried again a little later in a desultory sort of way. Almost anything—meaningful or not—is better than nothing when you're trying to teach. But in fact, there were precedents for it, and it was much more than it seemed at first sight. Miss H—— asked everyone in my class to connect dots that were located randomly on a sheet of paper—we all tapped our pencils with our eyes tightly closed—to make nifty patterns that could be colored in. Miss H——'s exercise was like the occupations in Frederick Froebel's famous kindergarten method. And I enjoyed this for a while—what a marvelous discovery. Miss H—— had something useful to show us about points and lines, and how they combined to make planes. The progression from one dimension to the next was kind of neat—these were relationships to remember. But my interest didn't last. How did I decide which dots to connect? I could sift through the possibilities counting them out one by one, but this didn't answer my question. I was connecting points blindly to get them all without looking at what I was doing. Everything seemed to be the same—it was numbing. Something had to change. Dots weren't numbered to make surprise pictures

4.   .3

        10.   .9

        11.
5.   6. 1   .2

        7.   .8

like the ones in my game books. (I learned later that computers handled shapes in this way with lists of points, here, segmenting two squares with ten lines—they're units— end to end.) And where did the colors go? At least Paul Klee got it right in his *Pedagogical Sketchbook*: boundary elements—points and "medial" lines

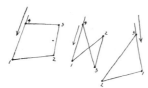

—formed meaningful planes. But I didn't know this. My results just didn't add up. Was this kind of counting a reductio ad absurdum? Miss H—— didn't say—it seemed to me, though, that it was what she wanted to show. It was something to discover on your own. My eyes were closed from the start—seeing and doing weren't tied. Figuring out the possibilities one by one in a mechanical process didn't go anywhere. It wasn't art unless you stopped to look, and then everything could change. Miss H——'s answer was the same, and now I knew why. There was a lesson to teach, and there was a lesson to learn—counting in this way wasn't seeing. That's why there were artists.

I was barely ten years old when I asked Miss H—— about lines, so I didn't know that my question was the private kind you kept to yourself. I looked around and asked again. And every time I did, I got the same kind of brusque answer I'd heard from Miss H——, or one of its mute derivatives. But I did get lucky. A year or so later, I found George Birkhoff's *Aesthetic Measure*. This was a real surprise! I turned the pages in awe—Birkhoff had a similar question and an articulate answer. Who was this guy, and how did it work?

Birkhoff was a famous mathematician at Harvard, and he knew that numbers could be used to describe how things change. He had great definitions of order—O— and complexity—C—and the guts to put them together in a wonderful formula

$$M = \frac{O}{C}$$

The measure—*M*—was perfect. You could use it to calculate with numbers to find the aesthetic value of polygonal shapes like these

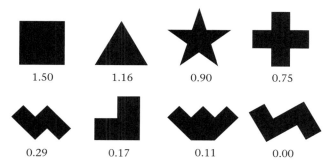

and other things such as ornaments, tilings, vases, music, and poems. So I calculated in earnest. But there were problems when I tried to see in the way Miss H—— implied I should. Shapes that looked different to me had the same aesthetic value. And the value of a shape didn't change when I saw it in a new way. One description didn't seem to be enough. You could just as well try Birkhoff's measure with your eyes closed. It was mechanical and misleading. There wasn't anything to see.

My question was still there, waiting to be answered. But my time hadn't been wasted—now I had Birkhoff's marvelous idea: that I could calculate to find an answer. Of course, this didn't seem to square with what Miss H—— had shown about counting. But I was young and didn't mind the inconsistency. Calculating was something I could do. And maybe it was too soon to tell if it worked. Only what could I use to calculate? Birkhoff's measure didn't work. Was there another formula that would—a kind of design equation that captured the right variables? No, that was out, too—it was still a single description. Seeing was the key. Maybe there was another way to paint by number that went beyond connecting dots. Suppose I could calculate with shapes. Was this calculating the way I learned in school? Was it just counting out? What did it mean to calculate anyway? There was more to find out.

Growing Up—How I Learned to Calculate

There are at least two ways to calculate that furnish practical answers to my original question about where lines go on a blank sheet of paper. There's the right mathematics *for* design, and the special mathematics *of* design. It's easy to see that my prepositions are opposites. They're almost mirror images—fo' and of. And if I concatenate them— the *r* is for reflection—they form the palindrome

forof

This is probably not what you expected. But it does use symbols to anticipate what I want to do with shapes. There are two sides to it. First, it suggests a way of calculating. I'm combining symbols in a deliberate way according to rules that define palindromes.

The mechanics of this is sketched a little later. And then, there's a trick that relies on a sudden switch in perspective. This is fairly common in puns, sight gags, and other practical things—for example, the word *bed* that children make with their hands

to distinguish the small letters *b* and *d*. There's just one way to do this—try a rotation. Well, I guess you can cross your arms to confuse *b* and *d* with *deb*. But maybe there's more to put this right. "Bed" is an especially nice mnemonic—the word *bed* looks like a bed, so the compound noun "word bed" contains what it means. The word

bed

is a word bed, and so, it appears, is forof. I'm going to play tricks like this as I calculate with shapes—in fact, every time I try a rule.

Ambiguity lets me change what I see as I talk about it:

—The shape

is a square and two diagonals. And it also shows triangular planes.
—Are you positive about that? Which planes are they?
—There are only four. They're easy to see. Sure, it's perfectly clear. Use your eyes.
—OK, let's see. You said it's a square and its diagonals. Sides and diagonals are single lines, aren't they? So you must be looking at the planes

with boundaries from these lines. What other choice is there?
—Don't be silly—use your eyes. What I said isn't what I see. Diagonals divide in four other triangles. My planes are obviously these

How can I do this with rules? And what does it mean for calculating? Let's get back to my distinction between the mathematics *for* and the mathematics *of* design, and see how this works out in the normal way.

(Seeing words for what they mean instead of as strings of letters for sounds is nothing new. I know a poet / visual artist who designed a wonderful word door

d r

as a way into or maybe out of her eye. Making things so that you see what they mean is harder than it looks. A lot of people have tried—the logical empiricist Otto Neurath is a recent member of this group—but it hasn't caught on. Nonetheless, the art is evident in Ezra Pound's eccentric enthusiasm for Ernest Fenollosa's *The Chinese Written Character as a Medium for Poetry*:

The Egyptians finally used abbreviated pictures to represent sounds, but the Chinese still use abbreviated pictures AS pictures, that is to say, Chinese ideogram does not try to be the picture of a sound, or to be a written sign recalling a sound, but it is still the picture of a thing; of a thing in a given position or relation, or of a combination of things. It *means* the thing or the action or situation, or quality germane to the several things that it pictures.

Fenollosa was telling how and why a language written in this way simply HAD TO STAY POETIC; simply couldn't help being and staying poetic in a way that a column of English type might very well not stay poetic.

As a shape, bed is asymmetric, and as a word, it's read from left to right. Still, I can't distinguish head and foot looking at it from the end or the side. The bed is firm, and written in this way simply HAS TO STAY FIRM. I like to think that poets know that nothing has to stay the same and take advantage of this. So a poet's claim that something does is pretty fantastic—pictures keep language poetic. I guess this makes poetry visual. At least pictures and words connect up. But are pictures of things and their relations shapes? What does

show as lines and planes? And there's an added dimension, too. Four small triangles make a pyramid with its apex or vanishing point where the diagonals cross—these alternatives may distinguish Chinese and Renaissance perspective—and four large triangles make a Necker-cube-like tetrahedron with its apex at either top corner of the square. Try and resolve the right triangles now. Things (parts) and relations in shapes aren't set once and for all. Which way does bed go? Poetry doesn't change—ambiguity makes the difference.)

I can calculate in design without saying much about designing. To begin with, I can analyze designs in a variety of ways. For example, I can look at their physical performance in mathematical models, or I can "rationalize" them—divide them up into components that I can manufacture and assemble. But analysis isn't the only use for calculating in design. I can be more synthetic. I can try functions or parametric representations to enhance my creativity. Equations define lines, curves, and surfaces that are used in pictures, buildings, and many other things that are admired today.

Computers are so good at this that I don't have to worry about any of the details. I can simply rely on experts and use the results. There's a lot of this in design right now. But personally, I'm more likely to try things I understand.

Three linear equations in the standard form

$$y = mx + b$$

define the lines that contain the shape

I can say how this works in a parametric model, but it's really the kind of exercise Miss H—— assigned. There's no design. The equations alone don't tell me what to see in the lines or what to do about it. They merely give me some stuff that might be valuable, to see and do with as I please. How do I see the triangle, or this A and that X? Suppose I've got a reason—articulate or not—to change the shape

into the shape

What makes this possible? I'd like to do more than borrow from mathematics. Good results answer the question "What kind of mathematics is useful in design?" But perhaps this isn't all I can do. Isn't there a mathematics of seeing and doing when it comes to designing? Shorten the question to "What kind of mathematics is design?" Better yet, "What kind of mathematics works when I don't know what I'm going to see and do next?" Can I look at designing as calculating in its own right? What kind of calculating is it if shapes are made in the ordinary way with pencil and paper—when thinking is drawing and seeing—with no equations and numbers?

This leads straight to the mathematics *of* design and to the corollary

design is calculating

that I want to explore. Right now this is no more than a heuristic, or perhaps just a metaphor to get things started. But by the end of this book, I want to have transformed it into a rigorous statement of fact with axiomatic certainty. Look at the verbal formula

seeing and doing

that I've already invoked a few times. It gives a pretty good idea of what I hope to accomplish. The formula translates easily into a rule of the form

see $x \rightarrow$ do y

where the variables x and y can have all sorts of things as values. But for most of my purposes, it's enough for x and y to be shapes. For example, the rule

that rotates a triangle turns the shape

into the shape

in a single step with two stages. I see the triangle

and trace it out. It's part of the shape

because its sides are embedded in the lines of the shape. And then I erase the triangle and draw another one

I'm going to be saying a lot about how to use rules like this automatically, so that seeing parts and replacing them by erasing lines and drawing more go together in a mechanical process in which the details are all worked out. And I'm going to show that being mechanical in this way and being creative aren't opposed when you calculate with shapes. It's mostly a question of getting embedding right, so that you're reasoning with your eyes. My rules let you see. But first, I need to say a little more about rules as they're normally defined and used to calculate. This takes me back to what happened as I grew up.

When I tried Birkhoff's measure, I knew how to calculate with numbers. That's what you learn in grade school and later. I was good at it. Numbers made Birkhoff's formula easy, yet it wasn't design. There wasn't anything to see, only to count. I had to find something else. I learned what I needed as an undergraduate at MIT. It still wasn't design, but it got me started in the right way. Marvin Minsky taught symbol manipulation—he explained Turing machines, Post's production systems and their nifty way of defining rules, and sundry equivalent or otherwise related devices. It was amazing how many different ways there were to calculate. The details varied, but a single idea tied it all together: one way or another, calculating is combining symbols according to given rules. An easy example is enough to show how this works.

Suppose I have two symbols, left and right angle brackets $\langle$ and $\rangle$, and I want to combine them in strings, so that left and right brackets are paired in the way left and right parentheses normally are. I'm after strings that have the following form

$\langle\ \rangle$

$\langle\langle\ \rangle\rangle$

$\langle\ \rangle\langle\ \rangle$

$\langle\langle\ \rangle\langle\ \rangle\rangle\rangle$

I'm using angle brackets instead of parentheses because the brackets look like something I'm going to do later on. You're probably getting used to this by now. One way to define strings of brackets is to calculate. I can use the two rules

(1) $\langle\ \rangle \rightarrow \langle\langle\ \rangle\rangle$

(2) $\langle\ \rangle \rightarrow \langle\ \rangle\langle\ \rangle$

Both rules let me replace the string $\langle\ \rangle$ whenever it's contained in another one, that is, if $\langle\ \rangle$ is part of it. When I use rule 1, $\langle\ \rangle$ is replaced with the new string $\langle\langle\ \rangle\rangle$. The idea is to put a pair of brackets around $\langle\ \rangle$, or equivalently to move the brackets in $\langle\ \rangle$ apart to insert a pair. And when I use rule 2, $\langle\ \rangle$ is replaced with $\langle\ \rangle\langle\ \rangle$. A pair of brackets is added either to the left or to the right of $\langle\ \rangle$. (When these rules add brackets to a string, everything else in the string moves to make room for them. Practical—concrete—details are ignored. This won't be the case for shapes. They aren't abstract in this way.) I always start to calculate with the same string $\langle\ \rangle$. It's the shortest string in which angle brackets are paired correctly. I can use my rules three times like this

$\langle\ \rangle \Rightarrow \langle\langle\ \rangle\rangle \Rightarrow \langle\langle\ \rangle\langle\ \rangle\rangle \Rightarrow \langle\langle\ \rangle\langle\langle\ \rangle\rangle\rangle$

  step 1   step 2   step 3

to generate the string $\langle\langle\ \rangle\langle\langle\ \rangle\rangle\rangle$ with four pairs of brackets. The double arrow $\Rightarrow$ indicates the process of applying a rule. The rule is used to replace the string $\langle\ \rangle$ that's bold. In step 1, I use rule 1, in step 2, rule 2, and in step 3, it's rule 1 once more. Every time I apply a rule, I define a well-formed string of brackets. And I can continue from where I've left off to get more strings of the same kind. Or I might want to start calculating from $\langle\ \rangle$ again to get other strings. That's all there is to it. That's all it takes to calculate anything that can be calculated. Find rules for palindromes. It isn't any harder than angle brackets. Palindromes are a special case in which only rule 1 is tried: $\langle\langle\ldots\langle\ \rangle\ldots\rangle\rangle$. Mark the centers of strings to insert matched symbols there.

Minsky didn't stop with symbol manipulation. He had other things to say, too. There was the bigger idea that rules might describe how we think. Minsky was passionate about this, and when I was a student, he showed it in his very public and uproariously impolite argument with Hubert Dreyfus—it was about what computers can and can't do. Dreyfus was one of my instructors in the humanities, and he didn't see how computers could think. The Danish philosopher Søren Kierkegaard and others showed why. It was about "results"—units and counting the distinct ways they combine. It seemed that there were things you could teach and count, and things you couldn't. Dreyfus and Miss H—— were saying the same kind of thing, but Dreyfus was explicit about it and had Kierkegaard to back him up. At the time, though, it didn't matter. It was all emotion. Dreyfus saw through what Minsky was trying to do—there was more to thinking than symbols in the way they're normally used—but Minsky wasn't listening to what Dreyfus was trying to say. It was the perfect academic argument—thinking was out! The line was drawn—you were either on the right side or on the wrong side of a new technology. Dreyfus never had a chance at MIT. Yet even today, no one knows for sure whether computers can think or not. It's the kind of question that will probably be resolved with a set definition. But the answer may be beside the point. If computers can't think, it won't be for the kind of reasons Dreyfus gives—because his reasons are included in calculating. Kierkegaard wasn't enough, even with the instinctive Miss H——. This was evident as soon as I started to play around with shapes and rules, and to get results—going from symbols to shapes changed everything. The difference was palpable. Calculating with shapes was an example of Dreyfus's way of thinking, and it let me see in the way artists do. The switch from symbols to shapes was my big idea—it really worked—but it was still a few years off.

Meanwhile, I heard Noam Chomsky talk about language. I learned that generative grammars—these are systems of rules something like Post's—show how words go together to make sentences. Almost everyone uses language in a creative way—you can say and understand things that you haven't said or heard before. But how is this possible? It's certain that no one knows every sentence in advance. Generative grammars provide the answer. With a limited number of rules to combine words, I can generate an unlimited number of new sentences. It's the same kind of recursive process I used to define strings of angle brackets. But what about design? It's creative, too. You can always make something different, but how? Chomsky's grammars got me thinking— why not shape grammars for languages of designs? With a finite number of rules, I might be able to generate an indefinite number of things. They might even hang together in the same style. I could finally say how to put lines on a blank sheet of paper. I could understand creativity in design.

When I started thinking about grammar and language in design, I had no idea that it was a bad mistake. From the start, people missed what I was trying to do. It's true that I had the following analogy in mind—

(1)   shape grammar : designs :: generative grammar : sentences

But sometimes, analogies imply a lot more than they should. My idea was that a grammar had a limited number of rules that could generate an unlimited number of different things, and that the resulting language was the set of things the rules produced. I didn't think that designs were sentences, but instead that grammars could generate both sentences and designs—whatever they were. Was this kind of creativity enough to make a language? It was only half of the formula. There were also words and sentences, and correct syntax and proper usage. Words and usage—was there anything to say about them in design?

On the one hand, what corresponds to words in design? There was plenty of loose talk around about the vocabulary of design—I still hear it today—only it was all pretty vague and never amounted to much. And I'm hardly blameless in this regard. Early on, I used vocabularies of shapes to define shape grammars, and for spatial relations to design with play blocks—cubes, oblongs, pillars, etc.—from Froebel's building gifts. This was standard practice calculating and designing. It was a mistake, and I said so both times in a wimpy sort of way. I wasn't ready to risk anything new. It challenged what I thought I knew from Turing and Post and from many designers. It was easier to be conventional and wrong. And it helped when I began to teach design. I learned that students were trying to define personal vocabularies in the rite of passage from novice to professional. In the same way, sophomores try to define their terms to resolve their endless arguments. But neither learning to design nor deciding to agree seems to have a lot to do with definitions—they're just a way to postpone thinking, never mind seeing. Definitions come afterward, when they don't matter. That's the problem I had with vocabularies. It's plain common sense. There are no words in design. For the analogy

(2)   designs : x :: sentences : words

—or in any subsequent refinement involving smaller features in phonetics or semantics—there's no rule of three to solve for the unknown x. It's undefined.

Susanne Langer explained why more than fifty years ago, when she tried to distinguish two separate kinds of symbolism—discursive forms having to do with language and the logic in Ludwig Wittgenstein's *Tractatus*, in a word, calculating, and then presentational forms having to do with drawing and correlative things in the arts.

Clearly, a symbolism with so many elements, such myriad relationships, cannot be broken up into basic units. It is impossible to find the smallest independent symbol, and recognize its identity when the same unit is met in other contexts. Photography, therefore, *has no vocabulary*. The same is obviously true of painting, drawing, etc. There is, of course, a technique of picturing objects, but the law governing this technique cannot properly be called a "syntax," since there are no items that might be called, metaphorically, the "words" of portraiture.

No words, no syntax, no sentences. Language is out of the question for design. That's OK with me. I'm not interested in language in that way. I can live without analogy number 2. But not so fast. The implications are broader. With no basic units—symbols that can be recognized wherever they appear—there isn't any way to calculate. Remember, calculating is using rules to combine symbols. What symbols? Without words, I can't calculate. My naive account of grammar and language in analogy number 1 doesn't bypass analogy number 2. Grammars need words to generate sentences. If 2 doesn't work, then neither does 1. Unless I can do something about units, it's either calculating or thinking, either counting or seeing, and Kierkegaard, Dreyfus, and Miss H———. There's nothing I can say about design. If you're lucky, you can do it, but this can't be taught. There's nothing to learn—no words, no syntax, no sentences. At least that's how it looks right now. Surely, there has to be a way to go on. Otherwise, there's only a mystery.

Then on the other hand, what can I say about usage? Are there rules that control technique? Langer acknowledges technique in drawing and the like, and a law governing it—as long as the law isn't syntax. Nearly all of the designers I know reject rules. It's easier to pick things out with a test than to generate them directly. Perhaps a test would work to check for good and bad technique in design. Why not Birkhoff's aesthetic measure? There are a handful of definitions for order and complexity that don't depend on words and syntax. And in fact, I can use the definitions in reverse to actually make things with high scores. If this works, I have an effective assay of technique—but it isn't a real option. The results don't match what I see. It's probably a lousy idea anyway. Everyone I ask agrees. Usage is impossible to gauge in design, even if it doesn't depend on words and syntax.

Words and usage don't work. They're dead ends in design. But let's look again before giving up. What can I do about rules and calculating, and numerical measures? First, I'm not keen on numerical measures of any kind, even if they distinguish good and bad technique. I'm not going to use them. In the past, I toyed with measures like Birkhoff's that did a lot of counting, only with algorithms, complexity, and information theory—perfectly modern stuff. They weren't any better—just one kind of description won't do. I'm glad I've moved on. I was wrong. So maybe there's another way to think about rules and calculating. If I can find a way to calculate without units—with rules that don't combine symbols—everything should be OK. I can get designs and not bother about words and syntax. I need to show that analogy number 1 and analogy number 2 are independent. And if I can, rules may govern technique—they might characterize usage. I could get back to words and syntax. What if they're defined when I stop calculating as a kind of retrospective summary of what I've done—perhaps in topologies that I can update as I go on? Suppose words and syntax aren't fixed but change—smoothly or in jumps—with ongoing practice. They're harmless as an afterthought, and they might help in teaching to trace a designer's intentions or to compare styles. That's when vocabulary is useful. It's only if I have to say what words and syntax are ahead of time that I have a problem. Designing isn't combining things anyway. How do I know what I'm going to use until I start? Where's the creativity?

I don't mean in the recursive sense Chomsky has in mind of forming combinations of elements from a given vocabulary—even if it grows with new words—but in the intuitive, open-ended sense, expected in the arts, of making new things where meaningful elements are never finally resolved. Can I apply rules to calculate without combining symbols? Can I give up on vocabulary, unless it's defined retrospectively? Are words and syntax necessary?

Thinking about these questions and others of the same kind—how to deal with the unknown x in the analogy

designs : x :: sentences : words

while I calculate—is another way to approach this book. But before I get to the answers, there's the question of grammar and language. Do I want to talk about them in design? Should I insist on the analogy

shape grammar : designs :: generative grammar : sentences

I don't care, as long as I can calculate without units or symbols, and so sidestep x. It's simply a matter of words. In logic and linguistics, grammar and language refer to rules and sets. If nothing is implied about vocabulary, then this is harmless. I'm easy about shapes and what I see, so why not about words and what they mean? And my use of grammar and language shows the origin of some of my ideas. Still, I'm ready to avoid both words for the sake of rules and using them to calculate with shapes. I started with shapes and rules, and Turing and Post. That's the history—in a word, rules. Yet language provides another way out that neither bends meaning nor bans words. Shape grammar is ironic, if grammar is vocabulary and syntax, and shapes are to see. It's an easy relationship—ambiguity in shapes is irony in words. What I say reinforces how I see. There's meaning in both.

Going On—How I Stopped Counting and Started to See

The problem is to figure out how to calculate without units or symbols. The solution is to see how to calculate with shapes. This has been my main interest ever since my student days. I've been lucky. I made a career out of it. There's a lot to see in shapes that's kept me going. I haven't seen the last of them yet. And I don't expect to anytime soon. But how I learned to calculate with symbols and rules isn't something to dismiss. It's too important for that. Rather, it's something to extend to shapes, so that the differences between shapes and symbols can be understood and reconciled. Symbols may be enough to handle language and most of thought. There are many people who think so. And I'm happy to think they've got it right, unless you want to design. Then thinking is seeing, and calculating means using your eyes. From what I've seen, learning how to calculate with your eyes isn't that easy. This isn't because it's hard to do—it's not—but because it works in a curious way. At times, calculating with shapes may not seem like calculating at all. In fact, it's always tempting to give up on shapes and simply calculate in the normal way with symbols. It's comfortable—there's a lot to do and you feel good about it. Getting used to something new is hard. You have to see how it works and really try it, that's what makes it fun.

Symbols are OK, but shapes do something different. They don't always look the same. Shapes are subtle and devious. They combine to confuse the eye and to excite the imagination. They fuse and then divide in surprising ways. There are endless possibilities for change. How to deal with this novelty while you calculate—neither limiting the alternatives nor frustrating the process—is the test. It's a question of what calculating would be like if Turing and Post had been painters instead of logicians, although Turing was a photographer. Painting and calculating together—what an exotic idea. Only the idea might not be that strange. Herbert Simon proposes as much in his speculative account of social planning without goals in *The Sciences of the Artificial*. Painting and language are creative in the same way. They rely on "combinatorial play" with simple things to make complex ones. There are symbols, and rules to combine them. (In fact, there's more. Chomsky and Simon are both keen on describing things— sentences and pictures—as parenthesis strings, that is to say, in "trees" or, identically, in "hierarchically organized list structures.") But my idea is not to show that painting is like calculating in Turing's sense—it's to make Turing's kind of calculating more like painting. This means giving up on symbols. And more, it means showing how my calculating as painting and Simon's painting as calculating are related. This is what my scheme for visual expression with shapes and verbal expression with symbols is all about.

The best way to see what's involved here is to try to use symbols to calculate with shapes. The trick is to segment shapes into lowest-level constituents—these are the symbols or units that are necessary for syntax—and to combine these constituents using rules in the same way that angle brackets are combined to define strings. Analogy number 2 is

shapes : lowest-level constituents :: sentences : words

I've given the unknown *x* a name, but the difficult task remains of defining the constituents to use. Which way of dividing shapes into parts makes the most sense in terms of what I want to calculate? Which analysis works best? The main difficulty may already be obvious. In design, it may not be evident what you want to calculate before you start. You may not know until you're finished. The constituents may change dynamically—is this possible?—as long as calculating goes on. That's one reason why the unknown *x* is undefined, why the vocabulary of design is so elusive. But let's try to find fixed constituents anyway, just to see how it comes out.

What constituents should I use to describe the shape

if I want to calculate with it? Well, it's going to depend on the rules I use—both the rules I apply to the shape itself and the rules I apply to the shapes produced from it in an indefinitely distant future. Maybe rules are like this

if there's a triangle, then rotate it

where a triangle is some combination of constituents. This is a symbolic version of the rule

that's defined for shapes. I've already shown how I wanted this kind of rule to work, so that it applies in terms of embedding, and erasing and drawing lines. But right now it makes sense to distinguish the triangle in the shape

to calculate in the right way with symbols. Three lines

were all I needed to draw the shape, except that a constituent for each line won't do for what I want. There's no triangle. So why not describe the shape as a triangle and three little angles that look like the angle brackets ⟨ and ⟩

That's good, but a triangle is normally defined to have three sides. So three lines and three angles might be better yet

And I may as well divide the angles up to make everything lines

The consistency is nice—the lowest-level constituents are lines of two different lengths—and I can find the triangle according to its standard definition—it's a polygon with three sides—and move it around. I'm also lucky. There are A's

and bits of hexagons

if I want rules to move them around, too. But what happened to the X's? I can't make them out with the lines I've got. Should I go back and segment the triangle in another way, so that it's cut up into angles? That's not a bad idea. Now I really have a triangle

(Or should I say trilateral? Words work in funny ways, too.) The whole shape is a kind of two-dimensional string of angle brackets. This is neatly consistent again—constituents are all the same angles. And I can find X's

not as intersecting lines, but as touching angles. That's a novel result. I hadn't thought of X's that way. Only now the A's and the bits of hexagons have disappeared. I need to reconcile the alternative ways I've segmented the shape

The divisions in

must also be divisions in

This gives the new constituents

There's a triangle

—a rather extraordinary one with six lines, but it's a triangle nonetheless—and there are the A's I want

each with eight lines, X's

with four lines apiece—they're sides of angles and also halves of intersecting lines, and that's a nice addition—and bits of hexagons

also with four lines. Everything is OK. I've got the right constituents, even if the definitions I need to pick out the things I want—a triangle, A's, X's, and bits of hexagons—are a little strange. That's just how constituents work. I can always explain how natural it is. I can define all of the things that interest me now and lots more that may interest me later—there's the chance to be creative—with a single constituent that occurs in different places. The numbers on a calculator display are a familiar example of this. There's something really seductive about it, and the effort to do it is very satisfying. I feel smart—well, at least awfully clever.

But let's suppose I want to find any A or X that I can see. What about these

Suppose calculating is truly visual, so that whatever I see is something a rule can find. Are any constituents going to work when I have to define them in this way? I might try to get around this by experimenting to determine what I can discriminate—I could do the psychophysics—and not try for constituents that go beyond the results. But then I'll need multiple rules for A's and X's that are segmented differently. And it's a blind anyway. I haven't solved the problem. I've simply avoided having to deal with it for now, until I get better glasses that let me see a bit more. Or maybe I can use rules that change constituents into new ones as I calculate. That's a good idea. Only I still have to figure things out to define these rules. Sometimes, this can get pretty complicated. Seeing seems much different. Why can't I calculate like that?

And there's a bigger problem to solve, too. It also depends on how sharp my vision is, only not as before. Stronger glasses aren't going to help, not even a tiny bit. My prevision is what matters. When I started to segment the shape

I said I had to do so first in terms of the rules I want to apply to it, and then in terms of the rules I want to apply to the shapes that are generated from it. I may have to use constituents for the shape—or rules to define constituents—that don't make sense now but that make sense later on. I need constituents to calculate, so I can't calculate with shapes to see how things are going to turn out—assuming there's a definite end. What should I do? Unless I'm a seer, this is a real bind. And in fact, I've been cheating all along to see what my rules do when they apply to shapes—for example, rules for a triangle, A, and X. It seems my rules work unofficially, but let's do it right.

Suppose I want to segment the shape

in terms of the rule

that rotates any of its three squares 45 degrees. This is a lot trickier than it looks. The sides of the small square cut sides of the large squares in half. Nonetheless, squares aren't four lines and eight lines apiece

as you might naturally intuit or guess from the way I segmented the shape

It's difficult to imagine all that's needed for everything to work out—the squares are twenty lines and forty lines instead

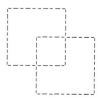

because of what happens when my rule is used to rotate both of the large squares, and how rotating the small square factors into this. Lines diffuse in analysis, as different parts (squares) interact dynamically. Look at my shape fade away (disintegrate) into finer and finer constituents. What I can draw with eight lines, and represent as sixteen equal segments to rotate each of its three squares, takes no less than eighty segments of two incommensurable lengths to describe completely. Every side of a large square corresponds with the palindrome

ababaababa

where $b = a\sqrt{2}$. The segments *a* and *b* in the string are related as the side and the diagonal of a square—this is too hokey to be wrong. Moreover, substrings are palindromes at *aba* and a half. Try these divisions and see how nicely segments align—especially when both of the large squares are rotated, so that sides match reversed at *aba*

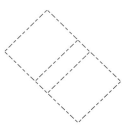

New relationships click as squares go around, rotating them in different ways connects everything to everything else.

These are hard earned results that should last. Yet they don't repeat in the shape

in which a small square is added to complete a copy of the shape

The number of segments looks to double in this way. Still, meaningful (exact) divisions are elusive—at least if I want to go on calculating with the options my rule provides, and do nothing extra. There's too much happening to get it to mesh. The five palindromes I need now, that is to say, the divisions I have to make symmetrically, clash. Specifically, the palindrome

ababaababaababaababa

that reflects my original one has substrings that are palindromes at *aba*, a quarter, and a half, but not at *ababaa* where sides of the largest squares overlap after they're rotated. This seems little to fix, only I can't find a way that doesn't loop forever. It's no use permuting *a* and *b* or refining segments in differences—restoring symmetry in one place breaks it in another. What works for three squares doesn't work for five squares. Langer's negative account of syntax for photography, painting, drawing, etc. is all the more persuasive as the outcome of a finite example that doesn't rely on "myriad elements and relationships." Words (segments) and sentences (palindromes) aren't set all at once and once and for all, as I rotate five conspicuous squares in twelve lines 45 degrees at a time. I can count the possibilities—looking at one, then drawing another—in an easy enumeration in which parts change. Sensitivity isn't necessary to see what's what. Yet the process is still ineffable. There's plenty that can't be said precisely in words. (My example takes time and may thereby imply something similar for music and dance—can it be there are no notes?) I guess I should settle for approximate results with itsy-bitsy units of equal length. This is the standard solution—it's being digital—and it's OK. Generality and convenience recommend it, but nonetheless, it's born of desperate practicality—meaning dissolves when segments are all the same. (Equal units answer to a single symbol, so strings and substrings are trivially palindromes. That's why units line up—approximately—as squares are rotated.)

Analysis gets off to a great start with the shape

only to fail with the next shape

and more spectacularly with succeeding shapes in the series

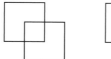   . . .

They're formed adding diminishing squares as before, but now nothing scales. New divisions aren't defined reflecting palindromes. This can be fixed by alternating segments that double, yet it doesn't pan out in other ways. Exact segments can't be sequenced from the start, so that I can calculate according to my rule. Meaningless units of equal length remain the lone choice. They work without helping, no matter how fine they are. This kind of analysis is blind.

Of course, once you're used to meaning, the habit is hard to break. Everything seems so senseless. But problems of the kind I've been discussing may not be as bad as they look, as long as I'm willing to calculate more than I see. After all, generating sentences requires more than speaking. There's plenty beneath the surface. If I'm sure about what's happening and positive the future will be the same—that's the perennial rub—I can use rules to replace constituents with others. As I go on, what's there and the way it's arranged may vary—but I know how. For rotating squares, two rules and their inverses work for constituent lines:

(1)   A line can be divided in half

————— —————

(1′)   Two halves can be combined.

(2)   A line be divided at $(2 - \sqrt{2})/2$

——— ————————

(2′)   The two pieces in rule 2 can be combined.

It's worth being explicit here about what I've been doing from the start, and to emphasize that arrangements of constituents and rules to define them are given symbolically (schematically) with words and diagrams. I can't draw constituents in shapes—lines fuse whenever they're combined. With shapes, the four rules I have all look alike. Visually, they're the same identity

—a line is a line. And certainly, these aren't the only rules I need for constituents. There are rotations of squares, as well, and many details to avoid unwanted results. These are mostly artifacts—products of abstraction that block my way unless I plan for them in advance. But the details aren't automatic—filling them in takes more than your eyes. Shapes aren't the same when constituents are defined. Structure intrudes. Logic becomes a necessary distraction.

The successors of the shape

show that finite limits on what I can see and do needn't make a difference. Words and syntax may not work even when I can draw everything. Just turning a handful of squares defies analysis, at least for exact constituents permanently arranged from the start. But perhaps it's worth seeing again how easy it is for analysis to fail when there's more to draw. I can use my original rule

to rotate squares 45 degrees with other rules like this one

to translate squares. Then together, the shapes in this series

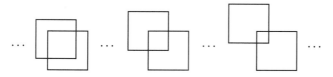

show what's wrong, in the way A's and X's do when the free ends of lines are cut. Lines can be divided internally anywhere at all when one shape is moved over another. And there are nice surprises

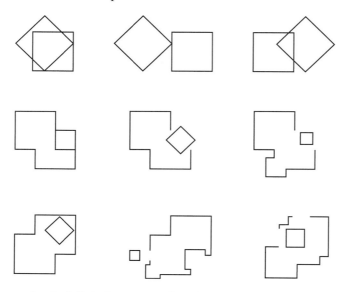

—also indefinitely many—that do the same thing as A's and X's. Squares and other parts combine in myriad relationships, with no meaningful constituents in sight. This has the feel of design. Certainly, it isn't classical—there's no module. But enough is enough. I don't want to think about constituents anymore—the whole idea is simply ridiculous. Is it worth missing all that seeing and drawing allow in order to calculate? No one can see everything in advance and plan for all of it all the time. And even when this kind of seeing is possible, there may not be a decent plan. Shapes aren't usefully described with constituents that are defined beforehand in some kind of precalculating. Seeing and drawing work perfectly without rational (analytic) thought. Lines fuse and divide. They meld without a trace of the past before I can look again. Then what you see is what you get. Analysis interferes, giving only approximate results, sometimes in what they show and always in what they don't. And if you're still not swayed, I have other examples. They're endless. There are nested polygons—triangles, squares, etc.—stars, and superstars. The wonderful surprises they contain are highlighted throughout this book. There's nothing more than meets the eye.

Shapes and symbols don't mix. Still, I need the latter to calculate. Is there anything I can do? Well, what I've been doing is fine, as soon as I give up on meaning and trying to understand what's happening. The best way to solve problems with shapes is to forget about seeing. I can grind things up uniformly into finer and finer constituents independent of calculating, so that whatever I want to see is a combination of these tiny bits. At least I can approximate what I want to see. There's a final granularity beyond which I'm blind. That's true. But if the bits are small enough, it doesn't matter. There are just a lot of them, and computers are fine with a lot of things. Anything I want to see—anything I want to calculate with—can be given as an appropriate collection of bits. I don't like any of this. In spite of its remarkable success in science and engineering—especially now in computer graphics, imaging, and visualization—the approach is ugly. But why not enjoy the results? Shapes made up of bits are ugly only underneath. What difference does it make? What I see is spectacular. Why am I so worked up?

The idea that shapes are bits bothers me because it violates almost every intuition I've ever had about seeing. I want to use these intuitions and develop them as much as I can. I would like to figure out how they work when I look at shapes, so that I can utilize them effectively when I calculate. In fact, I'm sure that as long as I take them seriously, I'm calculating, only I'm doing it visually in a special way where embedding is key every time I try a rule. This lets me use my eyes.

Giving up on shapes in a technique that isn't visual isn't a sensible option, when seeing is decisive in creative activity. I don't think about shapes in terms of the bits that combine to make them. There's no difference between what there is—merely bits—and what I see—lines, etc.—and do. Reality doesn't lurk behind appearance. There isn't a hidden structure under the surface to stop me from doing what I want. There's nothing to understand that my eyes can't tell me. I think about shapes directly in terms of how they look, and how they change if I look again. What you see is what you get. And it's all you ever need if there's embedding.

I could go on in this vein, but I wouldn't be any more convincing. Whatever I may see, simply grinding shapes to bits really and truly works. Whether or not you like this kind of mince surely depends on your personality as much as anything else. If you're even a little bit like me, you're going to be a curmudgeon. Bits (standard units) make me grumpy. I'm too attached to meaning to settle for anything less.

Of course, there are other ways to look at shapes in terms of bits—at least in terms of points that can't be ground more finely even in principle. Things are better if I use point sets for shapes, with their nice mathematical properties. I find this easier to take than finite collections of bits that aren't there to see. Points are too small to worry about. But there are the inevitable problems. Points aren't always like shapes, and neither are point sets. Most of all, boundary elements and parts get mixed up whenever points make lines, planes, and solids. Everything has to be "regularized" before it works the right way. I'm not opposed to the effort. It takes a lot of effort to see how shapes work, as well. But there's always something to be fixed when I define shapes in terms of something else. There's always a bit that seems to be left out. What makes shapes so hard to deal with in terms of bits?

The trouble with bits—including points—is that they're not the same as the things they combine to make. This worries me, because it gets in the way when I want to calculate with shapes. I'm going to say a lot about it in terms of embedding. But maybe others share my qualms. In fact, I have some pretty extraordinary company. Leonhard Euler was the first to classify polyhedra according to their vertices, edges, and faces, and thus to show how basic elements are related in shapes. (Miss H—— knew about this.) Points (vertices) are boundaries of lines. Then lines (edges) are boundaries of planes, and planes (faces) are boundaries of solids. These relationships were surprising at the time—this was a radically new way to describe polyhedra in terms of geometric entities of finite extent and increasing dimension, and with sensible properties.

These new elements are tactile, they are differences in texture. If you hold a model polyhedron you feel its flat faces, the ridges where they meet, and the sharp points at the corners.

But Albrecht Dürer more than two hundred years earlier had described polyhedra in terms of their "nets"

and so distinguished vertices, edges, and faces that are undeniably tactile, too. Just think of using your hands to fold a net to make a polyhedron. Maybe the hand is as perceptive as the eye. After all, I can trace parts with my fingers when they're embedded. Is this another way to calculate? There are vertices for Braille—it uses symbols—and also edges, faces, and polyhedra that allow for more. So I can calculate with shapes via hand or eye—they're reciprocally related in what I see and in what I draw and make. Sensory experience is sensory experience, in one modality or another. But let's get back to the point, and the higher elements that take up space. Euler wasn't keen on bits.

Only admit this proposition, bodies are compounded of simple beings, that is, of parts which have no extension, and you are entangled. With all your might, then, resist this assertion: *every compound being is made up of simple beings*; and though you may not be able directly to prove the fallacy, the absurd consequences which immediately result, would be sufficient to overthrow it.

Points aren't parts of (embedded in) lines, planes, or solids because points have no extension—neither length, area, or volume. And in the same way, lines aren't parts of planes or solids—there's no area or volume—nor are planes parts of solids. This idea is the heart of William Blake's spirited defense of "Republican Art."

I know too well that a great majority of Englishmen are fond of The Indefinite which they Measure by Newton's Doctrine of the Fluxions of an Atom, A Thing that does not Exist. These are Politicians & think that Republican Art is Inimical to their Atom. For a Line or Lineament is not formed by Chance: a Line is a Line in its Minutest Subdivisions: Strait or Crooked It is Itself & Not Intermeasurable with or by any Thing Else.

Newton's atoms are bits—points or infinitesimals—and they aren't in Blake's lines. Every subdivision of a line contains only lines—and planes and solids are alike in exactly the same way. Basic elements can only be divided into basic elements of just the same kind.

It's Blake versus Newton, art versus science, visual versus verbal, seeing versus counting—shapes versus bits includes it all. But this isn't good and evil or the Yankees and the Red Sox. Shapes and bits provide a way to blend these stark dichotomies. There's a nifty kind of equivalence between them that calculating with shapes helps to reveal. Dealing with shapes as if they were bits is a good practical idea that's also an example of calculating with your eyes. Yes, it can be visual, but then sometimes it's not. I'm going to tell you when and how. It's easy once you see how embedding lets you calculate with shapes without using symbols. Then everything falls into place. If I can calculate with shapes, then I can say how to put lines on paper in order to see what's there. I can design.

Trying to Be Clear

The rubric for the previous subsection—how I stopped counting and started to see—may need a little more explanation than I've given it. The explanation is implicit in what I've been showing you. But sometimes it pays to say exactly what you mean, at least if you can. Calculating with symbols has a lot to do with counting. You can always say how many symbols you've got. Whenever you add another one you don't already have, there's one more, and whenever you subtract one, there's one less. Only shapes don't work this way. Seeing takes over—shapes fuse and divide as they're combined. It's what happens when embedding isn't identity. If I have three squares

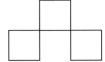

and add one more

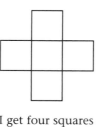

I get four squares or five

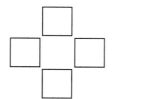

And if I take one square away, I may be left with none

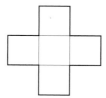

What kind of adding and subtracting is this? And a lot more follows—combining two squares gives me four triangles when I look at their sum

 + =

So maybe the shape

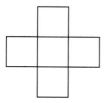

is really L's. There are orthogonal pairs of polygons—each has six sides, but no, that makes a chevron—and ordinary L's with two arms apiece. Let's try to count them. There are at least eight big ones with equal arms in twenty different ways, for example, like this

and twenty-four of these L's altogether. Yet indefinitely many bigger and smaller L's with equal and unequal arms remain. This kind of arithmetic is disconcerting. Counting symbols and seeing shapes aren't the same.

Of course, there are still rules. And they show in another way how counting and seeing differ just as symbols and shapes do. Rules to calculate with symbols are easy to classify in terms of how many symbols they contain. There are two symbols in each of the left sides of the two rules that I described earlier—the rule $\langle\ \rangle \rightarrow \langle\langle\ \rangle\rangle$ and the rule $\langle\ \rangle \rightarrow \langle\ \rangle\langle\ \rangle$—and four symbols in each of their right sides. This is the basis for the so-called Chomsky hierarchy that ranks alternative ways of calculating by their power and complexity. But the rules I use to calculate with shapes can't be classified in this fashion. There's no way to describe them by counting because there's no vocabulary. And even if there were, it might not help. Shapes don't have definite constituents. Their parts aren't numerically distinct. There were different descriptions of the triangle in the left side of the rule

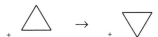

when I tried to count parts. The triangle was just a single constituent, then three constituents in two ways

or six

And the left side of the rule

had twenty constituents and also forty when I used it to rotate the trio of squares in the shape

This is silly. Visually, rules for shapes are all the same. Their left and right sides contain a single shape apiece. There's no complexity I can see—no constituents to count—before calculating; I can see it only retrospectively in the results of what I do.

One of the main reasons Dreyfus gives to show that computers can't think is that they're counting out. This is a consequence of using independent symbols in combination to represent salient features of the world that aren't independent themselves. Let's suppose I view symbols as numerals that I can place here and there according to a rule to produce numbers. Then I can search through what there is without looking at anything. The odometer on my car works this way. It simply keeps on turning. What symbols look like individually or together doesn't matter. Left and right angle brackets ⟨ and ⟩ might just as well be reversed for all the difference it makes. Or why not use left and right parentheses, standard dots and dashes, or 0 and 1? Any pair of symbols will work the same. That's why it's code. It's only the arrangements that count. I can enumerate the distinct possibilities—list them one by one—as if I were in a trance. There's no reason ever to use my eyes. Symbols are all I have to combine, and they don't change when they're put in place. Dreyfus doesn't think this is thought—it isn't seeing—and it's not design. (In fact, this is what Miss H——'s exercise showed in a reductio ad absurdum—counting without seeing isn't art.)

The string

⟪ ⟩ ⟪ ⟫⟫

doesn't look like

⟫ ⟨ ⟫ ⟪⟪

It may look a little like

(( ) (( )))

even though it's flatter and longer, and not as sensual. But how about

. .–. .–––

or

00100111

Symbols stand for features of the world that change as they combine. And as sensible things in the world, symbols have features of their own. But to make sure that symbols stay symbols, their features aren't allowed to interact. This prevents symbols from standing in for what they stand for. I started out talking about calculating in terms of prepositions—for and of—and now I'm doing it again. It still has to do with how things look. There's no telling what you might see next that symbols as symbols don't show. Going beyond symbols and counting alternative arrangements is exactly what thinking with your eyes is for. Design isn't combining symbols and sorting through the possibilities to find what you want—there's more to it than search. It's also seeing what you do as you calculate.

Still, there are alternative points of view—even ones that limit alternatives. Not everyone heeds more than how things are arranged. (Pound reads Chinese ideograms in this way as pictures of things and their relations.) Then meaning is easy to miss if you aren't trained to look. But sometimes, checking all variability repays the effort. C. S. Peirce is clear about this. Listen to what he says:

To believe that any objects are arranged among themselves as in Fig. 1, and to believe that they are arranged as in Fig. 2, are one and the same belief; yet it is conceivable that a man should assert one proposition and deny the other. Such false distinctions do as much harm as the confusion of beliefs really different, and are among the pitfalls of which we ought constantly to beware, especially when we are upon metaphysical ground.

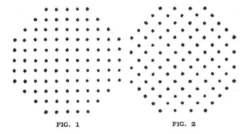

FIG. 1   FIG. 2

Figure 1 and figure 2 don't look the same. That's why Peirce uses them. Nonetheless, he knows more than his eyes do, and wants to credit less than they find. But if my behavior changes because I see figure 1 like this and figure 2 like that, is it a false distinction? To be sure, there's a 45 degree rotation between figure 1 and figure 2. But who says this identity makes things the same? How about left and right angle brackets? They're distinct symbols, even if twin lines are arranged in both, and one rotates into the other. No one believes ⟨ ⟩ is ⟨⟨, ⟩ ⟨, or ⟩⟩. (But there's always more when the eye is so easily fooled. The three new pairs one after the other form the meaningful arrangement, ⟨⟨ ⟩ ⟨ ⟩⟩. Angle brackets can be regrouped after they're combined. This is a useful trick in design, and in algebra and mathematics, too. What you see is what you get.) Or better yet, try the letters b, d, p, and q. My copy of *The American Heritage Dictionary of the English Language* shows them like this

b d

p q

They're equivalent with respect to a group of four transformations—rotations and reflections. Things that are arranged with respect to b

.b·

also have this spatial relation with respect to d, p, and q

·d   ·p·   ·q

The arrangements are indistinguishable. Peirce would probably agree that my four fig-ures are just like his two. Still, let's look at some possible consequences—well, at least one. What happens to reading? Is everything from beb to qeq in the following table the same?

beb   deb   peb   qeb

bed   ded   ped   qed

bep   dep   pep   qep

beq   deq   peq   qeq

No one thinks so. We're not trained to. There's the word bed to tell b and d apart, and p and q when bed is upside down. And surely, the alphabet doesn't bother Peirce. He's not worried about single letters, but about multiple objects and distinguishing arrange-ments that are the same. That makes the difference. But when are single letters not multiple strokes? What do arrangements of objects look like? Why aren't they shapes with parts? Let's see what I can say about Peirce's figures when I test them in various ways.

In figure 1, there are eleven horizontals and eleven verticals, while its twin figure 2 contains fifteen horizontals and fifteen verticals. Four squares arranged in the follow-ing way

on four adjacent points in figure 1 don't look the same as four squares—or is it five?—arranged in like fashion

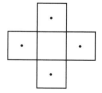

on corresponding points in figure 2. Even Birkhoff's aesthetic measure distinguishes the figures—without really looking! In particular, Peirce's figure 1 taken as a square in this orientation

has a higher value than figure 2 as the rotation

The score is 1.50 to 1.25. Does this miss the mark? What are the objects (parts) in Peirce's two figures anyway? Are they so obviously individual points, permanently fixed before I have a chance to look? Maybe they're different in each figure and vary unpredictably. Suppose they're horizontals or likewise verticals. Things don't have to touch to hang together. Stars don't in constellations. How does this change the arrangements the figures show? What happens to the identity between them now, when they aren't even numerically the same? Is any relationship ever going to be guaranteed? What if figure 1 is something else, perhaps the sum of four squares that touch at their corners

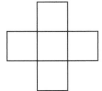

and figure 2 is five squares with common sides

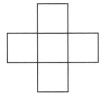

Is this really a false distinction? Perhaps it misses what's actually there—both of my figures contain sixteen lines

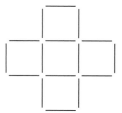

that depend on the same twelve points

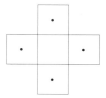

Or is it four points

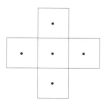

and five

Are boundary elements more meaningful than centers? Who's to say? Do I have to de-cide once and for all?

I can change my mind about what I see anytime I want. Is this automatically an error? Where's the pitfall? Seeing isn't stuck—it has no roots in metaphysical ground. Nothing is certain. It's merely a convenience to assume that the things in the world are so forever, and keep all of their original parts. It facilitates taking roll. But if I only count, I'm going to miss a whole lot. Once I begin, I lose my chance to change. There aren't any surprises with symbols. Parts don't fuse as long as I remember what they are. Everything divides in the same old way with the same old constituents. Combinatorial play makes perfect sense for games like checkers and chess, or for construction sets like

Tinkertoy or Lego. It's exactly what computers do best, and sometimes they're better at games than we are. But it's neither all I do nor all that computers should do. That's why I want to calculate with shapes. There are no constituents to stay the same. It's seeing, not counting. And what I see changes every time I try another rule. This is always more than counting out.

There's no denying that Peirce's figures are the same. But they may not look it. What's neat about calculating with shapes and rules is that they let me have in both ways. In fact, I can determine whether there's identity or not for anything I see using a single rule that doesn't imply an arrangement of objects. That's why I'm always free to go on to something new. Nothing is eternal and unchangeable. What you see is what you get.

Tables, Teacher's Desks, and Rooms

I started looking at shapes when I was a child and have been looking at them ever since. In fact, now that I have children of my own, I look for interest in shapes in what they do. I like the way William James describes reasoning as the ability to deal with novelty—to see and use new things in new situations. And I'm keen for my daughters to catch on to this. I can't imagine any better way to learn about novelty than to experiment with ambiguity in shapes. No, I don't talk to my daughters about ambiguity, although Catherine asked me once what it really meant. I just want them to be encouraged to rely on their eyes when they think. So what kind of visual education are they receiving? In school, there isn't much. Grade-school teachers haven't changed. Miss H—— would fit right in. The main emphasis is still on counting instead of seeing—at least seeing isn't taught. (I'm not alone in thinking so. Mel Levine is an expert in education and a pediatrician who helps kids whose learning styles don't fit in school. They see things differently and are difficult to teach. Dr. Levine distinguishes counting—"sequential ordering"—and seeing—"spatial ordering"—and is clear about which is the more important in today's classrooms.

Being great at spatial perception seems not to be a graduation requirement. So we may elect to do nothing about a shortcoming in this neurodevelopmental function. After all, we don't need to fix everything!

Some kids are good at seeing, and some kids aren't. But it doesn't matter either way, because schools don't know what to do about it. It's better to fix kids than schools. This is a strategy of convenience that's much too common—ignore strengths in the one to correct weaknesses in the other. After all, there's proof that schools teach what kids need to succeed. Is this kind of success worth it? What makes it so hard for schools to be inclusive? Why not teach to the strengths in all kids—visual, verbal, or whatever—as they come? It makes sense to assume that everyone sees the world in a novel way. The trick is to keep this advantage. There's no telling what's going to be useful. Everyone's point of view counts. There's a lot to gain, in school and afterward.)

My daughters were given rulers with the ABC's when they started kindergarten. Their teacher said it was to remind them that words and sentences could all be made with the same alphabet (vocabulary). Letters and inches were alike—only so many fit on a line. Naturally, counting was next. Both girls used manipulatives in the lower grades to see what was happening. They started with unit cubes (points) that were small enough to pick up with their hands and count. The cubes went together in groups of ten to produce a ten-bar (a line). Then ten ten-bars were placed side by side in a hundred-square (a plane), and finally ten hundred-squares were stacked in a thousand-cube (a solid). These materials weren't very attractive

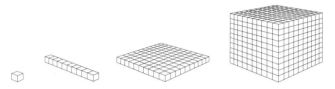

but the method was clever. There was counting and place value—even geometry and Cartesian coordinates—all at once. But it was odd, too. Units weren't independent in ten-bars, hundred-squares, or thousand-cubes. Lines were etched in their faces in a grid. You couldn't take units out. They fused in unusual sums when their number and arrangement were right. Number and arrangement—that's why Peirce said his figures were the same. Yet fusing things together was different. Somehow, shapes were involved. What was there to see? Did ten-bars, etc., always look the same? And it went on in this way—at ten thousand, there were alternatives. There might be a tesseract and cubes of higher dimension, or bigger bars and squares up to a million-cube. The recursion was neat either way. Only which one was it; how did you decide? Counting wasn't ambiguous—it was just the way it looked.

Of course, fathers can be silly when it comes to their daughters. Counting is something everyone needs to learn. And today, there are standards and tests to make sure you do. "A student who's tested is a student who's taught." Do your eyes make a difference? Do children see what I see, or use shapes in the same way? Listen to Alexandra when she was seven years old. What she shows is more than I could possibly make up. "This" (draws a loop)

"is a cursive l. You can use it in an i" (draws a small circle)

"It's chasing after a smaller fish" (draws eyes)

"that swims up to the top." And Alexandra's younger sister, Catherine, has a nice way of seeing, and of saying what she sees. Only sometimes she has a little trouble counting. In her class at school, she learned how to use maps and plans. One had a key that showed a table

her teacher's desk

and a flag, pencils, a globe, and a wastebasket

     flag

     pencils

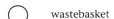   globe

wastebasket

When Catherine was asked how many tables were in the room

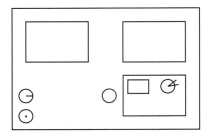

she replied, "three." I liked this—a desk is a table, isn't it?—but Catherine's teacher wasn't pleased. I thought it might be the room—it was a bigger rectangle. Or was the small rectangle on her teacher's desk a table? Maybe the room and the tables were desks—how many did her teacher have? Somehow, I missed the point. I was looking at it the wrong way. Flags, pencils, and globes weren't wastebaskets. And pencils—long, thin things—couldn't be globes—round, fat ones. This was right. Only Catherine didn't care. She looked at the six (?) drawings in the key and saw shapes. No one told her not to. She used her eyes to count. Rectangles made tables and desks. I didn't ask about things with circles. The room was magic—embedding was involved. It changed every time she looked. What good were standards now? But counting required identity. Why was this so important? Who said maps and plans worked that way? Were they hundred-squares? Why not the other way around, so that grids were to see? What happened to ambiguity and reasoning? (A math specialist at Catherine's school tells me she's amazed at how many children say her room has changed whenever they visit again. This may complicate counting or cause problems in metaphysics—it shows how artificial they are—but it doesn't worry children. The rooms they see are the rooms they draw.)

Alexandra and Catherine don't make definite things. They draw lines to see what they get—Catherine actually says so—and blithely go on from there to try it again. It's like an experiment, or more like painting. The outcome can't be known beforehand because there isn't time to look. Within the lines, Alexandra and Catherine are free to see as they please. It's easy to find new things in new situations. They're dealing with novelty all the time. Is this something to use? Seeing and counting aren't the same, but there's reasoning—yes, calculating—in both. Why not take advantage of it? To insist on counting may limit children, if they learn with their eyes and on their hands (digits). And it isn't necessary when you can go on from what they see. Seeing is as useful as counting. It's thinking, and there's a lot to show.

It Always Pays to Look Again

This book is divided into three parts that correspond pretty closely to the three stages in my autobiography. But the parts are presented in reverse order. I need to show you more about what it means to calculate with your eyes—how seeing and counting differ when you use rules—before I can show how to calculate with shapes. Then there are the formal details to make sure that it works. And you need to know how to calculate with shapes before you try it out to design. So the three parts are these—

Part I: What Makes It Visual?
Part II: Seeing How It Works
Part III: Using It to Design

"It" is in the titles on purpose, and sometimes it and pronouns like it are elsewhere and have no set antecedent. It can't be helped with shapes and rules—what you see is what you get, whatever was there before—and it can happen with words. Ambiguity is part of everything I do, so I try to use it.

In all three parts, the presentation is visual, in two senses. First, there are a lot of drawings. If I had a way of doing it—and I don't, even though I've worked to find one—I'd just have drawings and no words. Maybe this isn't so far-fetched. Pound recommends something similar for poetry, never mind that Chinese ideograms aren't shapes. And Klee gets close to what I'd like in his *Pedagogical Sketchbook*. But it's often obscure—it really only works with words. Everything is always ambiguous otherwise. Drawings punctuated with words are what I've got. You do have to look at what I've drawn to understand what I say. My drawings aren't like the figures in most books that are placed haphazardly with respect to the words, and that you're free to look at if you want or ignore. My drawings are parts of sentences. They're there with the words—you have to read them—and the words are sometimes there as drawings—there's the word

bed

for and of, and strings of angle brackets, etc.

Not long ago, I saw a figure in a book that was part of a quotation. The words were fine, but the figure looked odd, so I went to the source. The original was a right triangle like this

and was possibly a mountain, among a host of other things. But the copy I'd seen first was the rotation

I suppose the triangle in this orientation looks like a mountain, too, yet it isn't the same. For one thing, it's higher. And it's impossible to walk on both of its sides. Maybe it's Gibraltar. No, it's turned around, and the description fits the original triangle better. Everything has changed. It all feels different. The new triangle seems much better suited as an illustration of the Pythagorean theorem, when sides are given by symbols

$$a^2 + b^2 = c^2$$

to remind me how to count without having to see. The words were all that mattered in the quotation—they were perfectly correct—you could ignore a few miscellaneous lines. Only in this book, lines count as much as words, and most of the time, more. What you see is what you get. Drawings and words that are this close together make the point. They strike the right balance between visual and verbal expression, and after all, both are integrally related in everything that I'm trying to do. You have to see this book to read it.

Then, I've also tried to make the presentation visual in the way all of the ideas fit together. I like to think of this book as if it were a shape itself. There's a lot of redundancy in shapes—pieces recur all over the place—and I've tried to do this with what I show and what I say about it. This doesn't mean you'll notice anything twice, but only that you'll find the same thing in many different guises. There's plenty of overlap and interpenetration of this kind. I've found it's a useful way to describe how things work. Once you see that shapes and calculating with them aren't about what you think, you'll see what's going on.

There's another way in which this book is like a shape. The different parts of a shape are shapes themselves. And the shape and its parts can stand alone. In the same way, the three parts of this book can be read separately, and for the most part are self-contained. Each was written with the others in mind, and tried on different audiences. My guess is that if the parts work separately, then they'll also work together. Whenever shapes combine, they fuse.

Background

The following background notes mostly follow the order of presentation in the preceding text. When coordinates seem necessary, I have indicated earlier page numbers. I thought of this when I saw ten-bars. You can find them on page 42.

My use of references in these notes and elsewhere in this book deserves brief notice. To start with, my references aren't comprehensive. Nor are they useful for their technical content, although it's largely current. And they aren't select points in the locus of a new debate. That visual and verbal expression are different doesn't surprise anyone. No, the surprises are found in the relationships between seeing and calculating, and how they tie visual and verbal expression together. By and large, my references are about what it means to calculate—about what calculating is and isn't supposed to involve. Some of the things I cite are so well known that they may seem gratuitous. This is a convenient way to highlight ideas that have become too obvious to discuss. In particular, nearly everyone I talk to naively assumes that generative processes are framed in combinatorial terms, so that calculating and seeing are both diminished. There's a given vocabulary of symbols and rules to combine them. And some apply this to thinking (cognition)—"[humans] have combinatorial minds."[1] I try to show how there's more. I also use references without regard to their original purpose. This is easy—it's dealing with shapes. And it's just as easy to trust anecdotal evidence before facts and results. This also has spatial aspects. It's no good predicting what people will see and do next unless it shows how they're free to go on in another way. Anything that can happen can be useful. In the end, what you get is how things appeared to me at the time. This is all you can ask for calculating with shapes. And what this shows is what I really want you to see. I have one thing foremost in mind—to explain in whatever way I can what it's like to calculate by seeing and why this is different than counting. Design and calculating with shapes are much the same. The trick is to be creative. This is a licentious process in which nothing is fixed. There's always more when you design, and I don't want to miss any of it just because I'm calculating.

The lines from Plato at the beginning of this book are in the Jowett translation of *The Republic*:

Inasmuch as philosophers only are able to grasp the eternal and unchangeable, and those who wander in the region of the many and variable are not philosophers, I must ask you which of the two classes should be the rulers of our State?[2]

Wandering in the region of the many and variable may lack clarity, but any path that's traced can be perfectly coherent in retrospect. It's the right place for designers, with the chance to see and do as you like to make something new to talk about. This explains the personal style I use in which verbal and visual expression combine. It's a good way to show in words what it means to wander around freely seeing and doing with shapes. Only what does this say about the "eternal and unchangeable" when I calculate with shapes? This is "metaphysical ground." If shapes are eternal and unchangeable with permanent parts, then there's no calculating by seeing. It's easy to use the philosopher's voice and talk impersonally and objectively when everything is definite. But design is lost once analysis is complete. Design isn't philosophy—what remains to be created that's more than a combination of things already there? Luckily, there's another way to look at it. I can have set rules—call them eternal and unchangeable, or simply memorable—without implying anything definite about shapes. Their parts depend on how I calculate, and they can change erratically as I go on. Embedding makes this possible—it allows for what analysis overlooks with its constitutive results. Calculating with shapes is open-ended. Everything in this process varies freely. Opportunities abound for creative design.[3] With shapes and rules, I can answer Plato's question in the way he finds self-evidently wrong. And I like to think that this is as sensible in politics as it is in design. There's a kind of gestalt switch, and more. Calculating gives Plato's answer sure enough—then, presto, mine. In fact, there's equivalence in verbal and visual expression, in the relationships between counting and seeing that I describe. (The prospect of fixed rules without fixed results is neat. Yet it may be pointless. There's no guarantee I can say what these rules finally are. Looking at myself or anyone else seems scarcely different from looking at a shape. I can calculate in another way as I "wander in the region of the many and variable.")

I started playing around with shapes and shape grammars when I finished my undergraduate studies, but it was a hobby. I was an economist at the time, developing models of urban growth. I learned that I could make them do whatever I wanted. I became a full-time shape grammarist—not a grammarian; I've never been an authority on the proper use of shapes—when my first research paper was published, with James Gips.[4] This was the official beginning of the subject. Gips and I were doctoral students at Stanford and UCLA, respectively, interested in how you could calculate with shapes. We worked out the idea for shape grammars together, with surprises in mind. That's what we called ambiguity. But this was a problem when it came to putting shape grammars on a computer. Gips developed a couple of neat programs, but neither of them allowed for ambiguity.[5] You could calculate with shapes on a computer only if you could describe them with symbols. You had to segment shapes into lowest-level constituents to start. Then there was the combinatorial play with simple things to make complex ones. Meanwhile, I worked out the details of embedding, so that you could calculate with shapes in the same way you see.[6] Symbols were unnecessary for shape grammars—on a computer or not. I still see Gips today, and he's happy to admit the wonders of ambiguity in shapes and everywhere else. He likes to tell me I'm a fake. I look like a strict formalist interested in rigor and rules. But really, it's the ambiguity that counts. Being a fake is high praise for a shape grammarist. One use of shape grammars is to produce new things—fakes—in a known style, for example, villa plans that look like Palladio's.[7] Take a look at the pair of plans

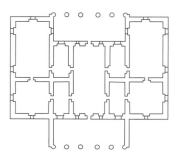 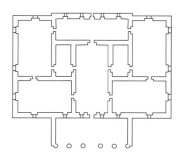

Which is the fake? No matter how you answer, you won't be wrong. Making fakes lets you see how well you understand a style. The idea is to be rigidly formal, and I'm to blame for it. Only it's the magic of shapes as they change that really fascinates me. I've never tried to hide it. It's magic everyone can see. And I want to show that it's rigidly formal without feeling that way. That's why I'm a fake. But use your own eyes. The enchantment is always there when you calculate with shapes.

One of the things that I like to say when I talk about shapes is this: "What you see is what you get." It pretty much sums up what this book is about. At the very least, it's the way I want to calculate. I wish I had been the first to use the phrase—it appears many times, initially on page 6—but it's from Geraldine Jones. Flip Wilson created and played the comic siren on American television.[8] Geraldine used the refrain to describe herself. She wasn't lacking in curves, and remember, she was Flip Wilson in drag. The refrain is always fitting when you're talking about shapes. Geraldine put seeing ahead of getting, and you can do this with a twist and a flip. I can use three lines to get the shape

and then see the triangle

Getting it first and seeing it later needn't match. Everything fuses and divides in between. The real secret to calculating with shapes is to see that there's always something new. No matter what I do, it's a surprise. What you see is what you get.

On page 6 and again on page 17, I talk about "results." The terminology is from Søren Kierkegaard's *Concluding Unscientific Postscript*. His marvelous discussion of this idea may just as well be about shapes, and what it means to calculate with them. The American pragmatists and today's neopragmatists also write in a way that describes shapes, and sometimes this is explicit. But for now, listen to Kierkegaard.

While objective thought translates everything into results, and helps all mankind to cheat, by copying these off and reciting them by rote, subjective thought puts everything in process and omits the result.[9]

When it comes to shapes, everything is up for grabs. There are no results—fixed constituents—to guide seeing. You can't cheat in this way with shapes. Nothing is given objectively to copy or recite by rote. There aren't any divisions to remember and get right. Seeing isn't a test. No one can do it for you. It's up to you now and whenever you look again. You're free to see whatever you want to see. You're the one to decide. And what you decide changes the way you go on in a process that's always open-ended. This kind of calculating is subjective and variable—the shape grammarist's voice is ineluctably personal. And once again, that's why I talk about shapes in this way because it's how seeing and doing work. In fact, whenever I use results, it may carry Kierkegaard's meaning to remind you to look again in your own way. (I have a peculiar habit of reading everything as if it were about shapes. I recommend this highly to everyone. It's a useful point of view. As soon as I saw how shapes worked, especially in calculating, nothing was the same. Things I didn't understand before were clear. It was a Kierkegaardian leap.)

Donald Schon's description of professional activity is in *The Reflective Practitioner*.[10] "Reframing" and "back talk" are at the center of ideal practice in design and elsewhere. When I first met Schon, he told me that everything I had ever said about design was wrong. I thought this was a nice way to start a conversation. And we went on and on about it in a professional way for a long time. It was the freewheeling, unscrupulous kind of conversation we both liked. It was the same calculating with shapes. Schon disliked shape grammars because he didn't trust calculating. It was moving symbols around with rules—as in a formal system with axioms and proofs—and this was entirely mechanical with routine results. Schon liked John Dewey, and so did I. We both agreed that his logic—that's his theory of inquiry—had a lot to do with design.

Inquiry is the controlled or directed transformation of an indeterminate situation into one that is so determinate in its constituent distinctions and relations as to convert the elements of the original situation into a unified whole.[11]

Shapes are indeterminate—ambiguous—before I calculate, and have constituent distinctions—parts—only as a result of using rules in this ongoing process. At least that's what I thought, and that's why I thought calculating with shapes had a lot to do with design. Schon didn't say one way or the other. Maybe he enjoyed the ambiguity. It's always there to use, and there's no reason to make up your mind when you can go on talking.

There's an illustration on page 10 from Paul Klee's *Pedagogical Sketchbook* that shows "medial" lines.[12] Points are connected to make lines that form planes in the way Miss H—— said. I like to think that Klee and Wassily Kandinsky, too—now it's explicitly *Point and Line to Plane*—might enjoy the idea of calculating with shapes. The first lessons in Klee's *Sketchbook* are wonderfully suggestive in this regard. I return to them in part II. And certainly, Kandinsky was trying something similar, although, at root, combinatorial.[13]

George Birkhoff's *Aesthetic Measure* is well worth looking at today.[14] It's one of the few books on aesthetics I know that actually contains pictures and worked examples. This alone is a major breakthrough. A technical account of Birkhoff's formula and new examples are in a later book by Gips and myself.[15] We also offer our own measure E_Z, with much else of independent interest. Like Birkhoff's formula $M = O/C$, E_Z involves generic ideas of unity and variety—richness of ends and economy of means—that apply to a broad range of things from paintings to music to scientific theories. But the definition of E_Z depends on algorithms and information theory. There's counting, and a ratio for relative entropy. As I said earlier, I'm not keen on it. But Gips is still very enthusiastic, and who knows, he may be right.

Elizabeth Goldring did the nifty word door I'm inviting you to enter—it's on page 13. This is a standard narrative device to begin stories and tales. Lewis Carroll's *Alice* pops to mind whenever things change like shapes without rhyme or reason. But there's also a rabbit-hole to start—or is it

rabbit h●le

—and then a little door. What's at stake here is not how good you are at this—Alexandra's l's, i's, and fish are better—but how to do it not knowing in advance that you're going to. (For more with an eye to children and calculating, and in particular, on counting things like tables and desks, see part I, note 14.) Otto Neurath talks about visual language in "Visual Education"—

Visual statements and verbal statements are different and not translatable element by element. An example: a boy walks through a door

and not

These are the only drawings in ninety-five pages, and they're key.[16] The shape *a-boy-walks-through-a-door* and the matching sentence are structurally distinct. The one has two parts, while the other has six, as above, or more at the nodes of a tree, like the one on the next page. Moreover, how do I divide the shape into the parts *boy* and *door*, and relate them? The boy may be a man, a girl, or a woman, and he or she can go either way or straddle the threshold. Maybe the boy walks left to right into or out of a house, so that the shape flips in neat ways. And the door may have an architrave with top and sides, or be otherwise embellished. Which of the many possibilities makes the best story? And I'm free to see novel parts, as well. Shapes and sentences aren't the same. But there's congruity, too, when Ezra Pound compares Chinese ideograms and poetry in his marvelous *ABC of Reading*.[17] In poetry, words are charged with meaning. For shapes, this varies as I calculate.

Marvin Minsky's book—*Computation: Finite and Infinite Machines*—is a good place to learn the ins and outs of calculating with symbols.[18] Minsky fell out with Hubert Dreyfus when he panned research in artificial intelligence (AI).[19] It was something Kierkegaard said. This started out as gossip and soon enough, there was a public debate—Seymour Papert represented Minsky who kept score, Dreyfus represented himself, and Jerome Lettvin was involved somehow. It ended in a free-for-all—ideas were flying all over the place. And the dust hasn't settled yet. At the time, everyone knew Dreyfus was wrong and had another reason why.[20] But it was almost twenty years later before Allen Newell managed to hit the mark.

Dreyfus's central intellectual objection, as I understand him, is that the analysis of the context of human action into discrete elements is doomed to failure. This objection is grounded in phenomenological philosophy. Unfortunately, this appears to be a nonissue as far as AI is concerned. The answers, refutations, and analyses that have been forthcoming to Dreyfus's writings have simply not engaged this issue—which, indeed, would be a novel issue if it were to come to the fore.[21]

In the AI community today, it seems that "discrete elements" still hold sway and continue to be a "nonissue." (The importance of units is also apparent in many related areas. For example, look at the wide-ranging use of Lindenmayer systems and cellular automata to model both biological and physical processes, and in evolutionary algorithms.[22] Claims for cellular automata as models of everything are perhaps overblown. But the automatic reliance on units everywhere is undeniable. In fact, AI and evolutionary algorithms are key in many computer applications in design.) Of course, the question of units is nothing new. It comes up over and over again without a solution. Susanne Langer was saying the same thing as Dreyfus twenty-five years earlier, only about Ludwig Wittgenstein's logic in the *Tractatus*, and with the arts—drawing, etc.— in mind. There's a lot riding on whether or not it's practicable to calculate without units or symbols. The whole reach of calculating as a creative way of reasoning depends on the answer. Isn't it high time for this "novel" issue to come to the fore once and for all?

I read Noam Chomsky's book *Syntactic Structures* when I was an undergraduate, and have barely glanced at linguistics since.[23] I checked some current sources, and the little I've said still holds up—from creativity to how sentences are described.[24] (In addition, there's the independent Cartesian hypothesis that rules are innate. Evidently, language and embedding are equally automatic—"Healthy adults [and children, for that matter] make very few errors on this test."[25] If our knack for language tells us about ourselves, then surely our knack for embedding does, too. Both are parts of what it means to be us.) A generative grammar is a model combinatorial system. Words and syntactic categories—sentences, noun phrases, verb phrases, nouns, verbs, etc.—combine in trees like this one

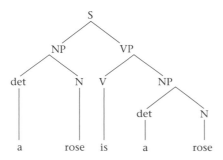

for the sentence "A rose is a rose."[26] (The identity is logically necessary, but Gertrude Stein repeats its predicate to be sure.[27] This makes another sound—Eros—so "a rose" is a shape. And the tree is twin structures in perspective—two sheds back-to-side. Or is this another trick, a clever facade to hide the truth? No doubt, the tree is a single edifice in elevation. Only "a house is a house" may be a better foundation. There's sound evidence indeed—seeing and hearing are calculating. Now it's eyes for shapes, hands for the vertices, edges, and faces of polyhedra, and ears for words to apply rules sensibly. The mind ties all of this together with symbols and counting to settle Plato's question in a surprising way. I said this before on page 47. Many things bear repeating—some never enough.) Chomsky is as well known for his anarchic politics as he is for his linguistics. And calculating with shapes seems to be as much like the former as the latter. In fact, deciding when things are alike is a key part of using rules. But it's more important now that shapes and rules go with many things they're not supposed to. I show this again in part I for Gian-Carlo Rota's phenomenology and combinatorics. On the one hand, there's how things look, for example, trees and hierarchically organized list structures—strings like ⟨⟨⟨ ⟩⟨ ⟩⟩ ⟨⟨ ⟩⟨ ⟩⟨ ⟩⟨ ⟩⟩⟩⟩, ((( )( )) (( )( )( )))), and 000101100100101111 in which symbols are combined in a certain way—and then on the other hand, there's counting distinct arrangements—the tree I've shown and my three strings are all identical. This is perfectly clear. But shape grammars let me see and count as I please. Moreover, they show how the contrasting things that people do hang together. Of course, this was evident from the start with Turing, photography, and machines.

Langer's book is *Philosophy in a New Key*. Her discussion of language and drawing, etc.—some of which I quote on page 18—is used to distinguish presentational and discursive forms of symbolism.[28] The distinction corresponds more or less to the informal one I make between visual and verbal expression. These are so obviously separate that it's easy to miss how they're related. Certainly, for me, there's a decisive link, and elaborating it to equivalence is what a lot of this book is about. I enjoy reading the initial few pages of Langer's final chapter, "The Fabric of Meaning." I like the opening line—"All thinking begins with *seeing* ..."—and more. First there's a strand of the idea that structure is a temporary (evanescent) record of our own activity. Topologies (vocabulary and syntax) are one way to show the structure of shapes. And I show that topologies are by-products of using rules—afterthoughts that evolve in fits and starts as calculating goes on, in the way a designer might explain a developing body of work. Then there's an apparent behaviorist twist—seeing is "sheer" response. Chomsky's old review of B. F. Skinner's *Verbal Behavior* puts this in doubt. But behaviorist ideas are of some use when it comes to saying what it means to calculate with shapes. One way to describe rules minimally is as stimulus-response pairs—I see this and do that. It's a stark reminder that shapes aren't represented either in rules or as the result of what rules do. Everything fuses and divides anew as I go on. Every outcome is a surprise.

I was pretty clear about the relationship between grammar and syntax in Langer's sense and calculating with shapes more than twenty years ago. I framed the contrast in terms of set grammars on the one hand and shape grammars on the other. Set grammars parody combinatorial systems, exaggerating their use of identity via set membership. Still, the technical details are unassailable—set grammars are equivalent to Turing machines.

Set grammars treat [shapes] as *symbolic* objects; they require that [shapes] always be parsed into the elements of the sets from which they are formed. The integrity of the compositional units in [shapes] is thus preserved, as these parts *cannot* be recombined and decomposed in different ways. In contrast, shape grammars treat [shapes] as *spatial* objects; they require no special parsing of [shapes] into fixed [parts]. Spatial ambiguities are thus allowed, as given compositional units in [shapes] *can* be recombined and decomposed in different ways.[29]

There's creativity in combining shapes and in dividing them. But the one without the other is just reciting by rote, merely counting out. It's all memory when shapes are divided in advance, but otherwise, everything is always new. No one took any notice of this. Maybe the difference between sets and shapes in calculating—between identity and embedding—is too subtle. Or perhaps rigor and formality don't work. I'm less technical now, and as informal as I can be. The message is the same, and I don't want it to be missed. It's all about seeing—there are no units; shapes fuse and divide when I calculate.

Langer also separates technique and syntax in her discussion of drawing and language. This is surely another version of the distinction between schemas and rules that contrasts a synoptic view of possibilities with mere combination. In architecture, for example, Gottfried Semper's *Urhutte* is an ample summary of buildings in the manner of Goethe's famous *Urpflanze*, while J. N. L. Durand's system of architectural composition is combinatorial à la Chomsky or Simon with a vocabulary of building elements, etc. Only the distinction isn't that clear-cut—there are usually combinatorial aspects to a schema when it's used. Goethe relies on transformations and permutations to vary the organs of his *Urpflanze*. Moreover, a system of vocabulary and rules with a starting "axiom" provides a synoptic view of possibilities that unfolds in a recursive process. The axioms of any formal theory do this, as well. Maybe schemas and rules are alternative ways of describing the same thing where the emphasis is differently placed. They may be distinct, yet they both show what's going on. Perhaps it's only the way you look at it, with the chance to switch back and forth. I'm used to conflating schemas and rules when I calculate with shapes. I can look at shapes as schemas animated by rules, or as something formed as rules are tried—either way without recourse to units, so that there's nothing explicitly combinatorial. And this is really what counts. In both ways, there's recursion, but there's no vocabulary. It's not words and rules. The shape

and rules to rotate and translate squares are a good example of this. Is the shape a schema, an axiom, one then another at different times, or something else when it's used to produce the nine shapes on page 30 and others like them?[30]

Herbert Simon's *The Sciences of the Artificial* is an old book for computer science, but it's still current today in science and design.[31] Things never change as quickly as people like to think, unless of course they're shapes. Big ideas that are in right now are in Simon's book from the beginning in sharp focus, for example, complex adaptive systems. I'm keen on the metaphor that calculating is painting—it's new in the second edition and stays in the third—even if Simon may miss some of its possibilities. I'll get back to it in part I, and to his way of describing pictures with hierarchies and his appeal to drawings to disambiguate sentences. The latter may be a version of Wittgenstein's picture theory of meaning. I'm not sure. But I am sure that there's a lot in Simon that bumps against shapes in really important ways.

Leonhard Euler's wonderful letters to the Princess of Anhalt-Dessau, the niece of Frederick the Great of Prussia, are popular accounts of various topics in physics and philosophy. The subject of ten letters from 25 April to 30 May 1761 is extension and the absurdity of dividing things with it into other things without it. The hortatory quotation on page 32 is from the penultimate letter of the series.[32] Euler's warning—deny parts that can't be divided—applies to all sorts of things from shapes to numbers and time. The way Euler came to describe polyhedra in terms of their vertices, edges, and faces—in terms of boundaries, boundaries of boundaries, etc.—is also enlightening.[33] Peter Cromwell goes on to describe the tactile quality of these elements in the short quotation on page 32.[34] And Erwin Panofsky mentions Albrecht Dürer's "nets."[35]

Euler and William Blake have the same politics. And Blake is a wonderful letter writer, too. His displeasure with "Newton's Doctrine of Fluxions of an Atom" and his stirring vision of the "Republican" line were conveyed on 12 April 1827 to George Cumberland.[36]

The quotation from C. S. Peirce and the twin figures

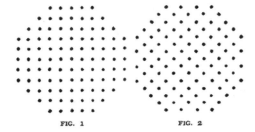

FIG. 1   FIG. 2

are from his famous article in *Popular Science Monthly*. It's called "How to Make Our Ideas Clear."[37] Ambiguity and clarity are opposites—it's one or the other. One way to be clear is to see that figure 1 and figure 2 show the same arrangement of objects. Only how can I tell I'm looking at an arrangement and not at a shape? Maybe if I divide a shape into parts, it's an arrangement of objects. But the shape comes first, and it's there to divide anew when I look again. Evidently, arrangements like sets are ideas and can be clear, whereas shapes are ambiguous. What can be seen can't be clear (unambiguous), and what's clear can't be seen (ambiguous). Shapes aren't ideas. Was Plato right that philosophers make better rulers than "those who wander in the region of the many and variable"? Is seeing mindless? Thinking with your eyes and dealing with ideas aren't the same. And sure enough, Peirce shows why in his neat discussion of habit, after the passage I've cited. It's another way to describe rules for calculating.

What the habit is depends on *when* and *how* it causes us to act. As for the *when*, every stimulus to action is derived from perception; as for the *how*, every purpose of action is to produce some sensible result.[38]

The arrangements in Peirce's figures are identical. But if perception is the test, then each supports different behavior. Is this a mistake? The philosopher finds ambiguity embarrassing and shuns it in logic and reasoning, even as the shape grammarist embraces ambiguity and exploits it in art and design. Rules are used in an open-ended process to decide when and how to change shapes with all of their ambiguity. It's asking too much to ask for less, and this is true when less is more. Doesn't anything hold still? One thing is clear. Arrangements like definitions and plans are mistakes—all four are made to check creative activity.

I mentioned William James on page 41. He links reasoning and novelty in *The Principles of Psychology*.[39] This relationship yields yet another telling way to characterize rules when I calculate with shapes. Rather than seeing and doing, the behaviorist's stimulus and response, or Peirce's when and how, it's sagacity and learning. These terms may sound quaint today—sagacity fails when learning ends with standardized tests—but they're valuable nonetheless. I'll return to both in part I. Meanwhile, it's the inverse of James's relationship between reasoning and novelty that explains why education is worth having. For James, "An 'uneducated' person is one who is non-plussed by all but the most habitual situations."[40] Learning how to behave in everyday situations whether at home or on the job is a vital goal in education. You know what to see and what to do as habits are fixed—when "the enormous fly-wheel of society" is put in motion—so that life goes by with relaxed certainty, and it pays to be on time and work hard. But in parallel, education acts against conservative inertia. This radical impulse resists final results. Even the humdrum is more than it seems and always merits another look. Seeing never stops. Blake saw a world in a grain of sand[41]—so much for units—and found "Republican Art" in this hackneyed line

———————

James has it going east and west not heeding the inconsistency.[42] Ambiguity is intrinsic in what there is to see, and has many uses. At its best, education makes it possible to experiment and learn how ambiguity works. You're encouraged to play around freely with whatever you see in an open-ended way. Novelty isn't routinely dismissed as confusion or noise, or as our Republicans imprudently demand, suppressed as a threat to high test scores, big business, civic pride, and homeland security. Order, predictable results, and steady plans aren't the goals. What's needed is creativity—the freedom to see and do. Education isn't all about standards and authority. It's to instill habits that bypass habit, too, to nurture the ability to go on seeing and doing when things are new. It's the same using rules to calculate with shapes.

Also on page 41, there's a quotation from Mel Levine's book *A Mind at a Time*.[43] The absence of a visual approach to education in schools is something that I hope calculating with shapes will help to address. At least it shows that it's possible to be formal with your eyes—as formal as mathematics—without losing anything that's creative in the process. With shapes and rules, novelty, seeing things in new ways, and experience that's ongoing and variable are emphasized. The social psychologist Ellen Langer calls this "sideways learning" and "mindfulness."[44] Means and methods of teaching make a difference in education—to learn by counting and more by seeing.

The triangle

on page 45 is in Mary Warnock's *Imagination* in a quotation from Wittgenstein's *Investigations*.[45] Transformations of shapes are easy to mix up. Sometimes it's good to keep them apart—a triangle this way or that may make a real difference, but sometimes not. You have to look and you have to decide. Shapes can be alike in many ways and may stand in for one another, too. The confusion, like ambiguity, is indispensable when I calculate with shapes. Embedding and transformations together make rules work. This is a neat relationship that lets me see what I do and change it.

I have given a rather lopsided view of bits. And in fact, it may be quixotic. There are many others who find bits inevitable, almost to the beginning of history. W. V. Quine gives a wonderful account of this in his discussion of atoms.[46] In his own mind, he "dreams of a meaningful perceptual atomism: a repertoire of basic features, noticed or not, in terms of which every neurologically possible human perception and perceptual distinction can be specified."[47] This appears to ask for something more than mere approximations, and in return, to end phenomenology. With meaningful constituents—mince won't do—combinatorics is enough. Even so, it isn't hard to see that noticed features have a property that unnoticed ones don't. And this makes me uneasy, as I've said before. But Quine finds bits undeniable in any subject that's a science.

What key trait makes the atomic approach effective in organizing a science? I say it is this: there may be indefinitely or infinitely many atoms, but they must be partitioned into a manageably limited number of kinds such that atoms of the same kind play identical roles within the laws of the theory. This much, significantly, is just what is required in order that a theory lend itself to the measurement of information.[48]

Atoms and laws smack of words and syntax. But it's the need to count—to measure information—that makes bits important. Is this the hallmark of rationality? Certainly, counting is included in reasoning at its very best. It's something to respect. And any claim to reason that goes without it is something of an embarrassment. In fact, visual reasoning—using your eyes to decide what to do next—always demands an apology. It isn't obviously counting and needs to be explained. It would make all the difference in the world if I could show it's a science. Maybe this isn't a dream. Seeing and counting are related—and that may just do the trick. (The value of counting is nowhere more apparent than in the measurement of reasoning itself. Francis Galton—Charles Darwin's cousin—was the first to think about this.[49] Galton never tired of saying, "Whenever you can, count." Counting was a habit worth having. It was the way to gauge mental ability by energy and sensitivity—the former as the capacity for labor and the latter as the response to physical stimuli. This seems ridiculous today given the accuracy of standardized tests of intelligence—IQ—cognitive ability, academic achievement, etc. And no doubt, standardized tests for tenure are around the corner to validate the rote results of peer review. This is what universities need—accountability and fairness demand it for faculty and students alike. Yet beyond what any test can show—even a bent for words and numbers—reasoning takes personal experience and has its own point of view. Visual analogies and puzzles on an IQ test don't have much to do with this. They work only if they're unambiguous. Is this ever possible? What's left that's visual or useful in new situations? Shapes are full of miscellaneous possibilities. How can you measure the ability to see in your own way if it's known in advance? Answers on a test are right and wrong without results to check seeing. At least energy and sensitivity are related to hand and eye. Shapes and rules bypass standards, tests, and the trivial idea that accountability makes a difference. Final answers are out of reach when there's more to see and do.)

My own field strives to be a full-fledged science. And there are many who work tremendously hard to make sure that this happens. Michael Batty is one of the most energetic. He's the long-standing editor of *Environment and Planning B*. This is the leading scholarly journal in which serious papers on shape grammars appear. Listen to what he says about shape grammars, urban morphology, and science. There are clear echoes of Quine.

With the exception of research at the architectural level involving shape grammars which do unpack the rule-based dynamics of how form is created, most conventional approaches to urban morphology such as those based on fractal geometry and space syntax are limited in their explanatory power.... There is no consensus in urban morphological research as to the fundamental [basic or atomic] unit of description.... What is required is research into what constitutes the most basic unit, but until there is consensus, little progress can be made. Only when there is agreement about the nature of the data can science begin. Only then can classifications and comparisons be made, alternative theories conjectured and falsified, and consistent methods of analysis meeting basic mathematical standards developed.[50]

I'm almost positive that shape grammars are mathematics—and not just as a method of analysis. I'm equally confident that Batty's fractal geometry (cellular automata) and Bill Hillier's space syntax are mathematics, too.[51] In fact, they're calculating with shapes when embedding is identity—in the special case where shapes behave like symbols. But shape grammars, cellular automata, and space syntax also differ according to Batty's measure of explanatory power. This highlights the split between shapes and symbols, even if standards and measures are likely to suppress novelty and exclude a lot that may be useful. The truth is I really don't like permanent standards and measures whatever they show, and try to work without them. So why am I sure that shape grammars are mathematics? I have some circumstantial evidence to support my claim. First, shape grammars let me calculate in algebras of shapes, and this sounds like mathematics to nearly everyone. It's the same whether you like shape grammars or not, and it may be the reason why. Words make a difference. More notably, though, math majors—graduate and undergraduate students—take my classes on shape grammars. And they do so voluntarily, without any kind of curricular coercion. Are there better judges of mathematics than students who want to do it? Our free choices let standards grow up and change within experience as part of it, whether they're haphazard everyday standards, rigorous mathematical ones, or something in between.

Shape grammars let me calculate with shapes—they let me use my eyes to decide what to do next. In this way, they "unpack the rule-based dynamics of how form is created." No one has complained yet that there's a loss of explanatory power because there aren't any units. In fact, shape grammars show it's possible to go on rigorously without "agreement about the nature of the data." You can call this science or not as you please. It's entirely inconsequential. It's calculating either way. Everyone knows that shape grammars are quirky, even unconventional as Batty implies. You put up with them. But there's surely another reason I haven't heard any grumbling about units. Their absence is overlooked. The assumption that there are units is so firmly rooted—it's automatic for calculating—that no one bothers to ask what shape grammars do. Or maybe they work so magically without units that no one cares. The results are spellbinding. Some things are difficult to see if you don't know how to look, even when they're right in front of your eyes. You need the rule and have to apply it. That's the reason for this book—to show how embedding makes it practicable to calculate with shapes that aren't given using units or symbols, and how calculating in this way includes creative design.

I   WHAT MAKES IT VISUAL?

To a large extent it has turned out that the usefulness of computer drawings is precisely their structured nature and that this structured nature is precisely the difficulty in making them. . . . An ordinary draftsman is unconcerned with the structure of his drawing material. Pen and ink or pencil and paper have no inherent structure. They only make dirty marks on paper. The draftsman is concerned principally with the drawings as a representation of the evolving design. The behavior of the computer-produced drawing, on the other hand, is critically dependent upon the topological and geometric structure built up in the computer memory as a result of drawing operations. The drawing itself has properties quite independent of the properties of the object it is describing.

—Ivan Sutherland

Use Your Eyes to Decide

Visual reasoning means using your eyes to decide what to do next. This formula looks just about right—it puts seeing and doing together in the way I like. But there's more to say about what makes visual reasoning useful in design. Just what makes reasoning visual anyway? How does calculating fit into this? And why are seeing and drawing an effective way of thinking? That's the nub of what I'm trying to do. In fact, I'm going to adopt the point of view of someone who thinks about design and how seeing and drawing help to make it work. This turns into a practical concern for shapes and rules, and their value in the design process. So there are some parallel questions that also require answers as I go on. How can I make anything that's really new when I calculate with shapes? How creative can I possibly be if I only use rules? Can I find another way to design? Am I any more creative if I don't use rules? Does this make sense? What's at stake?

A good way to see how all of this lines up is to try my first question,

(1)   What makes reasoning visual?

I'm not going to answer question 1 directly. Instead, I'm going to pose two ancillary questions that seem easier, probably because I have something to say about them. Here they are:

(2)   What makes calculating visual?

(3)   Does reasoning include calculating?

I'll take a meandering route through their answers that digresses now and then to explore other questions like the unnumbered ones in the previous paragraph. This isn't exactly what Plato recommends in the quote that heads the introduction, but wandering around aimlessly to see what's what—changing your mind freely—is a useful way to get new results. It's a nice way to see what calculating with shapes and rules is all about. It feels right, and there's some logic to it. If my answer to question 3 is yes, then I can argue by analogy that visual reasoning includes visual calculating. And if I can answer question 2, then I can use visual calculating to understand visual reasoning. It's reasoning by inference—from the properties of a part to the properties of the whole. Of course, this assumes that parts and wholes are alike. I've already said so for shapes and embedding. This makes calculating with shapes and reasoning (inference) the same in at least one respect. Plus, I'm more confident about the mechanics of calculating than I ever will be about reasoning generally.

I've always liked engineering, with its sensible outlook and palpable results. It's the same when I calculate. I can point to examples—some of my own invention—and go through them step by step. But it's hard to know about reasoning. My own reasoning when it goes beyond calculating is as suspect as any. Whenever I think I have a good argument, someone soon comes along and proves the opposite. And it's just the same if I try to follow the reasoning of others. I go from thinking I'm thinking to thinking I'm not. I'd rather stick with engineering and show how things work out sensibly. It's easy to do applying rules to calculate with shapes. I can't be sure until I show you, but I'm almost positive—you're going to be surprised at how much more there is to visual reasoning than you imagine, if it's anything at all like visual calculating. The kinds of things I have in mind don't come from complicated ways of counting or clever coding tricks that take real brainpower—from what's customarily valued and encouraged in calculating. They come straight from seeing. It's all there whenever you look.

I've framed my questions with respect to the following diagram

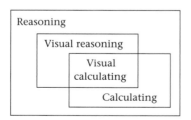

that shows how everything is supposed to fit together. This extends counting to calculating in what I said in the final pages of the introduction about reasoning at its best and why its visual counterpart is something to explain. Diagrams are meant to see.

But when I look at mine, I worry about which way the inclusions should go—what's embedded in what? What makes me think I have the right setup? There are a couple dozen ways to permute the names of the areas, with novel consequences that might be useful. Maybe the names should be reversed like this

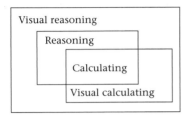

so that reasoning and calculating are special cases of visual reasoning and visual calculating. Is this an example of how visual reasoning is supposed to work? I don't know. There's a nifty change in perspective, with the kind of switch that's common in design in the interplay between results and goals. Many things alter freely the way drawings (shapes) do when I look at them a second time. Ambiguity is something to use. And no matter which diagram I try, visual reasoning and calculating need to be explained. My three questions still hold with undiminished force. What's more, I'm sure that each of my diagrams is correct on its own, for calculating by counting (this is the standard method of calculating that's taught in school) and then by seeing (this is my alternative that relies on shapes). And there are telling equivalencies, as well. It's uncanny how everything converges so quickly, and without any fuss. I'm right back to the scheme I outlined at the beginning of the introduction to relate verbal and visual expression. This depends on the contrast between identity and embedding—between points (symbols) of dimension $i = 0$ and basic elements of other kinds—lines, planes, and solids—of dimension $i > 0$. What this contrast means for reasoning and calculating, visual and not—why the value of i matters—is mostly what I'm going to explore.

Let's see how all of this works out in some detail. What about question 3?

Does Reasoning Include Calculating?

I want to show that reasoning includes calculating—or at least that there's a reason to think so. Most of the people I've asked agree that it does. Some see calculating as what the best in reasoning is all about, while others see it as a narrow kind of process among many of greater scope and use. Nonetheless, I only need the inclusion to go on, so that I can explain visual reasoning in terms of visual calculating. This isn't new territory. The relationship between reasoning and calculating has been described many times before—Thomas Hobbes was apparently the first to try—in a variety of ways from which I can select. Sifting through the possibilities may take some reasoning—at least a little judgment if not actual calculating—but the stakes aren't high. There's enough agreement to decide on pragmatic grounds alone. And in fact, this points the way.

Whenever I read William James, I always find something new about shapes and rules. What's more, there's an account of reasoning in *The Principles of Psychology* that works flawlessly for what I want to do. For James, reasoning is a compound process with interlocking parts. He divides the "art of the reasoner" into moieties:

First, *sagacity*, or the ability to discover what part, M, lies embedded in the whole S which is before him;

Second, *learning*, or the ability to recall promptly M's consequences, concomitants, or implications.

This is precisely what happens whenever rules are used to calculate. A rule $M \rightarrow P$ shows the part M to be embedded in the whole S, and specifies the consequences, etc.—call them P—of finding M in S. Remember how the rule

that I described in the introduction used embedding to rotate triangles. Any part I can see and trace I can change. In just the same way, the rule $M \rightarrow P$ applies to S to produce something new. Of course, this is only a sketch. It leaves out most of the important details. I have to say a lot more about how the rule $M \rightarrow P$ works when it's used. The trick is first to find a suitable embedding relation, and then to show how M can be embedded in S, and how together with P, this changes S.

James takes the syllogism (predicate calculus) as his example—this only confirms the link to calculating—with almost no attention to the underlying details that make rules work. James isn't an engineer. Sagacity and learning are taken for granted. He has something else far more interesting and weighty in mind. He wants to plumb creative thinking and describe the source of originality. In fact, James's overarching definition of reasoning is the ability to deal with novelty. This is why reasoning makes a difference.

If we glance at the ordinary syllogism—

M is P;
S is M;
∴ S is P

—we see that the second or minor premise, the "subsumption" as it is sometimes called, is the one requiring the sagacity; the first or major the one requiring the fertility, or fulness of learning. Usually, the learning is more apt to be ready than the sagacity, the ability to seize fresh aspects in concrete things being rarer than the ability to learn old rules; so that, in most actual cases of reasoning, the minor premise, or the way of conceiving the subject, is the one that makes the novel step in thought. This is, to be sure, not always the case; for the fact that M carries P with it may also be unfamiliar and now formulated for the first time.

For James, there are twin ways to be creative—using rules ("the way of conceiving the subject") and also defining them (connecting M and P in the first place). And he puts greater emphasis on the former. Perhaps this is surprising, but I think he's right about "the novel step in thought." Embedding—"the ability to seize fresh aspects in concrete things"—is the key. Of course, James also relies on learning. This isn't about the kind of facts that are taught in school where the emphasis is on counting things, but about finding rules and remembering them independent of things and their parts. I can decide what to see and do without "translat[ing] everything into results." There is no final analysis, only lots of temporary analyses that can change erratically as rules are tried. This is a dynamic process with plenty of ambiguity. Nothing ever has to stay the same. Novelty is everywhere. Once you see how this works—and it does depend on seeing—it's evident that the standard version of rules in terms of symbols—what Susanne Langer has in mind when she considers vocabulary and syntax—is neither James's nor mine.

So question 3 is easy enough, and the answer I have helps with question 2. First, I can use embedding to distinguish visual calculating and calculating in the ordinary way with symbols. And then, James's double take on creativity works for shapes and rules. There's always the chance for something new. Rules are defined when shapes are combined in pairs—there's learning what to try—and rules apply via embedding—there's sagacity seeing in alternative ways. Is this all that's needed? What does embedding allow that "results" miss? How does it work?

Reasoning is often surprising when it succeeds—at least for James—and may be equally so when it fails. I want to begin with an instance of the latter to illustrate a few details of embedding, and what these mean for shapes and rules. My example deals with line drawings, but this in itself doesn't make it visual. If drawings are handled logically—that is to say, rationally in terms of given parts—shapes aren't really defined. Neither reasoning nor calculating is automatically aligned with seeing. Things can break down. In fact, my example shows how easy it is for calculating and seeing to disagree. Of course, there's a way to reconcile them that I'm going to show, too. Visual calculating and hence visual reasoning are neatly practicable with shapes and rules.

A First Look at Calculating

T. G. Evans applies the rules of a "grammar"—it's syntax in Langer's sense—to define shapes in terms of their "lowest-level constituents"—or alternatively atoms, bits, cells, components, features, primitives, simples, symbols, units, etc. This illustrates some notions that have been used widely in computer applications for a long time. They're ideas that are as fresh now as they ever were. (Rules like this were applied early on in "picture languages" to combine picture atoms and larger fragments, and just afterward in Christopher Alexander's better known yet formally derivative "pattern language" for building design. The story today in AI, computer graphics, design, etc. is the one I told on page 51 about units, Lindenmayer systems, and cellular automata. My set grammars are also alike—but maybe more inclusive, being the same as Turing machines. Of even greater interest, though, set grammars work the way shape grammars do for points. For lines, things diverge with important consequences for visual calculating. The dimension *i* of basic elements makes a difference—what happens as rules are tried depends on the value of *i*, and whether it's zero or not.)

Evans's grammar contains rules like this one

Three lines → Triangle

that defines triangles in the ordinary way as polygons with three sides. In order to show how the rule works, I first have to give the embedding relation, and then tell what options there are to satisfy it. For Evans, embedding is identity among constituents. This is the same for points. The rule applies to a shape when all of its constituents (points) are also in the shape. Moreover, the constituents in the rule may be transformed as a whole arrangement—they can be moved around, reflected, or scaled—to determine the right correspondence with constituents in the shape.

Evans uses this shape

as an example. The shape has a finite set of constituents. It's twenty-four line segments, each one defined separately by its endpoints—first there are the four sides of the large square and their halves

then the two diagonals of the square and their halves

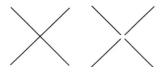

and finally the horizontal and the vertical and their halves

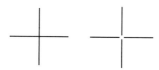

And Evans's rule—the one for three lines—applies without a hitch to pick out the sixteen triangular parts of the shape. There are eight small triangles, four medium ones, and four large ones

This is really pretty neat. In fact, it's a very clever bit of coding. If there were only eight long lines in the shape, then there would just be large triangles and no small or medium ones. And if lines were only halves, then there would be three distinct kinds of triangles

not all with three sides, that I would have to define in separate rules. In addition to the rule

Three lines → Triangle

for small triangles, I'd need a pair of new rules

Four lines → Triangle

Six lines → Triangle

for medium triangles and large ones. But how many representations does a triangle have? I thought there were always three sides. That's what I was taught in school, and that's what I normally say I see. Evans's grammar cuts through this confusion artfully. The grammar is seeing what I do, when a solitary rule of no great complexity—it's what you expect: three lines—is used to calculate. What else do rules and constituents imply? How far can I go with this?

I can give rules for squares and rectangles—four lines apiece; bow ties of distinct shapes—again four lines apiece; and congruent crosses—either two lines or their four halves

2 lines   2 lines   4 halves   4 halves

And my rules find all of these figures wherever they are in the shape. There are five squares, four rectangles, six bow ties, and two crosses of each type. This is great. But already there are signs of trouble. I can't tell the crosses apart just by looking at them, even if I can by the rule I apply. Calculating and seeing are beginning to look different.

Now suppose I go on to define an additional rule

Line →

that erases lines—the lowest-level constituents—in Evans's shape. What do I get if I apply my new rule to erase the lines in all small triangles, or in all medium or large ones? Whatever happens, I don't expect to see the lines I've removed in my result. If I do the erasing by hand to remove the lines I see in small triangles, the shape disappears. And for medium or large triangles—erasing what I see by hand without thinking about it—I get a cross that looks like this

But in all three cases when I calculate with the rule, my results look like this

Some parts are hard to delete when I use my eyes, even after I've applied the rule. The shape is visually intact whichever lines I erase. You can check me if you like. I haven't made any careless mistakes, yet I don't get what I expect. I must be seeing things. And, actually, I am. I always knew it would be this way. Seeing is believing, but not always. The lines I've erased with the rule aren't there. No two of the resulting shapes are the same. They're numerically distinct—what better way to tell things apart—with eight, sixteen, and eighteen constituents apiece, and they're all different from the shape

I started with.

Be careful, though. The problem is not that I can't trace eight or more distinct lines in Evans's shape—that's easy—but that for Evans there are four numerically distinct versions either with eight lines, sixteen, eighteen, or twenty-four. And these versions are hard to keep straight. How can I tell which is which by looking? What happens if they get mixed up? How can anyone tell, without consulting a higher authority or some kind of official record? God always has the right answer, but is apt to conceal it. Revelation comes from faith. But I'm left with experts and others who don't know. Whom do I ask to tell them apart? Answering this question is a real predicament—it just goes on and on. I'm lucky that I don't have to trust my eyes. There's a more effective way. I can calculate to find out. Think of this as an experiment on a computer to find the hidden (deep) structure of a shape. I can keep track of where the rule applies to decide what I can't see. There's some bookkeeping, to be sure, but the way seems clear. If I follow Evans and define constituents by their endpoints, then I can record horizontals (H) followed by verticals (V) and diagonals (D) in three different lists

1. 2. 3.

4. 5. 6.

7. 8. 9.

(H (1 (3), 4 (6), 7 (9)),V (1 (7), 2 (8),
3 (9)), D (1 (9), 3 (7)))

(H (1 (2), 2 (3), 4 (5, 6), 5 (6), 7 (8),
8 (9)), V (1 (4), 2 (5, 8), 3 (6), 4 (7), 5 (8),
6 (9), D (1 (9), 3 (7)))

(H (1 (2), 2 (3), 4 (5, 6), 5 (6), 7 (8),
8 (9)), V (1 (4), 2 (5, 8), 3 (6), 4 (7), 5 (8),
6 (9), D (1 (5, 9), 3 (5, 7)))

(Of course, these descriptions change if I rotate Evans's shape 45 degrees

The discrepancies between the new lists and the original ones are pretty much the same as the discrepancies between the original lists themselves, yet the former seem trivial and inessential. Who decides what's important?) Telling shapes apart may take

more than my eyes. It depends on lists. Look again. What difference do you see? There's no way to break the monotony.

Let's look at how the shape

is put together, and what this implies about what I can see. The twenty-four constituents (line segments) in the shape include the eight long lines

and their sixteen halves

Each long line contains two halves, and each half is contained in a long line. This gives me the sixteen triangles I want. But if I erase a long line, there are two halves that visually compensate for the loss. And if I erase any half, there's a long line that fills in. The shape is going to look exactly the same, even as its constituents change. Calculating multiplies differences I simply can't see. Is this a reasonable way for reasoning to work?

These are the facts I have so far—they go from what I can see to what I can't. It seems that

(1)   some shapes can look different and be the same,

while

(2)   other shapes can look the same and be different.

There are many examples of statement 1 in the introduction, including the three lines

part of Evans's shape

with triangles, pyramids, and tetrahedrons, and the pair of figures

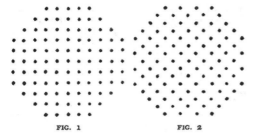

FIG. 1   FIG. 2

from C. S. Peirce. In fact, what I'm trying to show in this book is how the embedding relation makes statement 1 practicable for shapes like these when rules are used to calculate. Rules let me see in alternative ways. And then Evans's shape gives four examples of statement 2. This is solid evidence that's right to heed. Nonetheless, I'm uncomfortable with my taxonomy. I'm going to affirm 1 and deny 2—it's just not the way shapes work. I can vary how shapes look any time there's something else to do. Their parts change freely, so they can be anything they need to be. There's plenty of ambiguity to go on. That's why drawing is useful in design. But constitutive distinctions that are permanent and fixed—"eternal and unchangeable"—and lost out of sight get in the way. They have to be remembered and honored to go on. Seeing begins and ends with my eyes. There's nothing more than they can find. If shapes look the same, then they are the same. What you see is what you get. Really, it's simply a question of logic. Deny statement 2 yourself and see if I'm right.

(The best way to explore the occult properties of Evans's shape is to count the different kinds of triangles it contains. This is what descriptions—representations like lists, strings, graphs, networks, trees, schemas, sets, structures, etc.—that are given in terms of constituents are for. Small triangles all have three lines apiece, but medium ones can have three to five lines and large ones three to nine. Lines are taken from these schemes

There are five distinct configurations for each grouping of three collinear lines

Table 1
Census of Triangles in Evans's Shape

Number of lines	3	4	5	6	7	8	9	3–9
Number of triangles	16	48	124	180	120	36	4	528

So there are five versions of each medium triangle, and a hundred twenty-five of each large one. The census is given in table 1. More is happening in Evans's shape than I can possibly see. What use are my eyes when nearly everything is hidden? I've no doubt that Evans's shape contains sixteen triangles that meet his definition and mine. I simply have to look to find them. I can trace them out. But this is only a half—actually 3 percent—truth.)

Constituents are made to calculate, and they're supposed to work. Surely, I can debug what I've done. That's an important part of defining rules and understanding what they do. If I erase a long line, I can also remove its halves at the same time. This takes another rule

Three collinear lines →

but gives some interesting results. I get a cross (two lines) and another one (four halves)—at least this looks right—erasing the sides of large triangles

three crosses (either two lines or four halves)—for the sides of medium triangles

and Evans's shape—evidently, the version with eight lines—for the sides of small triangles

This is a marked improvement, plus it shows what's left to do. If I add the conjugate rule for halves

Two collinear lines →

so that the long line that contains a half is erased when the half is, then I get the visual results I'm looking for. I started with a single rule to erase a line, and now I have three rules that have to be applied judiciously. Who would ever think that triangles could cause so much trouble? Imagine the difficulties for harder shapes. But so what? Problems are there to solve any way you can. That's what reason is for. Evans's grammar is fixed—it's permanent and permanently repaired—even if my two new rules are ad hoc.

Only there's more to worry about. How does this square with statement 1 above, and what it implies? Seeing may be confused in other ways as well, when it comes to calculating in Evans's grammar. Many parts that are easy for me to see—there are no tricks; you can see the same parts yourself—are impossible for rules to find. Take the triaxial motif

with equilateral arms. I can define the Y in the rule

Three lines → Y

The Y appears indefinitely many times

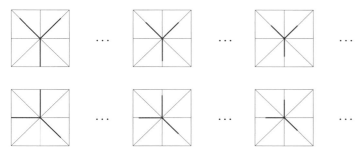

yet the rule—or any other rule for that matter—can't find it, not even once. And it's easy to check that this is correct. It's calculating, but it isn't seeing. What's gone wrong? All of a sudden, Evans's grammar is blind. Is there always something that's going to be missed when I calculate? It's not because I can't define precisely what I want to find. I can do that for any shape (part) I like. Maybe I should try the rule

Three lines → WHY

Why can't I see Y? (Words that sound alike can be different, just not in Evans's way.) It's part of sensible experience, and it's almost everywhere I look. What's going on with shapes and rules?

In Evans's shape, there are too many constituents for triangles, and not enough of them for even a single Y. One or two line segments can be found in a number of places here and there

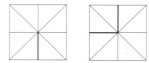

but never three equal segments all at once. I can always add new constituents to complete Y's

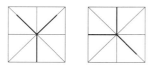

But additional constituents don't help when I try to erase lines in triangles. (They also change the census in table 1.) What's more, there are never going to be enough constituents to find all of the Y's there are to see. No matter what I do, I can't specify (anticipate) everything I might see before I've had a chance to look. What about other letters from A to Z—say, big K's and little k's? What about crosses

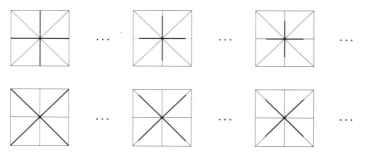

Evans's constituents miss almost all of them, even as they make two of them more than once. My analysis has got to stop sometime, and when it does, calculating goes blind. Analysis may be an essential part of reasoning—maybe it's a prerequisite—but it seems either to confuse seeing or to limit it.

Neither the surplus of lines nor the lack of Y's and everything else from A to Z seems right. What I see and what Evans implies I should when I calculate just aren't the same. Must calculating and visual experience be related so haphazardly? There's a huge gap between them now that I have to bridge if I'm going to get anywhere with visual calculating. Visual reasoning seems long out of sight. But hold on. Maybe the gap results from flawed reasoning about seeing. Maybe it's artificial.

The problems with Evans's grammar are unnecessary—if you're still with me, you've probably decided that calculating is, too—and they needn't ever arise. Evans uses a zero-dimensional embedding relation for points—namely, identity—to calculate with shapes made up of one-dimensional line segments. As a result, lines behave like points even though they take up space. This appears to be trivial enough—lots of things are the same; for example, Lego blocks and Tinkertoys—only the disparity between identity for points and embedding for lines has some bewildering consequences. Take two.

First, the shape

has no obvious constituents to serve as points. It's easy to see that lines come undivided. How can I cut these

into meaningful segments without knowing beforehand what rules there are and how I'm going to use them? Internally, both of the lines are homogeneous. And externally, their relationship is arbitrary. This is how it is for the lines in any shape. I can never be sure how many segments there are. Lines aren't numerically distinct like points. They fuse and divide freely. I can draw two lines to make a cross

and then see alternating pairs of L's

or I can turn this around and draw L's, and see a cross. Nonetheless, I've decided to calculate. So I have to define points explicitly in whatever way I can cook up according to my immediate interests and goals. Right now I'm looking for triangles. There's a kind of funny circularity here that's almost hermeneutic. I've got to find triangles in order to define a rule that lets me find triangles, or something of the sort. Seeing and calculating are linked. That's for sure. But perhaps their relationship isn't what I want. Seeing may be finished—completed if not done for—before I calculate at all. Is there any way to reverse this inequality, so that seeing and calculating are the same? Seeing and calculating might look the same if there weren't a problem to solve before calculating to solve the problem.

And second, after I determine these points, I have to keep to them for as long as I calculate. There's no way to start over with another analysis. I'm told constantly that it's cheating if I do. It's logically incoherent. Rationality depends first and foremost on points that are given once and for all—they're "eternal and unchangeable"—and then on showing how they're arranged. Otherwise, you can't tell what's going on, anything can happen. Without a vocabulary of units, it seems there's nothing to explain. (Emerson is famous for the reverse view. "A foolish consistency is the hobgoblin of little minds, adored by little statesmen and philosophers and divines. With consistency a great soul has simply nothing to do." So much for Plato and politics, but today the first phrase of the first sentence is really a cliché. As a student, I used it as a reason to be silly. But the following sentence is the real clincher. When the analysis I've already used is a special description that controls my ongoing experience, what am I free to do? There are no surprises left—only Kierkegaard's rote results. They're repeatable, sure enough, but they don't show anything new. This is neither drawing nor design. Where's the ambiguity and the novelty it implies? Why not change my mind? What stops me from seeing something new? I can't imagine a consistency that's not going to be foolish sooner or later if I calculate with shapes. What I see may alter erratically.) There's an underlying description of the shape

that depends on how I've defined constituents before I begin to calculate. The description isn't anywhere to see. It's hidden out of sight and isn't supposed to intrude. Only it limits everything I see and everything I do. There's no problem, as long as I continue to experience the same things and my goals are fixed—if nothing really changes. Otherwise, it's nearly impossible to try anything new—or merely to erase lines and to find Y's—without running into big trouble.

Evans isn't to blame for the embedding relation he uses. He applies definitions like "three lines are a triangle" to describe what he sees in the way that's normally expected in computer models. This follows what's become a de facto canon—

Calculate with things that aren't zero dimensional as if they were.

It's "being digital." And there's a plethora of examples, from computer graphics, imaging, and fractal modeling, to engineering analysis and weather forecasting, to complex adaptive systems of all sorts. Finite elements—units, big and small and in between— are combined to describe things that aren't sensibly divided. It's a powerful method with an ancient history and a superb record of success, and it works like magic. Yes, it's simply an illusion. And it's easy to expose when calculating and sensible experience are asked to agree. But this is nothing new. James says it squarely—there are "many ways in which our conceptual transformation of perceptual experience makes it less comprehensible than ever." What's gone wrong? Maybe there's no such thing as visual calculating. Do all of these negative examples mean that I should give up, or are they reason to try another way? What kind of evidence would make a difference?

I'm going to have to show that analysis—segmenting or dividing shapes into lowest-level constituents—isn't something necessary in order to calculate, but rather something contingent that changes or evolves—even discontinuously—as a by-product of what I see and do. Analysis is one way to show what happens as I go on calculating. What I do as I calculate—the rules I have and the way I use them—determines how constituents are defined. There's nothing to see or do before I start. There are still rules to try.

What Makes Calculating Visual?

Sometimes I try an informal rule of thumb to decide when calculating is visual. Both the dimension (dim) of the elements (el) and the dimension of the embedding relation (em) I use to calculate are the same. I can state this in a nifty little formula that's a good mnemonic—

$$\dim(el) = \dim(em)$$

I'm pretty sure the rule is sufficient—whenever my formula is satisfied, it's visual calculating. I'm just not sure the rule is necessary. There may be examples of visual calculating that don't meet this standard. Perhaps it would be better to try and make sense of the relationship $\dim(el) \leq \dim(em)$. But whatever the answer—and I'm ready to bet on equality, especially because the formula is so elegant—I want the equivalence (biconditional)

$$\dim(el) = 0 \equiv \dim(em) = 0$$

to be satisfied. I want to ensure that zero-dimensional embedding relations are only used with zero-dimensional elements, that is to say, with things that behave like points. This rubs against canonical practice when it comes to calculating. But I want to try something else.

As formulas go, mine is pretty vague. I don't say how to evaluate either side except in a few ad hoc cases. Still, the formula is enough for the time being. And there's no reason to avoid ambiguous or vague ideas when they stimulate calculating. In fact, they may be indispensable to what I'm trying to show. I can't imagine anything more ambiguous and vague than a shape that isn't divided (analyzed) into meaningful constituents, so that it's without definite parts and evident purpose. I'm going to use my formula to get to the idea that calculating is visual if it can deal with shapes like this. I want to use rules to determine what parts I see and what I can say about them, and to allow for what I see and what I say to change freely as I calculate. And I want this to happen every time I try a rule. I'm told calculating is a good example of what it means to be discursive—well, sometimes when I calculate it looks logical, but most of the time it's only desultory rambling with my eyes. Shapes should be ambiguous and vague—full of miscellaneous possibilities—and ready to use when I calculate, wandering in the region of the many and variable.

So what can I do to make Evans's example visual? My formula provides twin options. I can change the elements in Evans's shape from lines to points, so that $\dim(el) = \dim(em)$, or I can use another embedding relation that's one dimensional. Each of these alternatives is feasible and amply rewards a closer look.

Suppose that the shape

is the nine points Evans uses to define line segments as constituents

and that the embedding relation is the same—I'll continue to require identity among constituents. But with points, I really don't have much of a choice. Embedding works only in this way.

I can use the rule

Three points → Triangle

in place of Evans's rule to define 45-degree right triangles

Or equivalently, I can give the rule in this identity

→

in the way I normally do in shape grammars, where two shapes—in this case, they're the same—are separated by an arrow. I'll say more about rules like this a little later when I look at embedding for lines. My new rule in whatever form finds twenty-eight different triangles in the shape

· · ·

· · ·

· · ·

including the sixteen from Evans's example. But there are forty-eight other triangles in the shape in five different constellations

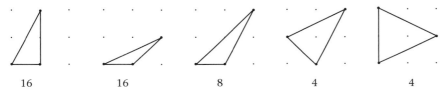

16   16   8   4   4

These are readily defined in additional rules. (Of course, it's easy to define all triangles using a single rule in the way Evans does, or as effortlessly, using a schema for rules in my way. This is also something I'll come back to again.) I can't find any other triangles. My grammar is seeing what I do.

Now what happens when I erase points or look for Y's? In the first case, my rule is just like it was before, but for points

Point →

Or equivalently, the erasing rule

When I apply the rule to erase the vertices of Evans's small triangles, the shape disappears the way it should. And if I do the same for medium triangles and for large ones, then I get the shapes

·   ·

·   ·   ·   ·   ·

·   ·

Everything looks fine, even if the cross appears in alternative ways. In fact, this may be a boon. I can decide whether I've erased the vertices of medium triangles or large ones simply by looking at the result. There's nothing to see that I can't understand. Points aren't like lines. They don't fill in for the loss of others because they don't combine to make other points and don't contain them. The grammar I've got for points is doing far better than Evans's grammar for lines. Perhaps visual calculating is really a possibility after all.

But what about Y's

·   ·

·

·

with equilateral arms that are defined in this rule

Four points → Y

or with the identity

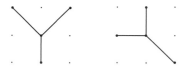

They're not a problem. I can't see the Y anywhere in my shape. It's possible there are other kinds of Y's—I can define additional rules to find them—but their arms are of different lengths

and that's not what I'm looking for right now. Calculating and seeing match again—this time with uncanny precision.

So here I am with the shape

·   ·   ·

·   ·   ·

·   ·   ·

that's just what calculating tells me it is. Nothing is ever hidden. Anything a rule can find, I can see. And what I see depends on the rule I apply. There's nothing to see that a rule can't find. This is just what I had in mind for visual calculating. But there's usually more to drawing than points—my example isn't completely convincing. Everything works because the shape contains points—lowest-level constituents once again—that don't interact. They're always independent when they're combined. Embedding means identity. The whole thing is strictly combinatorial—points are like marbles ready to count, and seeing is a matter of combining and rearranging them in alternative ways. Surely, there's something more to seeing than counting. To see what it is, I have to go back to lines and change the embedding relation, so that it's not simply identity. This isn't hard, and it makes a big difference.

Suppose I keep Evans's shape the same

I can draw it with eight lines—its maximal elements—the way an experienced drafts-man would. It might go like this—in sequence, the three horizontals

the three verticals

and the two diagonals

Only I'm not obliged to treat these lines as constituents. In particular, the parts of the shape may be combinations of maximal lines—just four of Evans's triangles are defined in this way—or, allowing for everything I can including the other twelve trian-gles, combinations of maximal lines and any of their segments. Now there are indefi-nitely many parts, and none trumps another. But segments aren't given all at once like points or the members of a set. They're not set out explicitly one by one; only maximal lines are. This is something new that looks almost Aristotelian. Parts are potentially infinite—I'm free to cut Evans's shape wherever I like—and not actually so. The parts I see—the limited number I resolve when I divide the shape or draw it—depend on my rules and how I use them. I need an embedding relation for this that's one dimensional and that works for lines. (Linguists like to say that languages are potentially infinite sets of sentences, and explain this with rules that combine words recursively. This is calculating by counting. It's why Chomsky's grammars are generative and it's what it means to be creative. Sets of shapes are the same—my rules are recursive, too. Only my rules do more when they divide shapes into parts. Seeing isn't counting, nor does cre-ativity end with words and recursion, or searching through the myriad alternatives they provide trying to find what you want. Combinatorial play goes just so far. But shapes fuse and divide as rules are tried. Sagacity makes a difference, along with learning that pairs shapes in rules.)

Let's agree that a line l is embedded in any other line l' if l and l' are identical

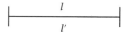

or—allowing more than embedding for points—l is a segment of l'

In general, a shape M is part of any shape S if the maximal lines of M are embedded in maximal lines of S. (I was drawn to this neat relation by necessity. When I started using a typewriter—I was eleven or so—I contrived an easy way to check my work against an original or if I had to retype a page to correct mistakes without making more. Proofreading was hard. It took too long, and mine was unreliable. So I would embed one page in another one. I would tape the first to a window and move my copy over it. This let me see what was on both pages at once. If things that were supposed to be the same lined up, I knew my typing was OK. Creative designers use tracing paper this way. Who would have guessed that it's just using rules?) Whatever I can see in S—anything I can trace—is one of its parts. This leads straight to calculating in the algebras of shapes in part II, and is almost exactly what James has in mind when he tells how reasoning works. For the rule $M \rightarrow P$ and the shape S, if I can see M in S, then I can replace it with another shape P by subtracting M from S and adding P. I'll add by drawing shapes together, so that their maximal lines fuse. And I'll subtract by adding shapes and then erasing one, so that segments of maximal lines can be removed. Remarkably, the embedding relation implies nearly everything I need in order to do all of this with axiomatic precision. I also need transformations of some kind to complete the correspondence between M and P and S in the way I did for Evans's kind of rules. But I'll skip the details for now because they're not too hard to fill in, even if they have a host of important consequences. It's enough to know that transformations are there, so that different shapes can be alike.

With lines and this embedding relation, Evans's rule to define triangles is simply the identity

I don't have to say what a triangle is in terms of constituents that are already given. I only have to draw it. It makes no sense at all to have the rule

Three lines $\rightarrow$ Triangle

because I don't know how the sides of triangles are divided—remember, there's no telling how many lines there are in a shape—or even if sides are parts. And I don't have to divide Evans's shape into constituents either for the identity to apply in the way I want, to find every triangle. The shape is OK as a drawing, too

When I use the identity, there are sixteen triangles—this is just what I see and can trace—even though the small triangles and the medium ones have maximal lines that aren't maximal lines in the shape. My erasing rule—the one I added to Evans's grammar—is

and it produces the results I get if I erase the lines I see by hand. In practical terms, this is just tracing again. If I apply the rule to the sides of small triangles, the shape disappears. And when I use it to take away the sides of medium or large triangles, I get the cross

This is the way it's supposed to work—seeing and calculating agree perfectly. When I see a part and change it according to a rule, nothing is hidden to confuse the result. Whatever distinctions a rule makes, I can see. There may be surprises—there are plenty to come—but they aren't conceptual ones caused because I've represented shapes with constituents that I can't vary after I begin to calculate. There's no hidden analysis that determines what I can see and what I can do. Surprises are perceptual. They're a natural part of sensible experience. And the rule

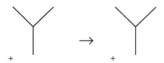

—another identity—finds as many Y's in the shape as you care to see. Seeing is never disappointed. There's no part I can see that a rule can't find. Novelty is always possible. What you see is what you get.

It may be useful to digress a little to compare Evans's example for points and for lines. For points, there are finitely many parts for rules to find, but for lines, there are indefinitely many parts. This is perfectly clear for Y's. And it's fundamentally so for the rules

The one can be used only a limited number of times, while the other's work may never be done. A point—just like a constituent—can be erased in exactly one way. I can't remove some of it now and some of it later. When it goes, it goes all at once. It's there or it's not. But I can divide a line wherever I like. I can take any piece now and another piece later. Its segments provide for endless possibilities. Points and lines just aren't the same kind of thing with their distinct dimensions and their corresponding embedding relations. If I confuse them in order to calculate, then I'm simply not calculating visually.

But there's a lot more. What about the constituents of the shape

How do these change as I calculate, and how are they finally defined? This is Evans's problem in reverse. He has to divide the shape before calculating, so that his rule can find all of the triangles there are to see. This analysis isn't part of calculating. It's more important. It's what makes calculating possible. I'd like to know how to define constituents, but Evans doesn't say. He probably doesn't think about it. It's just something you do when you're going to calculate. Only how do you do it without calculating? Even if it's obvious, I'd like to see what's involved. And it may not be that obvious. Evans gives twenty-four constituents when twenty-two will do. So I'll take a different tack and show how to define constituents as part of calculating. I'm not stuck in the way Evans is. I'm free to look at everything—including analysis—as the result of applying rules. This is precisely what I said visual calculating should do. Embedding makes it possible.

Let's look at something easy. I want to use the rule

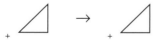

to calculate, so that constituents are defined dynamically again and again in an ongoing process. The rule is an identity: it simply tells me a triangle is a triangle without referring to its sides—Evans's definition—or to any other parts. I can't say anything about a shape in a rule—identity or not—that goes much further than pointing to it and announcing that it's that. I can name it—a triangle is a triangle—but there's nothing definite about its parts. I'll say more about this and what it means for visual calculating and reasoning itself as soon as I get to schemas for rules. Right now, though, I only have my identity for triangles. What good is it to know that a triangle is a triangle?

Identities are interesting rules. Rules are supposed to change things, but identities don't. Whenever they're used to calculate—let's apply one or more to a shape S a number of times—the result is a monotonous series that looks like this

$$S \Rightarrow S \Rightarrow \cdots \Rightarrow S$$

In each step ($S \Rightarrow S$), another part of S is resolved—that's the part I see—and then nothing else happens. The shape doesn't change. It stays the same. At least that's how it looks. Identities are constructively empty. They're useless! And it's standard practice to discard them. I've seen doctoral students do so with relish. There's something liberating about getting rid of unnecessary stuff. But this may be shortsighted—even rash. It misses what identities do. There's more to them than idle repetition. Identities are observational devices. They're all I need to divide the shape S with respect to what I see. If I record the various parts they pick out as they're tried, I can define topologies for S. These show its constituents and how they change as I calculate.

Suppose I apply the identity

to the shape

so that large triangles are picked out in a clockwise fashion in this four-step series

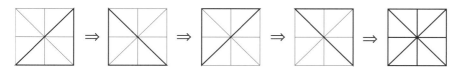

If I take the triangles the identity resolves—remember, these are the triangles I see—I can use them to define constituents. I'm going to calculate some more to explain how I've been calculating. There are a number of ways to do this. For example, I can work out sums and products, or I can add complements as well. Complements give Boolean algebras for the shape. They're a special kind of topology with atoms that provide a neat inventory of constituents.

The first time I try the identity to calculate, I get a Boolean algebra with two atoms

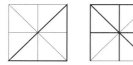

I see a triangle and its complement. It may be a little far-fetched to assume that I see the shape

—I have a hard time making sense of it until I try my identity again—but complements are sometimes like this. They're surely worth the added effort, though, because they simplify things as I go on. There are four atoms when I apply the identity the second time

Now I see a pair of triangles and their complements that combine in products to define constituents. And there are seven atoms the third and fourth times I use the identity

including the six individual sides of the large triangles and the interior cross. This is all pretty good. The constituents I finally get match my visual expectations. The sides of the triangles interact, while the cross is a figure on its own.

Of course, there are also medium and small triangles in the shape

And I can apply the identity

 →

to find these triangles in exactly the same way. Medium triangles—if I resolve all of them—define nine constituents

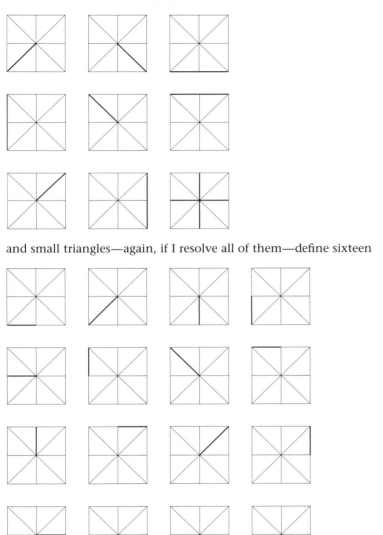

and small triangles—again, if I resolve all of them—define sixteen

The atoms I get for the small triangles—the half lines in Evans's example—are the most refined constituents I can define, regardless of how I use the identity to pick out triangles. All of the large triangles in the shape are made up of six constituents apiece, all of the medium triangles contain four constituents each, and all of the small triangles have three

But this doesn't mean—as it did in Evans's example—that triangles have to be described (represented) in three different ways for the identity to work in the way it's supposed to. For the identity

the embedding relation is given for lines, so that they can fuse and divide in any way whatsoever, but for Evans's rule

Three lines → Triangle

embedding requires that constituents—they neither fuse nor divide—match in an exact correspondence, as elements do in sets. Perhaps this is another way of seeing it. A shape—at least with lines, or basic elements that are planes or solids—is not a set. For points, shapes and sets coincide. Whether or not embedding is identity is key in saying how shapes work.

My identity applies to shapes, not to their descriptions. As far as the identity is concerned, a triangle is whatever I draw. It's simply this

with no divisions of any kind—no sides, no angles, and no anything else. And it's always there to see if it can be embedded. I only have to trace over it. Evans gets into trouble because of the way he calculates. He confuses a triangle—something sensible—with a solitary description—an abstract definition—that's only one of many conceptual transformations. This is the kind of thing that can happen whenever my formula $dim(el) = dim(em)$ isn't satisfied, and in particular, when the embedding relation is zero dimensional and elements aren't. Shapes and descriptions are different sorts of things. But more important, I can calculate with shapes without referring to their descriptions. This idea provides another useful way to think about visual calculating.

Only before doing so, let's look at Evans's approach in a slightly different way. Let's ask how to make it work, so that lowest-level constituents—points, lines, or whatever—correspond with what I see. They're numerically distinct, and I can pick them out whenever I look. This shows more of what's at stake—why lowest-level constituents are just another way of thinking about points.

There Is No Vocabulary—Well, Almost

Shapes containing points are numerically distinct. But shapes made up of basic elements of higher dimension don't have this property. For example, Evans's shape

has at least eight lines, and any number of lines more. Of course, I can cook up special ways to divide shapes—always with the concomitant loss of other parts—so that basic elements are numerically distinct. I can use maximal lines in the way I have or I might also choose maximal lines and the different segments they define when they intersect. The total number of segments for a line in that's divided n times and the line itself is the sum of the numbers from 1 to $n + 1$, as here for $n = 2$

Counting like this provides a nice way to describe shapes that's especially useful when you're looking for polygons. But it's already pretty clear that it isn't visual. It gives the twenty-four lines Evans uses so effectively to resolve triangles. Each maximal line is divided once in half to define three segments. But this seems profligate. Maybe the sixteen halves—the "minimal" elements—are all that I need. They're the segments I got when I applied the identity

everywhere I could. But let's try something else where there may be more than basic elements—maximal, minimal, or otherwise.

   Suppose I look at the lowest-level constituents in Evans's approach as symbols or units—basic elements or not—in a given vocabulary, and that I want to arrange them, so that it's always the same what's there. How can I use a vocabulary of shapes if they're taken this way when they're combined? How do the shapes look, and what kinds of arrangements are possible? Can I be certain that I can distinguish the shapes I give for symbols visually, with no ambiguity? This isn't always so. For example, this shape

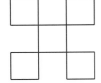

contains exactly five squares—no ambiguity. But if I slide the four outside squares in this quintet clockwise, I get the shape

Now I need only count four squares, yet may also find five. How can I lose a square that I haven't erased? Where did it go? I want the shapes in my vocabulary to be just like points that are independent and add up in one way when they're combined and moved around. How does this work if basic elements and embedding aren't zero dimensional—if I let

dim(el) > 0

and

dim(el) = dim(em)

What does this tell me about the difference between points and lines, or basic elements of higher dimension? What does it say about embedding and identity? How should I see to count?

Maximal elements work already as symbols in a vocabulary. Lines may all look alike—they're geometrically similar—but I can use standard lengths to define different symbols, in fact, everything from A to Z. And this isn't a problem for planes. There are triangles and squares

and plenty of other figures that aren't the same. Nor is it a problem for solids. But symbols needn't be maximal elements. They may be defined in the normal way as shapes of other kinds.

Suppose I stick just to straight lines. Then it's always possible to combine the shapes in any vocabulary whatsoever to produce ambiguous results that aren't numerically distinct. Suppose I start with polygons that by themselves are easy to tell apart—perhaps a square and two different right triangles

The sides of a square are the sides of four other squares that combine to make the shape

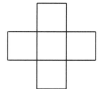

So there are four squares or five in the arrangement. I can also use squares to make triangles in the familiar Pythagorean fashion

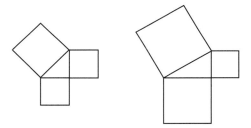

with three squares or three squares and a triangle. And in the opposite way, I can combine triangles to make squares

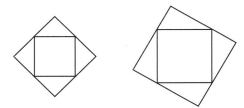

so that nothing adds up. It comes as no surprise that there are four triangles, or four triangles and a square. But because the sides of triangles fuse, there may only be two squares. This is a little weird. The triangles are there to start and aren't to end, while the squares are there to end and aren't to start. Combining the shapes from a vocabulary can be dizzyingly confusing, even when these shapes are visually distinct and all there is to see.

Perhaps the easiest way for shapes to be like symbols is to rely on the normal conventions for printing and reading. This uses the idea that shapes are connected when they touch. First, I'll make sure that the individual shapes in my vocabulary are connected—their parts touch directly or via other parts—and then that they don't touch when I combine them. This is how points work. Every point is connected. And two are the same if and only if they touch. Of course, there's more to say for lines. Two connect—they touch—if the boundary of a line embedded in one and the boundary of a line embedded in the other touch: schematically for collinear lines, so

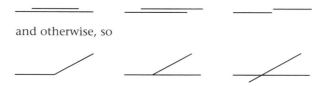

and otherwise, so

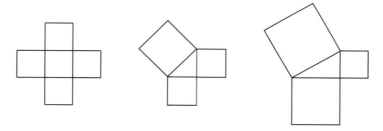

And the recursion is good for planes and solids, too, but that's not important now. (It's interesting to see how Turing machines do the same thing to calculate—there's a tape divided into cells, and each cell contains a single symbol. Being connected fixes the cells and the symbols at once.)

These requirements are simple yet awfully limiting when it comes to the shapes in a vocabulary and combining them in different arrangements. In fact, everything I've done with squares and triangles is barred. This goes for lowercase i's and j's, too, and some punctuation and technical signs. And the loss may be unavoidable. When lesser constraints of increasing strength are tried, they fail to ensure that shapes act like symbols. These constraints also highlight the difference between points and lines. Let's try them in sequence.

To begin with, suppose the shapes in my vocabulary are unrestricted—they may be connected or not—and that they're combined, so that a piece of every one is free— it's a tag to find the shape in an arrangement. I can say this precisely in terms of parts that are defined using embedding—there's a part of every shape that doesn't share a part with any other. This seems just about right, and it isn't hard to see. Now the shapes

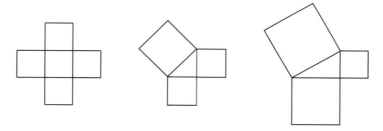

contain four squares or three with respect to the vocabulary

that I've been using. Each outer square has three free sides. But all of the sides of the inner square or triangle are sides of other squares. Nice, only there are some problems that aren't prevented.

Before considering these, it's worth noting that Nelson Goodman proposes an even weaker standard in *Languages of Art*. He endorses it wholeheartedly, without qualification. It's always enough for the shapes in a vocabulary to be "relatively discrete"— no shape has any other as a part.

Even inscriptions of different *atomic* characters may have common parts so long as no such part is an inscription in the scheme; that is, atomic inscriptions need be discrete relative to the notation in question only, as the "a" and the "e" [below] are atomic and discrete in a scheme that recognizes no proper part of either as an inscription.

Goodman uses the vocabulary

as an illustration. The two letters are relatively discrete—there's no E in A, nor A in E—so the shape

contains an A and an E even though they split an I between them. The I isn't relatively discrete with respect to A and E, so it's not in the vocabulary. But I'm free to augment the vocabulary with another shape

that meets Goodman's standard. Only now the shape

is either A and E, or A, +, and E. The + shares parts with A and E that are distinct

and aren't recognized in the vocabulary. So it's OK. The expression

$A + E = AE$

makes sound visual sense—whatever else it might mean

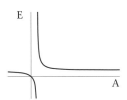

Is this a mistake? The symbols A, E, and + may be the problem. It's no big deal to trace smaller A's in A—A is just the same as the Y in Evans's shape—and in fact, I showed this earlier in the introduction, dividing the shape

The letters A and E and the arithmetic symbol + are all like Y. They aren't discrete with respect to themselves

But Goodman uses A and E, so I guess they work. Surely, he knows how his standard goes. It always helps to check with an authority when seeing is confused. This is a reliable way to clear things up. But my square and triangles

are OK, whatever the fine points. They're relatively discrete, and because they're polygons, they don't have the problem that Y has. Endpoints are shared. Lines don't dangle—they can't be cut little by little at their ends. Still, there are difficulties with the shapes

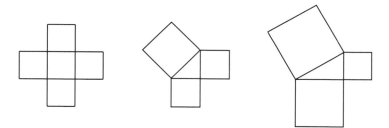

They aren't numerically distinct. Relative discreteness doesn't go far enough. I guess that's it for weaker standards. And in fact with my standard

is just that—A and E.

Nonetheless, the shapes

 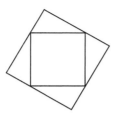

are either four triangles or two squares. Each count is fine separately. All of the sides of the triangles and all of the sides of the squares are free. Only the sum of the triangles includes the squares, and vice versa. And these aren't isolated examples that are safely ignored. It's also the same for the shape

in four different ways with two polygons, when three concave polygons, a trapezoid, and a pentagon

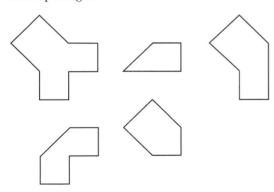

are added to my vocabulary

And possibilities grow exponentially for a vocabulary of polygons

   ...

and corresponding triangles in the shapes in this array

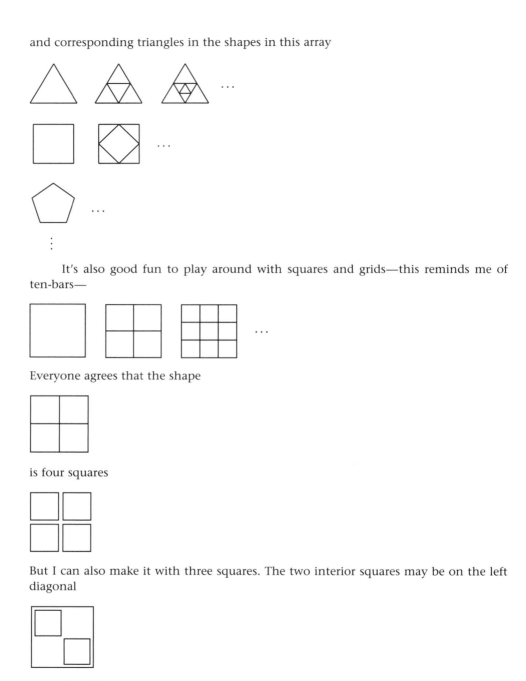

It's also good fun to play around with squares and grids—this reminds me of ten-bars—

Everyone agrees that the shape

is four squares

But I can also make it with three squares. The two interior squares may be on the left diagonal

or on the right one

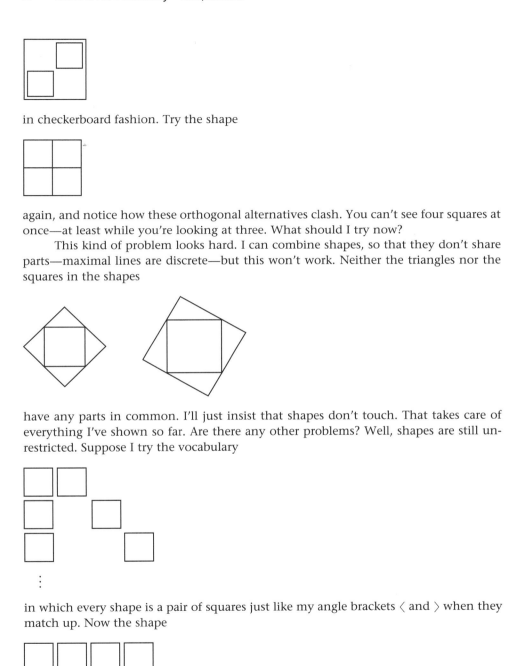

in checkerboard fashion. Try the shape

again, and notice how these orthogonal alternatives clash. You can't see four squares at once—at least while you're looking at three. What should I try now?

This kind of problem looks hard. I can combine shapes, so that they don't share parts—maximal lines are discrete—but this won't work. Neither the triangles nor the squares in the shapes

have any parts in common. I'll just insist that shapes don't touch. That takes care of everything I've shown so far. Are there any other problems? Well, shapes are still un-restricted. Suppose I try the vocabulary

in which every shape is a pair of squares just like my angle brackets ⟨ and ⟩ when they match up. Now the shape

is two shapes from my vocabulary in three different ways

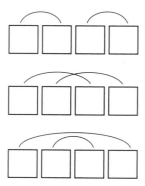

(Is ≪ ≫ ambiguous, as well? Perhaps—but only in two ways.) What's more, a string with n shapes from my vocabulary ($2n$ squares, although I have no way to resolve them) can be divided in $4n^2 - 8n + 3$ different ways. I'm ready to give up. I have Goodman's authoritative account—

Note how far astray is the usual idea that the elements of a notation must be discrete. First, *characters* of a notation, as classes, must rather be disjoint; discreteness is a relation among individuals. Second, *inscriptions* of a notation need not be discrete at all. And finally, even atomic inscriptions of different characters need be discrete relative to that notation only.

—but let's play it safe. It makes sense to require connected shapes that don't touch when they combine. Not even discreteness works all the time—discrete points never touch, but discrete lines may. How many are in the cross

It's twice in Evans's shape each time as two lines or four. But maybe it's three lines in two alternative ways, and in fact, it's three in indefinitely many ways and likewise for four lines or more when discrete lines are connected.

This way of defining a vocabulary of shapes and using it, so that shapes behave like symbols when they're combined, can be applied very broadly and is consistent with everyday practice. Nonetheless, it has a number of obvious drawbacks that limit its practicality in drawing and design. In particular, no connected shape can ever be divided. There are a myriad of possibilities that go unfulfilled—not even a triangle has three sides. Evans's exercise is pointless—there's nothing to say about his shape and no reason for his rule. Making shapes into symbols doesn't appear to be a very good idea. It just makes them look like points—but points are there already—and it's unnecessary to calculate with my kind of rules. What's more, I like the ambiguity that's involved. It's sheer novelty, and there are many ways to use it. Why should I stop seeing?

A Second Look at Calculating

I'm going to show a few additional examples of rules that aren't identities and the way they work to calculate with shapes. I want you to see how shapes are redescribed as I apply rules of a general kind that includes identities and more. There's no set way to divide shapes that rules can't alter. The ability to handle all of the ongoing changes in what I see—there's always a chance for more, even with a single rule—is what makes calculating visual. If you first want to check the formal technicalities that are needed for rules to work—there aren't many—you can jump to part II. It's safe to wait, though, because they aren't really necessary. It's always possible to follow along with your eyes. You simply have to look to understand what I'm doing. Nothing is hidden. I can draw it all when I calculate by seeing.

The rule

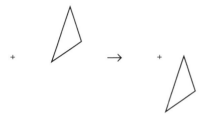

and its inverse

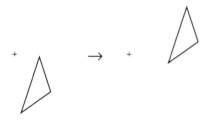

—it's the rule defined when the left and right sides of a rule are flipped—move triangles back and forth along a fixed axis

keeping their orientation constant. Together they're like the identity

and the rule

that are both instances of the schema

$x \rightarrow t(x)$

where x is a shape and t is a transformation or an operator of some kind. Only now, x is a new triangle and t is one translation or another instead of the identity transformation or a rotation. I want to apply my rules—the one and then the other—to change the shape

containing a triangle and a chevron into the shape

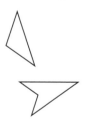

so that the triangle and the chevron are reflected as a pair through a vertical axis running through the chevron

This sounds OK. But if you think about it, it just can't be right. Perhaps that's the point—drawing trumps thinking. There's no reason to stop with what I can deal with in my head before I try my rules and see what they do. In my head, the whole idea is senseless.

The rule

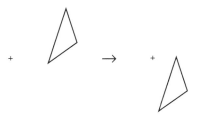

divides the shape

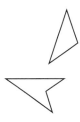

neatly into two distinct parts. It separates the triangle and the chevron, moving the triangle without changing its orientation, and leaving the chevron in place—it stays exactly the same. And when the rule

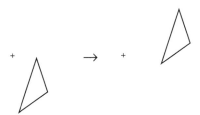

is tried next, the triangle should keep its orientation and move either back to its initial position or to an orthogonal one

There's a choice here because the triangle is bilaterally symmetric—if I reflect it, nothing changes in what I see. So I can apply the rule both ways. Moreover, the chevron should still be where it was to start—at least according to the rule. That's the pickle. What seems to be possible doesn't include what I want

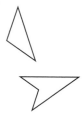

I have to replace the triangle and the chevron in the shape

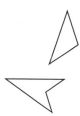

with another triangle in a new orientation, and a chevron that's been reversed. One after the other, the translations in my two rules don't add up in the desired way. No matter what I do with the rules, I can't reorient the triangle. There's no way to reverse its direction. And I can't apply either of the rules to the chevron. There's no way to change it, period. Reflecting these figures together as a pair is impossible with the rules I've got. The local changes they make are just too restricted to produce the global transformation I'm looking for. However, it's awfully hard to see everything in your head if you plan too far in advance—even a couple of easy steps with opposite translations—when there's visual calculating to do. Then, it's usually better to draw.

Let's stop thinking and see what happens. There's a way out of my predicament when I approach it visually, so that a shape can be a shape it's not. It's easy to apply my rules to define the shapes in this series

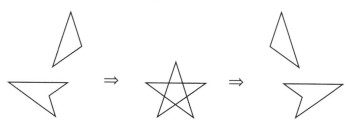

The five-pointed star

contains the translation of the original triangle exactly where it should be, right over the original chevron

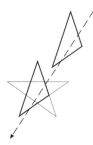

But lines fuse and divide. Look at the star again. In addition to the triangle from the initial shape

I can see four new ones

that are each over different chevrons. It's hard to see more than one triangle at a time. Still, all five are parts of the star. And when any one is moved, the other four disappear along with the corresponding chevrons—just like magic. If I apply the rule

  → +

to the triangle

using a reflection, then I get the result I want. My eyes show me how to do something I never had in mind. My representation of the initial shape as a pair of independent polygons—a triangle that moves around and a chevron that stays put—doesn't tell me what to see, and in fact it keeps me from seeing what I need. It's hard to believe, but there's actual proof. Calculating is creative. It conjures up a triangle and a chevron out of thin air. But the alchemy is real—it's all in the pentacle.

The rule

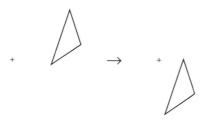

produces the star

from a triangle and chevron, and I can see both in the star. But when I apply the rule

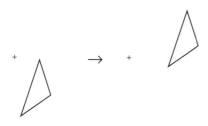

to the star, it changes what I see in a surprising way. Lines fuse whenever they combine, so that all prior divisions disappear. Then new divisions are possible—anywhere. I can find triangles, and chevrons along with them, to reconfigure the star. I don't have to foresee anything before I begin or have any idea of what's going to happen. And I don't have to intervene from outside later on if I see something new. I'm applying rules to define parts on the fly, not to match permanent constituents that are defined in advance. So long as lines fuse, there's no history that privileges some parts and disadvantages the rest. I can't tell parts apart—they're all the same. What you see is what you get. It's visual, and it's calculating.

The three shapes in the series

each contain a triangle and a chevron. But the star

can be divided in five different ways that are mutually incompatible as I go on. One of these divisions

is consistent with what I did to start—that's the constructionist's reason to keep it—while the other four

break with the past in a radical way. The process seems discontinuous, but as I show just below, it really isn't. It involves a gestalt switch, or maybe a kind of saltation, that I can describe in a coherent way. The constructionist's preference is no more rational, reasonable, or right than any other. Triangles are all alike with respect to my rules. I'm free to choose. So which of the five triangles in the star is it finally going to be? There's no way to tell until I try a rule. And then my decision is only ephemeral. It needn't carry over to what I do next. It may be entirely inconsequential—ignored and

Table 2
Constituents Defined by Calculating

Shape	Atoms

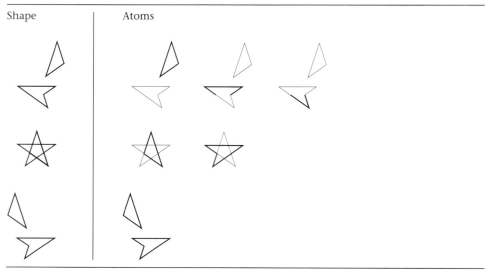

forgotten—as soon as I use a rule again. The parts I see can change at any time depending on how I calculate. It's entirely a matter of embedding—of tracing parts according to rules as I go along.

Descriptions aren't set when I calculate by seeing, but this doesn't mean that they aren't useful. They are—only in a retrospective account of what I've done. I can describe the shapes in the series

with topologies. These show that the reflection from the initial shape to the final shape is continuous, albeit triangles and chevrons are woefully tangled up in the star. They also show how the shapes in the series are divided into constituents as my rules are applied to calculate. My topologies for the shapes are Boolean algebras with the atoms in table 2. (The tips of chevrons are aligned to show how atoms compare from shape to shape.) There are different types of topologies that work just as well. But mine are nice and easy, and they're enough to illustrate what's important right now.

The atoms are defined retrospectively as a by-product of calculating. To quote Kierkegaard—at least as James does—"We live [calculate] forwards, but we understand backwards." I start with the final shape and go back to the initial shape. The final shape has no noticeable structure or complexity. It's an atom, since it isn't divided with a rule. But each preceding shape has the triangle picked out by a rule as an atom, and the atoms required to form its complement and to ensure continuity going forward. This may sound a little obscure—I know I mentioned Kierkegaard—but really neither is. Kierkegaard's "results" show one way to be clear when they're copied off and recited by rote. And I'm simply calculating again to explain how I've been calculating. This fabricates results to use until I change my mind. The details are fleshed out in part II, in another example.

The full value of my topologies as an account of how I calculate is easy to see if I record the divisions in the triangle in the right side of the rule

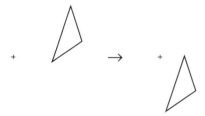

with respect to the lowest-level constituents (atoms) of the star. The triangle is divided into two parts

These combine with the twin constituents

of the chevron in the initial shape to form the triangle and chevron that are the constituents of the star. The pieces

make the triangle in the star that's picked out when the rule

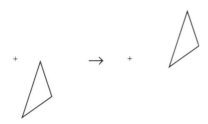

is tried, and the remaining pieces

combine in the chevron that's left after the rule works to produce the final shape. This requires looking back and forth to get right. But it's easy to summarize in a nice-looking lattice. The triangle and chevron that form the star—they're at the ends—and the triangle and chevron needed for the final shape are related as shown here

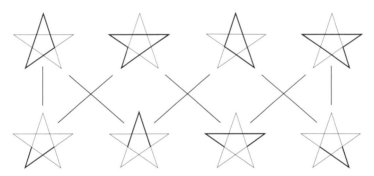

And notice that this is truly a lattice and not a tree or hierarchy. The shapes at the nodes—the quartet of pieces at the top and their parts at the bottom—are all tangled together and interact. Everything works visually when my eyes wander. Neither the pieces nor their parts are independent.

Looking forward, the constituents of the shapes in the series

anticipate what the rules are going to do when they're actually applied. This is what I tried to do in my head and failed. It seems to be divination, only it's not. It happens because constituents are determined as an afterthought. Whenever calculating stops, I can describe what's gone on as a continuous process in which shapes are assembled piece by piece in an orderly way. This makes a good story and a good explanation. It's the kind of retrospective narrative I hear all the time from people doing creative work, especially in design!

Look at it again in another way. Every time the rule

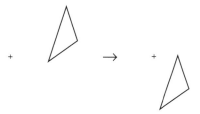

or its inverse is applied, its right side divides in a different way to produce the constituents in the shape that's defined. The triangle has alternative representations that change as rules are tried. First, the triangle is divided in two

as I've already shown, and then it's not divided at all

But perhaps this is starry-eyed. It isn't how I was trained in school—I'm positive every triangle has three sides. And Evans is, too. It's simply not a triangle otherwise. There's a problem somewhere, and not with my rules. Making up your mind too soon—saying what it is before calculating—ends seeing. Evans's shape

shows this brilliantly. The way I describe what I'm doing changes as I calculate, so I can always go on and calculate some more. It isn't fixed before I begin, it's merely an artifact of what I'm trying for the time being. Anything else is mere prejudice. Nothing stops me from seeing things again in a novel way. I'm free to fuse old divisions and make new ones.

Anticipating what might be is challenging, although embedding makes it unnecessary. Still, I wonder what Evans would do with the shape

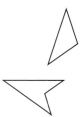

if he were asked to calculate with it in a grammar using his kind of rules. The problem is straightforward—segment the shape into lowest-level constituents, so that any rule I try works. If Evans is anything like me, he would probably say that there's a triangle and a chevron. Why not treat them as symbols from a given vocabulary? The figures are individually connected, and they don't touch. Or, with a little more sophistication than I'm used to, he might say the triangle has three sides and the chevron four. This rehearses the standard definition of polygons that everyone relies on. But neither option does the job. The right divisions are clear-cut in my topologies, and they provide constituents for the shapes in the series

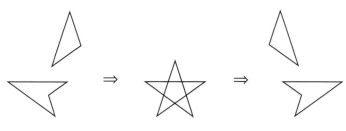

that are defined so that

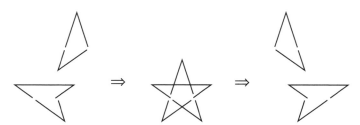

This is fine. It works perfectly when the rule

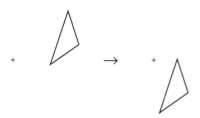

is represented in the following way

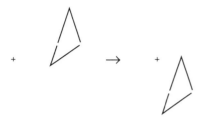

and has an inverse. The only rub is that my topologies are determined after the fact. I can't define them until I calculate, and I can't calculate à la Evans without the divisions they imply. What a terrible fix. I have to decide in advance—before any rules are given or applied—how to cut two randomly related, obviously homogeneous lines

That's one side of the triangle in the initial shape

and one side of the chevron. These are the same two lines I didn't know how to divide on page 75. I still don't know where to cut them. Anything I try would only be a guess, and this won't do. Science is out—of course, there are experiments, but then divisions are after the fact—and clairvoyants and seers are best silent with predictions that are hard to trust. What could possibly prompt a decision until I move the triangle to make the star

and then pick out another triangle and move it—remember, this isn't calculating—to get the final shape

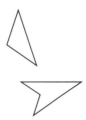

But even preknowledge that's perfect may not give an exact solution. I failed rotating squares in the introduction (pages 25–30)—the future was set shape after shape, only my answer for three squares didn't scale to five squares, seven squares, etc. And it's simply hopeless otherwise, when the future isn't clear. It's asking a lot to know what to expect, so that there's no reason for ongoing experience. The shape

may begin a longer series in which arbitrarily distant shapes determine what's necessary to segment it into constituents. This isn't an inference (induction) I know how to make. And really, who does? It's way beyond the reach of reason—visual or not. Think of all the things I would miss if I got it wrong—but how can you think unless you can see? That's the problem—thinking isn't blind. It's good that constituents aren't needed to calculate. I can draw without having to infer anything about what I'm going to see and do, as long as there's embedding. (Alternatively, embedding lets me anticipate everything without having to say what it is.) That's the secret that makes shapes and rules indispensable in design.

A technical problem of lesser importance is worth noting, as well. Suppose I have the foresight—or simply the blind luck—to represent the initial shape

in the right way, and I have the rule

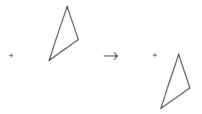

and its inverse. Does this settle the matter? As I said earlier, the triangle

is bilaterally symmetric. So this axis of translation

and this one

are equivalent when my rules are applied. But in order to represent the triangle in these rules, I have to cut its longest side unevenly. This breaks its symmetry. The axis

and the axis

aren't the same. They were originally equivalent—so in addition to the reflection

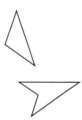

of the initial shape, I could get its rotation

However, this isn't a possibility if the side of the triangle is divided. Now each of my rules needs to be represented twice with different axes to include the distinct versions of the triangle. In particular, the rule

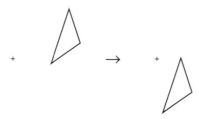

has twin representations—first

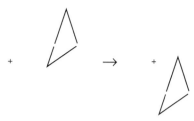

and then in addition

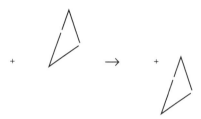

Of course, I can avoid this—but only after the fact—if I make further divisions in the initial shape

If there's one way to divide a shape to do what I want, then there are going to be other ways as well. It's easy to confirm, even if it isn't exactly obvious, that I can cut the sides of the triangle and the chevron in this way

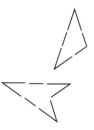

Then the rule

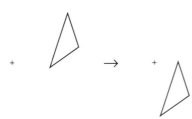

looks like this

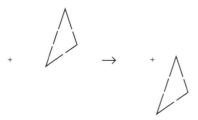

Added complication—above, it's preserving symmetry with finer and finer divisions—is bound to be a chance to make a lot of silly mistakes. But I guess it's good to have more to think about to keep busy. It may feel great to fix things that don't work. The effort is pointless, though, if your eyes are always right. Calculating shouldn't be this hard. Why not look instead? Dividing shapes into lowest-level constituents isn't a prerequisite for rules to work. It's always enough to draw shapes—in any way you choose—in order to define rules to calculate by seeing. There's no reason to do anything more. Embedding lets me trace out parts that aren't given beforehand and then replace them. There's sagacity and learning. That's all I need for both calculating and reasoning.

It's usually wise to have more than one example so you can be confident that what you're worried about isn't a rare phenomenon of no general consequence. It's easy to imagine the star

linking other shapes

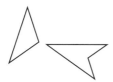

and their transformations when triangles like mine

are translated along different axes. And there are still other shapes

that can be transformed when triangles are changed in a more complicated way. Even so, these possibilities are merely a trivial beginning.

The five-pointed star

initiates twin series of stars and superstars that have the kind of ambiguity that I've been playing with. The stars in this series

   ...

have an odd number of points. And I can trace polygons in each one

   ...

that work just like triangles and chevrons in the five-pointed star. There are $2n - 1$ pairs of polygons—one with n sides and the other with $n + 1$ sides—in a star with $2n - 1$ points. Each of these pairs provides its own description of the star that's incompatible with the others when I calculate with two rules—and each description leads to different results. One rule is defined for the polygon with n sides according to the schema

$x \rightarrow t(x)$

and then there's its inverse. There's a transformation of the polygon back and forth. The process is already familiar for the series

and the rule

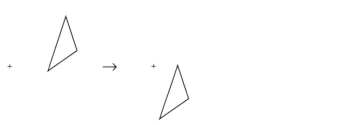

The five-pointed star is put together and taken apart in alternative ways. And there are comparable series for stars with more points. For example, the seven-pointed star

mediates the rotation from this shape

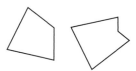

into this one

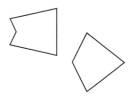

when the quadrilateral

is moved this way and that along the axis

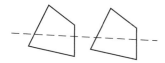

using the rule

and its inverse

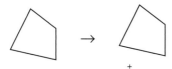

And there are other possibilities beyond these. Suppose I move every polygon in the same direction without inverses. Then the shape

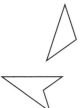

is changed in this way

when the triangle

in the five-pointed star is translated like this

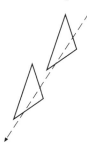

along its axis. That the triangle in the shape

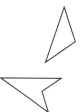

can be moved to the other side of the chevron

is not unexpected. But that these polygons are apparently rotated together as a pair once their positions have been reversed is a surprise. Calculating with shapes isn't for the faint of heart.

Stars are marvelously ambiguous. It seems that almost anything is possible with only a couple of polygons. Their sides interact, so that the parts at the start change in unforeseen ways. It's a really fascinating process, and one that implies much more for what my eyes can find to see.

For example, if I go on drawing and extend the lines in each of the stars in the series

so that every two lines intersect—no two are parallel and no three share a point—then I get the corresponding superstars in this series

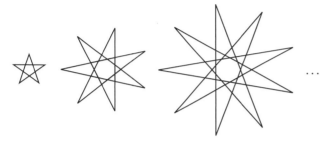

Only the five-pointed star is both a star and a superstar—five lines intersect in ten points. But all of the others stars have greater potential as superstars. For $2n - 1$ lines, there are $2n^2 - 3n + 1$ intersections. And I can count in additional ways, too. For example, every superstar is made up of $n - 1$ concentric shells—you can think of them as orbits—and $2n - 1$ intersections lie in each. Moreover, anywhere I look, $2n - 2$ intersections are on a line. It's all pretty neat. Still, some things about superstars are far easier to see than to count. Let's try—it turns out to be even neater with a host of real surprises.

Novel behavior is common when polygons interact. With stars, it's two polygons, and with superstars, it's two or more. In fact, there can be a cast of thousands that changes dramatically. It's a question of what I see as I calculate. Suppose I define rules according to the schema

$x \rightarrow t(x)$

so that x is any chevron and the transformation t keeps shapes similar—or congruent if you want. Then I have rules like this one

that I can apply recursively to separate chevrons and superstars in the following manner

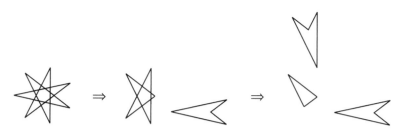

until there are only chevrons and a triangle. Whenever I try a rule, the convex vertices of the chevron that's moved are always outside points of the superstar. The number of chevrons in this process depends on the number of points in the initial superstar. In my example with a seven-pointed superstar, the number of chevrons is two. But in general for $2n - 1$ points, $n - 2$ chevrons are going to be pulled apart. In the full process, $2n^2 - 7n + 6$ intersections are lost. In particular, every time I apply a rule to move a chevron in a superstar of $2i - 1$ points, $4i - 9$ intersections disappear. This is readily confirmed in the equality

$$\sum_{3 \leq i \leq n} 4i - 9 = 2n^2 - 7n + 6$$

It's a worthwhile relationship, the kind that's found on tests in school. And today, knowing how to prove it is the mark of an educated person, a good citizen, and a reliable employee. After all, life unfolds with inductive regularity—once a rule is tried everything plays out according to plan.

Of course, I can always turn everything around and calculate in the opposite way. I can start with chevrons and a triangle

and then apply other rules from the schema $x \rightarrow t(x)$ to move the chevrons to make a superstar

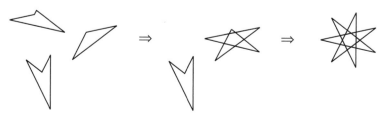

And when I connect this series and the previous one via the superstar—it ends the former and begins the latter—I'm left with what amounts to an extraordinary transformation

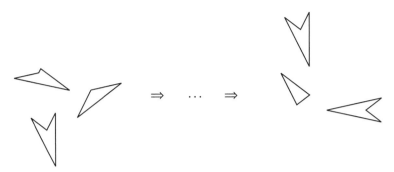

that seems unimaginable in any of the counting and corroborative arithmetic I've done. By calculating with rules that simply move chevrons—they keep their "shape"—I can change both a chevron and a triangle into dissimilar ones. It isn't normal for things to alter in this way. Still, there it is—not complete in a single rule that doesn't show much, but chevron by chevron and piece by piece as in the topologies in table 2. Neat things happen when shapes fuse and divide. Play around with rules and see what you get. It's the best way I know to learn how to calculate using your eyes. You can start over every time you look.

There's always more to see and do because superstars are ambiguous when they're divided into chevrons and a triangle according to the rules defined in my schema. And it's worth reinforcing, so that it isn't lost in more complicated cases where seeing may seem harder. Actually, the truth is that I enjoy this kind of stuff and want to do it again. It's exciting to see how many ways you can switch what you see looking at the same thing with the same rules. Visual calculating isn't just an isolated trick. Take a look at the nine-pointed superstar

Three chevrons may be picked out in this sequence

The first chevron is included in the initial superstar, while the second and third ones are contained in the superstars

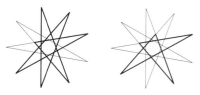

left when the first and second chevrons are resolved. The triangle

is defined at the conclusion of the process. Alternatively, the chevrons in the sequence

will do, with the intermediate superstars

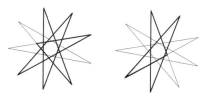

and the final triangle

This kind of ambiguity is overwhelming, exponentially so. And the urge to count the possibilities is unremitting. I succumbed to the triangles in Evans's shape, and I'm on the verge of doing superstars. Once you start out, you just want to add to the series until you get them all—it's the little matter of distinguishing one, two, and three. But the feeling of completion (exhaustion) that comes with an enumeration of constituents and their configurations is debilitating. The eye is sated, so that seeing more is superfluous. Still, there's always more to see. That's why visual calculating is so important. Seeing—using my kind of rules—trumps counting with its units, names, lists, and definitions. Shapes aren't everyday arrangements—their constituents can alter when I look at them. And taxonomies (topology or syntax) aren't stable—they change dynamically as calculating goes on. John Dewey applies this relationship that puts seeing ahead of counting in *How We Think*. He maps the hazards and drawbacks of "logical analysis" and "anatomical and morphological method" in education. Evans tries the former, and I use the latter in my catalogue of triangles in table 1. (In fact, Miss H——'s exercise—connecting dots in lines to make planes—also shows what Dewey finds. Sooner or later, counting is meaningless—and then it's time to see.)

Even when it is definitely stated that intellectual and physical analyses are different sorts of operations, intellectual analysis is often treated after the analogy of physical; as if it were the breaking up of a whole into all its constituent parts in the mind instead of in space. As nobody can possibly tell what breaking a whole into parts in the mind means, this conception leads to the further notion that logical analysis is a mere enumeration and listing of all conceivable qualities and relations. The influence upon education of this conception has been very great. Every subject in the curriculum has passed through—or still remains in—what may be called the phase of anatomical or morphological method: the stage in which understanding the subject is thought to consist of multiplying distinctions of quality, form, relation, and so on, and attaching some name to each distinguished element. In normal growth, specific properties are emphasized and so individualized only when they serve to clear up a present difficulty. Only as they are involved in judging some specific situation is there any motive or use for analyses, *i.e.* for emphasis upon some element or relation as peculiarly significant.

I'm not so sure there's a huge difference between intellectual (rational) and physical analyses. It's hard to imagine a final test for either. But in "normal growth," there's the logic of inquiry, and this is how parts are defined as rules are applied. In fact, had Dewey gone on to say that properties aren't fixed but change even erratically from moment to moment—that embedding isn't only identity—he would have said a lot more. But then, he wasn't thinking about rules and calculating with shapes. The damage done when logical analysis is taken too seriously is all too evident in the host of school subjects Dewey surveys, from reading, writing, and arithmetic to drawing and geography. The same kinds of problems are plain today in computer graphics (drawing, modeling, visualization, etc.) and geographical information systems. It's Evans's syntactic approach again, and the scientific approach to urban morphology, too, with atomic units of description, cellular automata, and fractal geometry. Drawing and geography are slow to change when there's only counting. But why is counting naturally assumed to be reliable and trustworthy—to get it all—when it leaves out so much? Repeatability isn't the goal when there's always creative work to do now. Counting misses everything that's new—there's nothing to see.

What Schemas Show

How descriptions of shapes change while I calculate is highlighted in another way when I use schemas to define rules. I've shown one schema already

$$x \rightarrow t(x)$$

without giving a general definition. That's because the idea is nearly transparent. But sometimes, a little formality is useful.

A rule schema

$$x \rightarrow y$$

is a pair of variables x and y that take shapes as values. These are given in an assignment g that satisfies a predicate. Whenever g is used, a rule

$$g(x) \rightarrow g(y)$$

is defined. The rule then applies as usual, as if it were given explicitly from the start. This works to express a host of intuitive ideas about shapes and how to change them.

Schemas can be very general. In fact, I can give one for all rules. I only have to say that x and y are shapes. Or schemas can be very restricted. Just a single rule is defined if x and y are constants—maybe the triangle

and the square

to give the rule

But usually schemas are more in the middle, so that shapes have useful descriptions. How to decide this and whether or not it makes a difference are hard to say. If you're interested in explaining everything of a certain kind once and for all, then it's nice to be clear about what schemas do. But if you take a historical view that looks at particular ways of calculating and how they go on, then there are other ways—topologies, etc.— to describe what's happening relative to rules that needn't be described themselves, and how these rules are used. Most of what I was told in school seems to support the first option. It isn't easy to ignore. And most work on shape grammars—including my early stuff, although sometimes there are hints of something new—makes this choice. Nonetheless, understanding how shapes work may be better served with the second option. What is it about schemas and how they work that makes me say this? Let's take a look at schemas and see what they can do.

Here's a rule

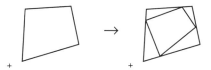

defined in a schema $x \rightarrow y$ that produces the shape

and others of the same kind

formed when polygons are nested or inscribed one in another. An assignment g provides values for the variables x and y that satisfy this predicate:

x is a polygon with n sides, and $y = x + z$, where z is a polygon with n sides inscribed in x.

The predicate can be elaborated in much greater detail. For example, I could say something more about polygons being convex, etc., and then go on to say that the vertices of z are points on the sides of x, etc. Thus, it's easy to see that the schema includes as a special case rules for shapes in the array

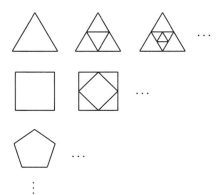

Here, g assigns regular polygons to x and z, so that the sides of the one have midpoints that are the vertices of the other, for example, like so

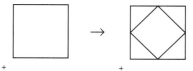

Still, this kind of detail isn't always necessary. I'm apt to take shortcuts whenever I can. In the schema

$$x \rightarrow x + t(x)$$

and others like it, I conflate the two variables x and y and the predicate. More technically, I should have said that x is any shape and $y = x + t(x)$. And the schema is developed further in the predicate above, in which x is a polygon and the transformation t is carefully spelled out. In like fashion,

$$x \rightarrow t(x)$$

provides a summary of the schema $x \rightarrow y$, where x is a shape and y is a transformation t of x. If t is the identity, then rules are identities themselves. And I can use rotations and translations as I did above. Or perhaps there's a boundary operator b to define rules that change lines to points and back again. If I write

$$b(x) \rightarrow x$$

as the inverse of the schema

$$x \rightarrow b(x)$$

in which x is a shape made up of lines, I get the rule

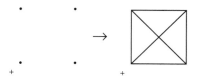

There's more about this in part II. But now, I want to show something different that goes to the heart of what it means to calculate visually. For this, it's enough to know what the variables x and y and the assignment g do. The main issue isn't technical.

For every predicate, there are indefinitely many others equivalent to it. It's clear that shapes made up of lines or higher-dimensional elements can be described in indefinitely many ways in terms of their different parts. It might go like this

x is the sum of the parts ... and y is the sum of the parts ... such that ...

For example, I can use maximal lines or their halves, thirds, fourths, etc. The principle is also true for shapes that contain points, because I can specify finitely many in countless ways with alternative expressions in logic. But of special interest right now, I can redo the predicate I have, so that y is n triangles rather than twin polygons with n sides apiece. If my rule is originally this

with two quadrilaterals, then it's also this

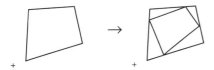

with four triangles. There are some wonderful twists and turns when I reason in terms of these contrasting descriptions.

This series of shapes

is defined using my new schema. It begins with a quadrilateral that's replaced with four triangles. And this is repeated in the same way to put four triangles in a quadrilateral. But this doesn't add up. The second quadrilateral comes from nowhere. And what's up with the four triangles? If I add four more, there are eight. I've said it before, and it bears repeating. The parts I see aren't fixed. They may alter at any time in number or by kind. Are there four triangles or two quadrilaterals? How I describe a rule and the shape to which it's applied don't have to agree. I can fool around with descriptions as long as I like to produce the results I want in a sensible way. Rules apply to shapes, not to descriptions. Everything follows, at least when I calculate with shapes. There's no such thing as a non sequitur or an inconsistency—only the elaboration that comes from looking again and then going on independent of anything that I may have seen or done before. Nothing is ever meaningless or contradictory. It's impossible to be irrational. I don't have to look back to look forward. There's nothing to remember to go on.

This sounds wrong. How can calculating be so confused? Definite descriptions define the shapes in a rule $g(x) \rightarrow g(y)$. But my description of $g(x)$ may be incompatible with the description I have for the shape to which I apply the rule. It just isn't calculating unless both of these descriptions agree. But what law says that shapes must be described consistently to calculate? The shape $g(x)$ may have indefinitely many descriptions besides the description that defines it. And none of these is final. Embedding works for parts of shapes—not for their descriptions—when I try the rule. My account of how I calculate may appeal to as many different descriptions as I like that jump from here to there haphazardly. It may sound incoherent or contradictory—even crazy or nuts—while I'm doing it. But whether or not the conclusion is favorable with useful results doesn't depend on this. I can always tidy up after I've finished calculating to provide a retrospective explanation that's consistent. Trying to be rational as I calculate may not be an effective way to go on. Rationality is simply a kind of nostalgia. It's a sentiment to end with, after everything has finished and a pattern can be established. A process becomes inevitable once it's completed and final. Then it's safe to say what happened in one way or another, and not worry that this could all change.

So when is calculating visual? I have another answer that may be better than my formula $\dim(\text{el}) = \dim(\text{em})$.

Calculating is visual when descriptions don't count.

Descriptions aren't binding. There's no reason to stick to any of them that's not mere prejudice. I'm happy with this, yet I'm not sure everyone will be happy with what it means for everything from reasoning in its widest sense to narrow technical specialisms like parametric design that go only as far as schemas with set variables. I use rules to calculate, but I don't have to play by them. I can cheat. And I can get away with it calculating. I'm totally free to change my mind about what there is, and I'm free to act on it. Children play games in this way, unless we intervene to make them follow the rules. But these are limiting, grown-up rules, not the kind that children must have already. Children's rules are surely more like mine. There are no definitions to conform to, and there's no vocabulary to build from. It's all fluid and in flux. Constituents—atoms, units, and the rest of it—are merely occasional afterthoughts. Is this going too far? What makes me think I'm calculating? But then, what's reasoning all about?

What's That or How Many?

I confess. I really don't know what reasoning is, and I'm not totally sure about calculating. For James, reasoning is sagacity and learning. And surely, this includes what I've been saying, especially about calculating with shapes and rules. Still, others may demur for one reason or another. Not everyone is as generous as James when he encourages alternative points of view and welcomes the novelty they bring—reasoning is at stake. There are standards to keep that decide exactly what's right and what's wrong—no doubt about it. But where does this lead? Wandering around is the best way to see. I'm going to look at some of the things a number of thinkers say about reasoning, calculating, and their relationships. This lets me explore visual reasoning and calculating in various ways. I want to reinforce the idea that shapes and rules do many things that calculating isn't supposed to do. (Shape grammars aren't what you think they are.) This opens the way to design. Mine isn't a logical argument that takes a predetermined route that's built up step by step. It really is wandering around—no map, no plan, and no final goal. I shift freely—perhaps even erratically—from here to there. And if I sometimes trace an idiosyncratic path that may seem discontinuous, it's to traverse the extent of this terrain—there's a lot to see and far more than I'm able to show. From my point of view, this makes what I say all the more convincing. Shapes and rules exceed standard expectations for logical analysis and rational thought when they depend on a given vocabulary of units. The trick is to get around analysis as a prerequisite for calculating. Shapes and rules let me go anywhere I like and see whatever I want. That's why they're worth the effort, and that's why it makes sense to talk about them in the open-ended, promiscuous way I do.

There's no better place to start than James himself—calculating with shapes and rules does what he says. It goes like this:

All ways of conceiving a concrete fact, if they are true ways at all, are equally true ways. *There is no property* ABSOLUTELY *essential to any one thing.* The same property which figures as the essence of a thing on one occasion becomes a very inessential feature upon another.

Meanwhile the reality overflows these purposes at every pore.

. . . *the only meaning of essence is teleological, and . . . classification and conception are purely teleological weapons of the mind.*

The properties which are important vary from man to man and from hour to hour.

Reasoning is always for a subjective interest, to attain some particular conclusion, or to gratify some special curiosity. It not only breaks up the datum placed before it and conceives it abstractly; it must conceive it *rightly* too; and conceiving it rightly means conceiving it by that one particular abstract character which leads to the one sort of conclusion which it is the reasoner's temporary interest to attain.

I may change occasions more rapidly than James expects, moving freely among parts whether they're details or overall features. I change occasions every time I apply a rule $M \rightarrow P$ to calculate—when I embed M and infer (introduce) P. And I string all of these occasions together in an ongoing series to produce useful but not necessarily logical (consistent) results. My temporary interests are in fact evanescent, and arbitrarily linked. They're shown in the rules I use to get the results I want. I think this is why visual calculating and reasoning can be a lot more effective in design than calculating and reasoning in some other way. Their appeal to seeing—to sensible, concrete experience—puts the ability to deal with novelty—"*the technical differentia of reasoning*"—at the center of creative activity.

Another famous philosopher, however, isn't sure that my kind of calculating with shapes—where rules automatically redefine parts as they're tried—is actually calculating. Ludwig Wittgenstein notices that numbers and shapes don't add up in the same way—there's a distinct difference between calculating and visual calculating—and he suggests that this shows that "mathematics is *normative*."

An addition of shapes together, so that some of the edges fuse, plays a very small part in our life.—As when

 and

yield the figure

But if this were an *important* operation, our ordinary concept of arithmetical addition would perhaps be different.

Let us imagine that while we were calculating the figures on paper altered erratically. A 1 would suddenly become a 6 and then a 5 and then again a 1 and so on. And I want to assume that this does not make any difference to the calculation because, as soon as I read a figure in order to calculate with it or to apply it, it once more becomes the one that we have in *our* calculating. At the same time, however, one can see quite well how the figures change during the calculations; but we are trained not to worry about this.

Of course, even if we do not make the above assumption, this calculation could lead to usable results.

Here we calculate strictly according to rules, yet this result does not *have* to come out.—I am assuming that we see no sort of regularity in the alteration of figures.

Now you might of course say: "In this case the manipulation of figures according to rules is not calculation."

Wittgenstein's curious manipulations in which figures alter erratically of their own accord have a familiar look and feel. It's uncanny—it's as if I were calculating with shapes and rules. And if the one skirts the comfortable norms of calculating as Wittgenstein implies, then so too does the other. Of course, norms may be effective or not. At first, Wittgenstein is tempted to check what can change and go on with business as usual.

And I want to assume that this does not make any difference to the calculation because, as soon as I read a figure in order to calculate with it or to apply it, it once more becomes the one that we have in *our* calculating.

Wittgenstein's first response is conservative—he's an instinctive constructionist. He joins with the rest of us to keep to the law that keeps everything the same. I count on figures to behave themselves when I use them to calculate. Making it that way is what training is for. (There are the basics—predefined constituents and their arrangements—rigorous standards, and tests to make sure that schools and students are held accountable for teaching and learning. But how basic are basics that have to be taught and tested? The push for standards is to exclude the unexpected. Standards limit present experience to what seemed to work in the past. Any prospect of novelty is gone. There are no surprises—just rote results. Nothing is ever ambiguous or vague. This is the end of anxiety and uncertainty, and it makes it unnecessary to trust others and give them a chance to think on their own. But is it a sensible way to educate people to recognize and exploit new opportunities? What good are my rules now? Of course, training needn't limit experience. It may be open-ended—for example, in studio instruction and situated learning. In the latter, master and apprentice interact during actual practice. They work on the same thing without having to see it in the same way. They go on. There's no underlying structure to control or guide the process—"structure is more the variable outcome of action than its invariant precondition." This is like visual calculating. Nothing guarantees that it's the same way twice.) But why not try something new? Is training necessary for a successful conclusion when I calculate?

Of course, even if we do not make the above assumption, this calculation could lead to usable results.

Ignoring "the above assumption" is what visual calculating is about. Whether or not you think it's real calculating doesn't actually matter. The ambiguity cuts in opposing ways: once to explain why greater attention hasn't been focused on visual calculating as a useful alternative to calculating with numbers—the one isn't calculating—and then again to explain why it's so easy to think that visual calculating is necessarily the same as calculating in the ordinary way. I like to calculate by seeing. But whenever I try, either no one believes it or they think I'm doing something else—that I'm calculating by counting. Maybe I'm wasting my time when it comes to visual calculating. Only what can I do? I want to see how far reasoning goes. And there's always something new to see that takes me somewhere else to look. My instincts aren't conservative when it comes to seeing shapes. There's simply no need to remember what was there before. I'm free to look again now to decide what to do next.

I guess my approach to shapes and rules isn't the norm. This much is evident in the quotation from Ivan Sutherland—one of the pioneers of computer graphics and computer-aided design—that I started with on page 61. Here it is again—

To a large extent it has turned out that the usefulness of computer drawings is precisely their structured nature and that this structured nature is precisely the difficulty in making them.... An ordinary draftsman is unconcerned with the structure of his drawing material. Pen and ink or pencil and paper have no inherent structure. They only make dirty marks on paper. The draftsman is concerned principally with the drawings as a representation of the evolving design. The behavior of the computer-produced drawing, on the other hand, is critically dependent upon the topological and geometric structure built up in the computer memory as a result of drawing operations. The drawing itself has properties quite independent of the properties of the object it is describing.

The preliminary appeal to structure and memory in early efforts to draw with the computer is unassailable today throughout practice and education. It makes the computer, and pencil and paper appear to be irreconcilably different kinds of media. The draftsman always has the option to draw it in one way and to see it in another—to forget what he's done, so that he can see and do more—while the computer produced drawing depends on the "topological and geometric structure built up in the computer memory as a result of drawing operations." This is precisely the difference between calculating visually and calculating the way Evans does with predefined constituents. And it's what worried Wittgenstein—figures on paper don't alter when you calculate, and if they do, you remember what they were. It's funny how things on paper—dirty marks, shapes, and figures—bother Sutherland and Wittgenstein for the same reason: they defy calculating. Of course, there may be an advantage. I can always count on the computer drawing to behave properly according to the way it's described. When its constituents are fixed in drawing operations, its future possibilities are circumscribed once and for all. The outcome of this is already clear in Evans's shape

And whether or not I can calculate to reflect the shape

depends on how the triangle and chevron are drawn. Sutherland is correct. The difficulty in making computer drawings is their structured nature. It's hard—no, it's impossible—to tell what constituents to draw without foreknowledge. That's the trick—not to need foreknowledge, so that the properties of computer drawings can alter freely to correspond with the properties of anything they're used to describe. That's why embedding makes a difference in design. It guarantees that shapes do what you want. There's no structure to remember. There's no reason for calculating to get in the way. Figures on paper and the computer drawing are the same.

Herbert Simon likes the idea that shapes are represented (structured) and well behaved in computers.

Since much of design, particularly architectural and engineering design, is concerned with objects or arrangements in real Euclidean two-dimensional or three-dimensional space, the representation of space and of things in space will necessarily be a central topic in a science of design. From our previous discussion of visual perception, it should be clear that "space" inside the head of the designer or the memory of a computer may have very different properties from a picture on paper or a three-dimensional model.

The representational issues have already attracted the attention of those concerned with computer-aided design—the cooperation of human and computer in the design process. As a single example, I may mention Ivan Sutherland's SKETCHPAD program, which allows geometric shapes to be represented and conditions to be placed on these shapes in terms of constraints, to which they then conform.

Yes, design is drawing objects and their arrangements! And Simon knows the kind of structure that works best in drawing and elsewhere—hierarchies make the difference. They're inherent in memorable experience and the reason it's comprehensible. Seeing things and their parts is impossible in any other way.

If there are important [things] in the world that are complex without being hierarchic, they may to a considerable extent escape our observation and our understanding. Analysis of their behavior would involve such detailed knowledge and calculation of the interactions of their elementary parts that it would be beyond our capacities of memory and computation.

How comprehensible are stars and superstars when I calculate with them? Aren't they important? Or do they escape observation and understanding, and exceed our capacity of memory? The structure of the five-pointed star

isn't close to being hierarchic when it's divided into elementary parts (lowest-level constituents) compatible with the shape

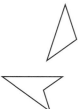

and its reflection. These parts combine to form triangles and chevrons in a pair of interacting ways

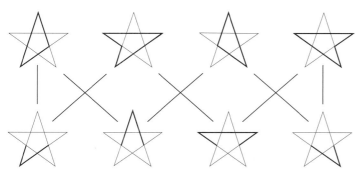

that block any chance of an underlying hierarchy. The practical necessity of hierarchical structure in calculating seems to be another good reason to deny the existence of elementary parts. It's easy to do without them. And once they're gone, new ways open up to restructure shapes dynamically. There's nothing to remember. Understanding changes every time a rule is tried.

I would like to think that the visual examples I've shown so far make this obvious. But Simon provides additional evidence, if there's still any doubt, in a wonderful analysis of representational drawing.

If you ask a person to draw a complex object—such as a human face—he will almost always proceed in a hierarchic fashion. First he will outline the face. Then he will add or insert features: eyes, nose, mouth, ears, hair. If asked to elaborate, he will begin to develop details for each of the features—pupils, eyelids, lashes for the eyes, and so on—until he reaches the limits of his anatomical knowledge. His information about the object is arranged hierarchically in memory, like a topical outline.

When information is put in outline form, it is easy to include information about the relations among the major parts and information about the internal relations of parts in each of the suboutlines. Detailed information about the relations of subparts belonging to different parts has no place in the outline and is likely to be lost. The loss of such information and the preservation mainly of information about hierarchic order is a salient characteristic that distinguishes the drawings of a child or someone untrained in representation from the drawing of a trained artist.

The way my computer works shows something different. Every time I turn it on, I see Apple Computer's Macintosh logo

The six maximal lines in this Picasso-Braque–like figure form a quartet of human faces. There are left and right profiles, and corresponding concave and convex front views with noses in alternating places

And if I cut the free ends of lines to treat the logo like the Y's in Evans's shape, there are indefinitely many more faces. Some even appear to wink. But this is unnecessarily indulgent. The four faces alone are already much too entangled for the logo to be described "in a hierarchic fashion." The hierarchies that describe the faces singly are incompatible. Which description is preserved when I draw the logo? Does it keep me from seeing the logo in another way? What about Wittgenstein's observation that figures on paper may alter erratically? The logo is like the five-pointed star. The parts of faces interact as copiously as the parts of triangles and chevrons, and don't fall neatly into independent groups. Try to draw some of the faces without drawing the others, or to erase one of the faces and keep the others intact. When it comes to calculating, there's no more to art—drawing, poetry, etc.—than to business, logic, mathematics, and science. Simon thinks so, and so do I. But our intuitions run in opposite directions. In art, there's no more than meets the eye. This changes what calculating is.

Of course, this isn't the whole story. Drawings can be used in myriad ways. In particular, Simon shows how drawings work "to resolve syntactic ambiguities" in sentences. This one

I saw the man on the hill with the telescope.

is a good example of what he has in mind. His account of the matter is perfectly straightforward.

This sentence has at least three acceptable interpretations; a linguist could, no doubt, discover others. Which of the three obvious ones we pick depends on where we think the telescope is: Do I have it? Does the man on the hill have it? Or is it simply on the hill, not in his hands?

Now suppose that the sentence is accompanied by [the] figure

The issue is no longer in doubt. Clearly it is I who have the telescope.

The figure has the list structure

SAW ((I, WITH (telescope)), (man, ON (hill)))

which does in fact disambiguate the sentence. But this list structure isn't the only possible description of the figure. It might also be

SAW (I, (man, ON (hill), WITH (telescope)))

Who has the telescope isn't all that has to be decided. The location of the hill is in doubt. The figure flips like a Necker cube, or Otto Neurath's picture *a-boy-walks-through-a-door* on page 50 where the boy goes into or out of a house. How does Simon know that he's looking up at a hill from its base and not down at a hill across a valley?

Why is he the big guy rather than the little fellow? It's the same watching a sunrise, with historical significance for astronomy. Is the sun rolling over you—the sun moves and the earth is fixed—or are you rolling under the sun? Simon's figure is just as ambiguous as his sentence, to multiply the confusion. But there's scant reason to take shapes seriously when you've already read what you're supposed to see! Nonetheless, shapes hold their surprises patiently. And it's a good thing, too. Otherwise, it would be easy to run out of new things to see. I'd have no reason to calculate with my eyes.

I've spent a lot of time quoting Simon. There are three main reasons for this. First, he doesn't pull any punches. You know exactly where he stands. So I can try to be clear, too, especially with the ambiguity and vagueness I'm trying to keep. Second, his take on computers, calculating, and hierarchical structure is canonical today. What Simon says is what everyone does—one way or another. I don't think this is entirely because of Simon—it may be, yet probably not—but because it's what we're taught calculating is from the time we're taught to count. Calculating by counting doesn't go very far in design and creative work. It's calculating by seeing that's worth a real try. And third, Simon makes use of spatial examples and analogies that give me something to see. I've looked at a few of these, and need only remind you of the truly marvelous idea that calculating and painting are linked. In fact, Simon's description of this relationship could be my own.

It is also beside the point to ask whether the later stages of the development were consistent with the initial one—whether the original designs were realized. Each step of implementation created a new situation; and the new situation provided a starting point for fresh design activity.

Making complex designs that are implemented over a long period of time and continually modified in the course of implementation has much in common with painting in oil. In oil painting every new spot of pigment laid on the canvas creates some kind of pattern that provides a continuing source of new ideas to the painter. The painting process is a process of cyclical interaction between painter and canvas in which current goals lead to new applications of paint, while the gradually changing pattern suggests new goals.

If situations are shapes, then this is what calculating is about. There's no need for consistency or to keep to prior decisions and goals. Nothing is ever finished. Everything is always up for grabs. Change may be sudden rather than gradual as Simon has it, but either way you look at it, things are different. Yet all Simon can think to do is to make change combinatorial—spots of pigment really are independent spots that can be identified. It simply doesn't work. It just isn't painting, nor is it visual calculating. There's more to seeing than rearranging units—

forms can proliferate in this way because the more complex arise out of a combinatoric play upon the simpler. The larger and richer the collection of building blocks that is available for construction, the more elaborate are the structures that can be generated.

Vannevar Bush wrote of science as an "endless frontier." It can be endless, as can the process of design and the evolution of human society, because there is no limit on diversity in the world. By combinatorics on a few primitive elements, unbounded variety can be created.

Primitives and building blocks—either a few or a lot—spoil the whole thing. It's easy to create endless (monotonous) variety and diversity in Chomsky's sense—you pay for it with growing complexity—only it isn't the creative kind you need your eyes to see. Then there's no complexity, just looking again—embedding this in that in a process where things fuse and divide and don't merely combine—to pick out what's new. Still, there's no reason to be upset. That calculating and painting are tied is in fact a remarkable idea, and when you turn the relationship around, without primitives and building blocks in combinatoric play, it's totally incredible. What's more, the interaction between calculating and painting in Simon's sense and painting and calculating in mine is another good way to introduce my scheme in which equivalencies for verbal and visual expression are shown. Simon gets it one way just about right. And he really takes seeing seriously when he talks about calculating. His visual approach is something special.

John McCarthy takes the kind of nonvisual approach to reasoning that I want to extend. (McCarthy and Marvin Minsky started artificial intelligence at MIT, and along with Simon and Allen Newell made sure AI was an important area of research in computer science.) In fact, McCarthy does pretty much what Simon says—he tries to structure problems before they're solved. This structure needn't be hierarchical, but there are still antecedent limits and constraints. McCarthy describes reasoning as circumscription in a nonmonotonic logic, that is to say, as common sense. His analysis of the missionaries and cannibals puzzle shows what's involved. The problem is easy to state.

Three missionaries and three cannibals come to a river. A rowboat that seats two is available. If the cannibals ever outnumber the missionaries on either bank of the river, the missionaries will be eaten. How shall they cross the river [?]

McCarthy counts numerical conservation among the primitive "facts" of "common-sense knowledge" that ground the puzzle—"rowing across the river doesn't change the numbers of missionaries or cannibals," nor, presumably, does it change individuals. In fact, McCarthy proves objects are limited to the ones that are given, in a circumscriptive inference for three blocks that applies equally to boats, cannibals, and missionaries. It's another way to be a constructionist. Still, is any of this sensible without more evidence? Why are missionaries and cannibals combinatorial units? Aren't they more like shapes? And what makes the puzzle a puzzle? It may be a parable instead that shows how missionaries convert cannibals as they cross the river. There's no reason cannibals can't be born again—they can change just like shapes. Or the puzzle may be an aboriginal tale. The magic is palpable. Missionaries needn't look the same in the new light on the opposite bank. The savage mind isn't trained to count. Cannibals are free to relish strange forms of life and digest what they see in alternative ways. But McCarthy's common sense is prudent—what doesn't have to be is excluded; keep to what's given. Ambiguity and novelty are just confusing and block simple logic. Calculating with shapes is outside the ambit of ordinary thought. Only shapes show that useful calculating is practicable when McCarthy's common sense fails. It's easy to see what happens without it. Try stars and especially superstars to mix up as many chevrons—"missionaries and cannibals"—as you like. Nothing stays the same for long. Otherwise, what's the reason for reason?

Of course, not everyone who thinks about computers has McCarthy's common sense. There's a lot of controversy in AI. Terry Winograd and Fernando Flores think blindness makes the difference. (Winograd took a starkly atomistic approach to computers and language as one of Minsky's doctoral students, but he may have changed his mind.)

We accuse people of lacking common sense precisely when some representation of the situation has blinded them to a space of potentially relevant actions.

This gets close to what calculating with shapes and rules is all about. If I follow Evans and describe (represent) the shape

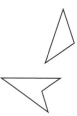

in terms of lowest-level constituents that are always independent when they're combined—there's a triangle with three sides and a chevron with four sides in the ordinary way—then I simply have no access to 80 percent of the triangles in the five-pointed star

I can't see them or move them. Because lines neither fuse nor divide, I miss the chance to produce the shape

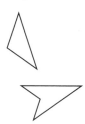

Limiting myself in this way seems a big price to pay in order to calculate, and it gets a lot worse for stars and superstars as the number of points grows. This is inevitable as

long as calculating depends on representations. No matter how carefully I describe things, there are going to be some things that I just can't see and some relevant actions that I can't take.

Whenever we treat a situation as present-at-hand, analyzing it in terms of objects and their properties, we thereby create a blindness. Our view is limited to what can be expressed in the terms we have adopted. This is not a flaw to be avoided in thinking—on the contrary, it is necessary and inescapable. Reflective thought is impossible without the kind of abstraction that produces blindness.

But Winograd and Flores do offer a glimmering of hope—in fact, a way to open up reflective thought (reasoning) and to get around the structured nature of computer drawings. Switching representations (visual reasoning) is how to avoid blindness.

[There's] the possibility of ... switching between different representations, or creating new representations. If this were possible, the blindness inherent in any one representation could be overcome. But if we look carefully at what is actually proposed, it does not really confront the issues.

If you think calculating is counting, then there are limits to what you can see. Your ability to handle novelty is circumscribed. With visual calculating in which rules apply to shapes in terms of embedding, the problem disappears. Descriptions (representations) don't count. I can calculate without them. Lines fuse and divide as rules are tried. Only this isn't my point right now. It's that common sense is outside of reflective thought. Common sense and calculating with shapes are excluded for the same reason—they don't work when you're blind. It seems that the value of common sense depends on whose it is. Is it common sense to see what ambiguity brings and to be open to it? Winograd and Flores think so. Or is it to check what you see with circumscription, conservation, constructionist scruples, and the like? McCarthy says so, and Wittgenstein wants to agree—at least until he thinks about it.

Winograd and Flores look at calculating in earnest Heideggerian terms like "blindness." Heidegger is hard work—first to ignore his politics and then to figure out what he's trying to do. I can approach both tasks spatially, and I guess it's worth the effort. A lot of what he says seems to be about shapes and how to calculate with them. But there are many other ways of talking—alternative terminologies—that aren't so inaccessible and that also apply to shapes. Earlier, I mentioned hermeneutics in a humorous way. Now it's time to be serious. Listen to what Hans-Georg Gadamer has to say about interpreting a text.

A person who is trying to understand a text is always performing an act of projecting. He projects before himself a meaning for the text as a whole as soon as some initial meaning emerges in the text. Again, the latter emerges only because he is reading the text with particular expectations in regard to a certain meaning. The working out of this fore-project, which is constantly revised in terms of what emerges as he penetrates into the meaning, is understanding what is there.

I may be projecting—this kind of writing is paradigmatic in the way it resists final understanding—but it seems to me that it's a pretty good description of what it's like to calculate with stars and superstars, or other shapes, in terms of a family of rules defined according to a schema. The schema bounds my expectations in a vague sort of way—I may not know exactly what it implies. Then embedding lets me project, so that meaning emerges and can be constantly revised. There's a lot of wandering around. It's easy to make quick and seamless transitions to other things. There are connections for all sorts of reasons. For example, I can count when I read in a kind of numerical exegesis. First there's *hermeneutics* that's spelled with twelve letters and then *phenomenology* that's spelled with thirteen. This may not be a logical progression, but that doesn't mean that the next term in my sequence isn't significant. What about phenomenology? How does it tie up with shapes and rules?

Shapes look trivial with lines. Their parts depend on the rules I use to calculate, but they act more like "pieces" than the tangled "moments" central to phenomenological analysis. Yet additional evidence supports an alternative view. Spatial wholes are described in terms of their profiles.

A profile of a spatial object is the impression made by the object from a certain point of view. It does not contain in itself the other views the object provides to other viewpoints. Rather, it points toward these other looks of the thing; they can be acquired only outside the present point of view. Each look is exclusive of the others. When one is present the others are absent.

Shapes are like this, too. Whenever I try a rule, I look at a shape from a certain point of view. The rule resolves one part of the shape, and puts its other parts outside of vision and use. I see the shape in a single way even though there are others, as when this triangle

oriented exactly as shown is first seen and then moved in the five-pointed star

Alternative divisions are possible only when rules are used again. And there's more in phenomenology that suits, as well. The renowned combinatorialist and phenomenologist Gian-Carlo Rota gives a number of examples—including reading and bridge—for Husserl's notion of *Fundierung* or founding. Bridge is a good example—what marks playing cards?

The point is that there is no one "what" that we "see" while watching four people around a table [an additional "what" with five named parts]—or while watching *anything*. All *whats* are functions in *Fundierung* relations.

The way rules handle ambiguity adds to Rota's examples. The *whats* of shapes depend on their parts, and these are resolved anew every time a rule is tried. For parts, "the only kind of 'existence' that makes any sense—if any—is the evanescent existence of the trump card." Parts are necessary now, and then go away as I go on calculating. The changing results contribute to the flow of meaning. Perception trumps logic to guarantee that there's something new to see that makes a difference. Wandering around is really wandering around. Is this existential? Maurice Merleau-Ponty suggests as much in an apt description of rationality.

Rationality is precisely measured by the experiences in which it is disclosed. To say that there exists rationality is to say that perspectives blend, perceptions confirm each other, a meaning emerges.

Like views are found elsewhere. James and Dewey both rely on the same kind of dynamic rationality in reasoning. Jacques Barzun admires the "artist mind" below. And my topologies keep a record of what I do as I calculate with shapes. So what's next? Is computational phenomenology in the cards? Don't be silly. This isn't what calculating is supposed to do, but there's no denying it—rules restructure shapes every time they're used. (Rota treats phenomenology and combinatorics as separate worlds— what's that and how many?—and has a cavalier answer when he's asked how he inhabits both—"I am that way." But it seems to me that there's an important relationship. It's combinatorics if shapes are made up of points, and phenomenology if they're not. The elements of thought either have dimension zero or greater. There's more than identity in embedding.)

Calculating and reasoning—visual or not—common sense, missionaries and cannibals, and other *whats* are no better off than shapes. But isn't this how it should be? The ambiguity is something to use, even with computers. Minsky is clever about this— he thinks that calculating and reasoning are the same without excluding my kind of rules that rely on embedding, the way McCarthy does, or impling that they're very difficult if not impossible to define, as Winograd and Flores do. Once you see the ambiguity, it's easy to make it work for you in many ways. In fact, what Minsky says about creativity is telling.

What is creativity? How do people get new ideas? Most thinkers would agree that some of the secret lies in finding "new ways to look at things." We've just seen how to use the Body-Support concept to reformulate descriptions of some spatial forms.... let's look more carefully at how we made those four different arches seem the same, by making each of them seem to match "*a thing supported by two legs.*" In the case of *Single-Arch*, we did this by imagining some boundaries that weren't really there: this served to break a single object into three.

However, we dealt with *Tower-Arch* by doing quite the opposite: we treated some real boundaries as though they did not exist:

How cavalier a way to treat the world, to see three different things as one and to represent one thing as three!

Minsky follows James with a neat example. For James, "Genius, in truth, means little more than the faculty of perceiving in an unhabitual way." It may be daring (cavalier), but Minsky welcomes alternative descriptions—at least a few of them. He's willing to apply "radically different kinds of analysis to the same situation" and sure that Thomas Kuhn's paradigm switches occur again and again in everyday thought. Only there's a nagging doubt. Minsky retreats too easily to the security of constituents and combining them. He splits thinking in two, just not the way James does. There's an initial analysis of "elements"—how is this done?—and then an independent heuristic search where "elements are combined in different ways until a configuration is reached that passes some sort of test." This is precisely the way computer models are supposed to work, and a far cry from James's sagacity and learning. How useful is analysis before search begins? Remember what happens when rules are applied to shapes. There's a paradigm (gestalt) switch every time a rule is tried. The elements of analysis aren't given beforehand but change as calculating goes on. In fact, Minsky's arches support this. They're the standard that shows what it means to be static, and more. The statics of arches—Minsky's Body-Support concept—works consistently in different cases because arches aren't static. Shapes aren't stable—they fuse when they're combined to make new divisions possible. Elements, configurations, and tests aren't the way to handle this kind of ambiguity. How well does Evans's grammar work? Like Winograd, he was Minsky's doctoral student, and he does what's right. An initial analysis to define constituents is followed by a search with a heuristic—try configurations with three lines—and a test—is it a polygon? But heuristic search is senseless once seeing stops. Yes, seeing—observing—is analysis, but you can always do it again in another way.

Minsky knows that quantitative models of reasoning are inadequate. Visual calculating—everyone says it's qualitative—might be the alternative worth searching for. But his reason to find something new is baffling.

[A number-like magnitude] is too structureless and uninformative to permit further analysis.... *A number cannot reflect the considerations that formed it.*

This is true for shapes. It's what lets me divide them freely as I apply rules. In fact, the idea is a corollary of my principle that descriptions don't count. When memory matters more than what I see, it isn't visual calculating. There's a conservation law of some sort to uphold the decisions I've made in the past—to recognize (remember) what I did before and act on it heedless of anything else that might come up. This looks away from visual calculating to calculating the way we learned in school. Once more, either visual calculating isn't calculating or it's misunderstood.

The idea that I can change how I describe things with rules is at the heart of visual calculating, but it seems to be an idea that's not easy to accept or use. And in fact it would be easy to dismiss if it only had roots in sensible experience. Art and such are important, but it's science that really counts. It's funny how things turn out. The idea that things have incompatible descriptions is strongly rooted in science, as well. Hilary Putnam tells the story.

Since the end of the nineteenth century science itself has begun to take on a "non-classical"—that is, a non-seventeenth-century—appearance. [Earlier] I described the phenomenon of conceptual relativity—one which has simple illustrations, like [mine for a few individuals], but which has become pervasive in contemporary science. That there are ways of describing what are (in some way) the "same facts" which are (in some way) "equivalent" but also (in some way) "incompatible" is a strikingly non-classical phenomenon. Yet contemporary logicians and meaning theorists generally philosophize as if it did not exist.

This contains a good description of the shapes in the series

that are produced when I calculate with the rule

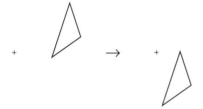

and its inverse. The five-pointed star is produced from the initial shape in one way, and then divided to produce the final shape in another way. This doesn't vex the eye, because it embodies my rules. All the same, the triangle and chevron at the start are incompatible with their reflection at the end. The star is made up of a triangle and a chevron in alternative ways. The facts are equivalent—"a rose is a rose." But the polygons consistent with the initial shape are inconsistent with the ones consistent with the final shape—"a rose is a rose." No one expects things to vanish if they're moved. Conservation is a solid law of physics. The outcome is never in doubt. The triangle in the initial shape must be in the star. Only how? Separate things can't occupy the same place at the same time. Impenetrability is another solid law of physics that has the ring of logic. It's impossible to jam two distinct triangles and their conjugate chevrons together all at once in the star—even visually. Try and see both alternatives at the same time—

But there they are—at least until I move one of the triangles. This is in fact a striking way to calculate. That it's left out of logic is no real surprise. But Putnam isn't worried about what logicians ignore. He wants to explain this nonclassical phenomenon. And what he finds meshes with some of the things I've been trying to say about visual calculating.

There are two important points. One works with visual calculating, and the other does—when it goes against convention—and doesn't—when it embraces counting. Counting is a reliable test of how things are, but it doesn't bother me if numbers change without rhyme or reason as I calculate. Let's see how this plays out. The first point is this—

[The] phenomenon [of conceptual relativity] turns on the fact that *the logical primitives themselves, and in particular the notions of object and existence, have a multitude of different uses rather than one absolute "meaning."*

And second,

Once we make clear how we are using "object" (or "exist"), the question "How many objects exist?" has an answer that is not at all a matter of "convention."

Putnam's first point is pretty obvious whenever I calculate with shapes. What I see before me depends on the rules I try. Evans's shape

isn't anything in particular until I apply the rule (identity)

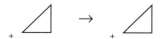

to pick out triangles. And if I try the rule

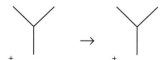

it's something different. Then Putnam's second point—at least my version of it—is also clear. It's not up to me how many triangles there are in the shape; the number is the result of calculating with the rule

to see how triangles are embedded. The only problem is that the rule can be used in different ways to get different results—"the figures alter erratically." Of course, I can always insist that the rule be applied everywhere there's a triangle. And I even have an algorithm for this—in fact, my algorithm is good for any rule. So maybe there's a definite answer after all.

But I have another way to look at counting that gives inconsistent results that aren't so easy to bypass. Suppose I start with the rule

that erases equilateral triangles—that's simple enough—and then apply the rule to the shape

In the series of shapes

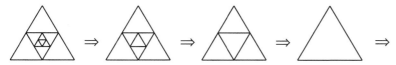

there are clearly four independent triangles. That's precisely how many I erase in order to make the shape

disappear. What better test for counting could I ever have? Every time I count a triangle, I take it away to define a one-to-one correspondence between triangles and numbers. Each triangle is counted once—that's how counting works—and all triangles are accounted for when the shape is gone, or my rule doesn't apply anymore. But I count five triangles in each series in this trio

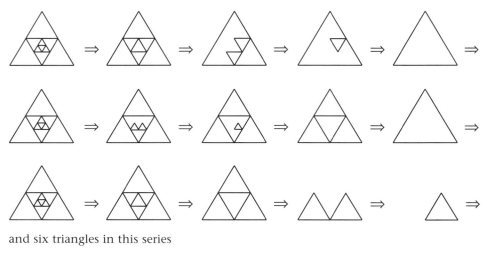

and six triangles in this series

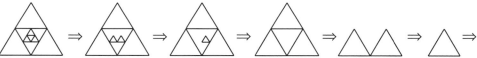

So what's it going to be? Does the shape

contain four triangles, five in one of three different ways, or six? The important thing to see is that giving rules to define parts isn't going to be enough. I also have to specify when and where the rules are applied. Being clear about what an object is before counting begins appears to be what everyone—from Evans to Goodman to Simon, McCarthy, and Minsky—is trying to do. The goal is to fix (rig) things, so that counting objects has the same result whenever you look. It's repeatable in exactly the way Kierkegaard dreads. But how much success has anyone actually had? Does Putnam know any more than Peirce about how to be clear? Can anyone say for sure how to distinguish shapes and arrangements of objects just by looking? I'm happy to pick out parts with rules that apply via embedding. That's as clear as I know how to be, so that I'm not tied to tendentious descriptions—even in schemas that define rules. But this can be messy when it comes to counting, unless I use points and other zero-dimensional things. What makes counting so decisive? Not everything has to add up. Meaning comes in other ways, too, when I calculate with shapes.

I've said all this before in one way and another. That's expected when you wander (walk) randomly with your eyes. But I'm thinking about my students. I show them how to calculate with shapes again and again. They nod knowingly and insist they've got it. Yet when it comes to doing it, they do exactly what they're used to. They try constituents, and rely on all of the other bad habits I thought I had managed to break. It's amazing how quickly they count things up and say they're complex before calculating. Variety is combinatorial with constitutive elements. There isn't much to see. James terms this "old fogyism" in *Talks to Teachers*. And my students—at least most of them in the PhD program—are old enough to feel its constricting grip.

In later life this economical tendency to leave the old undisturbed leads to what we know as "old fogyism." A new idea or a fact which would entail extensive rearrangement of the previous system of beliefs is always ignored or extruded from the mind in case it cannot be sophistically reinterpreted so as to tally harmoniously with the system. We have all conducted discussions with middle-aged people, overpowered them with our reasons, forced them to admit our contention, and a week later found them back as secure and constant in their old opinion as if they had never conversed with us at all. We call them old fogies; but there are young fogies, too. Old fogyism begins at a younger age than we think. I am almost afraid to say so, but I believe that in the majority of human beings it begins at about twenty-five.

James was a late bloomer and expects this in the majority of human beings. The truth is that there are telltale signs of old fogyism at thirteen. The trick is not to rush headlong into puberty and the reciprocal quest for rigidity. This may be unavoidable at twenty-five. But when I calculate with shapes, old fogyism is postponed indefinitely. Shapes have topologies that are rearranged extensively—in two ways: meaningful constituents alter both spatially and numerically—as rules are applied. But this is only calculating. In other things we do, the pull of old fogyism is more difficult to overcome. Barzun calls it the "rubber-band effect"—snapping back to what we thought before. When I teach, I repeat a handful of examples—like my stars and superstars—to stretch the rubber band. I do this as hard and as often as I possibly can. And from time to time, I actually get lucky—the rubber band breaks. Then teaching is its own reward.

I never tire of saying that the parts of a shape depend on what happens to it as I calculate. So long as I continue to try rules, parts change. But I like to be consistent about this whenever I can. If I take the series of shapes

seriously—and I still do—then the various parts of the shapes are the result of using the rule

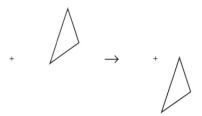

and its inverse in a specified way. Now look at the atoms in table 2. They take care of any inconsistencies in the way the five-pointed star is described, so that the series is a continuous process. And I can always do this somehow after I'm done calculating—with topologies, Boolean algebras, lattices of different kinds, or comparable descriptive devices. But more than the variability that's brought in as a result of this, there are alternative ways of going from the initial shape to the final shape that imply different parts for shapes as I calculate. Just what these parts are isn't a matter of convention, at least not in the way Putnam has in mind. I can't say what the parts are until I try my rules. There's real work to do to find out what's what. I have to interact with shapes in the same sort of way I interact with other things like letters or numerals when I read or do arithmetic. I can probably contrive some method to reconcile any differences that arise from calculating in this way or that afterward, if it's useful. Yet there may be no end of it. Differences—numerical discrepancies are only symptomatic—are bound to arise as I go along, because shapes are ambiguous. And there's no reason to think that these differences aren't real. It isn't necessary to define objects all at once in a coherent way. It's OK to go on calculating, so that objects (parts) are defined piecemeal with the possibility of revision every time a rule is tried. Things change with lots of surprises.

One way to check on experience is to require that parts be numerically distinct—to ask the question how many and get the same answer with the same parts every time. An accountant is trained for this, and a schoolteacher expects it when taking roll. My local selectman is proud of it—"I'm logical, I'm an accountant." I know just what she means. I count at the market to make certain that I have all of the items on my grocery list. Counting is an everyday practice that's useful in business and science. But perhaps it isn't that elucidating. Suppose I have a superstar with around fifteen points

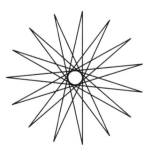

and that my schema is used, so that the dynamics (physics) of chevrons is known in full. Counting works OK—intersections vary predictably. The content of lines is also constant—their total length is conserved as rules apply. And it's not hard to find a dozen chevrons and a pair of triangles to form the superstar and take it apart—I simply look to read them off one by one. This is even nonclassical science in Putnam's sense. Only there are so many different ways to see—billions, in fact—that no one need ever agree about the chevrons and triangles to begin and end, or about the sequence of events in between. Or maybe I can show what's going on in another way. I have like problems and lots more when I use the schema

$x \rightarrow t(x)$

and let x be a line

_____

or a right triangle

and let t be a Euclidean transformation. See what you get as you replace lines embedded in lines or triangles in planes. Any shape can be changed into any other. (And notice that this doesn't work for points. There's no way to get more points than the ones you have to start.) I'm not sure how to count now. Nothing is fixed. Counting may not be as useful as I thought. It's one way to understand things among countless others. It may tell you a lot, but there's always more to see.

Wittgenstein looks at shapes and how they add up when lines fuse. And James muses about counting, and whether it distorts sensible experience.

The relation of numbers to experience is just like that of "kinds" in logic. So long as an experience will keep its kind we can handle it by logic. So long as it will keep its number we can deal with it by arithmetic. *Sensibly*, however, things are constantly changing their numbers, just as they are changing their kinds. They are forever breaking apart and fusing. Compounds and their elements are never numerically identical, for the elements are sensibly many and the compounds sensibly one. Unless our arithmetic is to remain without application to life, we must somehow *make* more numerical continuity than we spontaneously find. Accordingly Lavoisier discovers his weight-units which remain the same in compounds and elements, though volume-units and quality-units all have changed. A great discovery! And modern science outdoes it by denying that compounds exist at all. There is no such thing as "water" for "science"; that is only a handy name for H_2 and O when they have got into the position H-O-H, and then affect our senses in a novel way. The modern theories of atoms, of heat, and of gases are, in fact, only intensely artificial devices for gaining that constancy in the numbers of things which sensible experience will not show. "Sensible things are not the things for me," says Science, "because in their changes they will not keep their numbers the same. Sensible qualities are not the qualities for me, because they can with difficulty be numbered at all. These hypothetic atoms, however, are the things, these hypothetic masses and velocities are the qualities for me; they will stay numbered all the time."

By such elaborate inventions, and at such a cost to the imagination, do men succeed in making for themselves a world in which real things shall be coerced *per fas aut nefas* under arithmetical law.

The cost to the imagination is twofold. First the effort to think up "elaborate inventions"—the devices that make calculating hard, and so important—can be a lot of fun. There's evident wit in Evans's shape. But then the toll these inventions take on my future experience—limiting its scope and content—is no fun at all. My initial investment shows negative returns. I can lose much more than I put in. My imagination is free to work in any way I like when I calculate with shapes. Counting parts isn't the only way to check experience. There are many other things to see and do. There's ambiguity and all the novelty it brings.

When it comes to novelty, I try to take James as broadly as I possibly can. There's seeing new things—for example, visiting Los Angeles for the first time—and equivalently, seeing things in different ways—going back (looking again) to find out how the city has changed. Either way, the same question invokes novel experience. What's that? And of course, this leads directly to visual calculating, while the reciprocal question—how many?—continues with calculating in the usual way. In fact, James presents his own series of visual examples in *Pragmatism: A New Name for Some Old Ways of Thinking*:

In many familiar objects everyone will recognize the human element. We conceive a given reality in this way or in that, to suit our purpose, and the reality passively submits to the conception.... You can take a chessboard as black squares on a white ground, or as white squares on a black ground, and neither conception is a false one. You can treat [this] figure

as a star, as two big triangles crossing each other, as a hexagon with legs set up on its angles, as six equal triangles hanging together by their tips, etc. All these treatments are true treatments—the sensible *that* upon the paper resists no one of them. You can say of a line that it runs east, or you can say that it runs west, and the line *per se* accepts both descriptions without rebelling at the inconsistency.

Let's try to define the options in the star once and for all. How would Evans do it? His method is clear. I count twenty-four constituents—six long lines and their thirds—if I'm going to look for triangles. Halves don't work anymore. They were ad hoc from the start. But will these same constituents do the job if I jiggle the two big triangles a little to get another six small ones? What happens if I jiggle harder and harder? Or maybe lines stay put. What about diamonds, trapezoids, and the pentagon in Wittgenstein's addition? And what about the A's and X's—big ones and little ones? Only why should I try to limit my experience before I have it? There's always something else to see every time I use another rule—as long as I calculate by seeing.

James and other pragmatists got it right. At least I think so, whenever I calculate with shapes. And today "neopragmatists" walk James's line that runs east and west. Richard Rorty's ironist is a perfect example as he and she try to redescribe things to make sense of them in a kind of literary criticism instead of philosophy. The goal isn't coherence but to get around argument—reasoning—"by constantly shifting vocabularies, thereby changing the subject." Rorty's ironist always has another verbal trick to see things from a different angle. It's not a question of truth but of "making things new." It's embedding all over again. This is how Rorty puts it—

I have defined "dialectic" as the attempt to play off vocabularies against one another, rather than merely to infer propositions from one another, and thus as the partial substitution of redescription for inference. I used Hegel's word because I think of Hegel's *Phenomenology* both as the beginning of the end of the Plato-Kant tradition and as a paradigm of the ironist's ability to exploit the possibilities of massive redescription. Hegel's so-called dialectical method is not an argumentative procedure or a way of unifying subject and object, but simply a literary skill—skill at producing surprising gestalt switches by making smooth, rapid transitions from one terminology to another.

The ironist doesn't calculate—Rorty explicitly says so—yet the ironist does exactly what I do when I calculate with shapes. We both exploit a host of descriptions in order to do more. It's just like politics. There aren't any ends—big goals like truth or permanent parts—only the means to go on. I use my rules in a mechanical process, while the ironist relies on literary skill to glide from one terminology to another in a dialectic. But nothing stops me from changing descriptions as I calculate. I've been calculating with shapes for the past thirty years, and this is simply politics as usual. Shape grammars allow for as much irony as you want, and shape grammar—that is to say, the term itself—is ironic. Grammar implies units and definite parts that aren't defined for shapes. Rules don't mean words and syntax. Lionel March is good at saying what's involved.

Contrary to conventional wisdom, rationality does not flourish in the presence of objective certainty, but actually thrives around subjective volition. To be rational requires the willingness to restructure the world on each contingent occasion, or in just two words, TO DESIGN.

And again for me, each contingent occasion is every time I try a rule. Going on means always starting over. There's a new analysis that's independent of any given before. Parts fuse to erase all prior distinctions, and the resulting shape divides according to the rule I use now. It's visual calculating—calculating by seeing. I started out with the question

What makes reasoning visual?

and said I thought about it in terms of design. It appears that I've been dealing with design all along.

So how are calculating and reasoning, and visual calculating and visual reasoning related? When I posed my question, I made two suggestions in the form of diagrams. Only right now it's probably a better bet to try a new diagram

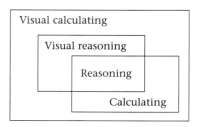

that reverses the relationship between reasoning and visual calculating. I didn't plan for this switch, but visual calculating seems to hold more than ordinary reasoning allows. Maybe this isn't worth the bother of figuring out. Perhaps the only relationships actually worth elaborating are these

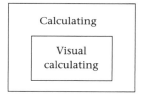 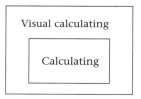

that chart equivalencies between calculating by counting that asks how many—the everyday kind of calculating we're all used to—and calculating by seeing that asks what's that. This is in part II. Still, describing reasoning and calculating is a little like looking at shapes. The relationships between them—both what there is and how it's connected—change as I try rules. I never promised more, and shapes and rules may be all I can get. Saying what they do is an ideal way to go on talking in an open-ended, free, and unprincipled way. James recommends this kind of conversation to teachers. He might just as well have been talking about shapes and rules.

A familiar example of the paralyzing power of scruples is the inhibitive effect of conscientiousness upon conversation. Nowhere does conversation seem to have flourished as brilliantly as in France during the last century. But if we read old French memoirs, we see how many brakes of scrupulosity which tie our tongues to-day were then removed. Where mendacity, treachery, obscenity, and malignity find unhampered expression, talk can be brilliant indeed; but its flame waxes dim where the mind is stitched all over with conscientious fear of violating the moral and social proprieties.

This is more than I said in the introduction about design and conversation. There are no proprieties in design—nothing commands respect. When I calculate by seeing, mendacity, treachery, obscenity, and malignity are unhampered, and in particular, mendacity holds sway. Conscientiousness doesn't work for shapes unless their parts are already decided. Then scruples make a difference—they keep me from looking again. My eyes are stitched all over with the certainty that what's been given before doesn't change. There's simply nothing new to see. It's just counting out. But then there's nothing new to design.

Background

Most of the material from William James is found in a pair of sections, "In Reasoning, We Pick Out Essential Qualities" and its successor, in chapter 22—"Reasoning"—in *The Principles of Psychology*.[1] The quotation on genius is in chapter 19.[2] It concludes an account of how our conceptions of things alter by being used and how old fogyism inhibits the assimilation of fresh experiences. "Old-fogyism, in short, is the inevitable terminus to which life sweeps us on." I like to think that visual calculating is a useful antidote. The longish quotation on numbers and experience is in chapter 28.[3] James talks about concepts and perceptual experience in *Some Problems of Philosophy*.[4] Kierkegaard's saying is found in James's *Essays in Radical Empiricism*, and is followed immediately with this observation.

Understanding backwards is, it must be confessed, a very frequent weakness of philosophers, both of the rationalistic and of the ordinary empiricist type. Radical empiricism alone insists on understanding forwards also, and refuses to substitute static concepts of understanding for transitions in our moving life.[5]

Fixed descriptions don't work in life or in calculating with shapes. Static concepts and the structure they imply are no substitute for rules and embedding. James's descriptions of the six-pointed star are in *Pragmatism*.[6] But also see his discussion of Lotze's descriptions of the star in chapter 11—"Attention"—in *The Principles of Psychology*. James's *Talks to Teachers* is worth reading from cover to cover, given the misplaced emphasis in schools today on basics, standards, and tests. It also contains some nice material on Francis Galton—I mentioned him in the introduction—and his seminal work on mental imagery and visual imagination. (Again, there are antecedent sections in *The Principles of Psychology*.) I have recorded James's delightful remarks on old fogyism and conversation.[7]

R. Narasimhan describes Evans's grammar and how it applies to his shape in the first chapter, "Picture Languages," in the book *Picture Language Machines*.

Recently, Evans has discussed a "grammar-controlled pattern analyzer" which he has implemented in LISP. "The inputs required by the analysis program consist of: (1) a grammar, and (2) an input pattern in the form of a list of lowest level constituents, with any desired information attached for later use in the analysis process. The output will be a list of all of the objects defined by the grammar which can be built out of the list of constituents forming the input pattern."

The following example taken from Evans' paper should give an idea of how such an analyzer would function: "Supposing we have a straight-line drawing as in Fig. 1, and wish to find all of the triangles (16, in the case shown). Suppose the input is to be the list of vertices (9, in this case) with, attached to each, a list of the others to which it is connected by a line of the drawing. The grammar rule we need to define a triangle might look like:

(TRI(XYZ) ((PT X) (PT Y) (PT Z) (ELS XY) (ELS XZ) (ELS YZ) (NONCOLL XYZ)) NIL)

which says a triangle consists of three points XYZ such that the predicate 'exists a line segment between' (ELS) holds, pairwise, between them, and that the 3 points are noncollinear (NONCOLL). When this grammar was supplied along with the input, the program found the 16 triangles."[8]

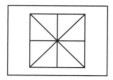

But where does the input pattern come from without prior analysis? How is this done today? To find out, I asked one of the stars in my shape grammar class how he would represent Evans's shape, so that it contained everything he could see. "I'd drag a point to make a square, insert the diagonals, and then rotate [and trim] them to make the horizontal and vertical." It works, but triangles may or may not be defined, depending on how squares are handled. If there are triangles, then there are four. No one questions the inevitability of this kind of structure when you calculate—well, almost no one. I do a seminar in design and computation. One of the participants knows exactly what it's about—"We only talk about *it* here." Her peers aren't so sure. They say, "It's theory—it can't be used to make things. What can you do without structure?" For a start, you might try and see. Picture languages, etc., encourage Evans's kind of thought, and have implications elsewhere. Christopher Alexander's "pattern language" is worth looking at, especially with its intended applications in design.[9]

I start with a quotation from Ivan Sutherland that's remarkably forthright about the importance of structure in computer drawing.[10] I like it a lot because it describes the crucial difference between pencil and paper—structureless stuff—and computer drawings so accurately. Herbert Simon's *The Sciences of the Artificial* is a classic. Every time I pick it up, I find something more of immediate interest in design. The quotes I use are from the second edition that includes the new chapter "Social Planning" in which Simon links painting and calculating.[11] John McCarthy discusses the missionaries and cannibals puzzle in a short paper in *Artificial Intelligence*.[12] The circumscriptive inference in McCarthy's example 1 shows how objects are limited from the start.[13] The material from Marvin Minsky is from two places. His thoughts on creativity and the Body-Support concept are found in *The Society of Mind*.[14] And the rest on paradigms, heuristic search, and structure is in his chapter in Patrick Winston's book *The Psychology of Computer Vision*.[15]

Terry Winograd and Fernando Flores show the limits of calculating with fixed representations.[16] But their conclusions seem much too pessimistic once embedding in its robust sense is taken into account. I quote from Hans-Georg Gadamer's *Truth and Method*,[17] Robert Sokolowski's *Husserlian Meditations*[18]—the few lines on spatial profiles—Gian-Carlo Rota's *Indiscrete Thoughts*,[19] and, finally, Maurice Merleau-Ponty's *Phenomenology of Perception*[20] to show that you may really be calculating even when you think you're not. The interesting thing is to figure out what kind of calculating it is. That's what I've been trying to do with shapes and rules.

There's no escaping a short list of miscellaneous stuff. Ralph Waldo Emerson does little minds in "Self-Reliance,"[21] and Jacques Barzun describes the rubber-band effect in *A Stroll with William James*.[22] Nelson Goodman's definition of relative discreteness in *Languages of Art* is neither consistent nor elastic.[23]

John Dewey dismisses logical analysis and morphological method in teaching in *How We Think*.[24] But Barzun finds Dewey's emphasis on the scientific method, even with his nascent logic of inquiry, a prime example of "preposterism." It puts recapitulation ahead of thinking and structure before calculating.

Dewey's plan is thus another piece of preposterism. When a good mind has done its work, idiosyncratically, it will no doubt submit the results to others in Dewey form. But this is no warrant for believing or requiring that the end[s] serve as a prescription of the means.[25]

"That expectation is pre-post-erous, the cart before the horse." Instead Barzun looks to James.

James . . . understands the child's mind (and the adult's, for that matter) as quite other. It is not an engine [computer] chugging away in regular five-stroke motion [there are five steps in Dewey's scientific method]; it is an artist mind; it works by jumps of association and memory, by yielding to esthetic lures and indulging private tastes—all in irregular beats of attention, in apparent wanderings out of which some deep sense of rationality rises to consciousness. There is no formula, for the trained or the untrained.[26]

There are no set answers when it comes to education. Training may help to get started—there's plenty of it at home and in school—but soon enough reasoning will follow artistic lines. This is what happens to figures when Ludwig Wittgenstein calculates. And I've tried to show that visual calculating encourages the creative wanderings of the artist mind. The artist mind is free to see and do in the unstructured flow of experience, to engage it directly without deciding beforehand what surprises it holds. That's why there are shapes and rules. And it's why embedding makes a real difference.

Wittgenstein adds shapes, so that lines fuse, and worries about what this entails for mathematics in *Remarks on the Foundations of Mathematics*.[27] I said earlier that going from combinatorics to phenomenology was something like the shift from identity to embedding, so that i exceeds 0. It strikes me now that this may be the same for Wittgenstein when he moves on from the *Tractatus* to the *Investigations*—he's going from points to lines. The value of the dimension i may explain some aspects of the split. It certainly helps to explain why calculating with symbols and calculating with shapes are different. William F. Hanks suggests that structure is an outcome of action, and that teaching and learning can occur in situations where master and apprentice act according to their separate representations of what's going on in his foreword to Jean Lave and Etienne Wenger's book *Situated Learning*.[28] This sounds like calculating according to rules that apply to shapes in terms of embedding. More accurately, though, representations (descriptions) as stand-ins for shapes aren't necessary to calculate.

The first quotation from Hilary Putnam is in lecture 2 in *The Many Faces of Realism*, and the other two are found in lecture 1.[29] Richard Rorty limns the ironist's literary skill in *Contingency, Irony, and Solidarity*.[30]

Lionel March and I enjoy talking about design at the Moustache Cafe in West Los Angeles, over a long lunch and a good bottle of wine. Neither of us is keen on scruples or conscientiousness—there are no proprieties when it comes to conversation and design. I have transcribed one of his wonderfully Kierkegaardian insights. Rote results blunt creative experience, too—they're the stuff of scruples and appeal only to the conscientious. It would be nice to have lunch again to see where all of this goes.

An interesting question for a theory of semantic information is whether there is any equivalent for the engineer's concept of noise. For example, if a statement can have more than one interpretation and if one meaning is understood by the hearer and another is intended by the speaker, then there is a kind of semantic noise in the communication even though the physical signals might have been transmitted perfectly.

—George A. Miller

Starting Over

In part I, I gave a visual account of visual calculating. Most of what I said could be checked with your eyes. Still, calculating is traditionally mathematics, and there are abundant reasons to make visual calculating look more that way. In particular, I can add the details to the scheme I outlined in the introduction that relates visual and verbal expression. And the mathematics repays the effort. It shows exactly how visual calculating includes symbol manipulation, and how symbolic processes by themselves are enough to calculate visually. What's more, the mathematics provides a range of technical devices that can be incorporated in rules, and that are very useful in design. In lots of ways, this is the heart of this book. Applying rules to design is what I wanted to do from the beginning, and now I'm going to develop some of the formal machinery that makes this practicable—always with seeing first and foremost. Everything I do meets the same test—is it confirmed by my eyes? I don't want to ignore anything that's visual. If seeing finally says no, then the mathematics is wrong. For example, taking lines in shapes as independent entities—treating them as members of sets—doesn't pass visual muster. You should use this test, too. Seeing always comes first. If something looks different than the mathematics implies, then there's something amiss. Trust your eyes. Only be sure that it's a matter of seeing, and not merely a consequence of remembering what's there before you look. It's easy to make the mistake that what something means now—what parts it has—determines what it looks like later. This is a semantic fallacy. Memory isn't necessary when you can always start over.

I once talked to a famous architect / computer scientist who insisted that the shape was three squares. He said this was its semantics—everyone agreed—and he went on to say what this implied. When you erased one square you got two

The squares were obvious, and the arithmetic was the standard stuff everyone learned in school. The tests I proposed to show how the shape worked without a given semantics went too far. You could do them, only they were meaningless. They weren't anything anyone of good will and sound mind would try. It was a question of morality and rationality. This was the simple truth: the shape had its semantics, and you handled the former—the shape—in terms of the latter—its underlying structure. The two were tied. But erasing didn't work no matter how I went about it

Experiment—use pencil and paper—try it yourself and see what you get. And the identity

$x \rightarrow x$

applied to more than squares when x was a rectangle

and to other parts, as well, when x was other things—maybe a long square bracket

or shorter ones of the same kind

At least the identity seemed to work in this way when I used tracing paper the way designers do to find what's there. See for yourself—the shape isn't a set of parts whatever they are. And drawing shows why. There's no semantics—descriptions don't count—and there's no syntax—words (units) fail. The usual distinctions blur and disappear. In fact, syntax and semantics are pretty much alike without words—neither is usefully engaged when shapes are involved. To do shapes the way I want to, you have to open your eyes to everything that seeing implies. It's the ambiguity that counts. The shape

is three squares, true enough—its semantics gets it right—and much more of equal value, too.

My protagonist isn't the only one to prefer the security of shared (definite) meaning to the open-ended uncertainty of more. In the quotation that opens this part, George A. Miller—an early cognitive scientist—tries the nifty formula

ambiguity = noise

And Miller and my protagonist may see eye to eye. The message seems clear in the din of agreement. They want to communicate with the received semantics in the way they're supposed to—what's meant is what's understood. There's no reason for ambiguity. Still, it's easy to misunderstand if there's too much noise. This is a problem in the shape

that's two squares

or four triangles

But twin variations seem perfectly manageable—I know how to count the variations in shapes like this that contain nested squares and concealed triangles. And this may be a way to measure semantic information with respect to a given vocabulary. What's more, the variations are fun to play with and something to explore. Only there's no end of K's. There are uppercase ones

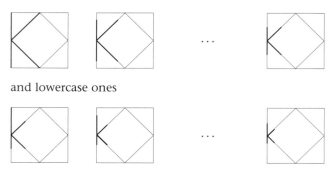

and lowercase ones

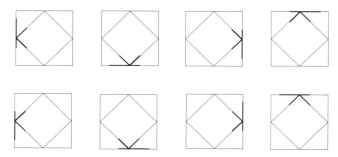

and their rotations and reflections. These are fixed in the symmetry group of the shape. All of its parts can be flipped and turned in eight ways

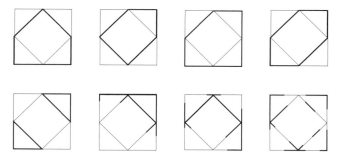

And I can go on and divide the shape in myriad myriads of other ways. There's always something new to see. Nothing stops me from changing my mind and doing whatever seems useful. I can always start over and try whatever comes up. These additional parts

scarcely begin to show how easy it is to switch from division to division without rhyme or reason. No semantics works all of the time. (Myriad myriads is a truly fantastic number that defies actual counting. It's one of Coleridge's many poetic inventions—changing a noun into an adjective—that look easy yet are hard to do. And it's a good example of the uncanny knack of artists and madmen—and sometimes, children who don't know any better—to see triangles and K's after they draw squares, and not to be bothered by it. I do the same trick every time I apply a rule to a shape when I calculate. There's no magic, just mechanics, and I can show exactly how this works. But perhaps I'm looking too far ahead. I still have Miller's problem.)

Ambiguity causes misunderstanding, confusion, incoherence, and scandal. Adversaries rarely settle their disputes before they define their terms. And scientific progress depends on accurate and coherent definitions. But look at this again. It's futile to try to remove ambiguity completely with necessary facts, authoritative standards, or common sense. Ambiguity isn't something to remove. Ambiguity is something to use. The novelty it brings makes creative design possible. The opportunities go on and on. There isn't any noise, only the steady hum of invention. The irony is hard to miss. No doubt, the formula

ambiguity = noise

is right, but this may not be what Miller has in mind. Ambiguity works in another way once a noise is a hum. Shapes and sounds are the same—they change freely.

Ambiguity lets me invent when I use rules to calculate with shapes. This is crucial in design. I don't want to postpone calculating until I've figured out what parts there are and what primitives to use. This is what happens, for example, in heuristic search. But design isn't search. It's far more than sifting through combinations of predetermined parts that are the set results of prior analysis, or evaluating schemas in which divisions are fixed in advance. I don't have to know what shapes are, or to describe them with definite units, for them to work for me as I design. Permanent units just get in the way. They keep me from seeing everything that's there because I have to see them. The semantics is fixed soon enough, but erratically. It's how I calculate that shows me what parts there are—only not all at once. Parts are evanescent. They alter as rules are tried. I have to go on to see how it all comes out. And isn't this the real reason for drawing—going on to see what happens? Representation isn't the problem. Seeing what's possible is. Ambiguity is a limitless source of novelty. Shapes are always new.

Both the intuitive idea and the mathematical idea that make this practicable are the same—

what's embedded is there

—but not always, only when I apply a rule. This is a finite, Aristotelian perspective that's well suited to visual calculating. I said this in part I, and there's more that bears repeating. First, what I add to a shape needn't be there when I look at what I've done—parts fuse. And then, I'm free to see as I choose. I can divide any shape wherever I want without knowing anything about its past. Parts are potential and not a matter of fact. They're only there as calculating goes on, and they're different every time I try a rule. The parts I use now are the parts that count. They change again and again, and aren't given in advance. Otherwise, seeing is pointless—I can adopt the received semantics and recite the expected results. But embedding always allows for more seeing and doing, and the kind of fusion and division in drawing and looking at shapes. This is as far as visual expression can go—there's simply no way to see and do any more. And rules make all of it happen. I'm going to show you how.

Back to Basics—Elements and Embedding

At the very least, shapes are made up of basic elements of a single kind—either points, lines, planes, or solids. Here are some examples of the first three

and these are drawings—just shapes containing lines and planes—of solids

Basic elements are readily described with the linear relationships of coordinate geometry. It's easy to extend this repertoire to include other curves and exotic surfaces, especially when these are also described analytically—for example, when lines are represented as conics to include segments of circles, ellipses, parabolas, and hyperbolas. But my results are pretty much the same whether or not I allow further kinds of basic elements. I'll stick with the ones that show what I need to. A little later, I'll say why straight lines alone are more than enough to see how shapes work—both as mathematics and as the stuff of design. It has nothing to do with approximation—using a lot of tiny segments to make curves. The real leap is to get over points and what they imply for shapes and rules.

Some of the key properties of basic elements are summarized in table 3. Points are undivided units. They're simple and yield nothing to analysis. But in contrast, I can cut lines, planes, and solids into discrete pieces—line segments, triangles, and tetrahedrons—so that any two of these pieces are connected in a finite sequence in which successive ones have a common boundary element—a point, a line (edge), or a plane (face). The construction is always possible. Still, it seems worth doing only for planes and solids that aren't triangles or tetrahedrons themselves. This is just

Table 3
Properties of Basic Elements

Basic element	Dimension	Boundary	Content	Embedding
point	0	none	none	identity
line	1	two points	length	partial order
plane	2	three or more lines	area	partial order
solid	3	four or more planes	volume	partial order

geometry—points are congruent and lines are similar, but planes and solids need be neither. It's easy to divide a hexagonal plane

in three different ways

But the bow tie (quadrilateral?)

isn't a basic element. No matter what divisions I try to make, there are going to be triangles that aren't connected in the right way—they don't share an edge, or begin and end a sequence of triangles in which successive ones do.

The way I construct lines, planes, and solids from segments, triangles, and tetrahedrons implies that they have finite, nonzero content, that is to say, extension measured by length, area, or volume. Yet reciprocal relationships aren't so easy. In particular, finite content needn't imply finite boundaries. Lines are no problem—each is bounded by a pair of distinct points—but what about planes and solids? Does finite content guarantee a finite number of basic elements in every boundary, or that the total content of the basic elements in every boundary is finite? The answer is no both times, and it's worth seeing why to emphasize that shapes are finite through and through.

Begin with the four lines

in the boundary of a square

Divide each line into segments, so that its first half, third fourth, seventh eighth, etc., are distinguished

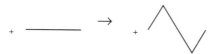

Then replace each distinguished segment with three others

that have total length twice the length of the segment. If this process is carried out sequentially—replacing four segments of equal length in each step—then the planes in this series

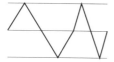

are defined. Each successive plane has the same area as the beginning square. Its boundary increases by twelve lines, and approaches twice the length of the boundary of the square. And, in fact, each successive plane is itself a basic element. But in the limit, there's finite area and a boundary of finite length containing infinitely many lines. What's more, a boundary of infinite length is defined if segments are replaced by others with constant amplitude—as shown here

for adjacent segments. When segments in the boundary of the square are elaborated as before, I get the planes in this series

Phenomena of this kind are found in fractals. Their approximations—as in my two series for squares—produce some nice visual effects. But the phenomena themselves have nothing to do with basic elements or the shapes they make. Basic elements aren't defined in the limit, but rather here and now. Everything about them is finite, except that I can divide lines, planes, and solids anywhere I want. Still, this is the potential infinite of Aristotle and not the actual infinite of sets where members are given all at once. I can see just a finite number of divisions at any time—and these may come and go as rules are used to calculate. Basic elements are the stuff of shapes and practical design before they're material for mathematics. Drawing a line in a single stroke with a pencil on a sheet of paper and tracing segments one by one are the twin examples I keep in mind.

Embedding is the main relation I use to describe basic elements, and by implication the shapes they combine to make. The only point that's embedded in a point is the point itself. Embedding is identity. But, more generally, every basic element of dimension greater than zero has another basic element of the same kind embedded in it—lines are embedded in lines

—schematically, like this

—and planes in planes

etc. Additionally, I can always embed these basic elements in other ones that are bigger. Content is finite for separate elements, but there are always other elements with more.

The embedding relation is a partial order. Most of the time, I take standard mathematical devices like this for granted, and use them without definition. But to start, it may be worth rehearsing the kind of ideas involved. A partial order satisfies three conditions. In particular, embedding is (1) reflexive, (2) antisymmetric, and (3) transitive. This isn't much help, so let's try it in everyday language. Then the conditions go like this—(1) every basic element is embedded in itself, (2) two basic elements, each embedded in the other, are identical, and (3) if three basic elements are such that each is embedded in the next, then the first basic element is embedded in the last. Drawing this doesn't show much. It's a problem with most abstractions that becomes more acute as I go on. That's what I like about shapes and their parts—they're always there to see. Even so, transitivity can look like this for lines

at least schematically.

There are some easy ways to play around with embedding to distinguish basic elements by kind—pretty much as I did geometrically with congruence and similarity, and then with content and boundaries. Different relations are defined when I look at all of the basic elements embedded in a given one. This isn't really Aristotelian where what I use is what there is, but the abstraction—agreeing that everything is actually there all at once—provides some structure. Think of it as one way of describing basic elements among many others, and remember that descriptions don't count when I calculate.

It's no big surprise that an equivalence relation is defined for a point—there's only one

•

Identity is identity. But, for a line

———————————

it's more interesting. A semilattice is defined with respect to joins—any two lines

—————— ——————

embedded in the line have a least upper bound

———————————

that's given by their endpoints (boundary elements). The least upper bound is the longest line of the four I can define with these points, and the shortest line that has both lines embedded in it. And, for a plane or a solid, there's only a partial order. There are plenty of upper bounds—the plane or solid itself always works—and if there are smaller upper bounds, then there are indefinitely many others. But least upper bounds aren't always defined, as, for example, in these three cases for squares

There are least upper bounds only when elements overlap or their boundaries do. Once more for squares, it looks like this

The same idea comes up later on for lines in addition to planes and solids when I define maximal elements in shapes, but in reverse. It's also worth noting that a lattice

isn't defined for lines because meets aren't always defined. In fact, it's the same for lines, planes, and solids—meets are determined only if these elements overlap. There's no other way for lines, planes, and solids to share an element and its content—shared boundaries alone won't do. For example, meets don't exist for three lines embedded in a fourth in this way

I can go on to consider embedding—again in a non-Aristotelian way—in terms of its properties on all basic elements of a given kind instead of just those basic elements embedded in a given one. This sort of generalization is especially useful when I define shapes and their algebras. But, for now, look at what happens with lines. I still have least upper bounds for lines that are collinear. However, joins in this case may or may not be defined for infinite sets of lines. The lines embedded in a given line have a least upper bound—the line itself. And the lines in this geometric series

have a least upper bound

However, the lines in this series of equal segments

don't, because there's no longest line. Content—now it's length—can increase without limit. Collinearity, however, is just a special case. Joins for lines that aren't collinear

aren't defined.

Even though I can get by with embedding alone, other relations on basic elements are helpful. In fact, I've used two of them a few times already—discrete and overlap.

Two basic elements overlap if there's a common basic element embedded in both. Otherwise, they're discrete.

Two points overlap only when they're the same. But, for lines and planes, there are other possibilities. These lines overlap

  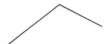

and so do these pairs of squares

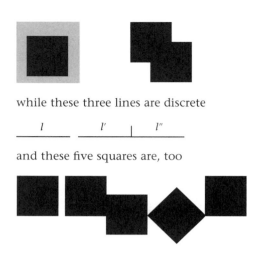

while these three lines are discrete

_____ *l*   _____ *l'* | *l"* _____

and these five squares are, too

Points never touch when they're discrete, but touching is allowed for discrete lines, planes, and solids either at points, lines, or planes. It's worth repeating over and over again—it was evident for meets earlier—that basic elements of different kinds are always separate. In particular, no basic element has content with respect to any basic element of higher dimension. This is why Euler was sure that points don't add up to make lines. Points aren't lines, or planes or solids. And this extends to lines and planes. Content is never zero.

It's easy to see that both of these relations—overlap and discrete—include embedding.

One basic element is embedded in another if every basic element that overlaps the first also overlaps the second, and conversely, if every basic element discrete from the second is discrete from the first.

For overlapping lines, it looks like this

and for discrete lines, like this

Whatever relation I use—embedding, overlap, or discrete—it comes to exactly the same thing. Any one implies the other two. But what about touching? I've used it without a definition. Points touch when they're identical, and more generally, other basic elements do when they overlap. Only lines, planes, and solids can also touch if they're discrete. Before I can say how this works, I need to say a little something about boundaries.

Basic elements that aren't points—either lines, planes, or solids—have boundaries. The boundary of any such basic element contains a finite number of basic elements, all of dimension one less than the original basic element itself. The boundary of every line

is just two points

while the boundary of a plane

contains three or more lines

More precisely, I should say maximal lines. Otherwise, there's nothing definite to count. Maximal elements are used to define shapes uniquely. And in fact, the boundary of any basic element that has a boundary is a shape. But before I deal with the details of this, let's try touching.

Points touch whenever they're identical. And basic elements of the same kind—two lines, planes, or solids—touch if there are basic elements embedded in each with boundary elements that touch. This is evident for basic elements that overlap. Any shared element has a boundary element that does the trick. For a pair of lines, I have

and for two squares

But the recursion is more general than this. It's clear in a few easy examples. When lines touch

there are endpoints that do

Embedded   Boundary
elements   elements

and when planes touch—for example, the equal squares

—there are lines with endpoints that do

Embedded
elements

Boundary
elements

Embedded
elements

Boundary
elements

I can go on to classify different ways of touching. For example, two basic elements touch externally when they're both embedded in a common element and touch without overlapping, as here for discrete lines

and in these twin cases for pairs of triangles

Of course, twins aren't always identical. In the first case, another plane is defined—boundary elements overlap—as this division into four triangles confirms

while in the second case, the bow tie still contains separate basic elements. And likewise, one basic element is tangentially embedded in another if the first is embedded in the second and there's a basic element that touches both externally. For lines, it's

and for planes, it's

  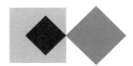

(But what happens if two basic elements are said to touch externally without both being embedded in a third? With three lines, I could have the first embedded in the second and cut by the third—schematically, like this

—so that embedding and tangential embedding are the same.) Moreover, I can define embedding, overlap, and discrete in terms of touching. One basic element is embedded in another whenever every basic element that touches the first also touches the second. I used the same idea to get embedding from overlap.

This has some history—touching externally and being embedded tangentially are from Alfred North Whitehead. He uses extensive connection to describe physical experience in *Process and Reality*. Intuitively, this relationship is having at least a point in common. It shows how continuous regions—they're the earlier events of *An Enquiry Concerning the Principles of Natural Knowledge*—interact, and touching for planes, but also for basic elements of other kinds, is alike in many ways. In fact, the discrepancies appear to be mostly irrelevant bits of formality. From what I can tell, Whitehead's regions and my basic elements are about the same. Notably, every region includes others—there are no units. And no region includes all of the others—there's no longest line, etc.—but any two regions are connected by a third. Disconnected regions don't combine to make a region, and it seems that connected regions may or may not do so. Whitehead gives the following evidentiary series of six diagrams à la Venn

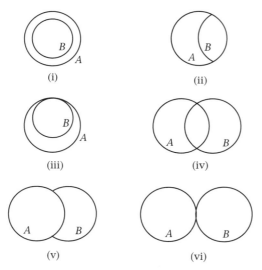

in which regions *A* and *B* are connected. In diagrams i, ii, and iii, there's inclusion (embedding), in i through iv, overlap, in v and vi, external connection, and in ii and iii, tangential inclusion. Presumably, the regions in diagram vi don't form a single continuous region, while the ones in i through v do. And surely, none of this is a surprise. Physical experience and visual experience coincide in many ways—surely, the latter is embedded in the former, and perhaps vice versa to establish identity.

The coincidence between basic elements and Whitehead's regions is a nice diversion. And there are other kinds of coincidence that are easy to see, too. Let a basic element of dimension *i* coincide with a basic element of dimension $i + 1$ if the first one is also a boundary element of a basic element embedded in the second one. Then points are coincident with lines

and lines are coincident with planes

But this definition may be too narrow. Lines that extend past the boundaries of planes

aren't entirely coincident with them, even though they contain lines that are. Only how about cases like this

where a line isn't coincident with a plane but can be divided into segments, so that each segment is coincident with the plane? (I can also say this for any basic element in terms of embedding. If I stick with lines, it goes like this: every line embedded in the line has a line embedded in it that's coincident with the plane.) Moreover, it would be useful for every basic element to be coincident with itself, and for the first term in a series of basic elements, each term coincident with the next, to be coincident with the last term. Once transitivity—that's the third amendment—is in place, points are also coincident with planes in various ways, either inside, on an edge, or at a corner

And with the final two amendments, I get a partial order. What's more, coincidence lets me define touching in another way. Two basic elements touch if there's a single basic element coincident with both. There's more here than in my initial definition, since basic elements aren't distinguished by kind—lines and planes can touch. This line touches three squares, each in a different way

And notice, too, basic elements and boundary elements touch, as here

for a plane, a line (edge), and an endpoint.

Embedding can be used to define many more things. For example, when do basic elements intersect, and when do they abut? There are properties like collinearity, coplanarity, etc. And there's inside and outside, and convexity. Defining things in this way to see how far you can go is a lot of fun, but it's high time for shapes.

Counting Points and Seeing Parts

Shapes are formed when basic elements of a given kind are combined, and their properties follow once the embedding relation is extended to define their parts.

There are noticeable differences between shapes containing points and shapes made up of lines, planes, or solids. First, shapes containing points can be made in just one way if the order in which points are located doesn't matter, and in finitely many ways even if it does. Distinct shapes are always defined if different points are combined. In contrast, there are indefinitely many ways to make shapes of other kinds. Certainly, distinct shapes contain different basic elements, but different combinations of lines, planes, or solids needn't define distinct shapes when these elements fuse.

The shape

can be made with eight lines

as a pair of squares with four sides apiece, with twelve lines

as four triangles with three sides apiece, or with sixteen lines—eight lines plus twelve lines with four lines in common—

as two squares and four triangles. But there's something very odd about how all of this works, too. If the sixteen lines are independent in combination like units that don't fuse or divide—if they're like points or behave like the members of a set—then the outside square

is visually intact when the squares or the triangles are erased, even though the entire shape should disappear. If it's squares that go, then the outside square has eight lines

and if it's the triangles, then the outside square has four lines

And that's not all. The shape

looks exactly the same whether or not the outside square as four lines is there, either as sixteen lines

or twelve

There are just too many lines. Yet they make less than I see. I can find only four upper-case K's

but each in five ways

with lines either from squares or triangles or both. Moreover, I can't find any lower-case k's at all. Lines don't work the way units do. And the same goes for planes and solids. Points are units, and they're the only basic elements that are. The shapes they make are separated from shapes of other kinds—those with lines, etc.—in some telling ways.

Of course, shapes are ambiguous with points and without—with lines, etc. They can be seen in different ways depending on the parts I actually find, or, as I show below, on how I apply rules to calculate. But the potential material for seeing isn't the same for shapes with points and for shapes made with other basic elements. Points can be grouped to form only a finite number of parts, while shapes of other kinds can be divided into any number of parts in any number of ways. This shape

.

.   .

with three points has eight possible parts

.   .   .   .

.   .   .   .

.   .   .   .

.   .   .   .

—one empty part and substantively, seven nonempty ones containing one or more of the points used to make the shape. I can show all the different ways I'm able to see the shape—at least as far as parts go—and count them. But the shape

has indefinitely many parts that needn't combine any of the lines originally used to make it. How the shape is made now and how it's divided into parts later are independent. What I find in the shape may change freely at any time. I can always see something new that I haven't seen before. There's no end to ambiguity and the novelty it brings when basic elements aren't points.

The contrast between points and basic elements of other kinds—lines, planes, and solids—implies alternative ways of calculating. In both, rules are applied to change one thing into another. There's recursion. But the properties of these things, and what they mean for rules, make a big difference. The first way of calculating is standard and uncontroversial, yet no less speculative for that. The idea simply put is this—

Calculating is counting.

Points make counting possible. They provide the units to measure the size or complexity of shapes—the number of points they contain—and the ultimate constituents of meaning. The second way of calculating comes from drawing with lines and looking at shapes. The main idea is this—

Calculating is seeing.

Now parts of shapes are artifacts of what I do as I calculate—they aren't given beforehand. There are neither predefined units of measurement nor final constituents of meaning. Before I calculate, all shapes are the same—each is a single, unitary thing, a simple it. And after I start, units change freely as I go on. They're different every time I apply a rule.

This contrast can be traced to embedding. For points, it's identity, so that each contains only itself. This is what units require, and it makes counting possible. But for all of the other basic elements embedding doesn't end. There are indefinitely many of the same kind embedded in each one—lines in lines, planes in planes, and solids in solids. This is the crucial difference between points and lines, etc. It explains the properties of the algebras I'm going to define for shapes in which basic elements fuse and divide. And it's how rules deal with ambiguity as calculating goes on, so that seeing never stops.

Yet the contrast isn't categorical. I have reciprocal models of calculating, but each includes the other in its own way. My algebras of shapes begin with the counting model. It's a special case of seeing when embedding and identity coincide. And I can deal with the seeing model via counting—and approximate it in computer implementations. These are telling equivalencies that show how complex things containing units are related to shapes without definite parts.

Whether or not there are units is the question used to distinguish verbal and visual expression—Susanne Langer's discursive and presentational forms of symbolism I mentioned in the introduction. It goes like this—

verbal expression (discursive forms) : units, symbols, or points
:: visual expression (presentational forms) : lines, planes, or solids

Verbal and visual expression aren't incompatible, though, as these relationships are sometimes thought to imply. Shapes with points and shapes made up of lines, planes, or solids aren't incommensurable. People calculate all the time. And art and design whenever they're visual are as much a matter of calculating as counting. This is what algebras of shapes and calculating in them show. The claim is figuratively embedded if not literally rooted in the following details.

Shapes in Algebras and Algebras in Rows

Three things go together to define algebras of shapes. First, there are the shapes themselves that are made up of basic elements. Second, there's the part relation for shapes that includes the Boolean operations. And third, there are the Euclidean transformations. The algebras are enumerated up to three dimensions—of course, there are more—in this series

$$
\begin{array}{cccc}
U_{00} & U_{01} & U_{02} & U_{03} \\
 & U_{11} & U_{12} & U_{13} \\
 & & U_{22} & U_{23} \\
 & & & U_{33}
\end{array}
$$

The series is presented as an array to organize the algebras with respect to two numerical indices i and j. In an algebra U_{ij}, the left index i determines the dimension of the basic elements, and the right index j is the dimension in which those basic elements are combined in shapes and in which the transformations are defined. This is easy to illustrate with points and lines. For $i = 0$, there are shapes like these

$j = 0$ $j = 1$ $j = 2$

when $j = 0$, $j = 1$, and $j = 2$. And for $i = 1$, shapes are like this

$j = 1$ $j = 2$

when $j = 1$ and $j = 2$. Evidently, i is greater than or equal to zero, and j is greater than or equal to i. Shapes can be defined and manipulated in any dimension at least as big as the dimension of the basic elements that are used to make them.

Every shape in an algebra U_{ij} is a finite set of basic elements. Only this isn't completely straightforward. When basic elements aren't points—if they're lines, planes, or solids—distinct sets needn't define distinct shapes. The easy way around this problem—it's the way ordinals are used to define cardinals as elements in equivalence classes—is to require that the sets given to define shapes have special properties to work the right way. In particular, I'll insist that their elements be maximal with respect to one another. Whenever two basic elements in a set are embedded in a common element—the common element is always outside the set—they're discrete and their boundary elements are, too. Distinct points are maximal

and so are the four lines

and the four squares (planes)

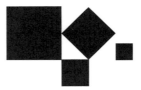

Maximal elements are discrete, but discrete elements may not be maximal, as these squares show

Boundary elements can't overlap.

(The equivalence relation I have in mind for sets of basic elements is this. Let the set S be included in the set T when every basic element embedded in a basic element in S has a basic element embedded in it that's also embedded in a basic element in T. Then the sets S and T are equivalent if and only if each is included in the other. Inclusion is the same as the part relation below, without maximal elements. That accounts for all of the complication. The smallest set in the equivalence class determined by S contains only maximal elements. The set of seven lines

is equivalent to the set of ten lines

And the four lines in the set

are maximal. In all three cases, the same square

is defined.)

I've described maximal elements in terms of embedding and boundaries because it's a cinch. But really, embedding is enough. The intuitive idea is this—basic elements of the same kind are maximal with respect to one another when they're separated by gaps. To be exact, every basic element that overlaps any two in a shape has a basic element embedded in it that overlaps neither. It's in the gap. This is clear for the lines

Any line that overlaps both has the line

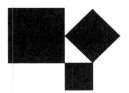

embedded in it that closes the gap between them. In fact, any line embedded in this line overlaps neither of my original lines. But notice that maximal elements can also touch. First, when they're not embedded in a common element, as for these three lines

but then, even if they are embedded in a common element, as for these squares

when boundary elements are discrete. Lines form boundaries of planes, while points form boundaries of lines.

Maximal elements stand the customary atomic (analytic) view of things on its head. Every shape is defined crudely with discrete elements that are numerically distinct, but with no implied granularity or structure. The list of maximal elements contains the smallest number of biggest things that combine to form the shape, instead of the biggest number of smallest things that do. Of course, the atomic view is no more than an approximation for shapes without points. Then every basic element has indefinitely many others embedded in it. And so, maximal elements don't behave like constituents. Otherwise, both approaches are the same—as for points. The part relation shows why.

Embedding is given for basic elements, and the part relation is defined for the shapes they make. The generalization looks like this

parts : shapes :: embedded elements : basic elements

and the supporting definition is remarkably easy to state—it's almost automatic—thanks to maximal elements.

One shape is part of another shape whenever every maximal element of the first is embedded in a maximal element of the second.

Thus for example, the lowercase k

with three maximal lines is part of the shape

with eight maximal lines, as this trio of embeddings shows

Parts don't require identity. The maximal lines in the two shapes are completely different. And it's worth making a big deal of this—

parts are there whenever I can trace them out

—so that the formality doesn't obscure the result. Nothing is lost in this two-tiered approach. There are basic elements and arrangements of them, allowing the former to keep all of their properties in the latter. Shapes are combinatorial after all, but not in the usual way where the properties of sets, list structures, graphs, etc., determine how elements behave. Formal devices come at the end to tidy things up. They don't make shapes the way they are. In a word, that's preposterous—at least as Jacques Barzun means it.

It's easy to see that the part relation is a partial order on shapes. In fact, I can use it to define lattices for shapes in the way I used embedding to describe basic elements, only now with far more generality. Meets and joins are defined for all shapes and for all values of i. This works because shapes can contain multiple elements and not just single ones, and also because there's an empty shape with no elements at all. Making shapes out of basic elements is a sweet thing to do. Even so, the lattice properties of shapes are usually framed in terms of Boolean algebras, and this is equally telling.

The familiar Boolean operations are used to combine shapes in various ways in the algebras U_{ij}. Sum (join), product (meet), and difference will do, or equivalently, symmetric difference and product. The part relation provides for these definitions regardless of the value of i. Once again, embedding is the key idea that supports my entire approach to shapes.

A unique sum is formed whenever two shapes are added together. Twin conditions are met—(1) both shapes are parts of the sum, and (2) every part of the sum has a part that's part of one shape or the other. (To make this perfect, I should say that every nonempty part of the sum has a nonempty part that's part of one shape or the other, because the empty shape is part of every shape. I'll avoid this detail again when I define difference.) With just condition 1, the sum can be too big, with condition 2, too small, but with both conditions, it's just right. Consider some examples for different values of i. The shape

with eight points is formed when the shape

with five points is added to the shape

with six points. The same three points

occur in both shapes to account for the eight-point sum. Every part of the sum— except, of course, the empty one—is a combination of points from either one or both of the shapes. In fact, for shapes with points, sum is set union—it contains exactly the points in one shape or the other. But, for other shapes without points, maximal elements can fuse when they're not identical—always if they overlap, and sometimes if they're discrete—and so may not be preserved when they're combined. The shape

is produced in the addition of the shape

made up of four triangles, and the shape with the two pieces

Neither of the shapes in the sum has any maximal element in common with the other. Their maximal elements fuse in combination. And the parts of the sum—for example, the shape

containing four triangles—needn't combine the maximal elements in the shapes. Set union is all there is to addition for shapes with points, but it's a different story with lines, planes, and solids when basic elements fuse and divide.

The way I've defined sum has a certain charm, but it isn't constructive. Unless I'm using points, I can't always list the maximal elements in a sum in an easy way. For this, I need an algorithm. I'm not going to give one for basic elements in general—it's too cumbersome. Rather, I'll give an easy algorithm for lines. It shows everything that's involved, and how it all depends on embedding. The three reduction rules in table 4 are used to produce maximal lines. The rules are independent, and they exhaust the different ways lines fuse. They apply recursively in any order—but with no

Table 4
Reduction Rules for Maximal Lines

Assume that lines are ordered by their endpoints, and let l and l' be any two of these lines. Then, a set of lines is changed into a set of maximal lines according to three reduction rules. The rules are used recursively in any order until no rule can be applied.

(1) If l is embedded in l', either like this

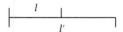

so that there's a common endpoint, or like this

so that there isn't, then remove l from the arrangement.

(2) If l and l' overlap but neither is embedded in the other

then replace both lines with the line l'' fixed by the leftmost endpoint of l and the rightmost endpoint of l'. This is the longest line with an endpoint of l and an endpoint of l'.

(3) If l and l' are collinear and discrete, and share an endpoint

then replace both lines with the line l'' fixed by the remaining endpoints of l and l'.

---

inconsistency—until maximal lines are finally defined. If I begin with the maximal lines in two shapes, I get the maximal lines in their sum. (It's worth saying, as well, that the equivalence relation I defined to catalogue sets of basic elements can be given in terms of these reduction rules—call the three of them working together R. The sets S and T define the same shape if and only if $R(S) = R(T)$. Be careful, though. The part relation isn't the subset relation. The set S can be included in the set T—then $R(S)$ is part of $R(T)$—without $R(S)$ being a subset of $R(T)$. The subset relation requires identity—embedding won't do.)

The four lines in this scheme

are reduced to a single maximal line after each of the rules in table 4 is applied once, perhaps in this sequence

Start

Rule 1

Rule 2

Rule 3

but in any other sequence, as well.

Shapes are also combined by subtracting. And as it did for sum, the part relation provides what's needed for a definition. There's a unique difference when one shape has another shape subtracted from it. Every part of the first shape that has no part that's part of the second shape is part of the difference—this makes the difference big enough—and every part of the difference is part of the first shape—this guarantees that it isn't too big. Some examples help to make this clear. The shape

made up of four points is produced when the shape

with five points is subtracted from the shape

with eight points. The difference contains the points in the first shape that aren't points in the second. This is precisely the way relative complement is defined for sets. But this doesn't work for shapes when basic elements aren't points. The shape contains no maximal plane that's a maximal plane in the shape

Nonetheless, their difference—the second shape subtracted from the first shape—contains none of the planes in the first. This part

of the first shape is produced instead. It results when the part

that the two shapes have in common is taken away. A nice way to confirm this is to draw both shapes together—to form their sum

and then to erase the second shape

It's easy to disagree about what the results of subtraction should be to satisfy intuition. Are there two squares when I take one away from this shape

Subtraction isn't an everyday operation for everyone, and it may take a little time and practice to get used to. A few more examples—for shapes made up of lines and planes—are helpful

A	B	Sum	Difference

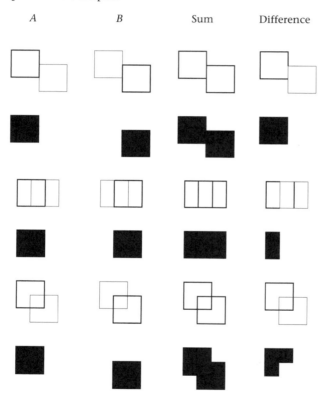

Drawing and erasing to define differences—this is feasible whenever j is one or two—always provide the correct result. It's also worth saying explicitly that the difference of two shapes is the first whenever their basic elements are mutually discrete, even if they have boundary elements that overlap, as here for lines and squares

or have coincident elements in common

The maximal elements in a shape formed in a difference are not defined automatically. Some work is needed to get them, just as it is to get the maximal elements in a sum. An algorithm for lines is framed in terms of embedding in table 5. The rules are independent, and they exhaust the ways any two lines interact when a segment

Table 5
Rules for Maximal Lines in Differences

Start with any two sets of maximal lines that are ordered by their endpoints. Let l be a line in the first set and l' be a line in the second. Then, the first set is changed recursively according to three rules that may be applied in any order until no rule can be applied.

(1) If l is embedded in l'

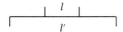

then remove l from the set.

(2) If l' is properly embedded in l, so that no endpoint is shared

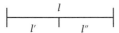

then replace l with the lines l'' and l''' fixed by the two leftmost and the two rightmost endpoints of l and l'. Alternatively, if l' is properly embedded in l, and there is a common endpoint

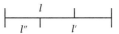

then replace l with the line l'' fixed by the remaining endpoints of l and l'.

(3) If l and l' overlap but neither is embedded in the other

then replace l with the line l'' fixed either by the two leftmost or by the two rightmost endpoints of l and l', so that l'' isn't embedded in l'.

---

of one is taken from the other. They apply in any order with exactly the same final result. A subtraction is finished when none of the rules applies to remove or replace a line.

The rules in table 5 may apply several times to produce a single line in a difference. In this illustration

Shape 1

Shape 2

all three rules are required to obtain the appropriate result in whichever way the subtraction is performed. In the sequence of rule applications

Shape 1

Rule 1

Rule 2

Rule 3

the second shape is subtracted from the first. And here

Shape 2

Rule 1

Rule 2

Rule 3

the first shape from the second. And notice also that maximal lines always result whenever one of my rules is tried. No matter how I subtract a line from a shape, I get another shape.

I've defined sum and difference for two reasons. First, they work to get the two other Boolean operations I said I was going to use—product and symmetric difference. It's best if I give the results in symbols—

Sum	$A + B$
Difference	$A - B$
Product	$A \cdot B = A - (A - B)$
Symmetric difference	$A \oplus B = (A - B) + (B - A)$
	$A \oplus B = (A + B) - (A \cdot B)$

When two equal squares

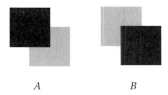

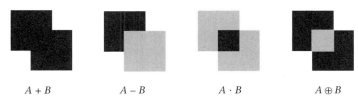

are combined, the results of these operations compare in the following way

(In the few places I use symbols to denote shapes in part I, they're the letters *S*, *M*, and *P* in accordance with William James's description of the syllogism. But henceforth I revert to my usual practice of taking letters from the beginning of the alphabet—in particular, *A*, *B*, and *C*. It's a habit that's hard to break. Rules and expressions don't look right otherwise.)

Keeping to symbols—I'll use $A \leq B$ when the shape *A* is part of the shape *B*, and I'll use 0 to denote the empty shape—it's easy to state the standard Boolean relationships. A few of these are in table 6. Evidently, facts 8 and 9 show that product and symmetric difference include both sum and difference. So starting with sum and difference is arbitrary, at least for the purpose of defining Boolean operations. My second reason for starting with sum and difference, however, isn't so easy to dismiss. It has to do with rules and how they work.

Algebras of shapes are perfect examples of Barzun's preposterism—most formal devices are. When I started playing around with shapes, I wanted to use rules to generate them. I tried this in many ways drawing with pencil and paper, until I discovered

Table 6
A Few Boolean Facts

(1) $A \leq B$ if and only if $A + B = B$	$A \leq B$ if and only if $A \cdot B = A$
(2) $A \leq B$ if and only if $A - B = 0$	
(3) $A = B$ if and only if $A \oplus B = 0$	
(4) $A + (B + C) = (A + B) + C$	$A \cdot (B \cdot C) = (A \cdot B) \cdot C$
(5) $A + B = B + A$	$A \cdot B = B \cdot A$
(6) $A + (B \cdot C) = (A + B) \cdot (A + C)$	$A \cdot (B + C) = (A \cdot B) + (A \cdot C)$
(7) $C - (A + B) = (C - A) \cdot (C - B)$	$C - (A \cdot B) = (C - A) + (C - B)$
(8) $A + B = (A \oplus B) \oplus (A \cdot B)$	
(9) $A - B = A \oplus (A \cdot B)$	

how it worked finding parts—using tracing paper to see what was there independent of what I drew—and replacing them in a recursive process. The part relation and a few transformations—they're given below—were what I used to find parts. And then subtracting and adding—that's erasing and drawing—and the same transformations let me replace the parts I found. So, what I did with rules told me what I needed to do with algebras. They're merely a summary of how things turned out. I didn't start with them or anything like them—that's preposterous. But that they're so nice in the end gives added support to my approach. The mathematics is too neat for rules not to work like this. In some ways, though, my algebras are profligate. In the theory of formal languages and automata—it's the mathematical basis for linguistics—algebras (monoids) are defined for strings of symbols using a single associative operation—concatenation. This explains strings, but it doesn't explain how rules apply. For that, you need other operations like sum and difference. The rules in a generative grammar need more than concatenation to work. To avoid this kind of problem for shapes, I started with shapes and rules at the same time. The two had to work together—the former without the latter left seeing a mystery. Without rules it was all magic.

The transformations that make rules work move shapes around, turn them over, and make them bigger and smaller. They're operations on shapes that change them into geometrically similar ones. They distribute over the Boolean operations, and may include, for example, translation

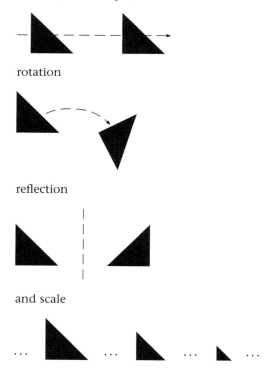

rotation

reflection

and scale

These transformations also form a group under composition. The properties of this group characterize Euclidean geometry. I use this group later to describe the behavior of rules when they're used to calculate with shapes.

That does all of it. I have shapes, parts, sums, and differences, and various kinds of transformations—some Boolean stuff and some Euclidean stuff—along with basic elements. This is what it takes to make seeing work. It blends a lot of well-known mathematics to handle shapes and rules. Let's look at it again all together. A few illustrations are enough to fix the algebras U_{ij} visually. And in fact, this is just the kind of presentation they're meant to support. Once the algebras are defined, what you see is what you get. There's no need to represent shapes in symbols to calculate with them, or for any other reason. Look at the shapes in the algebra U_{02}. This one

is an arrangement of eight points in the plane. It's the boundary of the shape

in the algebra U_{12} that contains lines in the plane. The eight longest lines of the shape are the maximal ones. And in turn, the shape is the boundary of the shape

in the algebra U_{22}. The four largest triangles in the shape are maximal planes. They're a good example of how this works. The triangles are discrete, and their boundary elements are, too, even though they touch externally. Points aren't lines and aren't in the boundaries of planes.

The properties of basic elements are extended to shapes in table 7. The index i is varied to reflect the facts in table 3. The algebras are linked via shapes and their boundaries—I'll say more about this in the next section. But for now, notice that an algebra U_{ij} contains shapes that are boundaries of shapes in the algebra U_{i+1j} only if i and j are different. That's why my examples ended at U_{22}. The algebras U_{ii} don't include shapes that are boundaries of shapes, and they're the only algebras for which this is so. How could they?—when $i = j$, j is one dimension too low. Of course, boundaries aren't the only way to distinguish these algebras. They also have special properties in terms of embedding and the transformations. And I'll describe these, as well, only yet farther on.

Table 7
Some Properties of Shapes

Algebra	Basic elements	Boundary shapes	Number of parts
U_{0j}	points	none	finite
U_{1j}	lines	U_{0j}	indefinite
U_{2j}	planes	U_{1j}	indefinite
U_{3j}	solids	U_{2j}	indefinite

Table 8
More Properties of the Part Relation

U_{ij}	Every shape has a distinct nonempty part—there is no smallest shape	Every shape is a distinct part of another shape—there is no largest shape
$0 = i = j$	no	no
$0 = i < j$	no	yes
$0 < i \leq j$	yes	yes

The description of parts in table 7 misses some important details. These require the index j. The additional relationships are given in table 8.

Boundaries of Shapes Are Shapes

Boundaries of shapes are another way to show how basic elements combine, and how embedding works. If a shape has a boundary, then its boundary is a shape. The boundary of each maximal element in the shape is a shape, and the sum of these shapes is the boundary of the shape.

Shapes containing points don't have boundaries. But the boundary of a shape made up of lines, planes, or solids is a shape containing points, lines, or planes. (The empty shape—when it's used with shapes with boundaries—is the only shape that has an empty boundary.) Some shapes and their boundaries are shown in these examples—first for lines

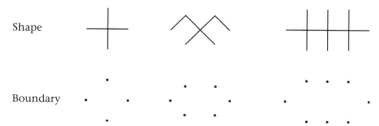

and then for planes

Shape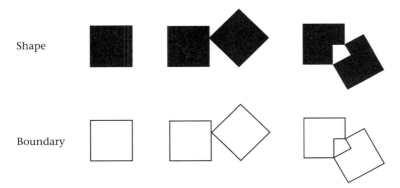

Boundary

Boundary elements are always reduced to maximal ones, so that boundaries are shapes. The boundary

of the four triangles

contains eight lines

instead of twelve

And the boundaries

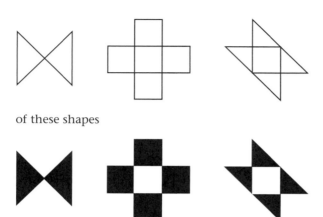

of these shapes

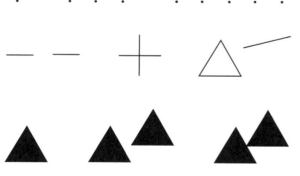

don't include all of the basic elements that are in the boundaries of their individual basic elements.

It's convenient to have a boundary operator b, so that $b(x)$ is the boundary of any shape x in an algebra where i is greater than zero. Moreover, b is a one-to-one mapping from the algebra $U_{i+1\,j}$ into U_{ij} when $j = i + 1$, and a many-to-one mapping otherwise. This is a precise but obscure way of saying that some shapes aren't boundaries, that some are the boundaries of exactly one shape, and that others are the boundaries of many. For example, none of the following shapes is a boundary with points, lines, or planes

However, these shapes with points and lines

are the boundaries of unique shapes with lines and planes

and this shape

is the boundary of many shapes—forty-one to be exact—of which these thirteen

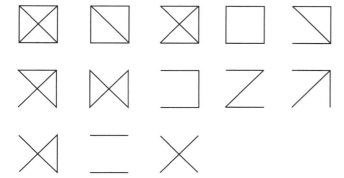

are geometrically distinct. And notice that of the thirteen, only two

are boundaries of shapes made up of planes

Right now, I'm going to illustrate the use of the boundary operator *b* in a few formulas with sum and difference. And somewhat later, I'll use *b* in schemas for rules. In this way, for example, I can calculate to connect points in lines to define planes. It's a nice transition that's useful in art and design.

The boundary of a shape is the sum of the boundaries of its maximal elements. But the boundary of a sum of shapes needn't be the sum of their boundaries, unless the maximal elements in the shapes are still so when they're combined. The rules in table 4 that define maximal lines show why. This is perfectly general—the same goes for planes and solids—and it's easy to see. Let's begin with the second case in the first rule in table 4 for one line embedded in another

and the second rule for two overlapping lines with a common segment not identical to either

In both, the boundary of the sum of the lines—that's the boundary of the maximal line they define—

and the boundary of their common segment

combine to form the sum of the boundaries of the lines

In symbols, it's

$$b(l + l') + b(l \cdot l') = b(l) + b(l')$$

(I'm using l and l' in two ways to denote lines and the shapes they define. I can be rigorous with added symbols—the shapes are $\{l\}$ and $\{l'\}$—but it's too fussy.) The third rule in table 4 shows another relationship. Two lines are discrete with a boundary element in common

The boundary of their sum—again, it's the boundary of the maximal line containing both—

and the product of their boundaries—their common endpoint—

come together in the sum of the boundaries of the lines

And in symbols, it's

$$b(l + l') + b(l) \cdot b(l') = b(l) + b(l')$$

But my two formulas aren't really independent—in the one, $b(l) \cdot b(l')$ is empty, while in the other, $b(l \cdot l')$ is. If I add everything up in Boolean fashion, I get the comprehensive formula

$$b(l + l') + b(l \cdot l') + b(l) \cdot b(l') = b(l) + b(l')$$

that describes how boundaries interact in all circumstances. And the first case in the first rule

is a nontrivial example of this. Neither $b(l \cdot l')$ nor $b(l) \cdot b(l')$ is empty. Both of the lines l and l' have a segment in common

and a common point in their boundaries

> The quartet of relationships in my final formula is exhaustive whatever basic elements are used—either lines, planes, or solids. But this can be expressed more concisely in another way using symmetric difference. The new formula has the feel of algebraic stuff. It's got the right look

$$b(e \oplus e') = b(e) \oplus b(e')$$

and the right sound—the boundary of the symmetric difference of two basic elements e and e' is the symmetric difference of their boundaries. Try it for the reduction rules for lines in table 4.

> I've been talking about basic elements—lines, etc.—but I might as well have been talking about shapes and their boundaries. In this respect, the formula

$$b(x + y) + b(x \cdot y) + b(x) \cdot b(y) = b(x) + b(y)$$

has a practical advantage over its dashing counterpart

$$b(x \oplus y) = b(x) \oplus b(y)$$

In the one, x and y can be any two shapes, while in the other shapes are restricted in a special way. In particular, the second formula is guaranteed to work only if all maximal elements are embedded in a common one—lines are collinear, planes are coplanar, etc. Once more, lines are enough to see what's going on.

> Look at this pair of lines

They're independent with respect to symmetric difference—their product is the empty shape. But this isn't so for the product of their boundaries

It's a single point. As a result, $b(x) \oplus b(y)$

is missing a point that's in $b(x \oplus y)$

More generally, common pieces of boundary elements in the maximal elements in the symmetric difference of x and y are lost in the symmetric difference of their boundaries. But it's easy to fix this when shapes are divided into parts according to whether or not their maximal elements are embedded in common ones.

The following equivalence relation does the trick.

Let two basic elements be coembedded whenever they're embedded in a common element.

The effect of this is clear in the shape A

that's divided into three different parts A_1, A_2, and A_3

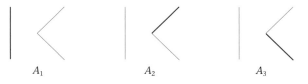

A_1 A_2 A_3

(This is a nice way to store maximal elements in a computer. After all, it's how an experienced draftsman would normally draw the parts of a shape made up of lines. But notice that the relation doesn't organize points, as it does basic elements of higher dimension—lines and planes and solids—when j is more than i.) Then two other facts—in addition to the fact that symmetric difference works for coembedded elements—are used to exploit this kind of division. First, the symmetric difference of two shapes is their sum, so long as no maximal element of one is coembedded with any maximal element of the other. In this case, the shapes have an empty product. But further, basic elements are maximal if they're not coembedded. So, second, the boundary of the symmetric difference of the two shapes is the sum of their boundaries. I can combine parts in one way if their basic elements are coembedded, and in another way if they're not, to get the result I want. Now suppose I take the boundary of the symmetric difference of the shape A

with three parts, and another shape B

that's also divided into three parts B_1, B_2, and B_3

according to my equivalence relation. Then, I get

$$b(A \oplus B) = b(A_1) + b(B_1) + (b(A_2) \oplus b(B_2)) + (b(A_3) \oplus b(B_3))$$

instead of

$$b(A \oplus B) = b(A) \oplus b(B)$$

The symmetric difference of A and B is

and both shapes have the same boundary

So, $b(A) \oplus b(B)$ is the empty shape, while the sum $b(A_1) + b(B_1) + (b(A_2) \oplus b(B_2)) + (b(A_3) \oplus b(B_3))$ is

.   .

.   .

Use tracing paper to test the results. It's easy to see that everything goes together exactly the way it should. This visual kind of demonstration always convinces me that I've got it right. It's so immediate, and it's something a designer would do. In fact, it's the way rules work when I calculate. Watching designers with pencils and tracing paper is watching visual calculating in progress. I'll get to it soon, but first let's see how algebras of shapes go together.

Boolean Divisions

I can classify the algebras of shapes U_{ij} in terms of their Boolean properties, and in terms of their Euclidean ones. This shows how the algebras differ, but more importantly how visual and verbal expression are related when the latter corresponds to the algebras of points. The Boolean classification relies on the variation of the indices i and j in table 8. The algebras U_{ij} are divided in this way

U_{00}	U_{01}	U_{02}	U_{03}
	U_{11}	U_{12}	U_{13}
		U_{22}	U_{23}
			U_{33}

according to whether or not i and j are zero. There are four regions to examine—the top row and each of its two embedded segments, and the triangular portion of the lower-right quadrant.

The atomic algebras of shapes are defined when the index i is zero

$\mathbf{U_{00}}$	$\mathbf{U_{01}}$	$\mathbf{U_{02}}$	$\mathbf{U_{03}}$
	U_{11}	U_{12}	U_{13}
		U_{22}	U_{23}
			U_{33}

Shapes are finite arrangements of points. The atoms—nonempty shapes without distinct nonempty parts—are the shapes with a single point apiece. They're the same as the units I've been talking about, but with respect to sets of points and the part relation instead of separate points and embedding. Any product of distinct atoms is the empty shape, and sums of atoms produce all of the other shapes. No two shapes are the same unless their atoms are. A shape either is empty or has an atom as a part. There are two kinds of atomic algebras depending on the value of the index j.

The only Boolean algebra of shapes is U_{00}

$\boldsymbol{U_{00}}$	U_{01}	U_{02}	U_{03}
	U_{11}	U_{12}	U_{13}
		U_{22}	U_{23}
			U_{33}

It contains exactly two shapes—the empty shape and an atom made up of a single point. In fact, it's the only finite algebra of shapes, and it's the only complete one in the sense that shapes are defined in all possible sums and products. The algebra is the same as the Boolean algebra for true and false used to evaluate logical expressions.

The other atomic algebras U_{0j} are defined when j is more than zero

U_{00}	$\boldsymbol{U_{01}}$	$\boldsymbol{U_{02}}$	$\boldsymbol{U_{03}}$
	U_{11}	U_{12}	U_{13}
		U_{22}	U_{23}
			U_{33}

Each of these algebras contains infinitely many shapes that all have a finite number of points and a finite number of parts. But since there are infinitely many points, there's no universal shape that includes all of the others, and so no complements. (It's easy to get around this for points and for basic elements of higher dimension if I look at shapes and their complements in a kind of figure-ground relationship. For example, here

the shape is either black or white, either the figure containing three points or all of the other points in the ground. And the same finite representation can be used to distinguish both cases by saying what is or isn't in the shape—the shape is three points or all points with the exception of three

This works without a hitch for points for any value of j, and for lines, etc., when i equals j. Otherwise, a little squinting is helpful. Try it for the shape

made up of three lines. Are the lines that define its complement

pure white or really gray? But this is a concrete problem without serious abstract implications. It's interesting, though, that a defining perceptual phenomenon finds its way
so naturally into mathematics. And figure-ground-like relationships come up in other
ways, as well, whenever complements are involved.) Shapes with points form a generalized Boolean algebra. It's a relatively complemented (table 6, fact 7), distributive
(fact 6) lattice when the operations are sum, product, and difference, or a Boolean ring
with symmetric difference and product. There's a zero in the algebra—it's the empty
shape—but no universal element because the universal shape that includes all points
can't be defined. As a lattice, the algebra isn't complete—every product is always
defined, while no infinite sum ever is. Distinct points don't fuse in sums the way basic
elements of other kinds do. The finite subsets of an infinite set, say, the numbers in the
counting sequence 0, 1, 2, 3..., define a comparable algebra.

Some of my technical jargon may be hard to take. Still, it's what the mathematics
is about, and it repays the effort to track down definitions for terms that aren't familiar.
Both the formalist and the artist need to meet each other halfway, so that they can join
at more than a boundary. There's much to be gained when each side heeds the other.
After all, I've been trying to show what calculating would be like if Turing had been a
painter. I try to use formal terminology only when it's helpful. Without it here, it
would be difficult if not impossible to make the rigorous contrasts that are implicit in
my series of algebras. At the very least, my appeal to these ideas should make it clear
that there's no reason to be flaky when you're talking about art and design. And at
the same time, I hope it's also clear that a formal presentation doesn't diminish the
expressive potential of drawings and the like. Shapes are always there to see with all
of their possibilities when rules are tried.

Algebras of shapes made up of points come up again when I consider algebras
of decompositions—they have a lot to do with spatial relations and set grammars. A
decomposition is a finite set of parts (shapes) that add up to make a shape. It gives the
structure of the shape by showing just how it's divided, and how these divisions interact. The decomposition may have special properties, so that parts are related in some
way. It may be a Boolean algebra on its own, a topology, a hierarchy, or something
else. For example, suppose a singleton part contains a single basic element. These are
atoms in the algebras U_{0j} but don't work this way if i isn't zero. The set of singleton

parts of a shape with points is a decomposition. In fact, the shape and the decomposition are pretty much alike. But decompositions aren't defined for shapes with basic elements of other kinds. There are too many singleton parts.

An algebra of shapes U_{ij} shows what happens when shapes are put together using given operations. But there are other ways to describe the algebra in terms of the shapes it contains, and to describe these shapes according to their algebras. Looking at the parts of a shape—whether or not these are finite in number—does the trick. This relativizes the algebra with respect to the shape, describing it with one of its subalgebras. Everything that goes on in the algebra goes on in the shape. A screen full of pixels, whether they're points or tiny areas, is a perfect example of this for U_{02}. But let's try it in general, and see how it works.

A shape and its parts in an algebra U_{0j} form a complete Boolean algebra that corresponds to the Boolean algebra for a finite set and its subsets. This is represented neatly in a lattice diagram. The Boolean algebra for the three points

in U_{02} is shown here

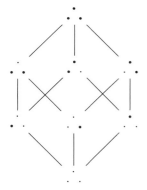

Pictures like this are compelling, and make it tempting to consider all shapes—whether or not they have points—in terms of a finite number of parts combined in sums and products. It's hard to imagine a better way to describe shapes than to resolve their parts and to show how the parts are related. This is what decompositions are for. But if parts are fixed permanently, then this is a poor way to understand how shapes work when I calculate. As I describe this later, parts—with and without Boolean complements—vary as I go on. Parts are decided anew every time I try a rule. Decompositions—Boolean algebras, topologies, and the like—change dynamically as a result of calculating. I don't know what parts there are until I stop using rules. Only then is there nothing new to see.

The Boolean algebra for a shape and its parts in an algebra U_{0j} is also a discrete topology. Every part of the shape is both closed and open, and has an empty boundary. Parts are disconnected. (Topological boundaries aren't the boundaries I've been describing so far that show how shapes in different algebras are related. Now the boundary of a shape is part of it and not a shape in an algebra of lower dimension.) This is a formal way of saying what seeing confirms all the time—there's no preferred way to divide the shape into parts. Any division is possible. None is better or worse than any other without ad hoc reasons that depend on how rules are used. This is where meaning begins, and going on is how it changes and grows. Shapes have meaning because I calculate. There's no meaning until I do.

Going on, the atomless algebras U_{ij} are defined when i is more than zero

U_{00}	U_{01}	U_{02}	U_{03}
	U_{11}	U_{12}	U_{13}
		U_{22}	U_{23}
			U_{33}

Each of these algebras contains infinitely many shapes made up of a finite number of maximal lines, planes, or solids. But every nonempty shape has infinitely many parts. The empty shape is the zero in the algebra. There's no universal element and hence no complements. (A universal shape can't be formed with lines, planes, or solids, as this would fill all of an unbounded space. Moreover in a bounded space where i is less than j, there would be infinitely many basic elements. It doesn't work either way.) This gives a generalized Boolean algebra, in the way this was defined for points. Only this time, the properties of sums and products are symmetric—for both, infinite ones may or may not be defined. When infinite sums are formed, basic elements fuse. But this alone isn't enough—for example, the sum of all singleton shapes isn't a shape.

In an algebra U_{ij} when i isn't zero, a nonempty shape and its parts form an infinite Boolean algebra. But the algebra isn't complete—infinite sums and products needn't determine shapes. It's worth seeing how this works, at least to emphasize once more that shapes are finite through and through. Every shape is the sum of the set of its parts. Only there are subsets of this set that don't have sums. Let's suppose that the shape is a single line

———————————————————

Then the series of shapes containing the first quarter of the line, the fifth eighth, the thirteenth sixteenth, and so on

———————————————— 1st $\frac{1}{4}$

———————————— 5th $\frac{1}{8}$

—————————— 13th $\frac{1}{16}$

$\vdots$

doesn't have a sum. No finite set of maximal lines corresponds to this infinite series of segments. This is similar to what I did earlier with boundaries of basic elements that were defined in the limit. And the construction applies equally to planes and solids if I divide rectangles or rectilinear rods. What's more, I can use fact 7 in table 6 to get the corresponding result for products. Now the shapes in my infinite set are these

and their product gives the gaps separating the segments in my sum

This is another kind of figure-ground reversal with formal implications.

Shapes made up of lines, planes, and solids have underlying topologies in the same way shapes made up of points do. Only instead of finite topologies, they're infinite ones. In particular, every shape has a Stone space topology. Parts correspond to closed and open sets. They have empty boundaries and are disconnected. In this, all shapes—with points and without—are exactly the same. They're all ambiguous. There's nothing about shapes by themselves, no matter what basic elements they have, that recommends any division over another. Stone spaces confirm what's easy to see, but they violate the Aristotelian scruples I invoked earlier on. Still, everything is grounded when I calculate. The parts I see—the ones that rules pick out—are the ones that count, with meaningful interactions and the possibility of substantial boundaries. And these parts, too, combine in topologies—finite ones—to describe shapes.

So far, my classification of shapes and their algebras shows that things change extensively once i is bigger than zero. And the pun isn't gratuitous. It applies spatially to basic elements, and then numerically to indicate the many differences between algebras when shapes contain points and when shapes are made up of lines, etc. Whether or not embedding implies identity makes a world of difference. But my algebras aren't the only way to think about shapes. There are two alternatives that deserve brief notice. They locate my account of shapes in a wider landscape of formal possibilities that includes philosophy and engineering.

First, there are the famous individuals of logic. Shapes are like them in important ways. In particular, both shapes and individuals can be divided into parts, now in one way and again in some other way, independent of any agreed formula. As a result, shapes, like individuals, aren't like sets. Henry Leonard and Nelson Goodman clarify this difference. The following quotation strikes at the heart of the matter.

> The concept of an individual and that of a [set] may be regarded as different devices for distinguishing one segment of the total universe from all that remains. In both cases, the differentiated segment is potentially divisible, and may even be physically discontinuous. The difference in the concepts lies in this: that to conceive a segment as a whole or individual offers no suggestion as to what these subdivisions, if any, must be, whereas to conceive a segment as a [set] imposes a definite scheme of subdivision—into [subsets] and members.

Embedding and the part relation are crucial. But the likeness between shapes and individuals fades as additional details are checked.

The way shapes and individuals are used distinguishes them most of the time. Rules are applied to change shapes—in fact, I defined shapes and rules in concert to make sure that this was so—while individuals aren't handled in this way. There's no distinction between individuals and individuals in rules. This is difference enough when there's calculating to do, but it may not seem decisive otherwise. And perhaps the contrast is simply a question of emphasis, with a common purpose. Individuals distinguish things in the total universe just as rules do in shapes. Only how? In the latter, it's calculating with parts that vary as rules are tried. Though here, too, there are worthwhile shadings. Goodman and W. V. Quine set up the machinery—"shape predicates"—to calculate with ink marks (individuals) in a "nominalistic syntax." Marks and lines, etc., are much the same in terms of embedding and parts, yet neither relation is exploited. Instead, shape predicates are used to recognize symbols and texts largely in accordance with the rudimentary conventions of printing and reading—pretty much as described in part I. Predicates are framed to block ambiguity and to discourage my way of calculating with shapes. But this is no surprise—symbols and texts are supposed to stay the same in a syntax.

Differences in definition are easier to compare. Individuals form a complete Boolean algebra that has the zero excised. The algebra may have atoms or not—it seems to, more often than not—and may be finite or infinite. Yet worries about zero—having something for nothing—pale against the possibility of taking infinite sums and products. I'm happy with zero (the empty shape) as an unremarkable technical device, because it makes a nice algebra and sticks to standard mathematical usage. And I'm unhappy with infinite operations, because I can't figure out how to do them in a practical way I can understand, or to see the extent of the results in every case. Still, this isn't all that's different. Unlike shapes, there are no added operators for individuals— transformations aren't defined. To be completely honest, though, the nonempty parts of any nonempty shape in an algebra U_{0j} are possible individuals. But if j isn't zero, then this isn't so for all of the nonempty shapes in the algebra taken at once. Shapes only go together finitely. Maybe the real difference is that logicians and philosophers don't have to make things, and artists and designers want to. At least, they can draw what they see.

This is a pretty tidy comparison, but there are qualifications. Not all individuals keep to the Boolean norm. Whitehead's regions and extensive connection are a good example. The relationships are usefully put like this. On the one hand, there are basic elements—Whitehead's regions—and then on the other hand, shapes—Boolean individuals. The analogy is worth showing explicitly—

basic elements : shapes :: regions : individuals

It seems there are twin intuitions that interact in a variety of ways. The one is about continuity—seeing that everything connects all over or touches throughout. This is evident for maximal elements, and also for basic elements that are coembedded. Then they occupy a continuous locus. Whitehead is explicit about this. He defines mediate connection—two separate regions A and B can be joined by a third C—in the following trio of cases

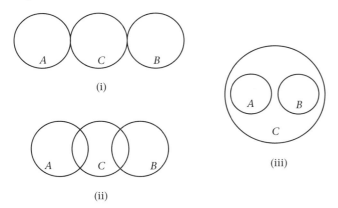

Coembedding is the third, and it's needed for touching in case i and implied in case ii. The second intuition is about combination—allowing everything to go with everything else—at least finitely for shapes but possibly otherwise for individuals—even with discontinuous results. Leonard and Goodman emphasize this. It sounds OK, yet may take some effort if you're trained to use a syntax where there's a difference between texts and symbols—the latter being connected shapes that don't touch. But no matter how it finally goes, it's nice that basic elements and shapes connect with so many other things. And this doesn't end. Engineers have something important to say, too.

The second alternative to shapes comes from solid modeling in computer graphics, as it was originally done in mechanical engineering. Solid modeling uses point sets. These are infinite, so there's a huge discrepancy with shapes. But, ignoring this, the topology of a shape in an algebra U_{ij} when i isn't zero and the topology of the corresponding point set are strikingly different. The shape is disconnected in the one topology and connected in the other. Among other things, the topology of the point set confuses the boundary of the shape that's not part of it—a shape in the algebra $U_{i-1\,j}$—and the topological boundary of the shape that is. Points are too small to distinguish between boundaries as parts and limits. To get around this, point sets are "regular" when they're shapes, and Boolean operations are "regularized." This seems an artificial way to handle lines, planes, and solids. Of course, shapes made up of points are point sets with topologies in which parts are disconnected. This and my gloss on individuals reinforce what I've already said. The switch from identity to embedding may seem modest—it's going from zero to one—but it has telling consequences for shapes and how rules work.

Euclidean Embeddings

The Euclidean transformations augment the Boolean operations in the algebras of shapes U_{ij} with additional operators. They're defined for basic elements and extend easily to shapes. Any transformation of the empty shape is the empty shape. And a transformation of a nonempty shape contains the transformation of each of the basic elements in the shape. This relies on the underlying recursion implicit in tables 3 and 7 in which boundaries of basic elements are transformed until new points are defined.

The universe of all shapes, no matter what kind of basic elements are involved, can be described as a set containing certain specific shapes, and other shapes formed using the sum operation and the transformations. For points and lines, the universe is defined with the empty shape and a shape that contains a single point or a single line. Points are geometrically similar, and so are lines. But this relationship doesn't carry over to planes and solids. As a result, more shapes are needed at the start. All shapes with a single triangle or a single tetrahedron do the trick, because triangles and tetrahedrons make the other planes and solids. For a point in zero dimensions, the identity is the only transformation. So there are exactly two shapes—the empty shape and the point itself. In all other cases, there are indefinitely many distinct shapes that come with any number of basic elements. Every nonempty shape is geometrically similar to indefinitely many other shapes. There's plenty of opportunity to move shapes around and to increase or decrease their size without changing the relationships between their basic elements—for example, the angles defined by lines.

The algebras of shapes U_{ij} also have a Euclidean classification that refines the Boolean classification I've given. Together these classifications form an interlocking taxonomy. The algebras U_{ii} on the diagonal provide the main Euclidean division

U_{00}	U_{01}	U_{02}	U_{03}
	U_{11}	U_{12}	U_{13}
		U_{22}	U_{23}
			U_{33}

The algebras U_{ii} have an interesting property. A transformation of every shape in each algebra is part of every nonempty shape. This is trivially so in the algebra U_{00}

U_{00}	U_{01}	U_{02}	U_{03}
	U_{11}	U_{12}	U_{13}
		U_{22}	U_{23}
			U_{33}

for a point in zero dimensions. Both the empty shape and the point are parts of the point. But when i isn't zero

U_{00}	U_{01}	U_{02}	U_{03}
	$\mathbf{U_{11}}$	U_{12}	U_{13}
		$\mathbf{U_{22}}$	U_{23}
			$\mathbf{U_{33}}$

the possibilities multiply. In this case, infinitely many transformations of every shape are parts of every nonempty shape. This is obvious for the empty shape. It's part of every shape under every transformation. But for a nonempty shape, there's a little more to do. Because i equals j, the basic elements in the shape are coembedded. And as a result, a single basic element contains them all. But infinitely many transformations of any basic element can be embedded in any other basic element. I can make the former smaller and smaller until it fits in the latter and can be moved around. So there are infinitely many ways to make any shape part of any other shape that has at least one basic element. The triangle

in the algebra U_{22} is geometrically similar to parts of a square

and in fact, to parts of itself

This has important implications for the way rules work when I calculate. A rule applies under a transformation that makes one shape part of another shape. Everything is fine if the rule is given in the algebra U_{00}. It's always determinate—if it applies, it does so under a finite number of transformations. In fact, the identity transformation is the only one. But in the other algebras U_{ii}, a rule is always indeterminate—it applies to every nonempty shape in infinitely many ways, as I've already described. This makes it hard, if not impossible, to control how the rule is used. It can be applied haphazardly to change shapes anywhere there's an embedded basic element—and that's everywhere. Indeterminate rules are a burden. They appear to be purposeless when they can be applied so freely. Still, indeterminate rules have some important uses that I'll get to later. They let me do things that seem beyond the reach of rules.

I like to think that shapes made up of lines in the plane—a few pencil strokes on a scrap of paper—are all that's ever required to study shapes and how to calculate with them. This is how I started playing around with shapes, and it's hard to stop because it's easy and fun, and it works so well. Nonetheless, there are other reasons for shapes with lines that aren't personal. In particular, they make sense historically and practically. On the one hand, for example, lines are key in Leon Battista Alberti's famous account of architecture—

Let us therefore begin thus: the whole matter of building is composed of lineaments and structure. All the intent and purpose of lineaments lies in finding the correct, infallible way of joining and fitting together those lines and angles which define and enclose the surfaces of the building. It is the function and duty of lineaments, then, to prescribe an appropriate place, exact numbers, a proper scale, and a graceful order for whole buildings and for each of their constituent parts, so that the whole form and appearance of the building may depend on the lineaments alone. Nor do lineaments have anything to do with material, but they are of such a nature that we may recognize the same lineaments in several different buildings that share one and the same form, that is, when the parts, as well as the siting and order, correspond with one another in their every line and angle. It is quite possible to project whole forms in the mind without any recourse to the material, by designating and determining a fixed orientation and conjunction of the various lines and angles. Since that is the case, let lineaments be the precise and correct outline, conceived in the mind, made up of lines and angles, and perfected in the learned intellect and imagination.

And it's the same today—try to imagine designing without lines. They let you find out what to do, and record the results of seeing and doing. Moreover, Alberti's idea of lines and angles comes up again a little later on: it's implicit in my use of spatial relations to define rules for design. Then, on the other hand, the technology of lines is uncomplicated and accessible to adults and children alike with minimal training. Pencil and paper are enough. Yet an algebraic reason supersedes anything I can find either in my personal experience, in history, or in technology. There are compelling formal arguments for drawing with lines.

Shapes containing lines arranged in the plane suit my interests because their algebra U_{12}

U_{00}	U_{01}	U_{02}	U_{03}
	U_{11}	$\boldsymbol{U_{12}}$	U_{13}
		U_{22}	U_{23}
			U_{33}

is the first algebra of shapes in the series U_{ij} in which (1) basic elements have boundaries, and the identity relation and embedding are different, and (2) there are rules that are determinate and rules that aren't when I apply them to calculate with shapes. For example, the rules I've already used to find and move polygons in stars and superstars are determinate, and rules in U_{11} are also indeterminate in U_{12}. The algebra U_{12} has extended basic elements and the right Boolean and Euclidean properties. It's representative of all of the other algebras where i isn't zero. This lets me show almost everything I want to about these algebras and the shapes they contain in line drawings. And that's mostly what I've been using. Pencil lines on paper are a perfect way to experiment with shapes, and to see how they work when I calculate. I rarely use anything else—perhaps a few points and planes now and again. Then the technology is still easy in the right way.

"Nor Do Lineaments Have Anything to Do with Material"

Alberti points out that lines—and likewise points, planes, and solids—don't have anything to do with material. This is a dogma in geometry, but sometimes the connection is worth making in design. And in fact, there are a host of things that can be connected with basic elements and shapes when I calculate. The path is clear when the algebras U_{ij} are elaborated and combined in different ways to define new algebras of shapes. This provides an open-ended repertoire of expressive devices that can be used in whatever way you please.

Shapes often come with other things besides basic elements. Labels from a given vocabulary, for example, $a, b, c \ldots$, may be associated with basic elements to get shapes like these

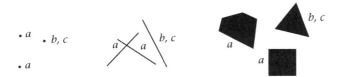

The labels may simply classify basic elements and so parts of shapes, or they may have their own semantics to introduce other kinds of things. In a more ambitious fashion, basic elements may also have properties associated with them that interact as basic elements do when they're combined. I call these weights. Weights go together with basic elements to get shapes that look like these

where points have area, lines have thickness, and planes have tones. Among other things, weights include different graphical properties such as color and surface texture, but any material property will do, and more abstract things like sets of labels, numerical values that vary in some way, or combinations of sets and values are fine, too.

Labels and weights let me put shapes together in alternative ways. I can place a triangle on top of a square to make the shape

in the algebra U_{12}, and then take away the triangle I've added. But the result isn't the square

that you expect from listening to the words—"take away the triangle after you add it to a square." The piece that the triangle and square have in common is erased from the top of the square in the way this happens in drawing to produce the shape

It's a mistake to assume that the things words pick out are always independent in combination. The intuition is common yet misguided, just another semantic fallacy. Language doesn't structure shapes permanently. You can always be surprised when descriptions don't count. But this is familiar territory—I experimented erasing squares in the shape when I started thinking about shapes and drawings. Yet there are other options. I can label the lines in the triangle in one way and label the lines in the square in another way, so that the square is still intact after adding and subtracting the triangle. Borrowing a term from computer graphics, the triangle and the square are on separate layers. The labels distinguish the layers to guarantee that the two shapes are independent. When I do something to one, it doesn't change the other. And I can handle this and more with weights. Either way, my example begins to show how labels and weights can be used to modify algebras of shapes.

When labels and weights are associated with basic elements, additional algebras of shapes are defined. Two new series of algebras are formed from the series U_{ij}. The algebras V_{ij} for labeled shapes keep the Boolean properties of the algebras U_{ij}, and the algebras W_{ij} for weights may or may not, according to how weights combine. A few technical details—enough to suggest that everything works—may be welcome.

Labeled shapes have labels associated with their basic elements, so that ones with the same label are maximal. A labeled shape A is part of a labeled shape B if for each label a, the shape formed by the basic elements labeled by a in A is part of the corresponding shape in B. This is easy to see in this example

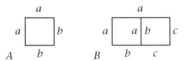

where the shapes A and B determined by lines labeled by a, b, and c correspond in the following way

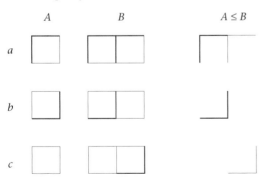

But the part relation fails if A is

because lines are classified differently.

Operations on labeled shapes are defined in the same fashion, when parts are combined according to their labels. It's plenty to do sum and difference. Only now, some simple notation is helpful. Let A_a be the shape formed by the basic elements in A labeled by a. If A is this labeled shape

then A_a is the shape

(Evidently then, A is part of the labeled shape B whenever A_a is part of B_a, for every label a.) Conversely, let A^a be the labeled shape defined when the basic elements in A are labeled by a. If A is the square

then A^a is

So the sum of two labeled shapes A and B is simply the collection of labeled shapes

$$(A_a + B_a)^a$$

for all of the labels a, and their difference is the corresponding collection of labeled shapes

$$(A_a - B_a)^a$$

For example, two labeled squares form a sum in this way

that contains the seven labeled lines

And this sum and another labeled square show how difference works when they combine in this way

The main thing to keep in mind is that basic elements interact if they have the same label, and combine independently otherwise. Parts of labeled shapes are considered separately "layer by layer" and then "stacked" to get the final result. But this isn't new—it's the same for coembedded parts where layers run every which way.

Of course, there are still the transformations. And it may be that they change labels, as, for example, when b is reflected to make d and then rotated to make p. Only for most of my purposes, it's easier not to allow this. After all, the relationships between b, d, and p aren't really between labels that are abstract symbols, but between concrete shapes. For my purposes, labels are invariant under the transformations—

$$t(a) = a$$

for every transformation t and every label a. And for a labeled shape A, $t(A)$ is the sum of the labeled shapes

$$(t(A_a))^a$$

for all of the labels.

It's fun to play around with notation occasionally, as I've been doing here with subscripts and superscripts. There's a spatial aspect to it that goes beyond formal content. But this isn't entirely gratuitous. When notation works, it helps to make formal content clear and effective, and to make it feel OK with perspicuous results. In fact, getting the right notation may be as important as getting the right idea—especially for its ongoing development. If I can transcribe the idea easily, then I can use it easily. This is another way that seeing counts.

Weights are a little more complicated to do formally, but the underlying idea isn't hard to see. Suppose I start with two lines labeled by a and b

and form a single line with weighted segments in this way

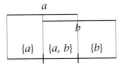

where each weight is a set of labels. Then the weighted shape made up of two lines {a}   {b}

is part of

{a}   {a, b}   {b}

Each of the lines in

{a}   {b}

is embedded in the line formed by the three segments in

{a}   {a, b}   {b}

Further, the weight of each of the lines is a subset of the weight of each of the segments it overlaps

{a}   {b}

{a}   {a, b}   {b}

It's also easy to form sums and differences. If I add

{a}   {a, b}   {a, b, c}

and

{b}   {a, b}

the picture looks like this

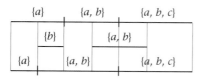

And if I go on and do the subtraction—the second shape from the first shape—I get

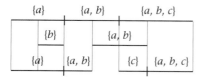

I've worked out the persnickety details of the part relation, and of adding and subtracting for weighted shapes, elsewhere—the references are in the background

section—and so will only give a brief outline. In fact, I'll just do adding and subtracting, as each normally implies the part relation (table 6, facts 1 and 2). The idea is to insert an algebra of weights—with labels, it's just the Boolean algebra for sets—in an algebra of shapes. Points are trivial. The problem is with lines, planes, and solids.

The basic elements in a weighted shape are maximal in the sense that ones of equal weight are. For a weighted shape A, let A^* be the shape defined when all of its weights are stripped away. Let's suppose A is the weighted shape

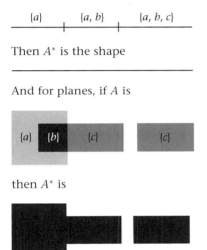

Then A^* is the shape

And for planes, if A is

then A^* is

The sum of two weighted shapes A and B in an algebra W_{ij} is formed by dividing the basic elements in A and B into separate pieces to assign weights. These new basic elements are distinguished according to whether they contribute to the differences $A^* - B^*$ or $B^* - A^*$, or to the product $A^* \cdot B^*$. These parts are distinct and separate from one another, and they totally exhaust the sum $A^* + B^*$

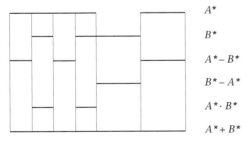

$A*$

$B*$

$A* - B*$

$B* - A*$

$A* \cdot B*$

$A* + B*$

The weights assigned to the basic elements that contribute to the differences are taken directly from A and B, while the weights assigned to the basic elements that contribute to the product are defined in unions. This process is easy to illustrate for lines

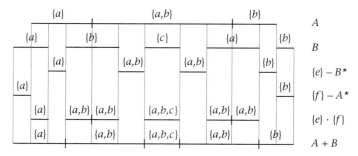

In particular, notice how singleton shapes are used to produce new basic elements. Let e and f be basic elements in A and B. Then for the twin differences $A^* - B^*$ and $B^* - A^*$, new basic elements are defined by $\{e\} - B^*$ and $\{f\} - A^*$, and for the product $A^* \cdot B^*$, by $\{e\} \cdot \{f\}$. And once this is done for all basic elements, resultant ones with equal weights are added together to make sure that everything is maximal. Basic elements defined in differences and products with singleton shapes are always discrete, but they may still have overlapping boundary elements.

In like fashion, the difference of two weighted shapes A and B is formed by dividing their basic elements into pieces that contribute to the shapes $A^* - B^*$ and $A^* \cdot B^*$. The weights assigned to the basic elements that contribute to $A^* \cdot B^*$ are defined in relative complements. However, weights can't be empty for basic elements to be included in the difference of the weighted shapes A and B. And once again, the process is easy to illustrate for lines

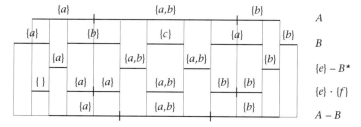

The Boolean algebra for sets of labels is nothing special. Nonetheless, it shows how a familiar abstract device is enough to change any algebra of labeled shapes into an isomorphic algebra of weighted shapes. Putting independent labels in sets lets me combine the labels. (I can do the same using individuals, only with atoms—one for each label—instead of members. But I like sets better. Labels are pretty abstract already, so there's no harm in sets and no reason to be like shapes. The contrast is worth keeping to stress the difference between classifying parts and finding them.) This trick makes labels unnecessary—weights will do. Of greater interest, though, there are more exotic algebras of weights that aren't Boolean. One is worth seeing in a little detail, because of its relationship to drawing and because of what it shows about cooking up algebras of weights where physical properties and mathematical ideas interact on equal footing to get a nice result.

Weights are already familiar in architecture, graphics, and the visual arts, where lines of different thickness are used in drawing

It's no big deal to extend this idea in a variety of ways—to points, for example, when they have area

and to planes and solids when they're filled with tones

as I've already shown. Such properties have a neat algebra with a relation and operations that correspond to parts and to sum and difference in an algebra of shapes.

Suppose that two lines of different thickness defined by numerical values—pen size will do—are drawn at the same time, either one overlapping the other

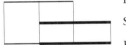

First line

Second line

Both lines

The thicker line appears at full length, while the thinner one is shortened. And if the two lines have equal thickness, then a single line is formed

First line

Second line

Both lines

In both of these experiments, the weight of the embedded segment common to the lines is the maximum of the combined weights. So for the weights u and v, it's just the case that

$$u + v = \max\{u, v\}$$

And for parts, it's easy to see that $u \leq v$ when

$$u + v = v$$

The way weights combine in differences, however, isn't as clear as it is for sums, and there's little in drawing that offers genuine guidance. But algebraic considerations suggest an interesting rule. Weights form a lattice in which the least upper bound of any two is their sum, and the greatest lower bound is their product or the minimum of both

$$u \cdot v = \min\{u, v\}$$

Clearly, $u \leq v$ when

$$u \cdot v = u$$

But in full Boolean fashion, I should also have the equality

$$u \cdot v = u - (u - v)$$

in which the product of u and v is determined in a double difference. If I make this so, then the rule where the difference of u and v is their arithmetic difference when v is less than u, and zero otherwise, is a felicitous choice. All of it—parts, sums, and differences—looks like this

$$u \leq v \qquad u + v \qquad u - v$$

Weights in the way I've been describing them have physical properties, so the transformations might make a difference of another kind. A color here needn't be the same when it's put over there, and area, thickness, and tone can vary as I move weighted shapes around. Nonetheless, I'll do what's easy and simply avoid additional complication—weights are invariant under the transformations. This makes perfectly good sense, too, being partly confirmed in everyday experience. My weight doesn't change when I go for a walk. No matter how I move, it's exactly the same.

Of course, it's always possible to elaborate the algebras U_{ij} in other ways that go beyond labels and weights. I can use labels and weights together, and it's a nice exercise to see how this sets up algebraically. But there's no reason to be parsimonious—and no elegance is lost—when new algebras are this easy to define. The idea is to get the algebra that makes sense for what you're doing, and not to make what you're doing conform to an arbitrary algebra that's in use. The mathematics is generous—even profligate—and it's no sin to be prodigal. It's worth taking the time to get the right stuff to express what you want to when you calculate. That's what I do when I select appropriate materials—pencils, pens, markers, different kinds of paper, etc.—to draw without thinking about how it's calculating. But there's mathematics for all of it. And I can even imagine doing it on the fly, so that algebras change dynamically as shapes do when rules are tried.

The algebras U_{ij}, V_{ij}, and W_{ij} can also be combined in a variety of ways, for example, in appropriate sums and products (direct products), to obtain new algebras. These algebras typically contain compound shapes with one or more components in which basic elements of various kinds, labels, and weights are mixed, as for example, in the shape

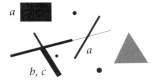

with points, lines, and planes, etc. In this way, the algebras U_{ij}, V_{ij}, and W_{ij}, and their combinations facilitate the definition of a host of formal devices in a common framework. The properties of these devices correspond closely to the properties of traditional media in art and design. Nothing is lost—certainly no ambiguity, and that's the main thing to check—and much is gained when things can interact in new ways. This lets me calculate in the kind of milieu that's expected for creative activity. I'm free to try any materials that work, and to experiment to find out how they work together.

The algebras I've been talking about give me the wherewithal to say what I mean by a design—not the activity, but its result. Roughly speaking, designs are used to describe things for making and to show how they work. This may imply a wide range of expressive devices—shapes and the kinds of things in my algebras—in myriad different descriptions that are linked and interact in many ways. As descriptions, designs are complicated and multifaceted. To begin, a design may consist of line drawings, with all their ambiguity, that I can use singly or multiply to determine form—for example, to show three-dimensional relationships in plans, sections, and elevations, or to describe the separate parts and their relationships in an assembly. Drawings, however, rarely give everything in a design. Sometimes, drawings are augmented with models and other kinds of geometrical representations. Or they're combined with labels and weights—even samples—to describe form further and to provide details of function, material, construction, etc. Drawings themselves can be described in different ways. I can decompose them into parts, and then assign parts to categories to clarify intention from different points of view and to allow for analysis, explication, and evaluation. These ends are also served when drawings are identified with other kinds of descriptions, including diagrams, graphs, and networks, and with numbers and mathematical expressions. And the use and scope of the various descriptions in a design may depend on special instructions and additional documents, or may be elaborated in an ongoing commentary—it's never too late to calculate some more, so that the design changes over time. Many things of many kinds connect to make a design. And all of this is possible in my algebras when I calculate.

It's easy to be precise about this—

designs belong to n-ary relations

The way of calculating I have in mind is meant to define these relations. "Languages" of designs defined in shape grammars are one example. And in fact there are more intricate examples as well—a few easy ones are given in this part and others in part III. Right now, though, it's good to see that my definition is more than bookkeeping. Not only does it imply that things connect up in designs in alternative ways, it also implies that specialists and users can communicate across domains—even at cross-purposes—to contribute to a single end. This is cooperation without coercion. There's no need for shared understanding or overarching control. Calculating with ambiguity and changing connections makes this possible. And it shows the kind of virtuosity that's expected in intelligent and creative practice. This goes beyond familiar slogans, like "form follows function," that are supposed to guide practice, and tiresome theory. And it shows the inadequacy of presumed generators of designs such as programme, context, technology, and material, and of studied accounts of how designs are produced whether formal, functional, rational, or historical. Practice is far more interesting. Designs result from a confluence of activities with multiple perspectives that ebb and flow. Changing interests and goals interact and influence one another dynamically. Nothing is set for long in this process. Designs are complicated and multifaceted—they're the very stuff of algebras and calculating.

Solids, Fractals, and Other Zero-Dimensional Things

I said earlier that decompositions are finite sets of parts that sum to make shapes. They show how shapes are divided for different reasons and how these divisions interact. Of course, decompositions aren't defined only for shapes in an algebra U_{ij}. More generally, they're defined for whatever there is in any algebra formed from the algebras in the series U_{ij}. And decompositions have their own algebras. Together with the empty set—it's not a decomposition—they form generalized Boolean algebras with operators. There's the subset relation, the standard operations for sets (union, intersection, and relative complement), and the Euclidean transformations. And, in fact, these are just the kind of algebras needed for set grammars. They make decompositions zero dimensional like the shapes in the algebras U_{0j}. The parts in decompositions behave exactly like points. Whatever else they are, they're members of sets—units that are independent in combination and without finer analysis.

I like to point out that complex things like fractals and computer models of solids and thought are zero dimensional. Am I obviously mistaken? It's easy to think so. Solids are clearly three dimensional—I bump into them. Fractal dimensions are neither whole numbers nor zero, whatever they are. And no one knows about thought, even though it's said to be multidimensional when it's creative. Only this misses the point. Fractals and computer models rely on decompositions that are zero dimensional, or like representations such as lists or graphs in which units are also given from the start. That's how computers work—they manipulate complex things with predefined divisions. Units are easy to count—fractal dimensions add up before calculating begins—and easy to move around to sift through possible configurations for ones of interest. Nonetheless, computers fail with shapes once they include lines or basic elements of higher dimension. I can describe what happens to shapes as long as I continue to calculate, and I can measure their complexity as a result of the rules I use to pick out parts. In this sense, shapes may be just as complex as anything else. There is, however, a telling difference. The complexity of shapes is retrospective. It's an artifact of the rules I try that depends on how they're actually applied. Without rules, there's no complexity. And with rules, complexity varies—up and down—as I calculate. There aren't any units before I start, and I have to finish to get an accurate and final count. I may not know what's going to happen until it does.

I've already shown that units in combination needn't correspond with experience. What a computer knows and what I see may be entirely different. The shape

is sixteen lines that describe two squares with four sides apiece and four triangles with three sides apiece. This explains how it works. But there are too many lines, and too few. Some parts are hard to delete—the outside square won't go away. And some parts are impossible to find—lowercase k's aren't there. But even if I'm willing to accept this because the definitions of squares and triangles are exactly what they should be—and for the time being, they're more important than k's—there's still a problem. I may not know how the shape is described before I start to use it. Does it include only squares, or some combination of squares and triangles? I can see the shape easily enough—there it is

—but I can't see its decomposition. I need to find this hidden structure. Experiments are useful, only they take time and may fail. I'm stuck without help and the occult (personal) knowledge of experts. Shapes aren't anything like this. What you see is what you get. This is a good reason to use shapes in design. There are times when I don't know what I'm doing and I look at shapes to find out. That's why drawing makes a difference. It's a little like listening to what you say to learn what you think. But there's nothing to gain if I have to ask somebody else what shapes are. Then I don't need to draw because I can see what they say.

Decompositions don't work. There are many reasons for this as just described, and maybe a few more to prove my point. First, there's the problem of the original analysis. How can I possibly know how to divide a shape into parts that suit my present interests and goals and that anticipate whatever I might do next? Nothing keeps me from seeing triangles and K's after I draw squares—even if I'm sure that squares are all I'll ever need and I'm blind to triangles and K's right now. It's much easier to see what I want to in an ongoing process than to remember or learn what to do. My immediate perception takes precedence over anything I've decided or know. But there's an option. I don't have to divide the shape into meaningful parts. I can cut it into anonymous units, small enough to model (approximate) as many new parts as I want. This is a standard practice, but the parts of the shape and their models are too far apart. Shapes containing lines, for example, aren't like shapes that combine points. This is what the algebras U_{0j} and U_{1j} show. Moreover, useful divisions are likely to be infrequent and not very fine. Getting the right ones at the right time is what matters. Yet even if units do combine to model the parts I want, they may also multiply unnecessary parts, beyond interest and use, to cause unexpected problems. Point sets show this perfectly. I have to deal with the parts I want, and also with the parts I don't. Dividing the shape into units exceeds my intuitive reach. I can no longer engage it directly in terms of what I see. There's something definite to know beforehand, so I have to think twice about how the shape works. It's an arrangement of arbitrary units that go together in an arbitrary way that has to be remembered. What happens to novelty and new experience? Memory blocks it all. Any way you cut it, there's got to be a better way to handle the shape. Decompositions are preposterous before I calculate. They provide a record of what I've done, not a map of what to do. They keep me from going on—at least in new ways.

But decompositions are fine if I remember they're only descriptions, and that descriptions don't count. They're what I get whenever I talk about shapes—to say what they're for as I show how they're used. Without decompositions, I could only point at shapes in a vague sort of way. Still, words are no substitute for shapes when I calculate. Parts aren't permanent but alter freely every time I try a rule. Shapes and words aren't the same.

How Rules Work When I Calculate

Most of the things in the algebras I've been describing—I'll call all of these things shapes from now on unless it makes a serious difference—are useless jumbles. This should come as no surprise. Most of the numbers in arithmetic are totally meaningless, too. The shapes that count—like the numbers I get when I balance my checkbook—are the ones there are when I calculate. I have to see something and do something for things to have any meaning. And seeing and doing can change things freely, even as calculating goes on.

Shapes are defined in different algebras. But how I calculate in each of these algebras has a common mechanism. Rules are defined and applied recursively to shapes in terms of the part relation and Boolean sum and difference—or whatever corresponds to the part relation and these operations—and the Euclidean transformations. This uses the full power of the algebras. You can't get away with anything less.

Rules are given by ostension. Any two shapes whatsoever—empty or not and the same or not—shown one after the other determine a rule. Suppose that these shapes are first A and next B. Then the rule they define is

$A \rightarrow B$

An arrow ($\rightarrow$) separates the two shapes. The rule has a left side that contains A and a right side that contains B. If A and B are drawn, then registration marks are used to fix the spatial relation between them. The rule

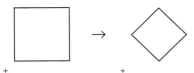

for example, turns a square about its center and shrinks it. The rule is a particular instance of the schema

$x \rightarrow t(x)$

I used in part I. The spatial relation between the squares in the rule—more accurately, their sum—is explicit when the mark

+

in the left side of the rule and the one in its right side register

This is a convenient device to show how different shapes line up. Likewise, the rule

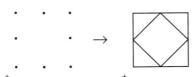

is one instance among many of the schema

$b(x) \rightarrow x$

when $b(x)$ is eight points. The shapes in the left and right sides of the rule line up just so to show the spatial relation between the eight points and two squares for which these points are the boundary. And if I define the supervening rule

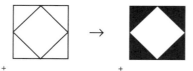

in the schema $b(x) \rightarrow x$, I show how two squares—eight lines—bound four triangular planes. But, in this case, this is the only rule with this left side. And no additional rule goes from planes to solids.

Two rules are the same whenever there's a single transformation that makes the corresponding shapes in both identical—left side to left side and right side to right side. The rule

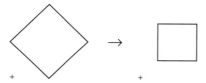

is the same as the rule

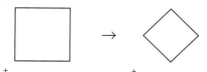

via a 45-degree rotation. But the rule

isn't, even though the shape

is formed when the registration marks in the left and right sides of the rule are made to coincide. The rule is the inverse of the rule

The square gets smaller or the square gets bigger. And this rule

moves a triangle to the right, while its inverse

does so to the left.

But inverses needn't be distinct when rules are defined in the schema $x \rightarrow t(x)$. An identity $A \rightarrow A$ and its inverse are evidently the same, only this is trivial. Of greater interest, the rule

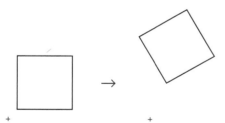

that rotates a square at a corner, and its inverse

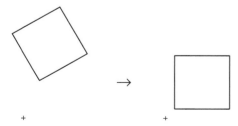

are the same. You can check this in general using the transformation $t' \cdot t^{-1}$, where t' is a transformation in the symmetry group of x in $x \rightarrow t(x)$, and $t'(t^{-1}(x)) = t(x)$.

It's also easy to see that $t' \cdot t^{-1}$ is in the symmetry group of $x + t(x)$. For the two squares in the rule

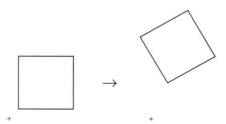

$t' \cdot t^{-1}$ defines the axis of reflection

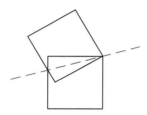

Still, in general, there's more to check to ensure that there are right answers. More generally, rules with symmetric sums have inverses that aren't the same—for example, this one

When the squares are reflected, the left one is the left one and not the right one. There's no flip.

The precise details of applying rules and saying how they work are straightforward. It's mostly using your eyes and saying what they see. A rule $A \to B$ applies to a shape C in two easy stages.

(1)   Find a transformation t that makes the shape A part of C. This picks out some part of C that looks like A. In symbols it looks like this

$t(A) \leq C$

(2)   Subtract the transformation of A from C, and then add the same transformation of the shape B. This replaces the part of C that's like A with another part that looks like B. And once again, it's nice to show it in symbols

$(C - t(A)) + t(B)$

In the first stage, the rule $A \rightarrow B$ is used to see. It works as an observational device. If A can be embedded in C in any way at all—no matter what's gone on before—then C has a part like A. In the second stage, the rule changes C in accordance with A and B. Now it's a constructive device. But once something is added, it fuses with what's left of C and may or may not be recognized again. The shapes (parts) in the rule are lost once it's applied. There's no record (memory) of the part identified in stage 1 or of the part added in stage 2. Calculating always starts over with an undifferentiated shape. And notice also that the two stages are intentionally linked via the same transformation t. This completes the visual analogy

$$t(A) \rightarrow t(B) :: A \rightarrow B$$

The rule $A \rightarrow B$ is a convenient example of the kind of thing that's supposed to happen. The rule $t(A) \rightarrow t(B)$ is the same and works for the given shape C. This is one way of thinking about context. It's evident when I transpose the terms in the analogy—the part of C that's subtracted is to A as the part that's added is to B. But the analogy stops there. It doesn't go on. It ends with A and B, and the transformation t. There are neither finer divisions nor additional relationships in A or B. The parts of shapes are no less indefinite because they're in rules, and they aren't differentiated when rules are tried.

The formal details of rule application shouldn't obscure the main idea behind rules. Observation—the ability to divide shapes into definite parts—provides the impetus for meaningful change. This relationship is nothing new, but it's no less important for that. As I've already said, it's seeing and doing, the behaviorist's stimulus and response, and Peirce's habitual when and how. And James has it at the center of reasoning. This is worth repeating.

And the art of the reasoner will consist of two stages:
First, *sagacity*, or the ability to discover what part, M, lies embedded in the whole S which is before him;
Second, *learning*, or the ability to recall promptly M's consequences, concomitants, or implications.

The twin stages in the reasoner's art are formalized in the stages given to apply rules. In fact, it's the same kind of analogy contained in rules themselves. I can show it in this way

$$t(A) : t(A) \rightarrow t(B) :: \text{sagacity} : \text{learning}$$

or, alternatively, so

$$t(A) \leq C : (C - t(A)) + t(B) :: \text{sagacity} : \text{learning}$$

in terms of what the rule does as it's used. Every time a rule is tried, sagacity and learning—redescription and inference—work jointly to create a new outcome. And it's sagacity that distinguishes rules the most as useful devices for calculating. Rules divide shapes anew as they change in an unfolding process in which parts are picked out, combine, and fuse. But learning isn't remembering how shapes are divided into parts—

that can change anytime. It's finding rules and remembering ones as examples of what to see and do. This makes a huge difference when embedding isn't identity. I can know how to go on without knowing anything for sure about the world. It's using your eyes to decide what to do next. (The root value of observation in calculating is reinforced when James quotes John Stuart Mill—"The observer is not he who merely sees the thing which is before his eyes, but he who sees what parts that thing is composed of." And again, for me this changes every time a rule is tried. But there's more. For Mill, observing and inventing are alike. This makes a neat metaphor for rules and a good heuristic in design.)

Trying It Out

The way rules are used to calculate is clear in an easy example. The rule

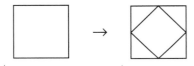

produces the shapes in this ongoing series

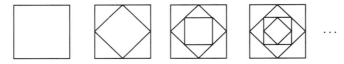

when I start calculating with the square

In particular, the third shape in the series is produced in two steps in the following way

and in three steps in this way

The rule finds squares and inscribes smaller ones. In the first series, the rule is applied under a different transformation each time it's tried to pick out the initial square, or the square inscribed most recently. But in the second series, equivalent transformations with respect to the right side of the rule (the details are given later, in table 10) are used in the first and second steps. The same square can be distinguished repeatedly without producing new results.

I can modify the rule

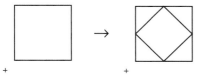

with a point in its left side and a point in its right side

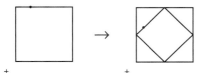

so that the rule has to apply to the most recently added square

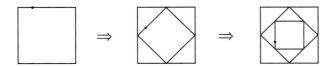

Points and labeled points are really good for this, and provide the kind of logic and control that's useful in calculating.

Playing around with the rule

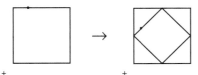

lets me introduce and use a telling asymmetry. If I tilt and stretch the smaller square

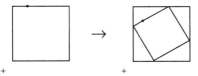

my rule applies only under rotations as it did before

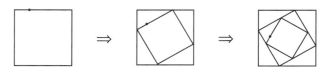

But suppose I move the points

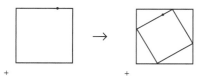

Now I have to use reflections to apply the rule, at least if I start with the same shape

Then both rules together let me rotate the inscribed square in any way I like.

This may be easier without points

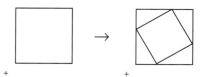

but in addition there's the chance of intersecting squares

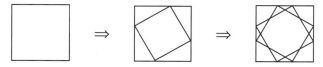

Two rules are better than one. Still, the single rule

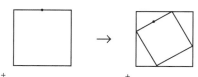

with a point on a symmetry axis of each of the squares is also enough

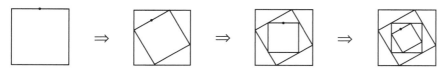

Notice, however, that the rule

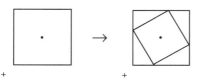

doesn't work—the centers of both squares are the same and so don't distinguish them. Of course, there are other places for points with different results, depending on the squares and how they're related, and the symmetries involved. Try the left side of the first rule and the right side of the second one to get what I've done—at least in a special case. And all of this can be extended with labels, for example, for rhythmic patterns of rotations and reflections. Things get interesting fast.

I can also describe the rule

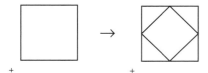

in a nice way, and its successors with points, too. A transformation of the square in the left side of the rule is part of the shape in its right side. The rule is recursive—I can apply it again in new places. But more generally for any shape x, I can define rules in terms of the schema

$$x \rightarrow x + t(x)$$

This gives parts of symmetrical patterns when the transformations t are the generators of a symmetry group. I can calculate with scalene right triangles using the rule

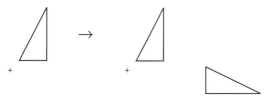

to get a shape with cyclic symmetry

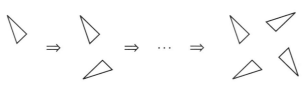

And together with a second rule

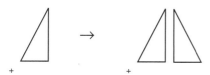

there's the shape with the corresponding dihedral symmetry

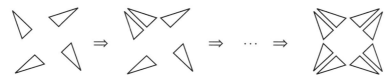

But x and $t(x)$ may touch—for example, perhaps basic elements in shapes overlap. If I use the rule

in which a square and a translation of it are added, I get a frieze

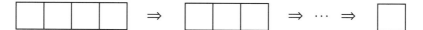

The inverse of the rule

takes me back to where I started

when I begin at the right, but it needn't once I turn the rule upside down

In fact, my rule for dihedral symmetry gives like results. Symmetry—now of shapes in rules—can't be ignored. And again, it's something to use. But I can also go on and calculate with my rule for squares to produce other shapes

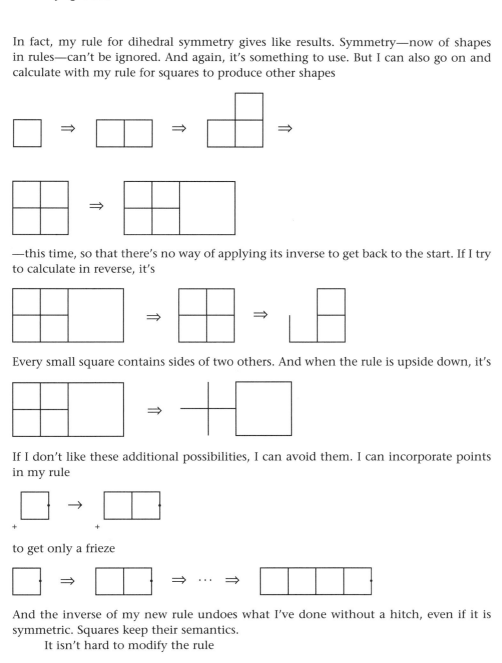

—this time, so that there's no way of applying its inverse to get back to the start. If I try to calculate in reverse, it's

Every small square contains sides of two others. And when the rule is upside down, it's

If I don't like these additional possibilities, I can avoid them. I can incorporate points in my rule

to get only a frieze

And the inverse of my new rule undoes what I've done without a hitch, even if it is symmetric. Squares keep their semantics.

It isn't hard to modify the rule

with points and labels in many other ways. I can use multiple versions of it—perhaps with additional rules—to produce shapes with myriad kinds of properties that may be desirable. Try it for shapes like the ones in the series

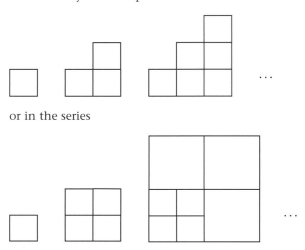

or in the series

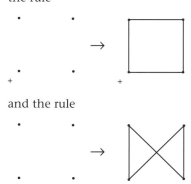

Or simply change the rule—again with points and labels—and see what you get. This is a good way to find the tricks that make rules do what you want. And it's always possible to be surprised—shapes are filled with ambiguities. Using them makes calculating worthwhile.

A variation of the schema

$$x \rightarrow x + t(x)$$

shows how shapes and their boundaries go together in spatial relations. In particular, the rule

and the rule

are both instances of the schema

$b(x) \rightarrow x + b(x)$

A shape is given in the left side of the schema and then added to a shape for which it's the boundary in the right side. I can calculate with my rules first to link points with a square and then with a bow tie—in much the same way Paul Klee describes "medial" lines, but now its points that are medial

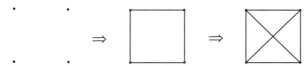

Or I can try something more ambitious—maybe the grade-school exercise I described in the introduction—the one Miss H—— assigned to show that seeing was more than counting. Suppose I begin with an array of points

The rule

gives it to me, along with every other shape in the algebra U_{02}. Points go anywhere I want because the rule applies to the empty shape, and it's the same under every transformation. (Any rule with the empty shape in its left side is indeterminate.) It's the same tapping my pencil on a sheet of paper to get random results. With the empty shape, there's no looking to see what to do. And I can go on in the same way I started and define additional rules using the schema $b(x) \rightarrow x + b(x)$—maybe these two with lines and planes

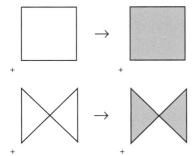

to fill in areas with tones that add up in an algebra of weights

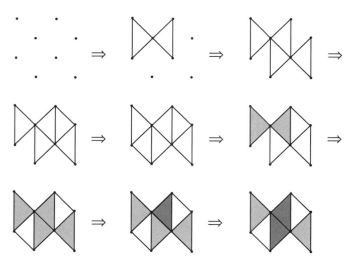

It's fun to see how maximal elements change in this process. There's plenty of opportunity to try all sorts of things with algebras, shapes, and rules.

Fractals introduce a different kind of symmetry. They're also formed when transformations of a shape are added up—now using rules in the schema

$$x \rightarrow \sum t(x)$$

What's different here is that scale may be conspicuously involved. Try the rule

to get the shapes in the series

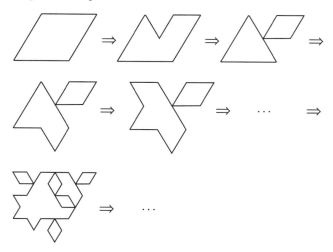

Fractals are zero dimensional, but this is scant reason not to define them using rules in algebras where embedding isn't identity. Fatal problems arise in the opposite way, if I try to describe things that aren't zero dimensional as if they were. This is the main point of part I, and it's a mantra worth repeating. It's the reason visual calculating makes a difference.

But there are some problems. The rule

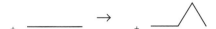

doesn't always produce the same fractals. I can apply the rule under alternative transformations—maybe inside out in rotations or reflections—to get the shapes

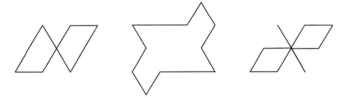

And because the line in the left side of the rule can be embedded in any line whatsoever, I can change scale in a host of surprising ways to get the shapes

in which units and divisions are incommensurable. (Units follow the series $1/2^n$ for $n \geq 0$, but I've used the rule for divisions at $3\sqrt{3}/2^{n+2}$. Other divisions would do, too.) Lines in fractals are units, but not in shapes when I calculate. Lines fuse, and divide erratically. You have to make them behave.

Good manners should be encouraged. My problems are easy to fix with a familiar device. I can change the initial shape in my original series with a handful of well-placed points

and I can change the rule in the same way

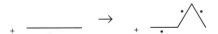

to limit the possibilities and thus guarantee the results I want. First, this makes lines behave like units—a point and a line together

_____
    •

determine a perpendicular

_____
    ⊥

and thus a constant scaling factor. And then, the point and the line break the fourfold symmetry of the line

so that rules apply in definite ways. (Turn this around and ask what a line does for a point that's invariant under indefinitely many transformations—rotations, reflections, and changes in scale. Points and lines interact with one another reciprocally when rules are tried. There's nothing to tell them apart that implies that points constrain lines or vice versa. Geometrically at least, basic elements are the same.) But apply the rule

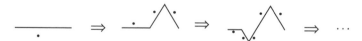

and see what happens

or other rules like it. (I count two hundred and fifty-six rules that can each be used for something different, and in combination to produce more. There are four distinct left sides and sixty-four distinct right sides, and no transformation matches left to left and right to right at the same time. But this is profligate—a few rules and other tricks do similar kinds of things. I can begin to think about this by moving points around with the pair of rules

+ _____ → + _____

+ _____ → + _____

to simulate what my other rules do. My new rules are defined in terms of generators for the symmetry group of the line. And the idea is good for other shapes with different symmetries.)

Modifying rules according to the symmetry of the shapes they contain is a useful ploy. More generally, though, I can vary the properties of the shapes in rules with basic elements, labels, weights, and so on, to get the outcomes I like. It's a lot like composing—there's symmetry, scale, balance, rhythm, color, etc. I'm still surprised at all the things rules do as they apply—with transformations, parts, and adding and subtracting in two easy formulas. That's all it takes to see and do—just calculating with shapes and rules.

Spatial Relations and Rules

There's more to calculating with shapes than symmetrical patterns and fractals or combining shapes and their boundaries. In fact, there are more generic schemas to define rules that include the previous ones with transformations and the boundary operator. And these new schemas are pedagogically effective—they make adding and subtracting explicit in rules before they're applied.

For any two shapes A and B, I can define addition rules in terms of the schema

$$x \rightarrow A + B$$

and subtraction rules in terms of its inverse

$$A + B \rightarrow x$$

where the variable x has either A or B as its value. (Evidently, addition rules—and likewise subtraction rules—are the same whenever the rules $A \rightarrow B$ and $B \rightarrow A$ are.) The shapes A and B define a spatial relation that determines how to combine shapes. They show how conjugate parts are arranged after I add one, or if I want to take one away and leave the other. But there's a caveat. A spatial relation is an equivalence relation for decompositions—two are the same when one is a transformation of the other. This is a nice way to describe how shapes go together to define rules in schemas. In fact, it provides a general model of calculating that includes Turing machines. Still, the spatial relation isn't preserved in the rules it defines. Descriptions have no lasting value, only heuristic appeal. They're something to use that helps to get started. Then you're on your own—you're free to see anything you choose. There's a lot more to shapes once they fuse than there is when they're kept apart in spatial relations. (That's calculating with sets in set grammars, not with shapes in shape grammars.)

Let's see how my twin schemas work. The shape

gives some good examples when it's divided into two squares to define a spatial relation. This keeps to the schema $x \rightarrow x + t(x)$ and its inverse, but nothing is lost in the simplification. There are still four distinct rules—two for addition

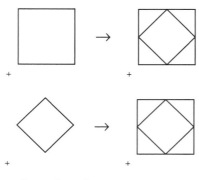

and two for subtraction

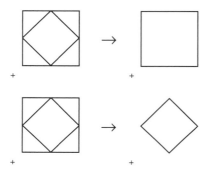

From the initial square

the rules apply to produce alternating squares in a series, with no beginning or end, that's centered on this segment

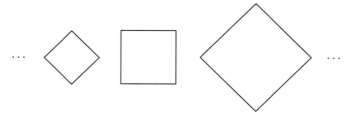

and any finite combination of these squares that you want for this reason or that—for example, the shape

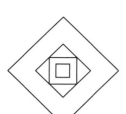

that contains four squares.

Decomposing shapes to define spatial relations for rules can be very useful. I can begin with shapes I like, and try to find rules to produce them and new shapes of the same kind. It's the beginning of stylistic analysis and a way to handle stylistic change. Or I can use these rules with whatever I'm doing to follow up an interesting motif or salient feature (part) in a way that's copying it and more. And it's especially nice that decomposing shapes is really calculating, too—for example, with identities defined in the schema

$x \rightarrow x$

or with erasing rules from the schema

$x \rightarrow$

But even better, there are telling decompositions no matter how I calculate. That's one of the things I showed in part I with rules from the schema

$x \rightarrow t(x)$

and stars and superstars.

Right now, though, the inverse schema

$A + B \rightarrow x$

is loaded with unexpected possibilities. Certainly, the cross

can be divided neatly into squares—either four of five of them—to define three distinct spatial relations

And the first of these in an addition rule

produces the cross in this way

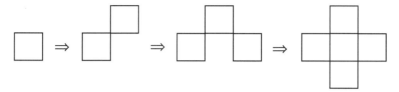

while the third in an addition rule

works so

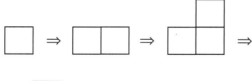

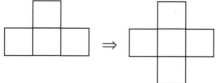

But suppose the cross without internal divisions is related externally to another square in the following way

Then I can use the addition rule

and the subtraction rule

to calculate

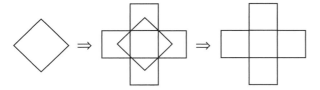

And the process continues

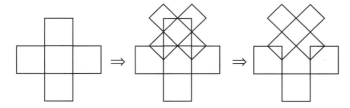

because squares are parts of the cross. But the location and size of the square that's subtracted—think of it as an armature—is really arbitrary. Any square or any other shape similar to part of the cross will do to define a productive spatial relation, for example

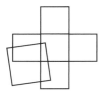

Whenever subtraction (erasing) is allowed, there may be a lot more to designs than meets the eye. Spatial relations are all over the place, just out of sight. Inference

(induction) is dicey at best given that shapes are ambiguous, and may be even more so when some parts have disappeared without a trace. But certainly there's a long tradition in design of using hidden axes, grids, regulating lines, different kinds of parti, etc. Spatial relations and rules defined according to my schemas simply generalize this idea—every shape is a grid

and any shape can be located with respect to it

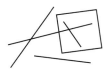

It's easy to be conventional and stick to classical lines and angles. Perhaps a pair is arranged orthogonally in this way

to get the addition and subtraction rules

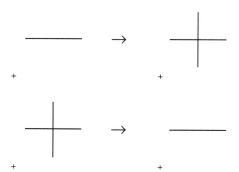

—they're both indeterminate—that let me calculate so

Or I might be adventuresome and try something else that isn't classical, where lines
are arranged promiscuously

to get different kinds of results

with new addition and subtraction rules. There's the same generative twist both
ways. Alberti, with his appeal to lines and angles, seems already primed for the
recursion—

All the power of invention, all the skill and experience in the art of building, are called upon
in compartition; compartition alone divides up the whole building into the parts by which
it is articulated, and integrates its every part by composing all the lines and angles into a single,
harmonious work that respects utility, dignity, and delight. If (as the philosophers maintain)
the city is like some large house, and the house is in turn like some small city, cannot the various
parts of the house—atria, *xysti*, dining rooms, porticoes, and so on—be considered miniature
buildings?

And Klee tries as much in the series of drawings that introduces his *Pedagogical
Sketchbook*

An active line on a walk, moving freely, without a goal. A walk for a walk's sake. The mobility
agent is a point, shifting its position forward.

The same line, accompanied by complementary forms.

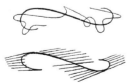

The same line, circumscribing itself.

Two secondary lines, moving around an imaginary main line.

What a marvelous way to start—adding complementary forms in spatial relations, and likewise adding lines and subtracting one that's then imaginary.

But decomposing shapes isn't the only way to define spatial relations to use in my schemas. I can start from scratch. I can begin with shapes—a vocabulary—and enumerate apt configurations. There's reason to be combinatorial after all. How things feel when I pick them up, move them around, and line them up with my hands is a natural way to approach this. It's similar to what Frederick Froebel emphasizes in the kindergarten. His famous building gifts and tablets (play blocks and plane figures), and categories—forms of beauty (symmetrical patterns), knowledge (arithmetical and geometrical facts), and life (buildings, furniture, monuments, etc.)—provide some nice material for experiments. Spatial relations determine rules to augment the categories, so that I can calculate. The spatial relations are neatly defined in kindergarten rhymes—

Face to face put. That is right.
Edges now are meeting quite.
Edge to face now we will lay,
Face to edge will end the play.

For pieces in the gifts, it might look like this

It feels right. But let's try it for geometrically similar polygons as boundaries of plane figures, instead of using play blocks. It's still the same idea, with the difference that everything goes together equal edge to equal edge, and vertex to vertex.

Suppose I begin with right triangles like this one

Then I get twenty-one spatial relations with distinct triangles

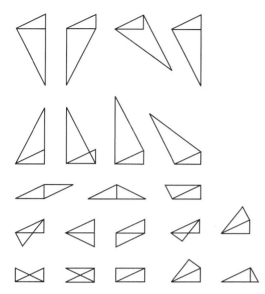

that answer to a group of transformations. In particular, two triangles share different edges that match left and right, and up and down—it's the symmetry of the line again. This is not unlike playing around with a T-square and triangles—even arbitrary ones— to see what you can do. Everything goes together in a marvelous catalogue of visual possibilities. And I can use these spatial relations in my schemas to define rules

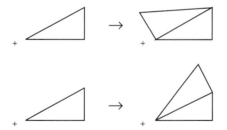

to calculate in a dynamic way

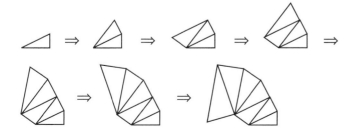

Or I can opt for a rule with symmetry

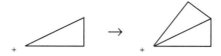

so that things stay the same when I calculate

But this rule and two others

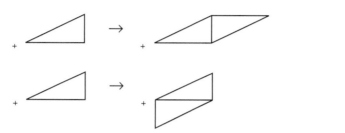

work together to produce tessellations like this

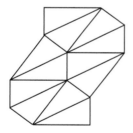

There's no telling when another rule might be useful—and it's always possible to add rules to the ones I've got.

When I started talking about the schema

$$x \rightarrow A + B$$

and its inverse, I said that what's changed needn't be what's added. For example, I can modify this rule

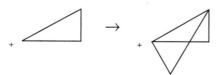

with points

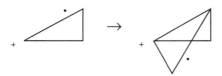

to calculate in the expected way

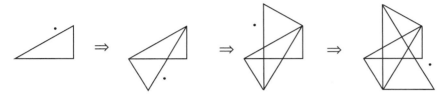

or I can forget the points and exploit the ambiguity using both addition and subtraction rules

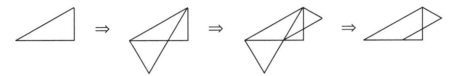

Parts change as I apply my rules. But there are other aspects of this, as well—distinct spatial relations can determine the same rule.

This shape

is the sum of two triangles in three different ways

Just looking at the pair of rules

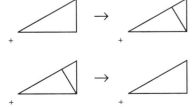

I can't tell which of the two triangles

I'm adding or subtracting. If I want a record of the triangles I've actually used, then this is a bother. Still, there are ways to keep track of things. I can resort to points again to distinguish the distinct cases—here for addition

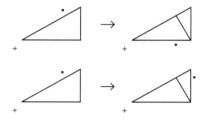

to get results like these

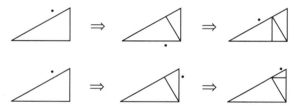

Or I can stop worrying about it, and take advantage of the ambiguity—perhaps in this marvelous series that concludes with triangles and rectangles

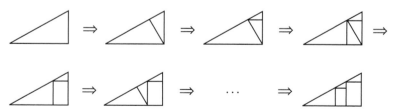

One of the reasons the catalogue of spatial relations I started with is so big is that the shape

is a scalene triangle. For triangles with more symmetry, the size of the catalogue decreases. In particular, for the isosceles triangle

there are six spatial relations

and for the equilateral triangle

just one

But there's no reason for me to stop. I can use my triangles together to get four more spatial relations

And I can break the symmetry of my triangles to define different rules that apply in definite ways. Again, points are useful if I put them in the right places—here in the isosceles triangle

and here in the equilateral one

And, in fact, these triangles with points have spatial relations that correspond to the ones for my scalene triangle. This is a nice way to show how symmetry works. Nonetheless, points are better used in rules. It's calculating with shapes that makes a real difference. There are addition rules like these

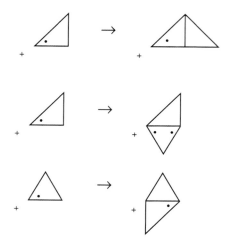

—and subtraction rules, as well—in which right sides contain a single point or several of them to show where rules apply next. New rules are always worth a try. With mine, I can get shapes like this

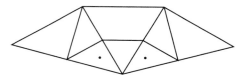

Let's look at something else—maybe rectangles and squares that keep their size and line up edge to edge and vertex to vertex in these spatial relations

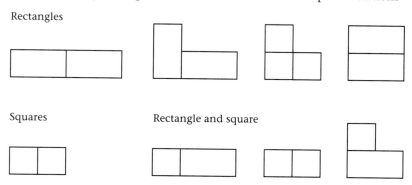

defined in my kindergarten rhyme. Points help to take advantage of the symmetries, and lined paper makes drawing easy. Try it.

Zero-dimensional devices help to tame rules in higher-dimensional algebras. In particular, points and lines show how visual ideas can be controlled in a comfortable, logical fashion. But rules draw distinctions as they apply, so ambiguities are always possible. Mistakes are easy to make even with tried and true devices, and may be worth keeping. Parts interact freely—doing something to distinguish one may unintentionally distinguish another with useful results. It depends on what rules there are, and on when and where they're applied.

Suppose I want to erase the horizontal line in the shape

in its entirety from end to end—maybe not right now, but sometime later. I can place a point so

and try the rule

This gives me

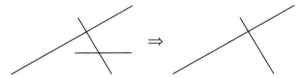

exactly as it should. But the rule also applies to each of the oblique lines to produce the shapes

The point isn't attached to a definite part. This relationship is determined over and over again, depending on my rules and how they're used. I have to think about the horizontal line and how it relates to the other two lines to place the point "correctly"

Now, no segment of an oblique line is long enough for the rule

to apply. Only the ambiguity needn't end here if I go on calculating. I may have to look farther out than I can see. Until I erase the horizontal line, the point can interact with any line that's defined—if there's a rule for it. Still, my answer may not matter. What if I also have the rule

that adds to lines. Dividing shapes into independent pieces to define rules rarely succeeds, unless I appeal to labels or comparable devices—for example, compound shapes in algebras formed in direct products—to keep things separate in an artificial way. But then what I see may not be what's there. Calculating with shapes is different when surprises are unavoidable.

There's a lot to see as I use rules to calculate with shapes. Everything works with everything else. But I've been showing only easy examples, special cases, and clever tricks. What can I say about rules generally to help me understand what they do? It's all in the two formulas for applying rules—either in the transformation t or in the part relation $\leq$.

Classifying Rules with Transformations

Rules can be classified in a variety of important ways. First, it's possible to decide whether they apply determinately or indeterminately—that is to say, whether or not there are a limited number of transformations t that satisfy the formula

$$t(A) \leq C$$

for the rule $A \to B$ and the shape C. The conditions for determinate rules vary somewhat from algebra to algebra, but can be framed in terms of a recursive taxonomy of registration marks defined with basic elements. It's usually a surprise that these marks aren't always the basic elements themselves or their boundary elements. Paradigmatically, lines in shapes intersect at points

Table 9
Determinate Rules in the Algebras U_{1j}

Algebra	The rule $A \rightarrow B$ is determinate
U_{11}	Never.
U_{12}	Three lines in A do not intersect at a common point. Further, no two of these lines are collinear, and all three are not parallel.
U_{13}	There are two cases. (1) Two lines in A are skew. (2) Three lines in A do not intersect at a common point. Further, no two of these lines are collinear, and all three are not parallel.

to fix transformations. The conditions that make rules determinate in the algebras U_{1j} are specified fully in table 9 to show how this works. When j is 1, there are no registration points—lines are always collinear. Otherwise, when j is 2 or j is 3, there are at least two such points and a plane. (What happens when i is 0?)

Many examples of determinate rules are evident in the previous section—and some contain more than lines. Of interest, all the rules made up of points and lines are determinate. But indeterminate rules are also easy to find, with and without points. The identity

is indeterminate in the algebra U_{12}. The K has three maximal lines that intersect at a single point. So the identity applies under indefinitely many changes in scale to find K's in the shape

However, bringing in a point

may not help. There's still just one registration point—the point and the intersection of the lines in the K are the same. Moreover, notice that different shapes may be equivalent in terms of the registration marks they define. The lines in the uppercase K and the lines in the lowercase k intersect at the same point, but this isn't all. Shapes made

up of segments of two or more unbounded lines intersecting at any common point—
for example

—are likewise related. Of course, with another registration mark, definite transformations can be defined, as in the identity

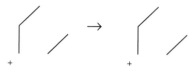

This works in the same way for the identity

And both identities are equivalent with respect to their registration marks, but just the
first finds parts in the shape

The part relation is needed, too, to tell whether rules apply or not.

The conditions for determinate rules in table 9 depend on the properties of the
shapes in the left sides of rules, and not on the shapes to which the rules apply. This
keeps the classification the same no matter how I calculate. It's also important to note
that the conditions in table 9 provide the core of an algorithm that enumerates the
transformations under which any determinate rule $A \rightarrow B$ applies to a given shape C.
If C is A, then the algorithm defines the symmetry group of A. But this is only an aside.
More to the point, rules can be tried automatically.

The problem of finding transformations to apply a rule $A \rightarrow B$ to a shape C looks
hard because embedding rather than identity may determine how maximal elements
correspond. Nonetheless, maximal elements in the shapes A and C fix registration
marks that coincide whenever a transformation makes A part of C. Certain combinations of these marks are enough to scale A and align it with C. Alignments needn't satisfy the part relation—distinct shapes may have equivalent registration marks. But the

alignments that do satisfy it exactly determine all of the transformations there are to apply the rule. This is clear for shapes in the algebra U_{12}.

A pair of points distinguished in the shape A—they're intersections of lines—may be transformed to register with any pair of points in the shape C in four ways. The ratio of the distance between the points in A and the distance between the points in C determines how A is scaled, and orientation left to right and top to bottom fixes alignment. The transformations so defined are distinct and include all of the ones that make the part relation hold.

Consider the rule

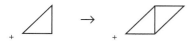

that puts triangles together. It's an instance of the schema $x \rightarrow A + B$—in fact, the special case $x \rightarrow x + t(x)$. The rule applies to each of the triangles in the shape

in two ways to produce four shapes

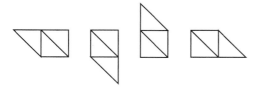

The transformations used for this purpose are readily defined. There are three points where maximal lines intersect in the triangle

in the left side of the rule

and any pair of these points may be distinguished to define transformations—I guess I'll take this one

Further, there are four points where maximal lines intersect in the shape

These combine in six pairs

The pair of points in the triangle may be transformed to register with each of the six pairs in four different ways

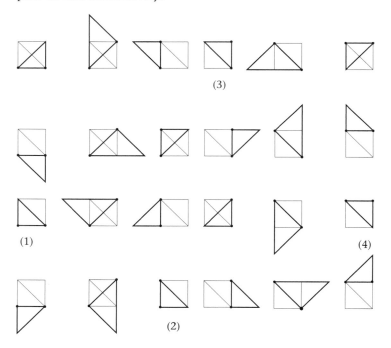

The part relation is checked for all of these transformations, and is satisfied by the four indicated by number. They're easy to see. The shapes

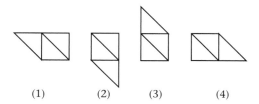

are produced when transformations 1 through 4 are used to apply the rule.

Of course, not every shape in the left side of a rule contains a pair of points where maximal lines intersect. The empty shape is one of these shapes, and K is, too. Moreover, there are shapes with parallel lines and shapes with lines that intersect at a common point—for example, these

Nonetheless, for parallel lines there are singular cases where rules apply determinately. Then lines are just the right length and are separated by just the right amount. This complicates things a little without changing much. Indeterminate rules are easy to identify and have many uses, even if ad hoc decisions are needed to apply them. Earlier, I tried the rule

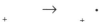

to get random shapes containing points. And I've used indeterminate rules to calculate with axes, and to extend lines. I'll show some other examples, too. Only now, there's more to say about rules and transformations. Surprisingly, the right side of a rule affects the way the rule is applied. How does this work?

The rule

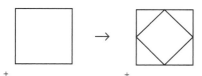

that inscribes a square in a square is determinate. The symmetry of the square in its left side lets it apply under eight distinct transformations—four rotations and four reflections. But for each transformation, the results are exactly the same. No matter how I replace a square

I get the shape

Why? The reason can be given in terms of Lagrange's famous theorem for subgroups, and provides another way to classify rules.

Let two transformations be equivalent with respect to a shape if they change it identically. In this example

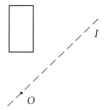

a clockwise rotation of 90 degrees about the point O

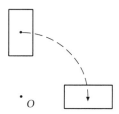

and a reflection across the axis I

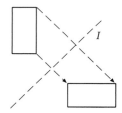

are equivalent relative to the rectangle. Both the rotation and the reflection do exactly the same thing—just look. And this gives a general result.

If a rule $A \rightarrow B$ has the property that the symmetry group of the shape A is partitioned into q classes with respect to the shape B, then the rule can be used in q distinct ways. And if the symmetry group of A has n transformations, then q divides n without remainder. The symmetry group of A has a subgroup containing n/q transformations with cosets given by the classes defined by B. Conversely, there's a rule for every subgroup of the symmetry group of A that behaves as the subgroup describes. The distinct uses of the rule $A \rightarrow B$ show the symmetry properties of A, and these properties classify every rule with A in its left side.

This is nicely illustrated with a square in the algebra U_{12} for clockwise rotations and for reflections named by these axes

Table 10
Classification of Rules in terms of Lagrange's Theorem

Rule	Subgroup	Number of cosets
$\square \rightarrow \square$	0, 90, 180, 270, I, II, III, IV	1
$\square \rightarrow \square$	0, 90, 180, 270	2
$\square \rightarrow \square$	0, 180, I, III	2
$\square \rightarrow \square$	0, 180	4
$\square \rightarrow \square$	0, I	4
$\square \rightarrow \square$	0	8

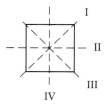

Rules behave in at least six different ways according to the six subgroups of the symmetry group of the square given in table 10. The symmetry group of the square has other subgroups that are isomorphic to these. One way to see this is in terms of equivalencies among the four axes of the square. There may be ten subgroups (the axes are all different), possibly eight (the horizontal axis and the vertical one are the same, and so are the diagonal axes), or the six in table 10 (the axes are all the same).

The rule

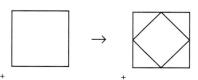

has the symmetry properties of the first rule I show in table 10, and therefore it acts like an identity with only one distinct use. The eight transformations in the symmetry group of the square in the left side of the rule are equivalent with respect to the shape in its right side. Try it yourself to make sure. And its also worthwhile to try this for the rule

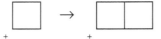

and its inverse that I used earlier, to show that calculating with shapes needn't be reversible. The rule has the symmetry properties of the fifth rule in table 10.

Classifying Rules with Parts

So far, I've been using transformations to classify rules. This relies on the Euclidean properties of shapes, but it's not the only way to describe rules. I can take a Boolean approach and think about rules in terms of how many parts there are in the shapes in their left and right sides. The classification of rules in this way by counting their parts is the crux of the Chomsky hierarchy for generative grammars. The hierarchy gives compelling evidence for the idea that calculating is counting.

Generative grammars produce strings of symbols that are words or well-formed sentences in a language. A rule

$$AqR \rightarrow A'q'L$$

links a pair of strings—in this case, three symbols A, q, and R, and three others A', q', and L—by an arrow. If the strings were shapes, then the rule would be like one of my rules. The rule is context free if there's just one symbol in its left side, context sensitive if the number of symbols in its left side isn't more than the number of symbols in its right side—my rule is context sensitive—and belongs to a general rewriting system otherwise. Languages vary in complexity according to the kind of rules that are needed to define them. Moreover, the class of languages generated by context-free rules is included in the larger class of languages generated by context-sensitive rules, and so on. How well does this idea work for rules defined in my algebras? What difference does it make whether or not i is zero?

There's no problem counting for shapes and other things when they're zero dimensional. Points—or whatever corresponds to them, say, the parts in a decomposition of a shape—are uniquely distinguished in exactly the same way symbols are. But what happens in an algebra when i isn't zero? What can I find in the algebra U_{12}, for example, that corresponds to points? Is there anything I can count on?

The rule

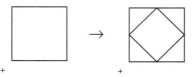

looks as if it should be context free, at least with respect to the unremarkable description

square → square + inscribed square

that I've been using all along. There's one square in the left side of the rule, and there are two squares in the right side. And in fact, the rule worked perfectly in this fashion when I used it to calculate before. I applied the rule twice in this way

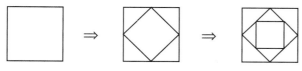

and three times so

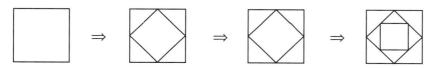

with a redundant step that repeats the preceding shape. Moreover, the final shape in both series matches the string ( ) ( ) ( ), where each pair of parentheses indicates another square, although the palindrome ((( ))) looks to be a better fit. (Parenthesis strings are paradigmatically context free. To see this, modify the two rules in the introduction—$S → (S)$ for ⟨ ⟩ → ⟨⟨ ⟩⟩ and $S → SS$ for ⟨ ⟩ → ⟨ ⟩⟨ ⟩—add the third rule $S → ( )$, and start with the symbol or "axiom" S.)

Other descriptions of my rule for squares, however, may be more appropriate. What if I want to use it together with a rule that finds triangles? The identity

shouldn't change anything. An identity

$A → A$

in a generative grammar is totally useless, either because it doesn't do anything or because A isn't a symbol I've used before. But any rule I add when I calculate with shapes will automatically work as intended with any rule I've already used. The part relation lets me recognize triangles—or uppercase K's and lowercase k's—after I've combined squares. So it might be necessary to look at the rule

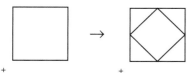

under the alternative description

square → four triangles

The rule is still context free, but it doesn't work. It applies once to the square

and then can't be applied again to the shape

Now there are four triangles and no squares. I can patch this up by dividing triangles and squares into three sides and four sides apiece. After all, this is the way they're normally defined. It's what Evans did in part I, and it gives me a new way of describing the rule

square with four sides → four triangles with three sides apiece

But if this is the case, then the rule must be context sensitive. Four lines are in the left side of the rule and twelve lines are in the right side. And it's easy to see that the increase in complexity pays off when I calculate in this way

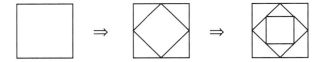

where the long sides of four triangles become the four sides of a square. This is convincing proof that the rule is context sensitive—or is it? There's still a lot more to worry about. The rule doesn't work in the longer series

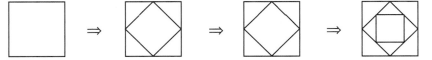

It has to apply to the outside square in the second step. Under the description of the rule I'm using now, each side of the outside square is divided in two. The outside square is four lines at the start, and then eight lines one step later after adding triangles. I can try another rule that changes how squares are described, maybe one with the description

eight lines → four lines

or a rule that applies recursively to fuse the segments in any division of a line

two lines → one line

Either way, a general rewriting system is defined. Alternatively, I can represent the rule

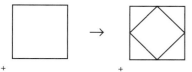

in two ways, so that squares have either four sides or sides described by their eight halves. And notice further that if I have reason to put four triangles in the right side of the rule, then its different versions are of different kinds—one is context sensitive (four lines go to four triangles) and then the other isn't (eight lines go to four triangles). What the rule is depends on how it's described. Maybe the rule is context free, maybe it's context sensitive, and maybe it's in a general rewriting system.

I can calculate with the rule

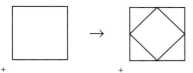

to get the shape

but I have no way of deciding how complex this is before I begin. Just looking at the rule isn't enough. I have to examine things anew every time I apply it, and determine how different descriptions of shapes interact. There are simply too many ways of calculating and too many different descriptions for this to be of any practical value.

In the introduction, I warned that the analogy

shape grammar : designs :: generative grammar : sentences

shouldn't be taken too far. And my discussion of the Chomsky hierarchy shows why in fairly rigorous terms. It provides a very useful taxonomy for generative grammars, but it doesn't work for shapes made up of lines, etc. Perhaps this is the fatal flaw in visual calculating—"Wouldn't it be wonderful if we could classify shape grammars the way Chomsky classifies generative grammars." Complexity is measured by counting symbols (units), and this is fine for shapes containing points and other things that are zero dimensional, for example, sets with members. They have definite descriptions that keep them numerically distinct. Nonetheless, there are no units for higher-dimensional things. The shapes in rules don't have parts that I can count before I calculate. These depend on how the rules are used. The description that makes sense for a rule now isn't binding later. What the rule is doing may change freely as it's applied. A square is four lines the first time the rule

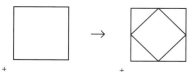

is tried and eight lines the second time around. Descriptions don't count. They alter too erratically for numbers to make sense.

The difference between rules defined for shapes and generative grammars is evident in other kinds of devices for calculating. They're described in various ways—spatially and not—but the method is always combinatorial. And, in fact, they're all easy to define in zero-dimensional algebras in which labels or weights are associated with points.

Turing machines are typical. They're defined for symbols on tapes—labeled points evenly spaced on a line—that are modified according to given transitions that work like my previous rule $AqR \rightarrow A'q'L$. But this is too obscure, and it's easy to be clear. The rule

in the algebra V_{02} corresponds to a machine transition in which the symbol A is read in the state q and replaced by the symbol A'. The state q is changed to the state q', and the tape is moved one unit to the left. I've assumed that the rule applies just under translations. Three points are needed to mimic the transition if all of the transformations are allowed. This rule

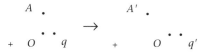

does the trick nicely. It's also a cinch to do Turing machines when i is more than zero. Try it with lines using triangles, and with planes using tetrahedrons, so that the parts that rules pick out behave like units. This series of scalene triangles

1/3   1/4   1/5

     . . .

where the apex is at $1/n$ for $n = 3, 4, 5 \ldots$ is enough for as many distinct symbols and states as I wish to have. Then I might define the rule

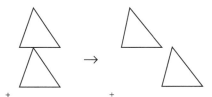

There are other possibilities, too. Stanislaw Ulam invented a device that's used widely to model physical phenomena of all sorts. Cellular automata are points with labels or weights. They're located in a grid—it's usually square—that has one or more dimensions. (Otherwise, points are solipsistic.) Neighborhood relations are specified in rules that are applied under translations. The rules work in parallel to change every point at the same time, with the sum of the individual outcomes as the overall result. The best-known rules of this kind are the ones for John Conway's game of life. In words, it goes like this—

Survival   If an occupied cell has two or three neighbors, it survives.
Death   If an occupied cell has four or more neighbors, it dies from overcrowding.
            If an occupied cell has one or no neighbors, it dies from isolation.
Birth   If an unoccupied cell has exactly three neighbors, it becomes occupied.
Stasis   If an unoccupied cell has less than three neighbors or four or more, it stays
            unoccupied.

—so that all 512 rules are divided into four equivalence classes. And for shapes, the 56 rules for birth are similar to this one

with black and white points—dots—at the centers of white grid cells. Colors are weights—the part relation ($\leq$) is identity, the sum of two is black unless both are white, and the difference of two is white. Or maybe I have cellular automata defined on a line of evenly spaced points. I can record their history by stacking strings of cells, and I can give explicit rules for this purpose. These eight rules

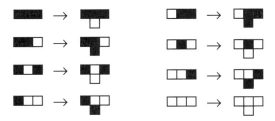

produce the shape

in fifteen iterations. Only this isn't necessary. Cellular automata are abstract symbol systems like Turing machines, and what they do can be presented in many ways. You can pretty much design the visual effects you want. My two examples, first with the game of life and then with strings of cells, begin to show this when the graphic devices used in each are switched. Or change the shape just shown, so that rows of cells are lined up to the left. There are new rules for this, and they're easy to define—in fact, I can use rules that apply to my original rules as shapes to get the new rules I want. Try it. Then after seven iterations, the result looks like this

Key (abstract) relationships stay the same, but what do you see? To find out when there's a fractal or "self-similar" pattern as intended, and not a checkerboard design— although this is interesting in its own way—apply the rule

that divides plane triangles and their boundaries, and use identities from the schema $x \rightarrow x$, so that x is one such triangle and its boundary, or any shape determined by the rule. These identities show exactly what it means to be self-similar, and they root the idea in seeing. What I've done lets me describe what I'm doing now and frame what I do later—learning and experience really matter. I can also see in novel ways— for example, let x be a polygon or A, B, C—or go on to something entirely different. Past experience and new are equally transferable in identities and in the left sides of other rules. What's useful here is useful there once it's transformed and embedded again—learning and sagacity go hand in hand in creative activity. And for shapes and rules, all of this works with nary a hitch.

   (Cellular automata are intriguing because they can be self-similar and can have other "emergent" properties; that is to say, they can form global patterns in time that go beyond points and local neighborhood relations. Once again, these patterns may be artifacts of how the cellular automata are shown, and certainly, finding patterns depends on this. But there's more to notice. Emergent properties are visible only from outside, not by calculating—we can see them because we've got a god's-eye view. This implies a perpetual gap between seeing and calculating. There's a kind of recursive ascent when there are emergent properties to see that calculating can't find, and no-where to stop—doing this three times, for example, it seems that you see what you calculate in your model of what you see what you calculate in your model of what you see what you calculate, or something similar. It's vertiginous without shapes. Then the series collapses when rules apply in terms of embedding and transformations—as with the rule and the identities I just tried. What you see is what rules do. Calculating or seeing, it looks the same.)

But let's get back to my enumeration of calculating devices. There are Linden-mayer systems for plant forms and other living things that are defined in algebras of labeled points. And there are production rules in expert systems, picture languages and derivative pattern languages in architecture and software design, and graph grammars in engineering design and solid modeling. There's no denying it—calculating as it's normally conceived is zero dimensional. My set grammars for decompositions give additional evidence of this. Rules are applied in my algebras in two stages. These are reinterpreted in set grammars in terms of subsets with members rather than parts, and in terms of set union and relative complement rather than sum and difference. The rules in set grammars use identity to check embedding, as rules do in all algebras where i is zero.

How Computers Do It

I've said a number of times already that calculating when i isn't zero with shapes made up of lines, etc., can be simulated in algebras when i is zero where shapes contain points. The story is easy to tell, and it goes something like this. Computers are Turing machines. But Turing machines are zero dimensional—they're defined in the algebra V_{02}. So if I can write a computer program that calculates visually with shapes, then whatever I can do when i isn't zero, I can also do when i is zero. Points are enough to calculate with shapes. And, in fact, most of the rudiments of this computer program are already in place, certainly for shapes with lines. And that's plenty, because embedding and identity aren't the same in this case. I just have to put it all together.

The central idea is to specify everything in terms of analytic expressions and boundary elements. There are, of course, the usual approximations. This is the same for points and other basic elements, because coordinates have real values. In one way, approximations have nothing to do with i being zero or not. Every endpoint of a line in an algebra U_{1j} is a point in the algebra U_{0j}, and vice versa. But in another way, i being zero does make a difference. In a computer, every shape—whatever its algebra—is represented with respect to the same shape in U_{0j}. There are just a finite number of points. Still, even with approximations, I can calculate to any degree of accuracy I wish.

Let's begin with the line defined in the familiar equation

$$y = mx + b$$

and its segments determined by distinct endpoints. Here the quartet of points on the line

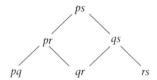

are such that $p < q < r < s$. Moreover, the segments pq, pr, ps, qr, qs, and rs are embedded in the line ps, as the semilattice

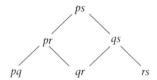

shows—a segment xy is embedded in a segment $x'y'$ whenever $x' \leq x$ and $y \leq y'$. But this kind of ordering isn't the only way to define embedding. There are metric devices, as well. For example, a point is coincident with a line whenever the length of the line is the sum of the two distances from the point to the endpoints of the line. Then, a line l is embedded in another line l' if the endpoints of l are both coincident with l'. When the embedding relation is defined, the part relation is, too. I need only maximal lines. The reduction rules in table 4 are for sum, that is to say, maximal lines for any set of lines. Similarly, the rules in table 5 produce maximal lines for difference. And a transformation of a line is determined by the transformation of its endpoints. So the result

$$(C - t(A)) + t(B)$$

of applying a rule $A \rightarrow B$ to a shape C is completely defined. Even better, I can find the different transformations t that satisfy the formula

$$t(A) \leq C$$

using registration points and the conditions for determinate rules in table 9. What a nice way for everything to turn out. There's an algorithm—a zero-dimensional Turing machine—for calculating with shapes of dimension greater than zero.

It doesn't take all that much to get the job done for lines. In practice, however, there are a host of complications to make sure that everything runs smoothly and efficiently. And extending this to planes and solids, and exotic curves and surfaces, is not without difficulty and real interest. Nonetheless, on the one hand, whatever I can do with lines—visually—I can do with points or symbols. And then on the other hand, calculating with points is a special case of calculating with lines, etc., when embedding is identity. Symbolic calculating and visual calculating—counting and seeing—are the same. There's inclusion each way, even if intuitions differ. Calculating is calculating no matter how you decide to do it.

Is this the final word? Probably not. Everyone seems happy with two cultures—the visual and the verbal—and bent on keeping them so, separate and equal. But it does go a long way toward showing that this is pointless and ironically reductive—calculating is just moving symbols around. Yes, it is—and look at what you can see and what you can do.

I Don't Like Rules—They're Too Rigid

The schemas I've used so far define rules of very broad, overlapping kinds. There are the identities

$$x \rightarrow x$$

and, more inclusively, transformations of shapes

$$x \rightarrow t(x)$$

Then I have schemas to define rules for myriad patterns with symmetry

$$x \rightarrow x + t(x)$$

for fractals

$$x \rightarrow \sum t(x)$$

and for adding

$$x \rightarrow A + B$$

and subtracting

$$A + B \rightarrow x$$

according to spatial relations. And, finally, there are rules connecting shapes and the shapes they bound—for example

$$x \rightarrow b(x)$$

to show the boundary of x, and

$$b(x) \rightarrow x + b(x)$$

to show $b(x)$ and a shape it bounds.

All of these schemas are worth having. Nonetheless, they're too loosely drawn to be decisive in practice to get shapes with specific properties or, more ambitiously, designs. My schemas give vague hints, not definite solutions. I can be perfectly general about this with the schema

$x \rightarrow y$

that says no more than try a rule—only which one? That's what everyone wants to know. And it's right to ask, even if the answer is never once and for all. But there's something remarkable about the schema $x \rightarrow y$ that goes beyond its practical value and that shouldn't be missed—whatever rule I try works. I can calculate with triangles and K's after combining squares. There's more than units and counting out. Still, starting with schemas may not be the way to go to get something useful in design. A better approach from a practical standpoint is to turn things around and extend rules to define schemas—to take something that works in practice and copy it in new ways elsewhere. And this is always practicable with shapes. The origin and history of the schema I used to show that descriptions don't count provides a telling illustration and reasons why schemas are useful in the first place.

The shape

is produced by applying the rule

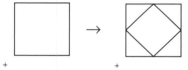

Squares are inscribed in squares in accordance with a single spatial relation between two geometrically similar shapes. But what happens if I want to produce the shape

and others like it by inscribing quadrilaterals in quadrilaterals? This is a natural generalization, and it's not surprising to find it along with squares

Easy enough—but the generalization presents a problem if all I have is rules. Squares work because they're rigid—hence the title of this section—while relationships between lines and angles can vary arbitrarily in quadrilaterals. Quadrilaterals inscribed one in another needn't repeat the same spatial relation. There's plenty of room for things to vary. And this is also true for squares—perhaps in the first black and white drawing above, but explicitly here

This kind of variation seems to imply that I need an indefinite number of rules to correspond with different spatial relations for squares. There are too many ways they can go together. But there's a neat way out using alternative spatial relations for points and lines—endpoints and interior points. I can modify my original rule

by replacing the square in its left side and the new square in its right side with their boundaries to get the rule

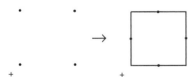

And this rule gives me exactly what I want, when I use it together with the indeterminate rule

that moves a point anywhere in the interior of a line, à la Zeno, half a segment at a time, and the rule

that erases a point. Then the boundaries of squares can be used to inscribe squares in squares, even as these boundaries are moved from place to place one point at a time. The details of this process are illustrated in the following way—starting with the topmost point—to orient squares as desired in a kind of distributed calculating.

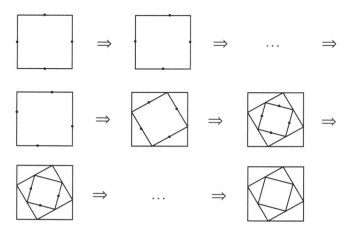

Indeterminate rules are really useful, but this trick alone doesn't work for quadrilaterals because they needn't be geometrically similar. That's why squares worked. With quadrilaterals, I still have to define an indefinite number of rules to get the shapes I want. I can avoid this embarrassment easily enough if I use indeterminate rules—including my rule to move a point on a line—in another way. But then the intuitive idea of inscribing quadrilaterals in quadrilaterals in a recursive process is nearly lost. I have to do almost everything line by line. I want to be able to define rules as naturally as I can, so that I can see how they work without having to think about it. Schemas make this possible—they describe shapes in rules without getting in the way when I calculate.

Let's rehearse the easy technicalities once more. A schema

$$x \rightarrow y$$

is a pair of variables x and y that take shapes—or whatever there is in one of my algebras—as values. These are given in an assignment g that satisfies a given predicate. Whenever g is used, a rule

$$g(x) \rightarrow g(y)$$

is defined. The rule applies in the usual way. In effect, this allows for shapes and their relations to vary within rules, and extends the transformations under which rules apply. It provides a nice way to express many intuitive ideas about shapes and how to change them as calculating goes on. It lets me do what I want with quadrilaterals in a natural way.

(I've shown, in outline, that there's an algorithm to find the transformations under which a rule applies to a shape. But is this also the case for assignments and schemas? What kinds of predicates allow for this, and what kinds of predicates don't? These are still open questions. Their answers are crucial to what I hope can be accomplished calculating.)

This

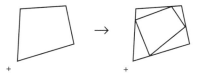

is an example of a rule defined in a schema $x \rightarrow y$ that produces the shape

and others like it from a given quadrilateral. An assignment g gives values to the variables x and y according to this predicate—

x is a quadrilateral, and $y = x + z$, where z is a quadrilateral inscribed in x.

The predicate is framed in terms of the schema $x \rightarrow A + B$ in the special case where the shapes A and B are quadrilaterals. Further elaboration is possible, but this is already familiar from part I. Nonetheless, some things are worth reinforcing.

    Rules have an advantage over schemas because I don't have to say anything definite about the shapes they contain—the intuitive idea is to draw them and calculate in terms of anything I see. But for schemas, I have to constantly remind myself that there are indefinitely many predicates equivalent to any one I've got. Shapes made up of quadrilaterals may contain triangles, etc. This defines the same rules, and it confirms the key idea that you can say almost anything you want to about shapes without it making the slightest difference when you calculate. And in particular, the description of a shape in a rule needn't match the description of the shape to which the rule is applied.

    These are things I've shown. But there are some details I didn't cover in part I. It's also worth noting that my schema for quadrilaterals produces the shape

and others like it, because the schema can be applied to a quadrilateral more than once under different assignments. This is easy to avoid in a number of ways. For example, I can put a notch in the most recent quadrilateral, so that the schema applies only to it, with rules like this

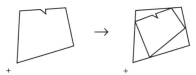

Or I can introduce twin points as I've done before for squares. Then the schema includes rules like this

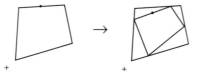

The tricks I have for rules are good in schemas, too. There are a lot of nifty ways to get what I want that depend on what I see—putting a basic element here or there to distinguish a part or to make it behave in a particular fashion relative to the other rules I'm using. The idea is to reason verbally—to say it in words—only after the real work has been done visually. There are many alternative ways to explain rules without getting into trouble calculating. Remember—descriptions don't count.

Schemas do many nice things. Another easy example shows how rules define my algebras. And it's one that illustrates again what indeterminate rules can do. Because points are geometrically similar and lines are, too, I can define the universe of shapes for the algebras U_{0j} and U_{1j} using first the rule

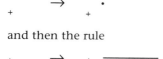

and then the rule

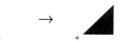

The empty shape is in the left side of both rules, and a point is in the right side of one and a line is in the right side of the other. But because planes and solids needn't be geometrically similar, I have to use schemas to obtain the universe of shapes for the algebras U_{2j} and U_{33}. These schemas $x \rightarrow y$ are defined in the same way. The empty shape is always given for the variable x, and either a triangle in U_{2j} or a tetrahedron in U_{33} is assigned to the variable y. Then a rule in the algebra U_{22} might look like this

Schemas are indispensable when I calculate, and there are many more of them to come in part III.

Parts Are Evanescent—They Change as Rules Are Tried

I keep saying that the parts shapes have depend on how rules are used to calculate. How does this work to determine decompositions? I'm going to sketch three scenarios—each one included in the next—in which parts are defined and related according to the twin formulas for applying rules. The scenarios are good for shapes with points and lines, etc. In fact, for lines, they're already familiar from part I. But my scenarios are just examples. There are other ways to talk about rules and what they do to divide shapes into parts. I'll show this below in an easy approach with identities and transformations. It expands a little on my second scenario to define equivalence relations that classify parts. Decompositions and other kinds of taxonomies are an ideal way for reasoning to conclude. There's a sense of accomplishment, and a real chance to understand what happened. Parts are charged with meaning. My scenarios provide the means to get them, and to change them whenever I go on.

In the first scenario, only rules of a special kind are used to calculate. Every rule

$$A \rightarrow$$

erases a shape A—or some transformation of A—by replacing it with the empty shape. So, when I calculate, it looks like this

$$C \Rightarrow C - t(A) \Rightarrow \cdots \Rightarrow r$$

I start with any shape C. Another part of C—in particular, the shape $t(A)$—is subtracted in each step, when a rule $A \rightarrow$ is applied under a transformation t. The shape r—the remainder—is left at the end of this process. Ideally, r is the empty shape. But whether or not this happens, a Boolean algebra is defined for C. The remainder r when it isn't empty and the parts $t(A)$, picked out as rules are tried, are the atoms of the algebra. This is an easy way for me to define a vocabulary, or to see just how well a given one works in a particular case.

In the next scenario, rules are always identities. Every identity

$$A \rightarrow A$$

has the same shape A in both its left and right sides. When only identities are applied, calculating is monotonous

$$C \Rightarrow C \Rightarrow \cdots \Rightarrow C$$

where, again, C is a given shape. In each step, another part of C is resolved in accordance with an identity $A \rightarrow A$, and nothing else is done. Everything stays exactly the same because $t(A)$ is part of C. Identities are constructively useless. In fact, it's a common practice to discard them. But this misses their value as observational devices. The parts $t(A)$ that are resolved as identities are tried, the empty shape, and C can be used to define a topology for C when they're all combined in sums and products. The first scenario is included in this one if the remainder r is empty, or if r is included with the parts $t(A)$. It's easy to do—for each application of an erasing rule $A \rightarrow$, simply use the identity $A \rightarrow A$. But a Boolean algebra isn't necessary when identities are applied. Complements aren't defined automatically. They may have to be specified explicitly.

In the final scenario, rules aren't restricted. Each rule

$$A \rightarrow B$$

applies in the usual way to define a series of shapes

$$C \Rightarrow (C - t(A)) + t(B) \Rightarrow \cdots \Rightarrow D$$

that starts with the shape C and finishes with the shape D. When the rule $A \rightarrow B$ is tried, a transformation t of A is taken away and the same transformation t of B is added back. But this is only the algebraic mechanism for applying the rule. What's interesting about the series is what I can say about it as a continuous process, especially when parts are resolved in surprising ways. For example, I can calculate so

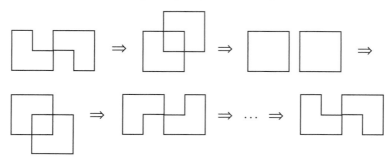

to turn a pair of touching chevrons into a pair of squares and back again, so that the pair of chevrons is reflected in between. The rule

that translates a chevron, and the rule

that translates a square, are used for this purpose. It looks hard—chevrons and squares stay the same when they're moved—but it works. What parts do I need to account for the change, so that there's no break or inconsistency? How are the parts the rules pick out related? When do chevrons become squares, and vice versa? What does it mean for this process to be continuous?

I'm going to build on a configurational (combinatorial) idea that's part of normal experience to answer these questions. It's the very idea I've been against as a way of handling shapes to calculate. Still, the idea works when it comes to describing what happens as rules are applied. Keep this foremost in mind—there's a huge difference between describing shapes and calculating with them. The latter doesn't depend on the former. In fact, the relationship is the opposite. Embedding isn't identity, but identity does play a central part in my approach to continuity. Things are divided into a finite number of pieces. I can recognize these parts—individually and in combination—and I can change them when I like for repair or improvement, or to produce something new. The pieces I leave alone stay the same, and they keep their original relationships. Changes are continuous, as long as they correspond in this way to how things are separated. Nothing that's not already divided is broken up. For example, if a motor goes bad in an appliance, I don't try to fix the motor. It's the smallest piece I can recognize that contains the problem—the motor is usually sealed—so I replace the whole motor and leave the other parts of the appliance alone. Everything else works exactly as before to make the repair a success. Anyone who worries about the motor has a finer decomposition than I do. Components may be complicated in their own right, but not in terms of the pieces I can see and manipulate, or the ones I can find in a catalogue.

This idea can be stated in a general way with mappings. They describe what rules do to shapes, and relate their topologies (decompositions). The details for different mappings may vary—and it's important when they do—but the core intuition is pretty much as in my appliance example. To get things going, I need another analogy that takes mappings from sets to shapes. It looks like this

mappings between shapes : parts :: mappings between sets : subsets

There are matching properties of mappings for sets and shapes, even if x in the analogy

x : shape :: member : set

has no meaning when i exceeds zero. What's evident for sets because they have members that are independent in combination needs to be said for shapes when there are no units. Consider, for example, one of these properties for the mapping h. If A and B are sets such that $A \subseteq B$, then $h(A) \subseteq h(B)$. And the same goes when A and B are shapes—$A \leq B$ implies that $h(A) \leq h(B)$. What h does to a shape, it does likewise when it's part of another shape. This works for mappings defined in the Boolean expressions I'm going to use.

Now suppose that a mapping from the parts of a shape C to parts of a shape C^+ describes a rule $A \rightarrow B$ as it's used to change C into C^+. Then this process is continuous whenever twin conditions are met.

(1)   The part $t(A)$ the rule picks out and replaces is closed, that is to say, it's in the topology of C. The rule recognizes a piece that can be changed—a motor or some other meaningful part.

(2)   For every part x of C, the mapping of the closure of x in the topology of C is included in the closure of the mapping of x in the topology of C^+, where the closure of a part is the smallest shape in a topology—it's a piece I can recognize—that contains the part. The closure of any part of my motor, whether rotator, stator, etc., or any nameless thingy, is the motor. In essence, the mapping is a homomorphism, and this in addition to condition 1 is why there's continuity. Moreover, if two parts are parts of

the same parts in the topology of C, then their mappings are parts of the same parts in the topology of C^+. The rule changes the shape C to make the shape C^+, so that the parts of C^+ and their relationships are consistent with the parts of C. There's no division in C^+ that implies a division that's not already in C.

The trick is to define topologies for shapes, so that whenever I apply a rule it's continuous. This is possible for different mappings—each in a host of different ways—working backward after I finish calculating. (If I'm impatient, I can define topologies after every rule application, or intermittently, but these definitions may change as I go on.) The mapping

$$h_1(x) = x - t(A)$$

is an obvious choice. It preserves every part x of the shape $C - t(A)$ that isn't erased when a rule $A \rightarrow B$ is used to change a shape C. It's right there as the leading term in the formula

$$(C - t(A)) + t(B)$$

that gives the result C^+ in which the supporting term $t(B)$ plays its part. Better yet, I can use the topology of the shape C^+ to get a minimal topology for C that guarantees continuity. In particular, x is a closed part of C just in case it's empty or y is a closed part of C^+ and

$$x = t(A) + ((C - t(A)) \cdot y)$$

The divisions in the piece $C - t(A)$ are fixed in the topology of C^+. Still, I may want something more profligate—perhaps a Boolean algebra for each shape. Then, for y in the Boolean algebra of C^+, x is as before, or

$$x = (C - t(A)) \cdot y$$

In both cases, distinguished values of x are easy to find. The empty shape is given explicitly, and C is given for $y = C^+$. And notice that $t(A)$ is defined when y is empty—condition 1 is included in condition 2. Then, there are sums and products. And in the Boolean case, the shape $x = t(A) + ((C - t(A)) \cdot y)$ has the complement $x' = (C - t(A)) \cdot y'$, where y and y' are complements. But be careful. Even though it looks it, the topology of C needn't be bigger than the topology of C^+—either by a single part or twice. Values of y may be equivalent in the sense that they define the same shapes.

If I try the mapping h_1 with identities, I get something rather different from what I described in my second scenario. This gives equal insight in an alternative way, and it's fun to compare. Even so, the mapping

$$h_2(x) = x - (t(A) - t(B))$$

works to include the second scenario in this one. Now

$$h_2(x) = x$$

and every part of C is left alone. Calculating is continuous if the topology of C is the same from step to step—from my previous formulas, I get $x = C \cdot y = y$. But then I need to update the topology every time an identity $A \rightarrow A$ is applied, so that $t(A)$ is a closed part. Conditions 1 and 2 are independent. It's no surprise, either, that there's a comparable account of any rule with a left side that's part of its right side—in particular, any rule that answers to the degenerate schema

$\rightarrow x$

with an empty left side, or to the familiar schema for spatial relations

$x \rightarrow A + B$

Mappings show how rules with widely different uses are alike.

Examples for both of my mappings show that what I can say about a shape that's definite—at least for parts—may have to wait until I stop calculating. Descriptions are retrospective—they record what I've done without limiting what I can do. In many ways, the past is reconfigured in the present, while the future is always open. My description of what happened before can change radically as I continue to calculate. What happens now makes a difference for the past because something else is going on whenever another rule is tried. History varies as I see and do more in new ways.

Before I turn to specific examples, it's worth emphasizing that describing what rules do is really the same as describing shapes in terms of their parts. There are alternative ways to do it—lots of them. I can be a purist and treat all my rules in the same way, or I can let my descriptions wander all over the place—even describing the same rule differently at different times. I've scarcely touched the surface with what I've said here about mappings and topologies and how they might be used. The foregoing presentation is pretty impressionistic—it's still about seeing. But I can fix things up a little with closure operations and closure algebras. And for those who enjoy mathematical depth and rigor, there's M. H. Stone's theory of representations. Only this means seeing in a complementary way that's abstract rather than concrete. Whatever you like— I'll stick with my finite Aristotelian perspective and what I'm able (need) to see—it seems to me that continuity is a good place to start. It develops the idea that things that coalesce can change at any time. In retrospect, unbroken community and licentious freedom are compatible. Playing around with descriptions of rules is another way to inform seeing, even impressionistically. It leads to a host of new insights about how calculating with shapes works and what it implies. There's plenty to do, but then calculating with shapes means going on.

Erasing and Identity

Some easy illustrations show how my three scenarios work. Suppose I want to use the first scenario to define decompositions for the shape

in terms of the rule

that erases triangles, and the rule

that erases squares. Five distinct decompositions result when these rules are applied to produce an empty remainder. They're illustrated neatly in this fashion

by filling in triangles. In the first decomposition, four squares are the atoms in the Boolean algebra that describes the shape. In each of the three succeeding decompositions, four triangles and two squares are picked out as the atoms in Boolean algebras, and in the last decomposition, eight triangles are resolved for this purpose.

There are two interesting things to notice. First, I can produce these illustrations in a direct product of algebras as I erase triangles and squares in the shape

This means calculating in parallel—seeing and doing different things at the same time in a coordinated way. I can recapitulate the use of the erasing rules

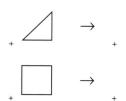

in the algebra U_{12}, and build up the corresponding decompositions at the same time in a combination of the algebras U_{12} and U_{22}, so that squares contain lines, and triangles are planes. Alternatively, labeled lines or lines with weights fix the twin layers in this direct product. So a combination of the algebras V_{12} and U_{22} or of W_{12} and U_{22} will do the whole job. The graphics is more concise, but perhaps not as clear. I need two rules whatever I do. These

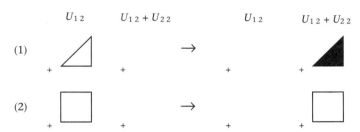

show my original idea. They're applied six times to produce the third decomposition. The rule used each time is indicated by number in the series

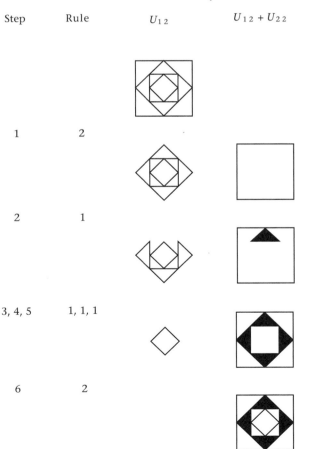

It's easy to see that the series could be different, so long as the same triangles and squares are picked out. In this scenario and the next one for identities, decompositions don't reflect the order in which rules are applied. The same rule applications in any order have the same result. But in the third scenario, decompositions are sensitive to when rules are tried.

Of course, I'm free to modify my rules to represent decompositions in another way. I can replace the algebra $U_{12} + U_{22}$ for lines and planes with an algebra W_{22} for planes and weights. Then triangles and squares are planes that are filled in with tones that add together to get darker and darker. Now my five decompositions look like this

and my rules are almost the same as before

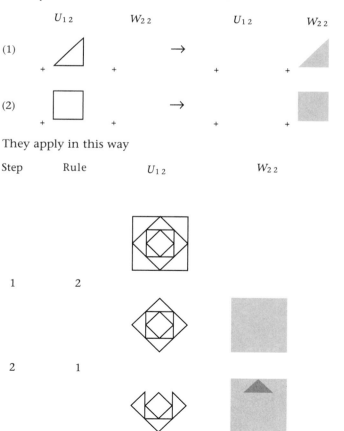

Step	Rule	U_{12}	W_{22}
3, 4, 5	1, 1, 1		
6	2		

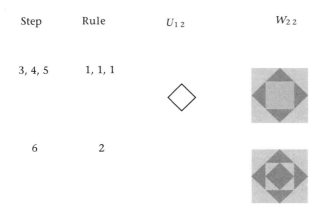

to produce the third decomposition. (Like results follow in the algebra $U_{12} + W_{22}$ with the schema $b(x) \rightarrow x$ for lines and the shapes they bound. I can do the third decomposition exactly as before in six steps or, alternatively, in two steps. The fewest steps for each decomposition is the number of gray tones it contains. Boundaries have some nice uses.) As I'm going to show next—this is the second point of interest—the number of decompositions for each of the shapes in the series

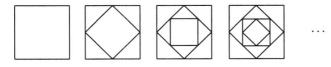

is fixed in a definite way, but how these decompositions are represented as shapes can vary freely. Decompositions are abstract in the same way words and sentences are in generative grammars, and they're abstract in the same way as Turing machines, cellular automata, etc. How I show them is independent of what they do—it's a question of design. Playing around with algebras and rules is an effective means to explore the possibilities.

The number $f(n)$ of distinct decompositions for any shape in the series

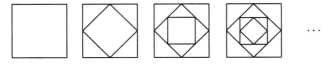

when the shape is divided into squares and triangles can be given in terms of its numerical position n. The first shape in the series is described in one way—it's a square—and the second shape can be described in two ways—it's either two squares or four triangles. Moreover, the number of possible descriptions for each of the succeeding shapes—so long as I keep the remainder empty—is the corresponding term in the series of Fibonacci numbers defined by $f(n) = f(n-1) + f(n-2)$. This works in the following way

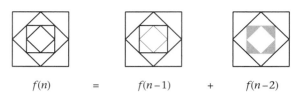

If a rule resolves the inmost square in the shape $f(n)$, then there are $f(n-1)$ ways to describe the remaining part of the shape—this part is one shape back in the series. Alternatively, if a rule resolves the four inmost triangles in the shape $f(n)$, then there are $f(n-2)$ descriptions—the remaining part is now two shapes back in the series. So the total number of descriptions is $f(n) = f(n-1) + f(n-2)$. I can prove this for any square and any four triangles that include the square. Still, the visual demonstration is immediate enough to make the formal proof superfluous. In this case, seeing is believing.

But that's enough counting. Let's try my second scenario. Suppose I recast the rules

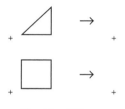

as the identities

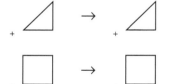

and then use them to define decompositions. Consider the shape

once more. If I apply an identity to pick out this triangle

and an identity to resolve this square

then the following topology (decomposition)

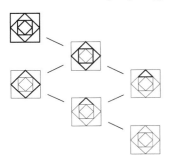

is defined. This time I've shown the topology as a lattice. It's easy to see that the right angle of the triangle and a corner of the square are distinguished. But other parts of the triangle and the square go completely unnoticed. If I recognize complements in addition to the parts I resolve when I use the identities, then a Boolean algebra is defined that has these four atoms

The first three give me what I want. Now the triangle and the square have two parts apiece and a common angle

Of course, I can always apply the identities everywhere I can. This determines another Boolean algebra with the twenty-four atoms

But then there are a couple more things to heed. Triangles come in three kinds

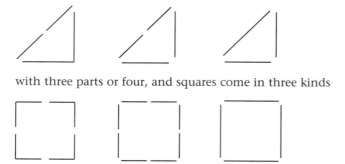

with three parts or four, and squares come in three kinds

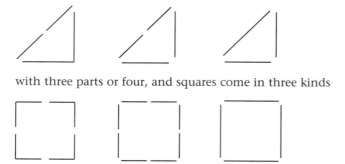

with four parts or eight. Moreover, the different decompositions of the shape may be regarded as subalgebras of the Boolean algebra, including all five of the decompositions obtained in the first scenario. Only there's no guarantee that things will always work out conveniently. A Boolean algebra needn't be defined for every shape when identities apply wherever they can. Other structures are also possible.

Classifying the parts of a shape in a decomposition is a useful practice that explains how the shape works and what it means. But topologies aren't the only way to approach this, and it's good to see something else to make the point. Let's try another easy example with identities that emphasizes the transformations instead of embedding and the part relation. After all, transformations are also needed to apply rules—they play the key role in deciding when shapes are alike. I won't show much detail, just enough to suggest that other ways of understanding are worthwhile, too. There are topologies to get back to. Still, there's no reason to stick with one way of describing things. If calculating with shapes shows anything, it's that nothing works all the time. It always makes sense to look again.

Suppose I have the identity

to pick out squares in the shape

In terms of this identity, there are fourteen squares that appear to be the same. But I can use the transformations under which the identity applies to define an equivalence relation. If I first pay attention to scale, then there are three classes of squares—nine small ones

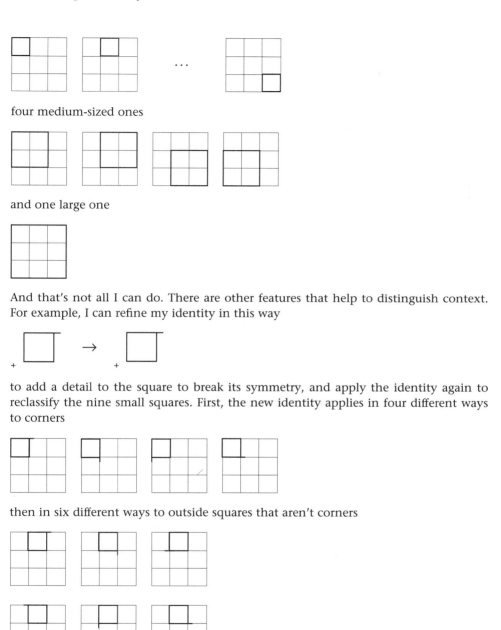

four medium-sized ones

and one large one

And that's not all I can do. There are other features that help to distinguish context. For example, I can refine my identity in this way

to add a detail to the square to break its symmetry, and apply the identity again to reclassify the nine small squares. First, the new identity applies in four different ways to corners

then in six different ways to outside squares that aren't corners

and in eight different ways to the central square

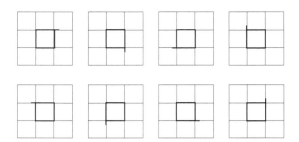

And, certainly, this isn't the end of it either. But the idea of using transformations and identities to classify parts seems well enough established. It gives a nice taxonomy for parts and their uses. Rules let me generate shapes and tell a lot about them. In fact, I like to think that whatever I describe—with transformations, with parts and topologies, or in some other way—is the result of calculating. Otherwise, what is there to talk about? Without something to see, there's nothing to say.

Calculating and Continuity

I'm going to try another rule—it's the very first one I used in the introduction—to show how the third scenario works. The rule

rotates an equilateral triangle about its center, so that the center point is permanently fixed. The rule is applied eight times to define the shapes in this series

This looks natural enough—and, no doubt, it is—unless you start thinking about what's going on. The final shape in the series is a rotation of the initial one about its center—that's the vertex shared by the three triangles in both shapes. But the transformation is surprising because the centers of the triangles in the initial shape change position when it's rotated

The rule doesn't move the centers of triangles, but they move just the same. What kind of paradox is this?

The answer is easier to see than to say. But let's give it a try. The rule can be applied to the fourth shape in the series in two ways. In one way, the rule picks out the three triangles that correspond to the three triangles in the initial shape. Only none of these triangles is resolved in the other way. Instead, the rule divides the fourth shape into two triangles—the large outside triangle and the small inside one—that have sides formed from sides of the three triangles that come from the ones in the initial shape. The rule rotates the two triangles in turn to get the fifth and sixth shapes. Now the rule can be applied in alternative ways to the sixth shape in the series. Either the rule resolves both of the triangles that correspond to the ones in the fourth shape, or it resolves the three triangles—one at each corner of the sixth shape—that have sides formed from segments of sides of the triangles in the fourth shape. The rule rotates the three corner triangles one at a time to complete the series. This isn't about thinking in a combinatorial scheme, but about seeing when lines fuse and divide.

The nine shapes in the series

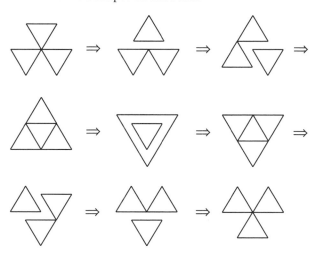

are all made up of triangles. Their numbers provide a nice summary of what happens as the rule is applied from step to step. Consider the following numerical series

3 3 3 │5 │2 │ 5 │3 3 3

3 3 3 │3 │2 │ 2 │3 3 3

3 3 3 │2 │2 │ 3 │3 3 3

The first of the trio shows the maximum number of triangles—these can be picked out using an identity—in each of the shapes. The next gives the number of triangles in a shape after the rule has been applied, and the last gives the number of triangles in a shape as the rule is being applied. In the second and third series, the number of triangles depends on what the rule does, either by rotating an existing triangle or by seeing a new one to rotate, and then counting in terms of the triangle and its complement. The resulting inconsistencies in the fourth and sixth shapes tell the story. Counting goes awry. Three triangles can't be two, and neither number is five. (It's blind luck that two and three make five. Usually, there's no easy relation to find.) But this way of calculating is a continuous process when topologies are given for the nine shapes.

The topologies for these shapes are defined as Boolean algebras with the atoms shown in table 11. This is practicable using the mapping $h_1(x) = x - t(A)$ and my formulas for closed parts. First a topology is given for the final shape. Any finite Boolean algebra works. I've used the trivial topology—the final shape is an atom—because the rule doesn't divide it. There's nothing to say—the final shape is without finer parts or definite purpose, ready for calculating to go on in any way at all. Once the topology of the final shape is decided, the topologies of the preceding shapes are defined in reverse order to keep the application of the rule continuous. Each topology contains the triangle $t(A)$ resolved by the rule—the topmost atom in table 11—and its complement $C - t(A)$ to form a Boolean algebra.

Keeping track of how rules work is a good way to see what's happening. I can record the divisions in the triangle in the right side of the rule

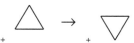

formed with respect to my topologies. This shows—again in the terminology of my formulas—what $t(B)$ does in C^+. The triangle is cut in alternative ways

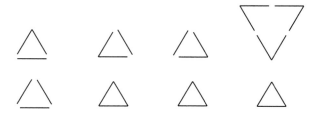

Table 11
Topologies of Shapes Defined by Calculating

Shapes	Atoms

in the eight steps of the series. The parts defined in the triangle combine sequentially to build up the different triangles that the rule picks out in its subsequent applications. The pieces

from the first three triangles combine in this way

and the remaining sides

combine in this way

to define parts (atoms) in the topologies of the second and third shapes in the series, and ultimately to define the large outside triangle and the small inside one in the topology of the fourth shape. Moreover, the pieces in the fourth and fifth triangles combine in like fashion to make the three triangles in the topology of the sixth shape that are needed for the production of the final shape. Looking ahead, the topologies of the shapes in the series appear to anticipate what the rule is going to do the next time it's applied. But this is because the topologies are given retrospectively. I can always describe what I've done as a continuous process after I stop calculating. This explains what I did and shows how everything goes together in a coherent fashion. Expecting more—so that the future is laid out in advance—is preposterous.

Every time the rule

is tried, its right side is divided with respect to a different topology. This shows in yet another way that the shapes in a rule have diverse descriptions that vary as it's used to calculate. The rule doesn't apply in terms of any one description that measures its complexity or anything else. How the rule is described is an artifact of what's been going on.

Before I finish up, it's also worth noting that the series

isn't isolated. There are many others like it. And in fact, they can be defined around each of the shapes in this array of nested polygons

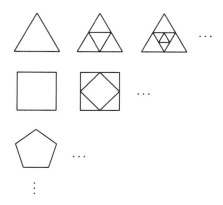

using only a single schema

$$x \rightarrow t(x)$$

where x is a triangle or a regular polygon, and t is an appropriate transformation of x. Then the number of ways I can apply the schema to a shape in the array without remainder corresponds to the Fibonacci number of its column. I showed this for the series of squares inscribed in squares in the second row. The rule

and others defined in the schema work like erasing rules. Shapes are filled with ambiguity. And there are always rules to take advantage of it, so that I'm free to look at things in new ways. Finding the right rule to apply may require time, effort, and a little luck, but nothing prevents it from being used.

Most of what I've been saying about rules and calculating with shapes is anecdotal. I've been presenting decompositions as case studies. This is no surprise. The way ambiguity is used now may have little to do with the way it's used later. Ambiguity won't go away. It's there whenever I apply rules to calculate, but it's not handled in the same way all of the time. That's why ambiguity is so interesting and valuable. The trick is to use ambiguity without limiting it by trying to generalize. There's no chance of this, as long as rules can vary as widely as shapes can. In this way, ambiguity always provides the chance to try things that haven't been tried before. It's keeping your eyes open when you calculate.

Design without Thought

What is design? No one ever agrees, but I used to side with Franz Reuleaux—

Invention, in those cases especially where it succeeds, is Thought.

In fact, he answers the overarching question I've been working on throughout this book when he links invention—creative design—and thought. And he recognizes the depth of the problem.

The mathematical investigations referred to bring the whole apparatus of a great science to the examination of the properties of a given mechanism, and have accumulated in this direction rich material, of enduring and increasing value. What is left unexamined is however the other, immensely deeper part of the problem, the question: How did the mechanism, or the elements of which it is composed, originate? What laws govern its building up? Is it indeed formed according to any laws whatever? Or have we simply to accept as data what invention gives us, the [mathematical] analysis of what is thus obtained being the only scientific problem left—as in the case of natural history?

But after thinking about it, I've changed my mind. Reuleaux's metaphor is dubious unless thought includes seeing. Then there's ambiguity to use in the combinatorial process he takes for granted. "How did the mechanism, or the elements of which it is composed, originate? What laws govern its building up?" Yet this kind of thinking is confirmed in cognitive science—"[humans] have combinatorial minds." There's no avoiding it—design has to be the way Reuleaux describes. But why, if it's as much seeing (observing) as thinking? The creative activity I have in mind tries new ways of looking at things—not just once or even a few times, but again and again on the fly. This is how calculating works as rules are applied to shapes. Shapes make a difference—ambiguity means creative choices all the time. Decompositions, definitions, and the segments and shards of analysis are mere afterthoughts of calculating, even if they're prerequisites in combinatorial minds. Combining constituents in increasingly complex arrangements isn't all there is to creativity. There's looking at what you've done and reacting to it in your own way. There are plenty of surprises, and whatever they are, they're possible with embedding. Anything can happen when basic elements fuse and divide as rules are tried.

Near the end of the introduction, I said that visual reasoning—using your eyes to decide what to do next—always seems incomplete. Because it isn't obviously counting, it needs to be explained. But even if counting gives right answers in the sciences—meteorology and social science are rife with reliable predictions—it still seems that there's room for something else. And the foregoing shows that visual reasoning is more than wishful thinking. What strikes me most about calculating by seeing is how easy it is to do, and how accommodating and generous it turns out to be. The relationship between embedding and identity is key—to show first that calculating by counting is a special case of calculating by seeing, and then that I can count to see. I've been trying to show that shapes with points aren't like shapes with lines, planes, and solids, and equally, too, that this isn't a categorical divide—in some ways, the differences don't matter. It's like seeing—I can switch back and forth. The leap from zero-dimensional shapes to higher-dimensional ones—from shapes where there are permanent units I can count to shapes where parts change freely—alters everything. Embedding and identity aren't the same, and counting obscures what I can see. But seeing isn't lost in my algorithms for rules. Still, I like to stress my visual intuitions more than algorithms. There's an imbalance today—rote counting passes for thinking far too often, with preposterous results. Everything is numbers and symbols without shapes. Seeing doesn't need to be explained, it needs to be used.

I can always see things in new ways when I calculate with shapes made up of lines, planes, and solids. I can draw to figure things out, and to see what I can do. This is my kind of design. But shapes with points—and likewise decompositions or representations in computer models—limit what I can see and how I can change my mind. A census of points doesn't offset the loss. The last thing I want to do while I'm calculating or thinking is to count. Showing how I calculate to see—that's what shapes and rules do—shows that calculating and thinking needn't be combinatorial. There's an alternative—I can always see something new. Counting is a bad habit that's hard to break, so count me out.

Background

James Gips and I published the original idea for shapes and rules in 1972.[1] That paper also describes the weights—shaded areas—in the five decompositions for the shape

on page 290. However, instead of algebras like W_{22} in which everything takes care of itself, we had an algorithm for "levels" (overlapping areas) and ad hoc "painting rules" given in Boolean expressions. Many of the formal devices I use go back to my book *Pictorial and Formal Aspects of Shape and Shape Grammars*.[2] There, I cover embedding—including parts ("subshapes"), representing shapes with maximal elements, and reduction rules—rules and calculating in the algebra U_{12}, calculating in parallel in direct products of this algebra, algorithms for computer implementations of shapes and rules, and equivalence with Turing machines. In fact, it's where I first used the beginning entries in Paul Klee's *Pedagogical Sketchbook*—I show them on pages 251–252—to link visual reasoning and calculating.[3] There's substantially more, too, that I haven't described here on sets ("languages") of shapes and how they're closed with respect to various operations on shapes and sets.

I introduced spatial relations and the schema

$$x \rightarrow A + B$$

in an early paper—"Two Exercises in Formal Composition."[4] The problem of defining styles from scratch (design synthesis in exercise 1) and from known examples (analysis using identities in exercise 2) is framed and discussed there. The first example of rules that generate designs in a given style—Chinese ice-ray lattices—was described in my next paper.[5] Perhaps more important, though, general schemas for rules were used for the first time. There are twin drawings from the Russian constructivist Jacob Tchérnikhov to illustrate this on page 278.[6] And also, basic elements of different kinds—points and lines—and labels were considered. This demonstrated the practical value—reaffirmed many times since—in the unlikely combination of algebras with atoms and without. I return to Chinese ice-rays in part III. Elaborations of the schema $x \rightarrow A + B$ and its inverse using Frederick Froebel's "building gifts" in design synthesis are in "Kindergarten Grammars," along with the rhyme on page 252, additional material on children's play blocks—for example, Abbatt building bricks in H. G. Wells's entertaining *Floor Games*—and a description of studio instruction in terms of both calculating and Froebel's kindergarten method with its gifts and categories.[7] The schema is instrumental, too, in analysis and design synthesis—including the seminal addition of stylistic change—in Terry Knight's book *Transformations in Design*.[8] Knight revisits these topics later, going on to compare work in design and composition in music.[9] The use of symmetry groups to describe rules is also explored in "Kindergarten Grammars." A little later, the connection to Lagrange is explicit.[10]

More background material of my own is spread out over a number of years. Froebel's building gifts are really zero dimensional because individual blocks neither fuse nor divide. And in fact they're better described in set grammars than with rules in my algebras if i is greater than 0.[11] Algebras of shapes are introduced in several different places, but comprehensively in the series U_{ij}, V_{ij}, and W_{ij} in "Weights."[12] The algebras W_{ij} subsume a pair of earlier approaches—Gips's and mine with levels and painting rules à la Venn, and Knight's with "color spots" that have a Goodmanesque tinge.[13] The idea of calculating in parallel with shapes and their descriptions in a multiplicity of algebras is considered in another way in "A Note on the Description of Designs," and the idea that designs are members of relations among descriptions of different kinds is introduced in "What Is a Design?"—although in neither instance with the algebraic generality and uniformity found in "Weights."[14] That calculating with shapes can be described as a continuous process using mappings and topologies is a recent development that awaits complete elaboration.[15]

Today, the literature on rules and the way they're used to calculate with shapes is much too extensive to cite item by item. Most of the relevant material has appeared in the journal *Environment and Planning B: Planning and Design*. Papers date from my first one in 1976—"Two Exercises in Formal Composition." With respect to the immediate themes covered in this part only, I recommend the authors in this list—alphabetically, Scott Chase (properties of basic elements and shapes, and computer implementations),[16] C. F. Earl (descriptive boundaries $b(x)$ of shapes x and their Boolean relationships, spatial relations with shapes and their descriptive boundaries, topologies of shapes and topological boundaries, computer implementations, and classifying arbitrary curves and surfaces in terms of their basic elements and the indices i and j for my algebras of shapes),[17] Knight (the previous work and other formal and historical papers with vanguard results that question the shape grammarist's habitual way of seeing and doing—Knight wants rules to apply in parallel in new kinds of algebras rooted in everyday design practice, and with taxonomic prescience defines types of emergence, anticipated and not, and ambiguity before rules are tried),[18] Ramesh Krishnamurti (the first computer implementation of shapes and rules—around 1980—and many improvements since in terms of shapes and their boundaries),[19] Djordje Krstic (algebras of shapes and decompositions),[20] Lionel March (miracles and what they mean),[21] and Mark Tapia (computer implementations).[22] There are other authors, though, of equal interest. More references are in part III.

George A. Miller's speculative comments at the beginning of this part are in "Information Theory in Psychology."[23] His extension of the engineer's idea of noise to define ambiguity in a theory of semantic information is captured in the neat formula

ambiguity = noise

Perhaps Miller is looking for a way to handle ambiguity to help with meaning, so that semantic errors can be usefully detected and corrected. This seems to be a goal today for advanced research in computer science. I recently saw the sign

in an office for PhD students in artificial intelligence (AI) who were working on "design rationale"—in particular, on a sketch-recognition language complete with a vocabulary of predefined shapes and a syntax for combining them.[24] It seems that ambiguity is something to stop in AI. But this seldom if ever happens with signs, and can't be expected for designs. In fact, it misses what drawing and sketching are for. Meaning is closed off in advance to anything new. There's no reason for reason. My retrospective account of meaning in terms of topologies provides a workable alternative in an open-ended process.[25]

I refer to Alfred North Whitehead and extensive connection in several places.[26] In particular, there are his diagrams from *Process and Reality* showing how regions are related, first on page 174 and then on page 211. Shapes connect both to Whitehead's regions and to Henry Leonard and Nelson Goodman's more comprehensive individuals.[27] These are also the focus of Stanislaw Lesniewski's earlier mereology (the theory of parts and wholes). Alfred Tarski describes it nicely.[28] Peter Simons provides an omnibus survey of the whole field—his discussion of extensional mereology is useful to compare shapes and individuals.[29] Goodman and W. V. Quine use "shape-predicates" to calculate with ink marks (individuals) in a "nominalistic syntax"—after discussing this with Tarski and Rudolf Carnap.[30] The brainpower is simply staggering. It seems almost comical, along with the results that suppress what marks can do. It's amazing how hard it is to make the world—even a small part of it—behave syntactically, and then everything is lost. Luckily, syntax isn't necessary to calculate. Leonard and Goodman, and Lesniewski, establish the Boolean standard for individuals, too, all with qualms about the zero.[31] Shapes are like "regularized" point sets, as well.[32]

Table 12
Alternative Ways to Describe a Shape A

	Points	Parts	Closed parts
Topology	Euclidean space	Stone space	Closure operation c
Closure of $x \leq A$	Point set + boundary	Parts are closed and open	Smallest closed part containing x
Boundary of x	Point set boundary	Empty shape	$c(x) \cdot (A - x)$
Connectivity	Multiply connected	Totally disconnected	Partially connected
Algebra	Boolean	Boolean	Heyting

Most of the mathematics I use is pretty elementary. In a few places, however, I probably exceed the limits of everyday familiarity. There are (1) M. H. Stone's generalized Boolean algebras (Boolean rings), (2) his extension of these systems to standard Boolean algebras, and (3) his theory of representations.[33] Earl presents a nice review of the techniques in the latter—Stone spaces, etc.—with respect to shapes and their topologies.[34] For example, closure for shapes and Stone's filters describe parts by the parts containing them. But, of greater interest, Earl summarizes alternative ways of describing shapes in terms of sets and parts. These are in table 12, and are familiar from what I've covered, using point sets, parts made up of points as well as lines, etc., and closed parts. Still, table 12 is only a snapshot, and there's more to see and do. It's crucial to what I've been trying to show that the closure operation c in the rightmost column is defined as rules are applied—for example, using the mapping h_1 on page 286 and either the first or both of the formulas that follow there. This allows for anything to happen as meaning unfolds in an Aristotelian process that's finite and continuous. Nothing is fixed before I begin to calculate, and everything is free to change as I go on. A Heyting algebra in which the complement of a closed part is the closure of its Boolean complement is defined via c. This is especially telling for h_1 and the first formula alone. (Heyting algebras also suggest a link with logic that I haven't followed up.) The Stone space topology in the middle column is really neat once you see how it works—even as an artifact of mathematical abstraction—and confirms what I've been saying about shapes with all of their concrete properties. And the mathematics for parts and closed parts—this goes together in closure algebras ($+$, $\cdot$, $-$, and c)—doesn't intrude in what's going on. It shows how shapes and rules work as if it weren't there. With parts and closure, you're free to think with your eyes—to see and do whatever you want. That's the real mathematics. And it doesn't need to be formalized to be used, even if that provides an impressive pedigree. Elsewhere, I show how generalized Boolean algebras and Boolean algebras are related, using figure-ground-like properties of shapes.[35] Monoids (page 194) are used in the theory of formal languages and automata instead of algebras with more Boolean-like properties.[36] Concatenation is the sole operation on strings of symbols from a given vocabulary. But, in general, monoids won't do for rule application.[37] Concatenation isn't enough to recognize and replace segments of strings. Noam Chomsky counts symbols to classify rules and to measure the complexity and power of generative grammars.[38]

Generative grammars aren't the only way to calculate where complexity is the measure. Steven Wolfram does cellular automata in remarkable detail—including John Conway's game of life—and provides useful background for like devices—for example, fractals and Lindenmayer systems.[39] To his lasting credit, Wolfram prefers graphic depictions of cellular automata to numerical summaries of data.

Looking through this book, one striking difference with most previous scientific accounts is the presence of so many explicit pictures that show how every element in a system behaves. In the past, people have tended to consider it more scientific to give only numerical summaries of such data. But most of the phenomena I discuss in this book could not have been found without such explicit pictures.[40]

Who needs sex when you've got "explicit pictures?" They're better than the real thing. All of them are zero dimensional—they "show how every element [point] in a system behaves." This might as well be Herbert Simon in *The Sciences of the Artificial*. In fact, Simon and Wolfram see pictures the same way. Try this one of an array

and ask the following questions—(1) how many cells does it contain? (2) how did it grow? and (3) how did it start? Individual cells behave as might be guessed. They're black if any of their eight adjacent neighbors is black—horizontal, vertical, and diagonal

But this doesn't make the picture explicit. Neither question 1 nor question 3 has a definite answer, even if I can answer question 2—at least experts can, the ones who watch cells do it. The picture is an $n \times n$ square, for any n. And there's no end of initial configurations—maybe these four

Really, though, I'm not being fair. I can't tell how many cells there are, but I can experiment. Subsequent pictures determine cell size if cells do what they're supposed to, and I have an accurate clock that tells me when to look. I just need a couple of measurements. Only what if there are finer and finer divisions in space and time? And the initial configuration may still be in doubt. Alternative histories are equivalent. But even with open questions, Wolfram's notion of "picture" has an uncanny appeal in art and science—for C. S. Peirce with arrangements of objects, Ludwig Wittgenstein in the *Tractatus*, Ezra Pound with Chinese characters, and Miller and Quine with information, and also for Simon, Ivan Sutherland, T. G. Evans, et al. This is an awesome lineup. Still, don't be swayed. There's more to a picture (shape) than any arrangement of predefined units can show. Moreover, formal languages and automata—generative grammars, cellular automata, etc.—are abstract symbol systems. There are many ways to depict how they work—after all, form follows function—but none is necessary to what's going on. Explicit pictures may reveal new phenomena, though the new phenomena could be otherwise in different depictions that don't change what cellular automata do. Algebras of shapes are needed for seeing and calculating to be the same; but then, shapes are ambiguous. Neither what pictures show nor their connection to cellular automata is definite. Wolfram is right to prefer pictures over numbers—there's more to see than to count.

(Do explicit pictures show the eternal and unchangeable, or are they a harmful vice? It's nice to be clear about what's happening unit by unit. There's plenty to admire in the precision and insight this implies, and in what it has to teach. Yet there's the numbing sameness of pornography when everyone calculates one way—counting out unit by unit in combinatorial play. There must be an alternative. A meaningful complaint takes an effective remedy, and that's what shapes and rules provide. Ambiguity is to use, while explicit pictures indulge an idle fantasy. Plato asked us to choose between explicit pictures and ambiguous ones, but he fixed the results. There's scant reason to vote. Counting yeas and nays matters only when ambiguity is noise without an inventive hum.)

I enjoy reading Leon Battista Alberti. He has a nice way of saying things and a nice way with lines, as well. I quote him on lines and architecture on page 214.[41] Alberti appears again on page 251, where he talks about compartition (spatial composition) and about the recursive relationship between cities, houses, and rooms.[42]

William James says many things that work. I rely on the relationship between sagacity and learning, first on page 64 in part I, and then again in this part on page 233. It's a striking way to describe rules. But I also go on parenthetically on page 234 to James's reference to John Stuart Mill. I find it as hard not to quote James as James does Mill. "To be sagacious", says James, "is to be a good observer. J. S. Mill has a passage which is so much in the spirit of [this] that I cannot forbear to quote it."

The observer is not he who merely sees the thing which is before his eyes, but he who sees what parts that thing is composed of. To do this well is a rare talent. . . . It would be possible to point out what qualities of mind, and modes of mental culture, fit a person for being a good observer: that, however, is a question not of Logic, but of the Theory of Education, in the most enlarged sense of the term. There is not properly an Art of Observing. There may be rules for observing. But these, like rules for inventing, are properly instructions for the preparation of one's own mind; for putting it into the state in which it will be most fitted to observe, or most likely to invent.[43]

To be sure, Mill would agree that freedom (liberty) to observe and to say what you see is key throughout education "in the most enlarged sense of the term." Education isn't about morality and good and bad manners, or testing what you know. Good answers and right behavior aren't set in advance—they're always a surprise. This isn't a question of logic but of unfolding experience. That's why I'm so keen on shapes and rules. My rules let me focus on this while going freely to that, without having to represent anything in between. They let me see "what parts that thing is composed of" in new ways as I go on. Only my rules aren't Mill's. His rules encourage getting in the right frame of mind. This is important enough—and for me, it involves marshaling an array of schemas $x \rightarrow y$ to define rules. That's the main job of part III. Then using these rules to calculate with shapes puts observing and inventing in a working relationship—I do the one to do the other.

The quotations from Franz Reuleaux that link "Invention" and "Thought" are in *The Kinematics of Machinery*.[44] In keeping with this, Reuleaux divides design into direct and indirect synthesis. He prefers the latter to the former, although this seems inevitable when invention is thought—sooner or later, the one is bound to be organized in the same way as the other.

Diagram of the Synthetic Processes

The importance of this part of the subject is so great that I have thought it worth while to add the accompanying diagram in the hope that it may make the connection between the different synthetic methods somewhat more clear to the reader.

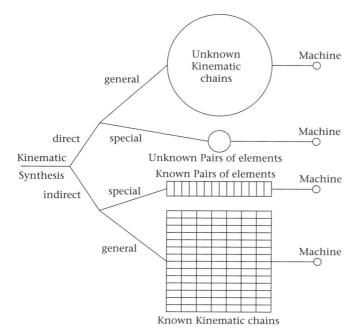

Kinematic synthesis as a whole divides itself into direct and indirect, and each of these classes again subdivides into general and special. The direct synthesis should combine the kinematic elements at its command into the required pairs or chains according to the laws of pair- or chain-formation. In part it strikes upon insoluble difficulties, in part it furnishes results that have no practical value. The indirect synthesis first (as special synthesis) forms and arranges all the possible pairs of elements, and then (as general synthesis) finds all the combinations of these pairs into chains. From this systematized arrangement of pairs and chains the special combinations best suited to each particular case can then be chosen by an inductive process. When the required chains have thus been found the remaining processes of forming them into mechanisms and machines present no difficulties.[45]

In a way, Reuleaux's diagram reframes Plato's question for design to minimize the chance of wandering anywhere unexpected. There are units to combine in both direct and indirect synthesis. They're combinatorial. But direct synthesis crosses the "Unknown" as luck takes it to what's fruitful and not, while indirect synthesis uses a logical (inductive) process to search through all possible pairs and chains that are "Known" in advance. Perhaps this is OK insofar as invention (synthesis) is independent of observation when parts fuse and divide. But even then, always knowing the way to go may miss something useful that's found only by taking an uncharted route. It seems that certainty guarantees getting it right by limiting what there is to see. In most cases, this is probably fine. In most cases, there's nothing to design.

Steven Pinker considers the kinematics of thought and mental machinery. I used his apt description of human minds—they're combinatorial—earlier, in the introduction, on page 46, and it follows Reuleaux on page 302. Pinker recommends an assortment of generative paraphernalia in cognitive science. His favorite devices are from linguistics, logic, and computer science—words and rules, individuals and kinds (members and sets), compositionality (the meaning of a complex expression depends on its constituents, what they mean separately, and how they're combined), and facts in a mental database.[46] This implies that design is thought—indirect synthesis is compositional in a database of known pairs and chains. And there's evidently more—for example, Simon's hierarchically organized list structures extend words and rules to pictures and drawings. But is this enough? Without embedding, human minds may seem naively combinatorial. In practice, Pinker's list leads away from drawing with shapes and rules to vocabulary and syntax—from design to philosophy and permanent results. There's no way to see anything that hasn't been described (represented) before. This splits thinking and experience, and explains why design isn't thought. When given units combine in novel ways, there's always more to count and no reason to see. This, no doubt, is wonderfully creative, but it's barely half the story—simply being generative (recursive) à la Pinker, in the way Chomsky and Simon urge, doesn't include everything that experience holds. There are endless surprises once embedding and recursion are put together. Shapes and rules—shape grammars—are as creative as words and rules, and then more so. Parts change freely as rules are tried, even identities in the schema $x \rightarrow x$ that keep shapes the same. There is no final vocabulary—meaning is renewed whenever I choose to look again. This is calculating by seeing, and it includes design.[47]

III   USING IT TO DESIGN

We began utterly wrong in England, and we have gone on wrongly, and the consequence is that it is only the exceptional person who learns to draw very well. Now in my experiments I have reversed that process, and I find that not only does every person when he is taught rationally, and intelligently in the same way that he is taught Latin, and Greek, and mathematics, learn to draw well, but also to paint well, and to design well. But it is on a wholly different principle from that on which he is taught here in England.... We have developed an intellectual method of teaching drawing, more industrial, more practical, more artistic, and infinitely more successful.... I propose to show how art education can be as sensibly treated as Latin and mathematics. I have a great wealth of illustration here, which, if you allow me, I shall be very happy to submit to you. Probably it would interest you if I showed you some of the actual work of the children in the public schools of Boston and Massachusetts.

—Walter Smith

Design Is Calculating

Metaphors are good heuristics. In fact, there's this metaphor for metaphors and heuristics. And there's also the one I started with

(1)   design is calculating

as something to try and to prove. An alternative to it is an equivalence when I use the mathematics of part II. It's this

(2)   drawing is calculating

where drawing is both seeing and doing. Whenever I put pencil to paper, I'm calculating with shapes or symbols. But there's nothing to code in a drawing, so I don't have to use symbols in place of shapes to calculate. Shapes are fine by themselves without underlying descriptions or representations. In the introduction, I said that I wanted to do this book in a rigorous way with shapes and no words. Now I can, and in a sense, this part is a first try—at least there are a lot of drawings that are all just as rigorous and formal as symbols and code. Shapes in rules show how to change shapes in an open-ended process for drawing and design. This is to see, but it's also included logically in statements 1 and 2. They combine in the formula

(3)   design is drawing

and I like to think that the corollary

(4)   design is calculating when you don't know what you're going to see and do next

follows, as well. This completes the transition from the mostly verbal discussion in the introduction through the unfolding visual argument in parts I and II to the mostly visual presentation now. It's going from calculating by counting to calculating by seeing with the shifting (subjective) viewpoints this implies.

Statement 4 pretty much sums up how I want to approach design with shapes and rules. I've been trying to show that calculating with shapes and rules is inclusive enough to deal with anything that might come up in design when it's done visually. That's the reason embedding and transformations are needed to apply rules. First, the embedding relation—what you see is there if you can trace it out, no matter what has gone on before. Second, the transformations—what you see is like given examples of what to look for, maybe things that were noticed in the past and used. And together—embedding and transformations interact as rules are tried to calculate with shapes.

The details aren't too far from drawing when you pay attention to what you're seeing and doing. The trick is to slow this process down a little bit to describe what's going on in a mechanical way. It's easy to say and, more important, easy to see. The beginning isn't much—start with any shape

C

Intuitively, there are lines on paper, but C can also include points, planes, solids, labels, weights, etc. Shapes can have any dimension you please, both in terms of basic elements and how they're combined. In drawings, lines are one dimensional and located on planes that are two. It all depends on the algebra in which you calculate. Then a rule

$A \rightarrow B$

that shows two shapes A and B applies to C whenever

$t(A) \leq C$

that is to say, there's a transformation t such that the shape $t(A)$ is part of (embedded in) C. The rule $A \rightarrow B$ is an example of what I want to see and do, and $t(A)$ is some part of C that catches my eye because it looks like A. The result of this is another shape

$(C - t(A)) + t(B)$

The shape $t(A)$ is taken away from C, and the shape $t(B)$ that looks like B is the new part that's added back. This is the same drawing with pencil and paper, although replacing parts with new ones isn't set out explicitly. The beauty of the process—with rules, or pencil and paper—is that what I do now doesn't restrict what I see next. Shapes fuse and divide freely, whether or not they're drawn according to rules.

For example, I can add a square to a square with the rule

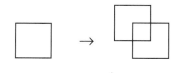

and then rotate a third square

that's neither one of the two squares I put together originally

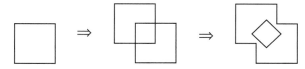

Or I can translate a chevron

to make a cross, and move another chevron in the opposite way to rotate squares

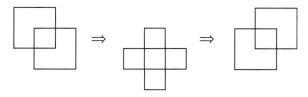

But my rule for adding squares

does more when I apply it in another way

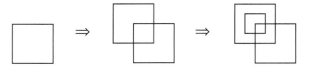

Then what I'm doing can repeat with plenty of surprises—here are four of them

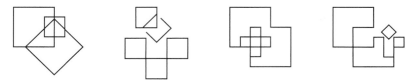

It's a lot easier to follow this with your eyes than to be consistent about it in words. Certainly, I haven't succeeded, fooling around with the squares I add and the squares I see and moving chevrons that pop up in unexpected ways. It's all a little crazy when I can change what I see and do this freely. It's hard to know what to say that isn't misleading or wrong. And really, that's the whole story. I can use rules to change shapes without being consistent about what I see. This doesn't sound like calculating, but it is. And it's what you need to design, so that you can change your mind about what you see and do as you go on. What it shows is that statement 4 isn't that far-fetched—

design is calculating when you don't know what you're going to see and do next

What a shape is depends on what rules are used, and when and how. This can vary for different rules, and, in actual fact, it changes every time any rule is tried. Yet there are some other things to consider that open up calculating even more.

As an example of what I want to see and do, the rule $A \to B$ may be too narrow. This was the problem in part II for squares and quadrilaterals. But there was a straightforward solution I could try. Instead of drawing rules or pointing to specific shapes, I could use schemas. This made calculating easier in some nice ways without compromising the embedding relation.

The new setup is pretty much the same as the one I have for rules, with the addition of variables, assignments, and predicates. There's a shape

C

and now a schema

$x \to y$

where x and y are variables that take shapes as values. These are given in an assignment g that may be restricted in some way by a predicate. The assignment defines the rule

$$g(x) \rightarrow g(y)$$

according to the predicate. This can go from any rule—then the values for x and y are simply shapes

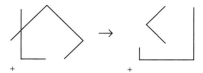

—to rules with certain prescribed properties. Maybe $y = x$ to define identities for polygons

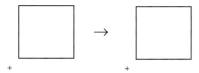

Or perhaps $y = t(x)$ for a transformation t of x

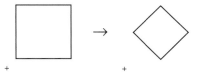

or $y = x + t(x)$

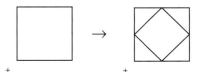

so that once a rule is applied to a part like x it can be applied again to a part like $t(x)$. This kind of recursion is neat, but it's not all that can happen in shapes, as the rule

demonstrates with the surprise square in its right side. And single rules are also possible—then x and y are given shapes, say, this square and its diagonals

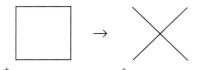

that I draw or point to in the usual way to show what they are. But no matter what rule is defined, it applies exactly as my two formulas describe. Still, it may be worthwhile to say this for schemas directly. The schema $x \to y$ applies to the shape C whenever an assignment g and a transformation t define a shape $t(g(x))$ that's part of C

$$t(g(x)) \leq C$$

The result of this is another shape

$$(C - t(g(x))) + t(g(y))$$

produced by replacing $t(g(x))$ with the shape $t(g(y))$. In most of the examples that follow, I'll be using schemas. I'll usually define them with one or two of the rules they determine under specific assignments with a short verbal description of the predicate involved, just as I've been doing. This avoids the need for a lot of technical details and lets me present everything visually. We'll just agree that predicates can be filled in as necessary. And I promise not to do anything where the details are mysterious.

A useful way to explain my formulas for schemas is to notice that the composition $t \cdot g$ in the expressions $t(g(x))$ and $t(g(y))$ generalizes the transformations. What it means for shapes to look alike can range very broadly and be decided in all sorts of different ways. I tend to show examples that depend only on Euclidean transformations—for example, shapes are alike if they're copies of the square

either because they're congruent

or because they're geometrically similar

but really anything will do. All rectangles may be alike

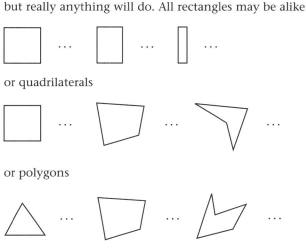

or quadrilaterals

or polygons

In fact, I can make the predicate that defines the assignment g as wild as I please. Maybe x in the schema $x \rightarrow y$ is a blob of some special kind

or any simple closed curve—whatever makes sense when you look is OK as long as there's a general transformation $t \cdot g$ for it.

It's also worth repeating that the predicates I use to define rules needn't be preserved as I calculate. I can put two quadrilaterals together

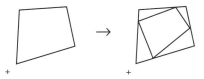

not unlike adding polygons and their transformations in the schema $x \rightarrow x + t(x)$, and then move triangles

according to the schema $x \rightarrow t(x)$. Predicates are simply a convenient way of describing rules—a way that doesn't carry over to calculating. Then descriptions don't count. There's no reason for me to be consistent about the things I see. Consistency is at root conservative—insisting that the language I've used in the past is kept as I see and do more makes calculating much too rigid. Certainly, it's logical—words make sense, so that things stay the way you say they are, and behave properly in the way you expect them to—but it isn't necessary. Why should words trump shapes when their parts can change freely in an open-ended, creative process? There's plenty of ambiguity and the paradigm (gestalt) switches that go along with it—what you see is what you get, any time you try another rule. And you can go on from whatever it is you see without ever thinking about it. There's always more to do. Ambiguity is to use. There's no reason to hesitate—

No one ever says "Stop!" Nothing blocks my way. Whatever I see is OK. Neither descriptions nor representations of shapes are needed to calculate—they don't intrude when rules are used to see and do.

So far, so good, but what about design?—that's what I want to use rules and schemas for. The problem here is to convince you that design is calculating. This is harder than it looks—not because it's difficult to produce designs by calculating, but because whatever I do may not be what you call design. Design varies so widely and unpredictably from person to person and from time to time that any calculating I do isn't likely to cover very much of it. Calculating to make designs will just have to do, with the promise that if you want to do it in another way, then shapes and rules are up to the task. And this doesn't mean starting over from scratch every time you have another idea or want to try something new, but rather adding rules or relaxing the ones you've already got to allow for more, so that designing, like seeing, is an open-ended process. This seems OK, but maybe I should look for a way to prove my claim that design is calculating. Well, this probably won't work—it's more a question of confirming a thesis in ongoing practice, and, in fact, there's a strong precedent for this in the argument that algorithms are Turing machines. I like to think that there's plenty of solid evidence in my examples. I'll trace these in a kind of personal history that shows some of the things I've tried to design by calculating. Most of what I say is pretty impressionistic, although not because I have to be so. The details are given elsewhere, so they needn't be a distraction here. It's more important now to emphasize key ideas that run through what I try and how they're expressed in rules and schemas. There's a lot to see that shows what rules can do, and most of it is just like drawing—but surely, this is already evident from statement 3

design is drawing

and what follows in statement 4 for shapes of all kinds.

Tell Me What Schema to Use

I started out with shapes and rules to generate paintings that were mostly about seeing—designs like this one

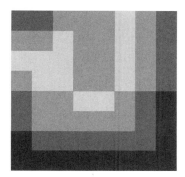

It's defined in an algebra $U_{12} + W_{22}$ for shapes made up of lines, and planes with weights—here, weights are colors that change from dark to light as they add up to produce an ambiguous kind of layering. My original rules were a little different from the rules I use now. They separated shapes and colors in order to generate designs, but in concert they worked pretty much as the rule

The idea was to connect squares in continuous paths that followed one another and intertwined. This elaborated the rule

that's much easier to describe in words without confusing what's going on. The rule colors square regions in a recursive process

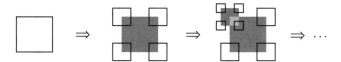

The lines in the left side of the rule

fix the boundary of the square plane in the right side, and they're replaced with lines for additional squares at the four corners of the plane. This is expressed inclusively to allow for other shapes besides squares in the schema

$$b(x) \rightarrow x + t_0(b(x)) + \cdots + t_n(b(x))$$

It's a little too complicated for my taste, so breaking it down into a pair of easier schemas is helpful. First, I have

$$b(x) \rightarrow x$$

to produce areas or regions (maximal planes) from the sum of their boundaries, and then next comes

$$b(x) \rightarrow t_0(b(x)) + \cdots + t_n(b(x))$$

to replace a shape with a number of geometrically similar copies. But I've already shown this in summary form

$$x \rightarrow \sum t(x)$$

for fractals. In fact, the design

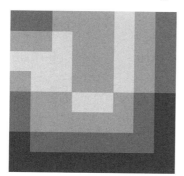

was inspired by David Hilbert's famous curve. More generally, though, I was applying two easy schemas from part II—schemas that did a lot of other things, as well, and that I still use today. This is something to keep in mind. The same schemas can be used to produce widely different results in different contexts, although the calculating doesn't change. This provides a positive reply to students when they try to calculate with shapes and rules for the first time—"What schema should I use?" It's a good question that experience finally answers. But, in the meantime, schemas and the rules they define can be shared and used in your own way—it's copying without repeating the past. There's something to learn in the classroom that works in the studio when students ask, "What should I draw?" Creative design can be taught like language and mathematics in school, with examples, rules, and practice and the opportunity to experiment freely. Rules make this possible because they apply to shapes in terms of embedding and transformations. But I'll come back to teaching a little later on, after I've presented more evidence to back up my claim that calculating with shapes and rules is creative.

I've been talking about schemas and rules for my designs. I did a lot of them, but one of the key ideas that worked over and over again in surprising ways was to add shapes and their transformations. This is minimally expressed in the schema

$$x \rightarrow x + t(x)$$

that defines the rule

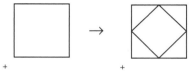

used for the shapes in the series

And, in fact, this provides for the six designs in figure 1 that keep to what I did with the schema $b(x) \rightarrow x + t_0(b(x)) + \cdots + t_n(b(x))$ to explore alternative ways of coloring regions. Whatever I've said about counting in the past, permuting colors is sometimes informative—as long as you know there's always more to see in another way. And as I went on, it seemed obvious that with all I could see and do with shapes and rules—my two examples merely begin to scratch the surface—designing and calculating weren't too far apart. But not everyone agreed.

The problem was evident—I was calculating to make designs in my own way. I could do anything I wanted and call it design. How about producing things that were designed by others with sensitivity and skill? What about some real examples that had the stamp of prior approval? Certainly, this wasn't possible, especially for things that weren't as regular and hard-edged as my designs. But, as luck would have it, I didn't have to search very far to go on. There were plenty of things to design with shapes and rules wherever I happened to look. It was surprisingly easy, and there were others to help who saw this, too. Design was calculating. But in fact I knew that, and I already had a way to go.

Figure 1

What the Thinking Eye Sees

After I tried schemas for my own designs and saw how well they worked to define rules, I tested them out on examples from Paul Klee's *The Thinking Eye*. I've already talked about the opening lessons in Klee's *Pedagogical Sketchbook* and the way they suggest a kind of visual calculating with shapes and rules. But there are more examples in *The Thinking Eye* of far greater variety. It's a perfect laboratory for schemas with exciting experiments ready to try.

There are plenty of designs like these two

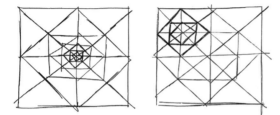

that I can get directly with rules. The rule

that's defined for squares in the schema $x \to x + t(x)$ is already familiar. And two additional rules introduce the idea of dividing shapes or the regions they bound—here, for the diagonals of squares

and for horizontal or vertical cuts

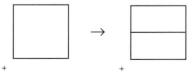

This implies division rules in a new schema

$$x \to \mathrm{div}(x)$$

—divide *x*—that extends my kind of calculating. In fact, $x \rightarrow x + t(x)$ and $x \rightarrow \text{div}(x)$ overlap in some nice ways. The rule

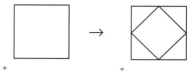

answers to both—its right side is the sum of two squares, or it's divided into four triangles and also a square. Together, the two schemas do a lot of neat things, and in the next section, I'll show this in a series of interrelated examples. But first I need a more typical example from *The Thinking Eye* where schemas are conspicuously required. There's something useful on almost every page—something surprising to see—but one design is especially right for how it looks and for what it shows. This is the "palm-leaf umbrella"

and it's within the immediate reach of the schemas I have right now, in particular, the pair of schemas above: $x \rightarrow x + t(x)$ and $x \rightarrow \text{div}(x)$. Only a couple of small changes are needed for the job. In many ways, schemas are like shapes—they're easy to change.

The palm-leaf umbrella is a playful design, yet Klee presents it under a serious rubric—

Irregularity means greater freedom without transgressing the law.

But is this the kind of freedom calculating allows? Certainly, calculating is a rigorous process that means following the letter of the law. The rule

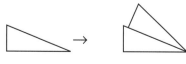

is defined in the schema $x \rightarrow x + t(x)$, and it evidently produces a pinwheel that's cyclically symmetric

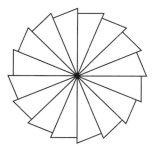

when calculating goes like this

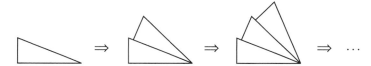

Not a bad design, easy to get, and a little something like Klee's palm-leaf umbrella. Nonetheless, everything seems far too regular in the way you'd expect when recursively applying a single rule that adds two congruent right triangles hypotenuse to side. But this is readily fixed in the new schema

$$x \rightarrow x + x'$$

where x and x' are both triangles, and not always similar ones x and $t(x)$. (The schema is another version of the schema $x \rightarrow A + B$ for spatial relations. I showed how to use it for arbitrary shapes A and B, along with its inverse $A + B \rightarrow x$, in several examples in part II.) The rule

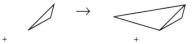

is defined in my new schema, and so is the alternative rule

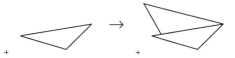

In fact, I can show how all of the triangles in the palm-leaf umbrella are related—no surprise. This sort of parametric variation in rules is already allowed in my schema for quadrilaterals that includes the rule

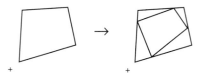

Perhaps the schema $x \rightarrow x + t(x)$ would be more productive if it were expressed in some other way that's a little more relaxed, maybe as

$$x \rightarrow x + t \cdot g(x)$$

in terms of a general transformation defined in a composition $t \cdot g$. There's probably some abstract algebra here that's worth pursuing. I'd have to be more explicit about what I wanted, but really that's an exercise to try. Right now, it makes more sense to go on calculating with its concrete results. The various rules in the schema $x \rightarrow x + x'$ give me the series of shapes in figure 2.

   Still, the final shape I show in figure 2 isn't Klee's palm-leaf umbrella—there are also quadrilaterals

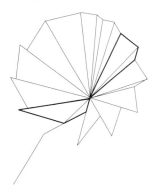

and a pentagon

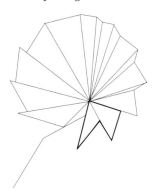

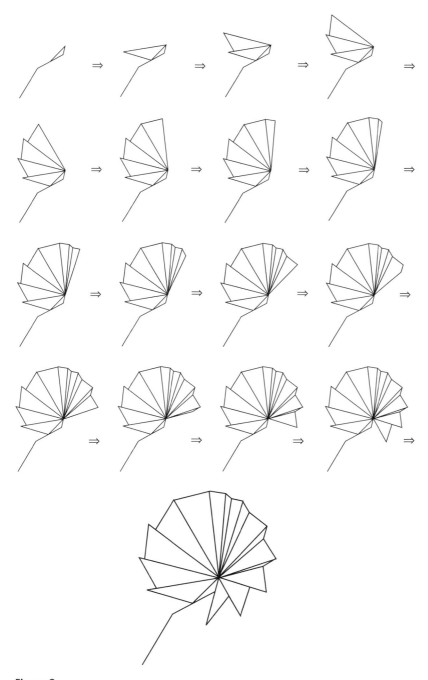

Figure 2

I seem to be stuck. But no, this isn't the end of it—I can do much more with my schemas to get exactly the results I want. Look at it another way and see how it works. The diagonal of a quadrilateral forms twin triangles

and it's the same for a pentagon with a concavity, at least in the special case where a diagonal and an edge are collinear

Shapes are always ambiguous, and the ambiguity is something to use. It seems that I already know how to go on. If I apply the inverse of my division schema $x \rightarrow \text{div}(x)$, that is to say, the schema

$\text{div}(x) \rightarrow x$

I can erase diagonals in polygons in just the right way. For quadrilaterals in the palm-leaf umbrella, I need the rule

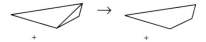

and this one

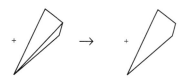

and for the pentagon, the rule

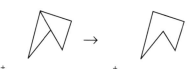

is fine. Inverses often come in handy—the schema $x \rightarrow b(x)$ determines the boundary of a shape with lines, planes, or solids, while its inverse $b(x) \rightarrow x$ works to color regions in my designs. And then there's the palm-leaf umbrella

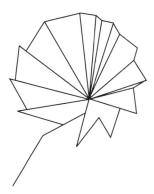

But be careful. Inverses may not do what you expect. For example, the inverse

$$x + x' \rightarrow x$$

of the schema $x \rightarrow x + x'$ doesn't work for quadrilaterals and pentagons. When I use the rules it defines, I'm left with an ugly gap

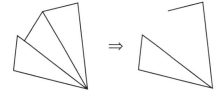

Yet beauty is in the eye of the beholder—perhaps this outcome is good for something else. And I can always go on from anything I have with shapes and rules.

Working through Klee's drawing in this way isn't meant to recapitulate what he did—no one knows for sure, and it's no good relying on what he says. Rather, I'm trying to show that schemas are up to Klee's kind of designs. The rules I need are included in a handful of schemas that are easy to use. And the rules themselves are easy to apply to shapes in terms of embedding and transformations. Embedding ensures there's no letter of the law—I can calculate with triangles and see quadrilaterals and pentagons—and general transformations allow for as much irregularity as I want—parametric variation of any kind is possible. Rules and freedom go hand in hand—the one implies the other.

I'm staking the plausibility of the metaphor "design is calculating" as a heuristic and equivalence squarely on my success with schemas, especially as I'm able to use them more and more to calculate with shapes and to make designs in different styles from different places and times. This is another kind of freedom, and it provides a very practical kind of proof that calculating works. There's seeing and doing, and that's all it takes when rules apply to shapes. I guess "design is calculating" really is more of a thesis than a theorem. The evidence adds up, but not to logical certainty, just to empirical belief.

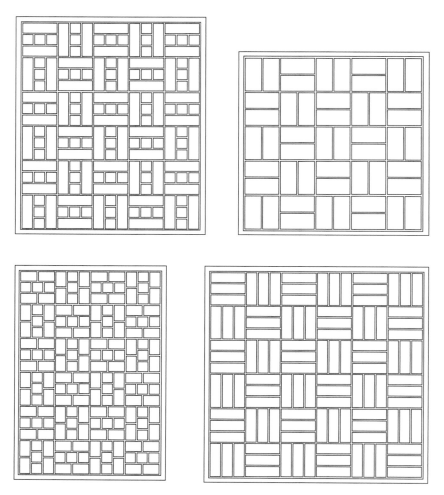

Figure 3

Chinese Lattice Designs—Seeing What You Do

There are myriad ways schemas can be used to produce designs. I especially like the Chinese lattice designs that fill window frames. Most of these form regular patterns of the kind shown in figure 3. They're taken from Daniel Sheets Dye's *A Grammar of Chinese Lattice*. It's a wonderful and extensive catalogue that's hard to put down. It's a joy to see. And in fact, like *The Thinking Eye*, it holds the material for endless experiments with your eyes.

The four lattices I've shown are checkerboard designs like this one

in which a given motif

is inscribed in squares in a rectangular array. The "H" alternates this way and that, left to right from side to side

to correspond to contrasting colors or distinct labels (symbols). This makes it easy to use my schemas—first, $x \rightarrow x + t(x)$ to produce the checkerboard pattern, followed by $x \rightarrow \mathrm{div}(x)$ to inscribe the H and divide squares. There are two rules for the checkerboard

(1)

(2)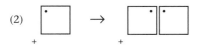

where x is a square and an asymmetrically placed point to orient the H with respect to left and right diagonals. And going back and forth from rule 1 to rule 2, I get the series of shapes

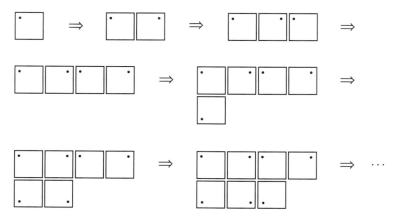

Then there's a single rule for the H to divide squares

Of course, the H I've given isn't the only motif I can use. Squares are divided in many different ways in Chinese lattices to make checkerboard patterns. In the designs in figure 3, the motifs vary in the following way

to define new regions, and in this lattice

there's a surprising checkerboard pattern, too, when squares in a diagonal grid are divided into regions so

This raises an important issue. I began with a corpus of shapes—designs in a given style—and specified rules in my schemas to define the corpus and to produce other designs of the same sort, and nothing else. There's even an easy kind of stylistic change where I add rules to divide squares with new motifs. In many ways, this is all very convincing. I can recognize what's in the style—do my rules generate it?—and I can produce novel instances of the style that haven't been seen before. I can go from known to new, and I can say exactly what's happening in terms of the rules I try. And that's the problem. When I look at the lattice just above—or the one with the H motif, for that matter—I don't automatically see the checkerboard or how its squares are divided. In other rule-based systems in which shapes are represented in terms of symbols (vocabulary and syntax), this is just something to get used to—learning the "right" way to see according to given rules. There's no ambiguity. Nonetheless, I have a creative way to handle any discrepancies between the rules I apply to produce designs and what designs look like. This is what I set out to do at the beginning of this book with embedding and transformations, and the effort pays off handsomely when I calculate with shapes and rules. That's why the mathematics was worth doing and getting right in the first place. Now calculating seems almost too easy, and it may be something of an anticlimax. I simply augment my rules with identities defined in the schema

$$x \rightarrow x$$

to pick out any other parts I see—according to Dye, "octagons"

"octagon-squares"

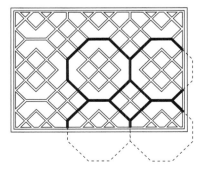

and "supplemental squares"

But, really, I can try any identity or rule—I'm free to see and do as I please.

A strictly generative account of style may not be enough. Saying what you see as you make what you want matters, too. Ambiguity isn't noise, it's something to use. And this is how shapes and rules work. I can always add the identities I need to see what's important and describe it independent of the rules I apply to produce designs. Embedding and transformations make this possible once shapes fuse, so that generative and descriptive aspects of style are on equal footing and can change with ongoing experience. Understanding a style is more than connoisseurship and forgery. There are other things to see and to say, as well, that go beyond recognizing instances and copying them in a particular way, or branching out to make new ones. And I needn't miss any of this when I calculate with shapes and rules.

There's always more to see and do. Not all of the lattice designs in Dye's *Grammar* are regular patterns. In particular, there are marvelous "ice-rays"

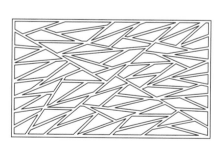 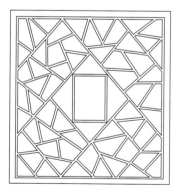

To appreciate [these] designs ... one needs to see ice forming on quiet water on a cold night. Straight lines meet longer lines, making unique and beautiful patterns. The Chinese term this *ice-line*, or lines formed by cracking ice; I have described it as the result of a molecular strain in shrinking or breaking, but more recent observations and photographs seem to prove that it is a conventionalization of ice-formation which has become traditional.

And by now, it shouldn't be a surprise that ice-rays are made by calculating.

Let's try the ice-ray lattice

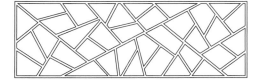

It's one of my favorites—in this case because what I see looks hard to do, but isn't. I need four kinds of rules like these

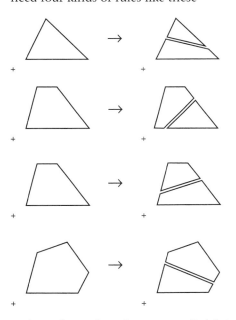

perhaps from the schema $x \to \mathrm{div}(x)$ to divide triangles, quadrilaterals in alternative ways, and pentagons. Then it's one more case of parametric variation using general transformations $t \cdot g$. Dye summarizes the process nicely—

In the case of the ice-ray pattern [the artisan] divides the whole area into large and equal light spots, and then subdivides until he reaches the size desired; he seldom uses dividers in this work.

Or I might think of my rules in another way in terms of a fractal-like schema

$$x \to x' + x''$$

where one polygon x is replaced by the sum of two, x' and x''. Whatever I do, it's the same—visually, there's the series of shapes in figure 4. Maybe the series is excessive and even a little indulgent—I like to draw—but it seems to me that it's worth seeing once for ice-rays that rules work throughout; and after all, I'm only showing half of

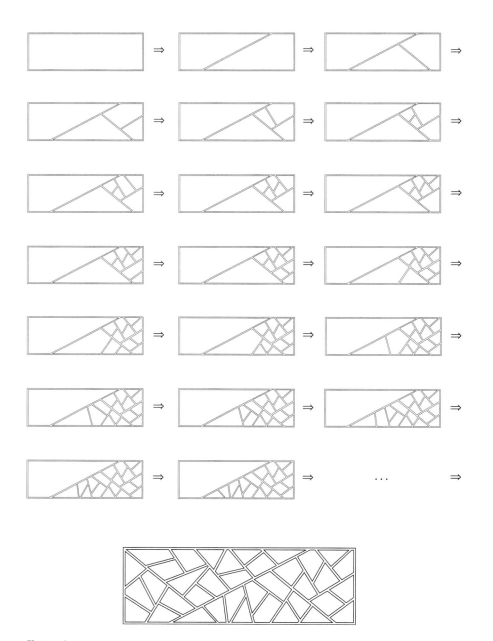

Figure 4

the process. In fact, the process isn't hard to describe. When I first thought about making ice-rays, I had Dye and the schema $x \rightarrow \mathrm{div}(x)$ in mind. This is what I said—

One can imagine a Chinese artisan, summoned to a building site, bringing with him tools and implements and a collection of finely finished sticks. Shown a rectangular window frame, he is asked to create an ice-ray lattice. He begins his design by selecting a stick of the appropriate length and carefully attaching it between two edges of the existing rectangular frame, thus forming two quadrilateral regions. He continues his work by subdividing one of these areas into a triangle and a pentagon. He further divides the triangle into a triangle and a quadrilateral; he divides the pentagon into a quadrilateral and a pentagon. Each subdivision is made in the same way: attach an appropriately sized stick between two edges of a previously constructed triangle or quadrilateral or pentagon, so that it does not cross previously inserted pieces. Each stage of the construction is stable; each stage follows the same rules.

Ice-rays make it easy to be a "rationalist"—to believe that available technologies, properties of materials, and methods of construction determine designs. And, to some extent, these constraints do matter as they're expressed in schemas and rules. Rules allow for freedom and constraints—going back and forth from one to the other is always possible. In a way, though, it's ironic. Many times, the truly hard problems are to fix constraints that aren't immediately spatial, for example, so that rules apply in the right logical or temporal sequence. But the seemingly effortless switch from constraints to freedom via identities and other rules is more impressive. That's where embedding and transformations really make a difference.

I've tacitly assumed all along that rules are nondeterministic, that is to say, they can be applied in various sequences under alternative transformations. This is the source of creativity, in Chomsky's sense, for vocabulary and syntax when different things are produced combining the same constituents, and there's a kind of ambiguity, too, when the same thing results in different ways. But shapes and rules give much more. Creativity and ambiguity have an Aristotelian origin, as well, that's evident when I use the schema $x \rightarrow x$ to define identities. Then I can divide shapes to see as I please.

For lattice designs, there are unlimited opportunities for variety and novelty in a traditional style. Even so, rules may apply in more specific ways. For example, not counting the pair of leftmost divisions, the ice-ray

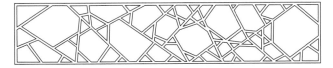

is produced from left to right

But this may be a fluke—lucky accidents and surprises where there's something unexpected to see are a wonderful part of art. Nonetheless, I can also use some familiar tricks from part II to make rules work the way I want, to guarantee reliable results. Perhaps it's important for the main divisions in ice-rays to be "orthogonal" as my example shows—then rules like this one

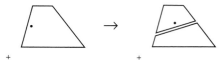

that incorporates a point will do the job

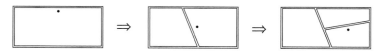

Or maybe "parallel" divisions that don't intersect are more desirable—then I can use a point in the rule

and in other rules like it to calculate so

And I can also give rules for lattice designs with other kinds of symmetry, for example, where divisions rotate in a nice way

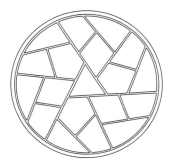

It's easy to do this for any transformation—simply show how it works in both sides of a rule in the schema $x \rightarrow \mathrm{div}(x)$. In particular, the rule

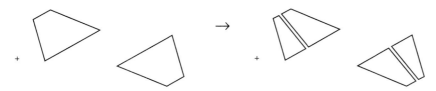

is good for a half-turn π. Then the compound schema

$$x + \pi(x) \rightarrow \mathrm{div}(x) + \pi(\mathrm{div}(x))$$

gives rules for any polygon x, even if it looks a little complicated. Still, there's no reason to worry. I can recast what the schema does in a two stage process in which the schema $x \rightarrow \mathrm{div}(x)$ is applied first to x and next to $\pi(x)$. This guarantees that $\mathrm{div}(x)$ and $\pi(\mathrm{div}(x))$ are both in the design as long as $\mathrm{div}(\pi(x)) = \pi(\mathrm{div}(x))$. Or equivalently, there's the schema

$$x + \pi(x) \rightarrow \mathrm{div}(x) + \mathrm{div}(\pi(x))$$

But in fact, $x \rightarrow \mathrm{div}(x)$ alone may really be enough—simply let

$$x + \pi(x) \rightarrow \mathrm{div}(x + \pi(x))$$

I can always divide more than polygons. Schemas and the rules they define work with remarkable ease.

Of course, there are other ways to change ice-rays that are of equal interest. Just as checkerboard lattice designs contain different motifs, ice-rays can be divided in alternative ways. In particular, there are axial motifs with three to six arms

Usually, these devices are used once centrally to start

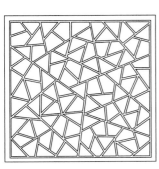 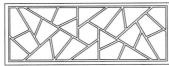 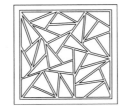

but occasionally they repeat in some delightful ways

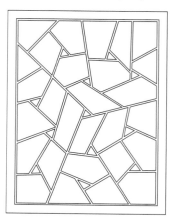

With shapes and rules, it's easy to add new motifs and to take advantage of what they do. It requires nothing more than a drawing to show what I want to see and do. That's how rules are defined. And that's all I need to calculate.

Earlier on, near the beginning of this part, I said that the same schemas worked in different contexts to produce different results. The schema $x \rightarrow \mathrm{div}(x)$ that I've been using to divide regions in ice-rays is a perfect example of this. I've already shown that the schema is good for other kinds of lattice designs and, as an inverse, for Klee's palm-leaf umbrella. But more conspicuously, it works in various algebras for painting and architecture. The painter Georges Vantongerloo did a large number of designs like this one

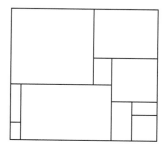

in which he starts with a pinwheel division and then makes orthogonal cuts. No one would ever call it an ice-ray, but it really is. And then the Portuguese architect Alvaro Siza relies on the same idea in designs for floor plans in his ongoing housing project at Malagueira—about twelve hundred units to date that repeat at least thirty-five plans. Here's one design that's produced with a biaxial cut followed by three more divisions

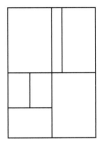

Ice-rays can be used widely in many different ways; but, of much greater importance, schemas can, too. This is certainly prima facie evidence that design is calculating, although showing that calculating pays off in studio teaching and creative practice is the real test. Professional disciplines are apt to have stubborn customs and recalcitrant standards—that keeps them exclusive. And art and design are hardly exceptions to this rule, so it helps to have more to go on before asking artists and designers to try something new that breaks with traditional methods of teaching and practice. Whatever they are, teaching and practice simply can't be calculating with shapes and rules. No—calculating is never ever creative.

They're Shapes before They're Plans

I'm going to do Andrea Palladio's famous villa plans, with the Villa Foscari as my main example

They form a style apart, vital and never diminishing in the capacity to entice others into emulation, but evasive of definition.

I'm interested in Palladio, just as I'm interested in Klee and Chinese window grilles, and my paintings, as well, to show that design is calculating. But of greater importance for buildings is that functional, social, and aesthetic relationships—things in the architect's Vitruvian canon of firmness, commodity, and delight—aren't beyond shapes and rules. Many find this surprising, even though these relationships are expressed in form. They're all about shapes, so calculating according to rules makes sense. However, I'm not going to do Palladio's system of proportions as part of what I show. Numerical relationships are easy in my schemas and rules, yet calculating with numbers doesn't buy anything new and may give the wrong impression. Rather, it's the look of Palladian villa plans—this is more than the usual stuff of calculating—that's my central concern. But first, notice a few additional things that this isn't about. Architects can be remarkably insecure when it comes to what they do, so it's worth trying to avoid common misconceptions from the start. Some ambiguity is lost in prefatory disclaimers, although there may be more to gain in other ways. What I'm doing isn't a commentary on contemporary architecture and how it's practiced, or an argument for classical principles of building or for the plan as a method of designing. Nor is my interest in Palladio historical. I don't know what he did to get his villa plans, although he's pretty good at saying how to design them in *The Four Books of Architecture*, and that's really as far as my scholarship goes. What Palladio draws, not what he builds, is what I'm interested in—plans are shapes before they're plans. That's why I can calculate with them. But the technical devices I use aren't necessarily the same as Palladio's—showing how to calculate always takes precedence, even if the results I get and the steps along the way are like his in many ways. My only stake in this is to show more about calculating with shapes and rules, and that calculating includes design, at least to the extent that I can make convincing plans without too much fuss. In fact, the schemas and rules I use are not unlike the ones I've used multiple times before. This buttresses my repertoire of schemas and recommends them again for teaching and practice—in particular, it extends what I can do in the classroom and how this works creatively in the studio. My way of calculating with shapes and rules is always open-ended. Knowing how to design something spatial—Palladian villa plans—may go farther than you expect.

It seems intuitive enough that there's more to villa plans than there is to Chinese lattice designs to make my case that design is calculating. Yet it's difficult to be sure about judgments like this when every shape of dimension one or more—even a single line

------

—has indefinitely many parts. There's a lot going on in shapes, all of them, that encourages wandering around in an aimless way. You never know how it's going to turn out. What there is in a line is always a surprise. And in fact I've been arguing from the start that being able to handle whatever comes up—to deal with the ambiguity—is a prerequisite if calculating is going to be of any use in design. It's calculating by seeing, yet once you can do it, you can also proceed with a plan in mind. Sometimes, it helps to calculate in stages—now, so that villa plans are produced in a straightforward manner that's easy to follow and explain. Four stages work perfectly for the schemas and rules I want to use, and they make good architectural sense—there are (1) walls, (2) rooms, (3) porticoes, and (4) windows and doors. What works for one thing, though, shouldn't be taken too far in a different direction. This is a sequence just for calculating, and it doesn't imply a hierarchy in plans. Hierarchies and such are always possible in other ways, for example, retrospectively in my topologies, but they aren't something I'm going to pursue seriously here. Defining villa plans is my only practical concern, and it's a must before I can try anything else.

This is the grid of walls

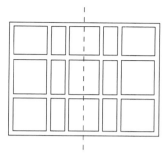

for the Villa Foscari, with an axis running through the middle column of rectangles. Bilateral symmetry is a characteristic feature of villa plans, and it's preserved in everything I do.

The rooms ought to be distributed on each side of the entry and hall: and it is to be observed, that those on the right correspond to those on the left, that so the fabrick may be the same in one place as in the other.

I can define the grid in terms of the schema

$$x \rightarrow x + x'$$

where x and x' are rectangles with dimensions that fit in Palladio's system of proportions. And the trick I used for symmetric ice-rays works perfectly again, to reflect the schema in this way

$$x + R(x) \rightarrow x + x' + R(x + x')$$

so that both sides of the grid are produced at the same time. Rectangles are added either vertically or horizontally. This is evident in two separate cases. First consider what happens when x is on axis, so that $x + R(x) = x$

Then, either $x' + R(x') = x'$, as in the rule

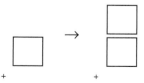

that builds a column of rectangles, or this isn't so, and I have a rule

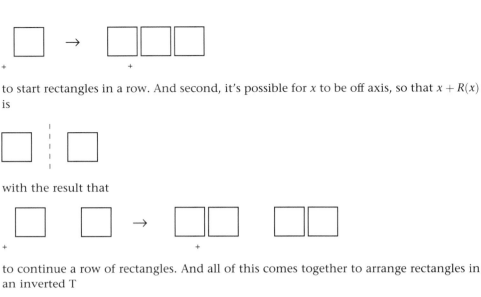

to start rectangles in a row. And second, it's possible for x to be off axis, so that $x + R(x)$ is

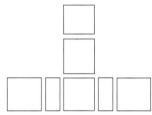

with the result that

to continue a row of rectangles. And all of this comes together to arrange rectangles in an inverted T

But I still need rules to fill in open areas, and to add a bounding rectangle. Two schemas do the job, and they make a good exercise—draw what you see and then what you want to specify the left and right sides of a rule of the kind you need. I'll say a little more about defining schemas in this way later for the Villa Barbaro, with a drawn example. In the meantime, there's something else I need to do of more immediate concern.

The problem is to combine rectangles to get the right room layout. To me, this is the heart of Palladian design—

A unique feature of Palladio's sketches or the plates to his *Quattro Libri* is the uniformity of schema in plans.

The schema $x \to \mathrm{div}(x)$ provides for the details that are needed to make this work. More precisely, I'll use the reflection of the schema's inverse—it's the opposite of what I did in ice-ray lattices—in this way

$$\mathrm{div}(x) + R(\mathrm{div}(x)) \to x + R(x)$$

Rules of the following kind are defined in this schema to form larger rectangular spaces in a recursive process

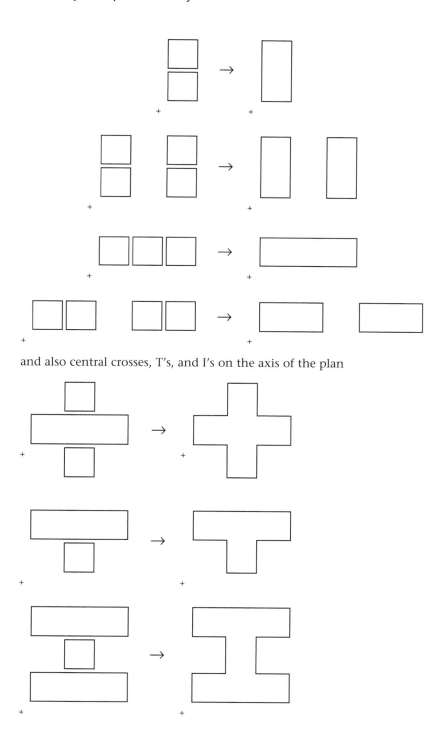

and also central crosses, T's, and I's on the axis of the plan

The rules are applied in this four-term series

for the Villa Foscari. Of course, additional room layouts are readily defined as well. And it would be nice to know how many.

Among the twenty surviving villas and twenty-odd projects known from drawings and the *Quattro Libri*, there are few instances of a repeated plan, motive or composition in mass; Palladio would produce at most two or three versions of a particular scheme before reaching out in an entirely new direction. The common core within this variety is a particular conception of architectural harmony and composition.

Questions of proportion aside, this depends on the number of rectangles in the original grid of walls. For a three-by-three grid

there are twenty distinct possibilities

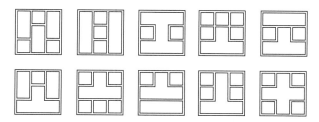

of which two—the fourth one with a central rectangle surrounded by seven squares, so that there's an open side, and the last one with a cross—appear in *The Four Books of Architecture* in the Villa Angarano and the Villa Barbaro. Then for the Villa Foscari and a five-by-three grid, there are two hundred ten alternative room layouts. Palladio includes seven of these in *The Four Books*, and one twice—it's remarkable how much more there is to do. Of course, this is the kind of configurational enumeration that I've been loath to recommend. Nonetheless, it's not without precedent in design. In fact, there are pattern books and the like—ones of late vintage and of combinatorial interest include polyominos, rectangular dissections, and Lionel March's remarkable taxonomy of all floor plans in terms of planar maps. It's useful to know what's possible, unless it interferes with seeing. Then the course is clear—stop counting!

Porticoes come next.

Often the porch is the only antique reference in the design; all the rest of the detail is simple geometry, which is consistent with the concept of a hierarchy of elements.

Porticoes and like devices line up with interior walls, and when there's more than one portico or whatever, they line up together, as well. There are various schemas for this that form a kind of architectural lexicon—I show how to define one entry below for the Villa Barbaro—but the logic of schemas is pretty straightforward. On one side of the plan, there's almost always a portico—either in antis or prostyle, as in the Villa Foscari. And then on the opposite side of the plan, there's a portico in antis, a wall inflection like this one

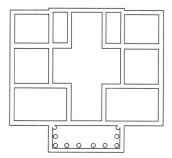

at the back of the Villa Foscari, or nothing at all.

Everything is ready for windows and doors. On axis, there are main entrances— at least one and usually two—that are obligatory, and interior doors line up with them. By now, the schemas for this should be evident. But off axis, things are a little more challenging. There are also enfilades, that is to say, windows and doors are aligned as the main entrances and interior doors are on axis. Drawing makes this practicable in rules. Put a line between two external walls and insert windows—vertically to respect the symmetry of the plan in the obvious way

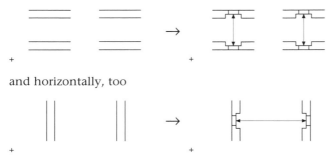

and horizontally, too

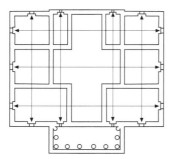

with this result

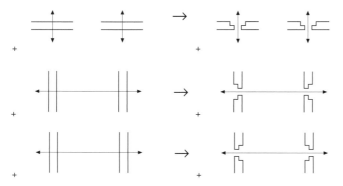

Then, where lines cut internal walls, put doors

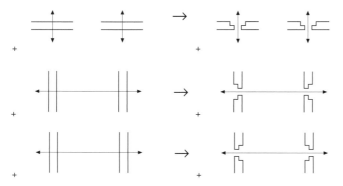

It's really kind of neat to see how easy this actually is, just seeing and doing wall by wall and door by door

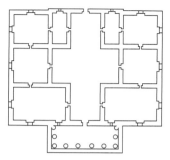

so that enfilades are formed automatically.

That's it. There's the Villa Foscari, only what else is possible? That's what schemas are for, to define rules that do more. And the examples in figure 5 show a representative sample of results—some of them are from Palladio and others are forgeries, and the two kinds aren't easy to tell apart. This can be a lot of fun, and it seems to me that it's in the spirit of *The Four Books of Architecture*. I can't help thinking Palladio meant his treatise to be used, and not simply as a static record of his designs. Drawings without instructions would have been enough for that. With shapes and rules, I have drawings and, in fact, drawings as instructions. Once again, design is calculating.

But there's a lot more to Palladio than I've shown with my schemas. I can use them speculatively in various ways, perhaps to track down Palladio's kin in design or to explore a host of novelties that bear a family resemblance. Palladio's most famous design is the Villa Rotonda

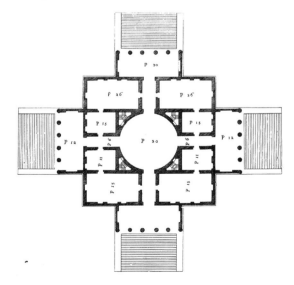

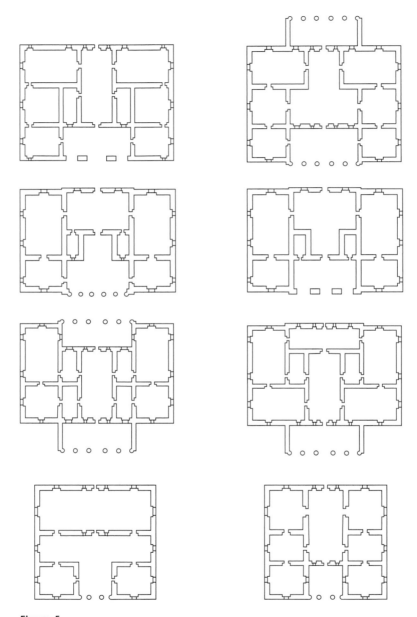

Figure 5

But this is probably too easy given the schemas I already have. It's enough to reflect them with respect to a second axis of symmetry located in a few distinct ways, and then to add the little more that's needed to handle centrally placed domes. The technique is already established in what I've been doing. So let's try another design that doesn't seem as straightforward at first blush and see how it goes. The Villa Barbaro at Maser—I mentioned it earlier when I set out my catalogue of three-by-three room layouts—is a good example. This is how Palladio draws it in *The Four Books of Architecture*

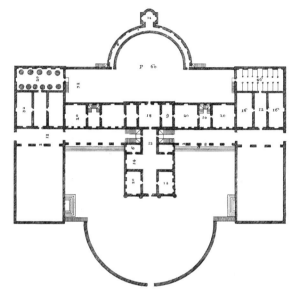

To understand how this design works tests schemas and rules in a new way. The villa was built for Daniele and Marcantonio Barbaro. It includes common public spaces in the main rectangular block and a row of private living spaces that the brothers shared equally, one of them to the left and the other to the right. And certainly, the design is different from the villa plans shown in figure 5. In particular, look at the stairs that divide the building close to its middle. What kind of entranceways are these, from the sides, symmetric but off axis? Moreover, the villa is complicated in other interesting ways. I like to describe it as separate buildings, one in front of the other, and there's good evidence for this in the actual villa, in photographs, and in other drawings (notably, the famous drawings of Bertotti Scamozzi). But is there anything to suggest two distinct buildings in Palladio's plan as it's actually drawn in his *Four Books*? Suppose this is exclusively an exercise with respect to the schemas I have for villa plans. The austerity and rigor smack of logic and reason, and this isn't at all misguided. Schemas and rules can be applied forensically to explain existing designs, just as they're used creatively to produce new ones. And my schemas give a definite answer—the Villa Barbaro is, in fact, the sum of two buildings.

Let's see how this works in terms of specific schemas and rules. First there's the main rectangular block

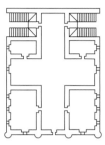

and then, just behind it, a single row of nine spaces

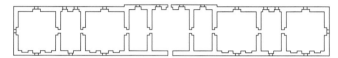

The central space in the row and the twin flanking spaces abut the main block, but the row and the block must be separate structures. This is the only way to ensure that there are enfilades—otherwise, windows and doors wouldn't make any sense. They would look like this

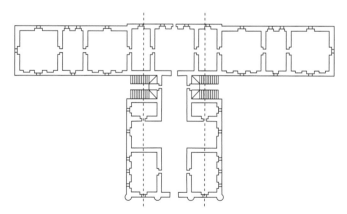

in a haphazard arrangement where not everything aligns as it should. My schemas don't allow for this, and Palladio simply wouldn't do it.

Now, it's easy to make plans. The back building is merely a symmetric row of rectangles—not a typical Palladian room layout, yet one nonetheless with a wall inflection and a horizontal enfilade—and the front building is in my catalogue of three-by-three room layouts, here as a plan with the correct dimensions

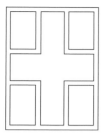

Still, there are the stairs—what should I do about them? They partially fill the two corner rectangles at the top, according to the rule

and thereby provide an alternative "portico." The rule is easy enough to define in the following way: draw what you want to change—that's the left side of the rule—and then draw what you want this to be—that's the right side. This seems almost trivial given the usual difficulties writing computer code, when I have to divide things into constituents, define them separately, and specify how they interact now and forever. But nothing has to be segmented or rationalized in this way to calculate. Drawing the rule works flawlessly, precisely because I don't have to say what anything is. Shapes don't have definite parts. I just trace what I see and do, with no divisions whatsoever, and go on—perhaps next to entrances that are put in like windows to define enfilades. And with a little jiggling, the rule is in a schema that applies generally. Shapes show how to change shapes as I calculate. This is calculating by drawing, first to define rules and then to use them. It's exactly what I want, and it's perfect for design.

But don't rules freeze Palladio in an academic style, so that his villas are set permanently outside of ongoing experience? This is the question I asked earlier for checkerboard lattice designs, and my answer remains exactly the same—

NO!

Now it's an emphatic "no" to academicism and the reductive nothing-but-ism it inevitably implies. And it's a rigorous "no" that I can justify on technical grounds, not a romantic response that simply feels good. The romantic "no" is an answer that's easy to give, easy to believe, easy to applaud, and hard to prove. It's right, but not at the expense of calculating. When you look at it another way, there's no reason for a split between romantic freedom and doing it by the numbers with shapes and rules. Calculating and freedom aren't incommensurable. Because rules are defined in terms of embedding and transformations, I can apply the same rules in different ways to change myriad parts of shapes, and I can alter rules and add them any way I please without ever having to stop what I'm doing and start over. There's no discrepancy between what I do and what I see next to go on—the one includes the other as shapes fuse and divide. It's calculating, through and through. The identities defined in the schema $x \to x$ may not do very much, but they let me see lattice designs in novel ways and show how calculating can be open-ended. In fact, the way identities work guarantees this kind of freedom and flexibility for all rules. The ease with which I can define schemas and use them to play around—for example, with the plan for the Villa Barbaro—is added proof. No wonder styles change and evolve freely. It's the chance to go on to something else whenever I look again that makes calculating with shapes and rules worthwhile. Calculating and experience are the same—there are rules for whatever I see and do. But these aren't rules for the academy—not with a grammarian's small "a" to enforce current standards, conventions, and norms, and not with Plato's capital "A" to grasp the eternal and unchangeable, either. There's no vocabulary in practice to distinguish good and bad usage when it comes to design. Shapes are filled with ambiguity—there's a lot to see and do wandering around. Calculating and experience are always new.

Seeing Won't Do—Design Needs Words

I'm afraid I may be giving a false impression. Design is drawing—true enough, it's calculating with shapes and rules. Yet most of the time words are involved, too, to say what designs are for and to connect them to other things. I've already done a lot of talking to describe rules as they apply to produce Chinese lattice designs and Palladian villa plans. Take my rules for villa plans—they're about villas and not just the shapes that go together to make them. When I combined the spaces in a grid of walls, I was describing rooms—central ones and the symmetric ones to their left and right. And when I defined an additional rule to alter the corner spaces in my room layout of the Villa Barbaro, I wasn't thinking about rectangles per se but about entrances, stairs, and porticoes. Villa plans are of functional, social, and aesthetic interest—they involve more than shapes—and different aspects of these concerns play into design at different times. What I say matters as much as drawing and calculating. Seeing won't do—design needs words. How can I manage this with rules, and how can I connect these rules and the rules I use to calculate with shapes in a single process? Filling in the details is important to make design seamless, so that a confluence of diverse and changing interests can be handled all at once. Designers and especially architects like to say that they're "generalists," and maybe it's really true. Design may not be about anything in particular but about a host of different things at different times. I'm going to show how this works using rules to calculate with shapes and using rules to calculate with words when both kinds of rules are used together.

I already said pretty much what's involved in part II, with topologies and combining algebras in sums and products. On the one hand, I showed how to define topologies for shapes retrospectively in terms of the rules I tried—with particular attention to erasing rules in the schema

$x \rightarrow$

that help to count, and identities and other rules in the schema

$x \rightarrow t(x)$

Topologies are simply descriptions that show how I'm calculating and how shapes and their parts change continuously as I go on. But I may want to name parts and give them meaning in alternative ways. So, on the other hand, I sketched a general approach in which different algebras are combined in sums and products to define compound shapes. It includes both what I did in algebras like $U_{12} + W_{22}$ with lines, planes, and colors (weights) to produce paintings and what I did originally when I handled shapes and colors separately. Now I'm going to give a couple of examples to illustrate some of the things I proposed, strictly with shapes and words—actually numbers, but these are words as well, and are largely equivalent in practice. Using words and using numbers both require looking at what's there. Words and numbers divide shapes, naming their parts, although numbers do it sequentially in order to count them up. The two work together to describe visual experience. They're there to give shapes meaning and they tend to keep it constant. The consistency seems right, yet it isn't necessary. Ordinarily, it's expected, and it lets us anticipate the future and plan for it without having to worry that everything might change without rhyme or reason. Perhaps this explains why creative activity, drawing and playing around with shapes when their parts alter erratically, is apt to seem ineffable. Yes, there are always topologies, although they aren't exactly everyday descriptions in words. But words and descriptions don't have to be used in design all the time, only if they're useful. And they are in my two examples. The second is the more elaborate. It uses schemas and rules for Palladian villa plans to explain how shapes and words (numbers) work and what this shows.

The main idea is easy enough—I'm going to associate description rules with the rules I apply to shapes, and use both kinds of rules to calculate in parallel. Every time I give a rule for shapes, for example, this one

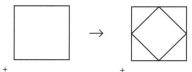

there are description rules for something else:

(1)   If the new shape is not the previous one, then the total number of squares I've inscribed increases by one, where squares are defined in the identity

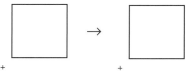

(2)   Furthermore, if there are more squares, then there are four more triangles, where triangles are defined in the identity

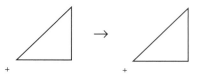

These description rules apply in conjunction with the rule

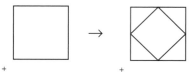

to say what happens as I continue to draw lines in a certain way—I get additional squares and triangles. Symbolically, I might summarize this with the rules

(1′)   number of squares → number of squares + 1

(2′)   number of triangles → number of triangles + 4

Then, for the series of shapes

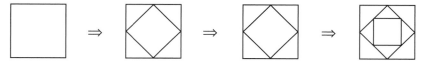

there's the corresponding series of descriptions

from step	0	1	2	3
number of squares	1	2	2	3
number of triangles	0	4	4	8

I'm calculating in parallel to produce shapes and the descriptions that go with them. And notice that I can even distinguish descriptions that are the same, if I count the steps in which they're produced. To start, there's a zero for bookkeeping, and then, the description rule

step → step + 1

There's a lot going on to tell me what I'm doing. The mechanics for all of it is straightforward enough, and extends neatly to many other things. For example, I can record the transformations I use to apply rules and define my topologies to show how rules pick out parts of shapes. Then there's more than mere mechanics that concludes with dry numbers. Well, the mechanics still isn't much—that's the way I like it when I calculate—but it shows that knowing how to count means first knowing how to see. This is where meaning starts and how it grows, and the process is far from dry. "To [observe] well," notes J. S. Mill, "is a rare talent." Shapes are filled with meaning as rules are tried. And it seems to me that this is the only kind of meaning that matters for shapes, whether in words, numbers, or topologies. Perhaps it's the only kind of meaning, period. It depends on what I see and do, and on what I make of it as I go on to see and do more. Rules apply to shapes and bring in words and numbers to make this possible. It's a process in which everything can interact and connect, and it's all calculating.

Let's try something that appears to be a little harder, although meaning doesn't have to be when it's a question of seeing. Suppose I'm looking at the rooms in a Palladian villa plan, and that I want to count them. Once again, there are numbers, and this involves distinguishing spaces and naming them in terms of what they're for. And, in fact, both naming and counting depend mainly on the rules I apply to pick out parts and change them as I calculate to produce the plan.

Let L and R be the number of polygons in the left side and the right side of a rule, and let k be defined as follows

$$k = L - R$$

This seems to be OK, but there's really a lot more to it than I've said. Rules are made with shapes that aren't divided in advance, and not with distinct symbols that are ready to count. This isn't generative grammar or syntax and words, so I have to figure out a way to count polygons. But remember what I did to define squares and triangles with identities from the schema $x \to x$. In much the same way, I can use erasing rules from another schema

poly $\to$

to count what I want. These rules pick out polygons—there are rectangles, crosses, T's, and I's—so that I add plus one every time a rule is tried with no chance of double-counting. There's an example of this kind in part II for squares and triangles in the shape

only it gives multiple answers between four and eight, and there's another example in part I for triangles in the shape that works in the same way with answers from four to six. But now, the erasing rules in my schema apply to give definite results—polygons are numerically distinct. And now, these rules apply to shapes in rules. This is important. Shapes are shapes wherever they are—it doesn't matter whether they're in rules or not. Either way, they're exactly as they're given, without finer divisions. Divisions are determined as I calculate.

Once k is defined, it's easy to say what rules do. First, there's an $m \times n$ grid of walls that's described by the coordinate pair (m, n), where m is the number of rectangles in a row and n is the number of rectangles in a column. (This counts columns before rows. It's interesting how things can get switched or turned around in shapes and words alike.) These values are set in the inverted T used to produce the grid. If I try a rule like this

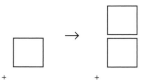

to add a rectangle vertically, my description rule is

$$(m, n) \rightarrow (m, n - k)$$

where $k = -1$. And in the corresponding way, if I apply a rule to add rectangles horizontally

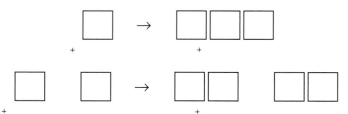

then my description rule is

$$(m, n) \rightarrow (m - k, n)$$

and $k = -2$. So, in the Villa Foscari with the inverted T

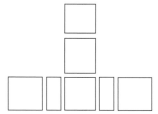

I have descriptions that look like this

from step	0	1	2	3	4
m		1	1	1	3	5
n		1	2	3	3	3

if the central column of rectangles is produced before the row that forms the base of the grid. And likewise, I can have the descriptions

from step	0	1	2	3	4
m		1	3	5	5	5
n		1	1	1	2	3

when I do all of the horizontal additions before the vertical ones. Both of these series begin and end in the same way, although the start is obligatory, and they have different terms in between. The variation isn't always gratuitous. It may be useful to guide or structure an assembly or manufacturing process—there are different numbers of rectangles at different times, so supplying and managing components, or resources generally, may be better in one way than another—or the variation may help to define and sequence the stages in a construction project. But for my purposes right now, both series are just the same because they end that way. This can be useful when rules apply to shapes nondeterministically. Then a successful conclusion may be the only thing that matters, not the different things that happen along the way. Still, there's a little more to do—an inverted T isn't a grid of walls. The T has to be completed—I need to fill in spaces and add a bounding rectangle. The description rules for this are given in the numerical identity

$$(m, n) \rightarrow (m, n)$$

The grid of walls for the Villa Foscari

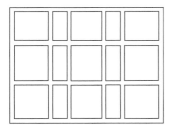

is produced in nine more steps after the inverted T is in place. This gives the following descriptions as the grid is finished off

from step	4	5	...	13
m		5	5	...	5
n		3	3	...	3

with the same repetition of numbers—5…5 or 3…3—at the end of both series. Evidently, the order in which rectangles are added continues to be irrelevant, and there's no reason to keep a running count.

Given a grid of walls and with its description (m, n) in hand, I know there are N rooms, that is to say, N is given in the formula

$$N = mn$$

This changes according to the description rule

$$N \to N - k$$

as I use rules to combine rectangles. In particular, for rules like these

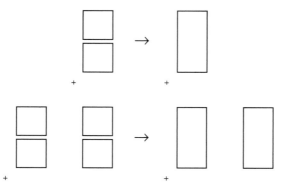

that put rectangles together vertically, $k = 1$ and $k = 2$. Then, for rules like these

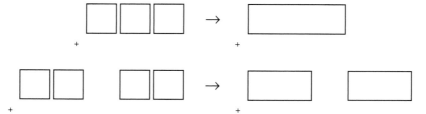

where spaces change horizontally, $k = 2$. And for the cross that combines three rectangles—two small ones and a big one—

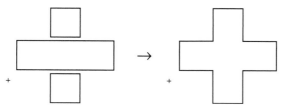

$k = 2$. As rooms are formed in the Villa Foscari

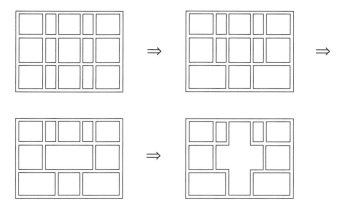

three descriptions change in this way

from step 13 14 15 16
N   15 13 11   9

My descriptions for grids of walls and room layouts fit together with almost classical precision to explain what my rules are doing as I apply them to shapes. In fact, there's a common parameter k in different description rules that's a kind of underlying module—the unity is undeniable. It's uncanny, but everything has got to be right once it's so clearly understood. That's why words and numbers work for a lot of design—to make it understood. Nonetheless, there are many aspects of design that seem exclusively visual—for example, mannerist details and more experimental devices are sometimes like this. Then, words and numbers—descriptions of all sorts, for that matter—may actually intrude. Words can bias the eye and obscure what there is to see and do. Luckily, there's plenty of opportunity to use rules and descriptions promiscuously in the kind of open-ended process I'm talking about. Even so, unbounded freedom may be burdensome when I have set responsibilities to meet and there are important goals to achieve. Goals and such are also descriptions, and they can be used to circumscribe the options I have as I calculate with shapes and rules—but this story is better told a little later on to add to my picture of design. Meanwhile, descriptions do something else in design that's worth a closer look. They help me organize what I'm doing in a variety of useful ways.

Descriptions determine relations to classify designs and to order them. In fact, I've already used descriptions to classify Palladian villa plans according to the values of m and n in the coordinate pair (m, n) that gives the number of rectangles in a row and a column in a grid of walls. In this sense, all of the entries in my catalogue of three-by-three room layouts are alike—they're the same "size." In particular, the plans for Palladio's Villa Angarano and Villa Barbaro

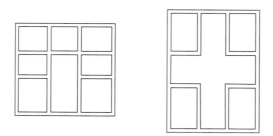

are equivalent. This is a little crude, but descriptions allow for finer distinctions, as well. I can also group $m \times n$ villa plans according to the number N of rooms they contain, where, once again

$N = mn$

in a grid of walls and varies according to the description rule

$N \rightarrow N - k$

Then my catalogue of three-by-three room layouts is partitioned in this way

Number of rooms

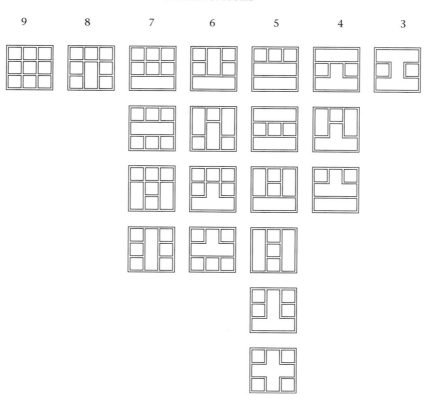

I guess it's about time that I call room layouts plans or villa plans. This may be overly optimistic—even reckless—but I've been leaning in that direction for a while, and words can change meaning as I calculate, just as shapes can when rules are tried. Now, two plans in my catalogue are equivalent when they have the same number of rooms, so the Villa Angarano and the Villa Barbaro are no longer the same. Nonetheless, there are five other plans that are still equivalent to the Villa Barbaro's, even if it's the only plan with a central cross. If I wish, I can augment my description rules to take care of this and classify central rooms, too. Then four plans are equivalent, with central rectangles, while one has a T and the other one has the cross. I can also go on to distinguish the plans with rectangular rooms in terms of description rules—it's a good exercise—but it may not be necessary. Descriptions give me a way of focusing on the kinds of things I want generally, with a free choice among equivalent designs. And this is how a lot of design seems to work in practice. It's a common occurrence that there are many designs that satisfy the same constraints and requirements. There's plenty of room to play around. And in fact, that's one reason why neat formulas like "form follows function" are always heuristics and only partially explain what happens in design. It seems that whatever I say about function is never enough to determine a unique form. And in fact, I may not want this. Otherwise, the myriad "undefined" things—at least there aren't any words for them—that I contribute as a designer are likely to be lost. Free choice or not, I'm calculating—it's just a lot more fun when things are open-ended. But descriptions work in another way to help with important decisions. Descriptions classify designs, and they order them—there's equivalence and also value. How does this work, and how is it part of the design process?

Once again, my catalogue of three-by-three villa plans is a pretty good place to start. I can count rooms and order plans up to equivalence according to the distinct numbers I get. The Villa Angarano

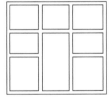

contains more rooms than the Villa Barbaro

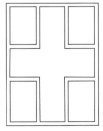

and in fact, more rooms than any other plan in the catalogue except the complete grid of walls. If I want to move beyond the grid and get something that's a little more expressive, and the number of rooms in a plan is the only additional thing I'm considering—the number should be high—then the Villa Angarano is the best I can do. But numbers may measure other properties, perhaps to optimize physical performance or social interactions. I might even try and apply George Birkhoff's aesthetic measure

$$M = \frac{O}{C}$$

to get something of delight from the plans in my catalogue, or use the corresponding measure of my own—E_Z—that I described along with Birkhoff's in the introduction. I wasn't keen on any of this then, and in practice I'm still not. Nonetheless, E_Z makes an instructive example without my having to rehearse any technical details. The results are enough. In terms of E_Z, the Villa Barbaro is better than the Villa Angarano, but it's only the second best among the plans with five rooms, after this one

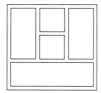

And notice that the three remaining plans with only rectangular rooms

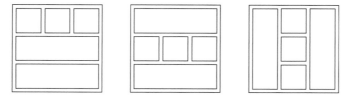

are the same. In fact in many ways, they look it—each with twin three-by-one or one-by-three spaces. But really, the main thing to get from all of this is that equivalence and value both depend on how descriptions are defined as I calculate with shapes. And there's plenty of room for descriptions to vary—they can be given in lots and lots of ways, and the ones to use are up for grabs. The perfect description now needn't be right the next time I look, and it's easy to forget as I go on. Things change whenever I try a rule. I'm always free to design some more.

I've kept shapes and descriptions together in the way I have so that when I apply rules to shapes, descriptions are automatically defined in parallel. But it's time to flip this around in an inverse way to show something else that's important in design. Descriptions can be defined independently to provide design specifications and requirements—even architectural programs—that set goals to guide and control the design process. For example, I can give a number N of rooms and then search through villa plans to find those with exactly N rooms. My description rules can be applied by themselves to define N, and this in turn tells me how I should try rules to produce plans. Suppose that $N = 8$ in a three-by-three villa plan. Then my description rule is

$$N \rightarrow N - 1$$

and I have to apply the rule

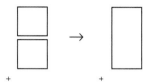

as I did for the Villa Angarano. But if $N = 5$, there are six options. In particular, if the number five is obtained in a three-step series—maybe this one

from step	8	9	10	11
N		9	7	6	5

—then the plan

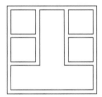

is the only one I can produce. Two other three-step series are also possible

from step	8	9	10	11
N		9	8	6	5
N		9	8	7	5

The first results in the same plan—remember that rules apply nondeterministically—while the second is simply a dead end. No plan can be produced according to the descriptions in the series—there's no way to go from step 10 with seven rooms to step 11 with five rooms, that is to say, from the plan

to the plan

Descriptions combine too copiously in too many series. You can ask for something that's meaningful according to my description rules—at least it's "grammatical"—that you can't get calculating with villa plans. It seems to me that sometimes imagination works in this way, too, when words promise more than I can do with shapes. Only perhaps this is just my imagination. And even if it's not, it doesn't make up for anything words miss. What I can say never trumps what I can see and do. But let's go on. The single two-step series

from step   8   9   10
N   9   7   5

already gives the Villa Barbaro, and also these four plans

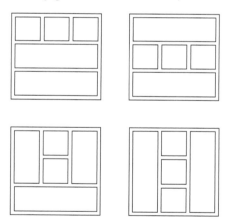

But notice that the plan for the Villa Barbaro is the only one that's defined uniquely—two rules are applied: first, one to produce a three-by-one rectangle, and then another to produce the cross. Each of the plans above, however, is defined in two ways—again rules apply nondeterministically. In three plans, large rectangular rooms come in pairs. Horizontally, the rectangles can be formed either one before the other, and vertically, from the top or the bottom. And in the remaining plan, the two symmetrical rectangles can come before or after the large rectangle at the base. Next, suppose $N = 9$ and the grid of walls is five by three to start—as in the Villa Foscari. Then, there are forty-three possibilities, of which these eight are a nice sample

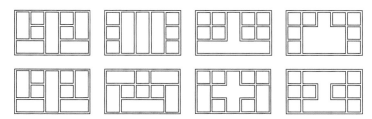

There are plans with central rectangles, crosses, T's and I's. But of far more interest now, plans fall into two separate and distinct groups. There are fourteen where descriptions are produced in a four-step series, perhaps this one

from step   13   14   15   16   17
N   15   13   11   10   9

of which the plan

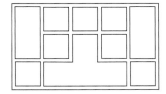

and the four in the top row are examples. And there are twenty-nine plans where descriptions are produced in the familiar three-step series

from step   13   14   15   16
N   15   13   11   9

for the Villa Foscari. The series also works for the four plans in the bottom row. Still, in practice things may not be as straightforward. Programs like plans can always be revised, and in fact the real goal may be to optimize both as they influence one another in various ways. This means changing programs and plans in parallel. Form and function, etc., interact, so that to some extent each implies and affects the other in a confluence of mixed interests and goals. This is beginning to feel like real design, and it continues to look like calculating.

The descriptions I've been using are fairly rudimentary, and they aren't anything to recommend in practice, although sometimes the descriptions that are used in practice aren't any more sophisticated. But it's not really descriptions that are at stake here, but rather description rules and how they're defined and used to describe what happens as I calculate. The idea is to combine shapes with words and numbers in a recursive process. Doing multiple things at once with shapes and words seems natural enough when you're in the middle of it—there's a knack to drawing and talking at the same time. But giving rules for this can be confusing at first, especially when the rules that describe what's going on interact in parallel and in other ways with the rules that apply to shapes. To get things off the ground, I've tried to avoid unnecessary details in a few very easy examples. Nonetheless, the key conclusions are pretty evident, and they're the same whatever descriptions are used. Design may be about more than shapes, but this isn't more than calculating allows. There are a host of different things involving functional, social, and aesthetic relationships that can be defined in myriad ways. Using models and mathematics is one way, as in the formulas $N = mn$ and $M = O/C$. I guess the formulas are kind of silly, but bringing in mathematics (topology, etc.) is a serious step. Description rules are made for it—they describe designs and can help to guide the design process. But none of this is what descriptions are actually about. The trick to descriptions is that they're never the final word. Things change as I go on calculating. It's worth saying over and over—there's more to see. This may coincide with what I've already said, but it's independent of the past. I may not remember what there was before, and in fact I may just as well be looking for the first time with no one to tell me what to see and do to go on. There's no reason to be coherent. Logic (rationality and science), morality, history, the authority of the ancients, and like imperatives are simply beside the point. Yes, consistency and words are useful more times than not, and they make a difference when I look again—but they don't have to. Otherwise, there's nothing really new to create. It's all been said before. Design goes away. Perhaps that's why the identities in the schema

$$x \to x$$

provide such good examples when it comes to seeing what rules do. Identities show everything new about shapes and calculating, and they can always be tried once more in another way.

Getting in the Right Frame of Mind

The picture of design I've been painting is all about schemas and rules, and about calculating in parallel with shapes and words, especially when shapes aren't divided into units in advance. Seeing is at the heart of it. I made a point of this near the end of part II, quoting William James, who was quoting John Stuart Mill on the importance of observation. Observing well—dividing things into useful and meaningful parts—takes a rare talent.

It would be possible to point out what qualities of mind, and modes of mental culture, fit a person for being a good observer: that, however, is a question not of Logic, but of the Theory of Education, in the most enlarged sense of the term. There is not properly an Art of Observing. There may be rules for observing. But these, like rules for inventing, are properly instructions for the preparation of one's own mind; for putting it into the state in which it will be most fitted to observe, or most likely to invent.

Mill's rules for observing and inventing have to do with getting in the right frame of mind to see and do. From my point of view this is marshaling schemas and rules to use. In fact, the schemas and rules I've proposed up to now provide a pretty good course in design—at least they're something to teach to "fit a person for being a good observer"—but there's more on education to come. Right now, it's time to take stock of the various schemas I have to use in teaching and practice, and to organize them in a catalogue raisonné.

I can go through schemas $x \to y$ in a more or less systematic way in terms of the variables x and y in their left and right sides. In the easiest case, both x and y are empty

$$\to$$

This seems inane, but it nonetheless defines a rule that's indispensable when I'm applying rules in parallel to everything at once and want to leave what's independent of my immediate concerns alone. Next, I have the erasing schema

$$x \to$$

and, in particular, the restriction

$$\text{poly} \to$$

for polygons, maybe with additional qualifications that make them convex or regular or that number their sides. The rules defined in both of these schemas let me count in another way, and they do in fact change what's there. The inverse of $x \to$ gives the schema

$$\to x$$

that appears to produce something from nothing. This seems like magic, but $\to x$ like $\to$ proves its worth calculating with rules in parallel—I can add to one thing in terms of something else that's not part of it. There are a couple of nice examples of this in the product of the algebras U_{12} and $U_{12} + U_{22}$, and in the algebra $U_{12} + W_{22}$ in part II, and my paintings work in the same way. Furthermore, the rules defined in $\to x$ help me to get going. When I calculate, I always need someplace definite to start. Nonetheless, $\to x$ may be unnecessary for this. If I wish, I can use identities in the schema

$$x \to x$$

to start with something interesting I happen to see instead. And then, of course, there's the general schema

$$x \to y$$

Most of the time, the variables x and y in the schema $x \to y$ are related in some way. This is already evident for the identities in the schema $x \to x$. Moreover, I have the schema

$$x \to t(x)$$

that includes the identities, and the schema

$$x \rightarrow b(x)$$

where there's a Euclidean transformation t or a boundary operator b that changes x. Or I might define another schema as an extension or counterpart of $x \rightarrow t(x)$, maybe

$$x \rightarrow x'$$

where x' is a parametric variation of x. Then I can relax the relationships between lines in the rule

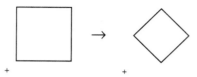

for squares with a pair of arbitrary quadrilaterals

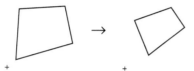

And for each of these four schemas, there are the sums formed when I add their left sides to their right sides. Ignoring the identities that stay the same, I get the trio of schemas

$$x \rightarrow x + t(x)$$

$$x \rightarrow x + b(x)$$

$$x \rightarrow x + x'$$

for rules that apply without erasing anything. Again, quadrilaterals are a good example

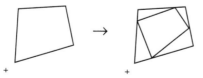

Inverses are very useful, too. The following ones are different from the schemas from which they're defined

$$b(x) \rightarrow x$$

$$x + t(x) \rightarrow x$$

$$x + b(x) \rightarrow x$$

$$x + x' \rightarrow x$$

while the schema $x \rightarrow x$ and its inverse are equivalent, along with the twin schemas $x \rightarrow t(x)$ and $x \rightarrow x'$ and their inverses. But notice, too, that in practice $b(x) \rightarrow x$ works for $x + b(x) \rightarrow x$—here, for a square and its boundary

I've also tried a few general-purpose schemas of another sort. For example, there's

$x \rightarrow \text{div}(x)$

to divide shapes in various ways—typically, the shapes are polygons as in ice-ray window grilles, housing plans, and paintings, although polygons aren't required for the schema to work—and then there's my old standby from "Kindergarten Grammars"

$x \rightarrow A + B$

for spatial relations that are defined either from a given vocabulary of shapes, maybe a square and a triangle

combined side to side in the following ten ways, where squares and triangles vary in size and orientation

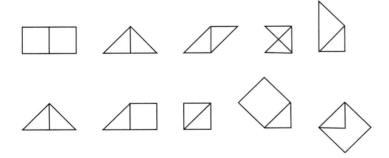

or from parts selected using identities in the schema $x \rightarrow x$, perhaps when x is a polygon and identities are applied to the shape

These were the exercises I tried for shapes and rules in "Two Exercises in Formal Composition." They set everything up for design synthesis and stylistic analysis. Spatial relations were enumerated in terms of a given vocabulary of shapes, but calculating with shapes wasn't restricted in this way. And once more, inverses are defined in the additional schemas

$\mathrm{div}(x) \to x$

$A + B \to x$

I used polygons in $\mathrm{div}(x) \to x$ for rules like this one

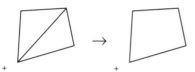

to complete Klee's palm-leaf umbrella. Of interest, too, I can recast the schema $x \to x + b(x)$ in terms of the schema $x \to A + B$, so that x in the left side of $x \to x + b(x)$ is a variable over A and B, and in the right side, x is A and $b(x)$ is B. This isn't exactly normal mathematics—it's more like Ludwig Wittgenstein's kind of calculating where "the figures on paper alter erratically"—but it does let me add the "usable" schema

$x + b(x) \to b(x)$

to my list of inverses for rules like this one

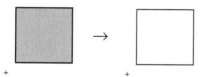

when $x \to b(x)$, that is to say

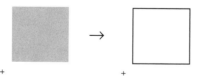

applies too broadly—perhaps to the shape

to produce

instead of

I can combine schemas in a variety of ways, too. For symmetrical arrangements and fractal designs, there's the easy schema

$$x \rightarrow \sum t(x)$$

when the schema

$$x \rightarrow x + t(x)$$

is used repeatedly with the generators of a symmetry group, or with transformations that include a change of a scale. Then, for shapes and fractal-like boundaries as in my paintings at the beginning of this part, there's

$$b(x) \rightarrow x + \sum t(b(x))$$

And, in special cases, there are rules like this one

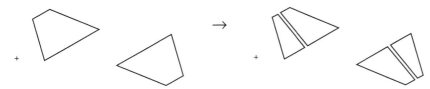

for symmetrical ice-rays that suggest schemas for grids

$$x + R(x) \rightarrow x + x' + R(x + x')$$

and schemas for villa plans (room layouts)

$$\mathrm{div}(x) + R(\mathrm{div}(x)) \rightarrow x + R(x)$$

in which transformations are used—in the two schemas here, there's a reflection R—to ensure symmetry of a certain kind. In particular, villa plans are bilaterally symmetric with respect to an axis that runs through rooms.

All of this gives me a handle on style and stylistic change, where schemas, assignments, and transformations in given algebras play important if not exclusive parts. It's easy to imagine one or more designers with a core repertoire of schemas that they combine and then apply in their own fashion to define a style that can change—even erratically—as different assignments and transformations are tried. This begins a good story, although designers are merely incidental. The problem, put simply, is to find rules that explain known examples of some kind that appear to hang together, with the ability to go on to new things like them, either recognized later somewhere else or produced from scratch. What designers say about what they do can help to define the rules, but personal testimony isn't indispensable and may be misleading or wrong. It's the same trying to find a grammar for a natural language like English—the speaker is only one of many who have a stake in what's said and how this works. And in literary criticism, writers are related to their work in the same way. What they say isn't decisive—others have a say, too. The evidence I need varies in a community enterprise. There are no necessary facts. Anything can contribute to the definition of a style at any time, especially when it's something new to see. Even if there's a definition that's affirmed and widely accepted, it's never final and conclusive. Everything can change as I go on. And that's exactly what new schemas allow when they're used to define rules to calculate with shapes. Minimally, of course, I can always add the schema $x \to x$ for identities. But in fact, keeping schemas the same—adding to them only once in a while, as I did for the Villa Barbaro—may be enough. Then there are assignments and transformations to stir things up.

Earlier, when I was first talking about style, I showed how a single schema

$$x \to \mathrm{div}(x)$$

could be used in diverse ways for Chinese lattice designs—checkerboard patterns and traditional ice-rays—floor plans in a major housing project, and nonrepresentational paintings. And it's easy to go on. The schema also works for paintings in the style of Fritz Glarner—his own, of course, and a host of new designs, maybe this one

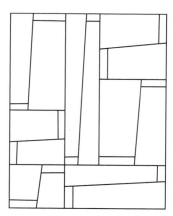

Then there are vernacular building plans in medieval Treviso—in two floors, for example

and many other things. There's plenty to see and do in various algebras as the schema is applied in terms of different assignments and transformations. Perhaps there's a formal method here—combining schemas from a common pool and trying a range of assignments and transformations to define styles and to change them. Terry Knight has shown with remarkable precision and scrupulous attention to detail—her taxonomy is uncanny—that the schema

$$x \rightarrow A + B$$

and its larger sums, first off

$$x \rightarrow A + B + C$$

where x is a combination of A, B, and C, work to distinguish workshops and periods of ancient Greek art in the Geometric style. There are battlement meanders

single (running) and multistage meanders

and spiraling meanders

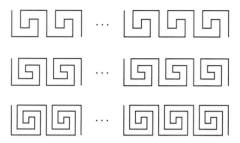

that vary in terms of the spatial relations given to define rules in her schemas. Assignments allow for shapes to be rearranged in spatial relations and for new shapes to be introduced. For example, I might start with the spatial relation

between two triangles, flip the large triangle to get the spatial relation

and then replace the large triangle with a square

all in accordance with the enumeration I set out before. And I can continue this in other ways, perhaps "dragging" points

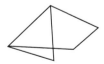

to turn the square into a quadrilateral with corresponding changes to the triangle. The repertoire of schemas from the series $x \rightarrow A + B$, $x \rightarrow A + B + C, \ldots$ is more or less constant, while rules are defined in alternative ways to produce different results. Knight proves the general paradigm in a special case. It's marvelous—styles and how they change depend on schemas, assignments, and transformations in given algebras. But undoubtedly I've missed a lot in my gloss of the essential facts. Knight would probably see it another way, as well, and there's no one better to believe than the author. One view is as good as another calculating with shapes, and no view lasts forever. This goes for styles themselves and ways of defining them. It strikes me that my description of style is simply a generalization of what's been tried, with more freedom and flexibility when it comes to schemas, using them, and changing them, and with greater emphasis on how assignments and transformations vary to tie things together. In addition, my approach to style corresponds to what I'm doing now with schemas and rules in different algebras of shapes, etc. It's a useful fit that's temporary if not evanescent, yet no less rigorous for that. It's being right without being eternal and unchangeable. It's just calculating with shapes.

Choosing assignments and transformations is another way to get in the right frame of mind to design, although I really don't have anything more specific to recommend than what I've already shown by haphazardly dividing shapes, defining spatial relations, etc. Building up a repertoire of examples and motifs that can be used in assignments—perhaps this is what designers mean by defining a vocabulary—repays the effort. In fact, this is as much as I know how to do, in addition to augmenting my catalogue of schemas. Even so, it seems there are too many options to be systematic. In principle, anything will work. However, the idea is clear. Given an assignment g and a transformation t, the composition $t \cdot g$ determines when parts are alike and how they change as rules are tried. There's plenty of room for variation and a myriad of expressive possibilities. The proof is easy to see in a small way in ice-ray lattice designs. Starting with a rectangular frame, orthogonal compositions produce

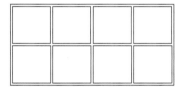

and parallel ones

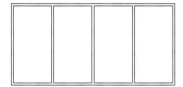

But then there's also this

I said I could augment my catalogue of schemas and rules, and indeed, it's never set once and for all. I can add to it as I please, and I have no reason to be parsimonious. Actually, I enjoy being messy and prodigal. There are many ways to frame schemas that are useful, even if the new ones I get are included in the ones I already have or are derived from them in some way. For example, six of the schemas I've given are ordered in terms of inclusion in the lattice

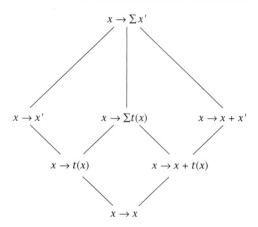

with a new schema at the top—

$$x \to \sum x'$$

—that extends the second schema $x \to x' + x''$ I gave for ice-rays. And building from scratch, the schema $x \to A + B + C$ and larger sums are defined when the schema $x \to A + B$ is applied recursively. But why should I bother with relationships like this? Trying to decide whether one schema is included in another or whether to reduce everything to a few "primitive" schemas seldom repays the effort. In general, each is difficult to do, and either way there's an inevitable loss of immediacy—all of a sudden, things are harder than they look. It's better to define schemas, so that they capture what I want to see and do now—whatever that is. Schemas should be easy to use. Some organization may help to remember what I have in my catalogue, although it doesn't go much farther than that. There's little to gain—the descriptions schemas contain don't carry over to shapes as I calculate. Seeing more to get new designs is what's important, not elegant schemas in a formal catalogue. Nonetheless, my catalogue is a database, and I'm told that's vital for cognition and thought. But more rigor and formality seems unnecessary, and even what there is may be too much. Adding to my catalogue, so that there are always schemas to use, is all that counts.

Where do I find schemas to add? Well, I've already given some hints. I can combine the sides of the ones I've got in sums, or switch sides to define inverses. Or I can combine schemas in various ways—as above in $x \to \sum x'$, or by incorporating transformations, etc., for grids and villa plans. (Many of the technical devices in my *Pictorial and Formal Aspects of Shape and Shape Grammars* are useful in this regard.) Moreover, I can learn from experience, adding to my catalogue as I try new things and see what they do. Perhaps I have a list of identities that are useful, and expand it according to what I produce when I calculate. Then what I see next depends on what I've done before. And, in fact, I did this for fractals in part II to show how they were self-similar. I defined identities according to the shapes—lines and planes—I produced calculating with the rule

in the schema

$$x \to \sum t(x)$$

for a triangle and its boundary. Alternatively, I could use the schema

$$x + b(x) \to b(x)$$

where $x + b(x)$ is anything I produce with my rule, to play around with triangles made up of lines

      $\cdots$

But getting back to my catalogue, I can apply the schema $x \to A + B$ a couple of times and use identities to define rules in the schema $x \to A + B + C$. And I can go on in this way for larger sums. Shapes go together when I calculate, and they go together in rules, as well.

But there's still another way to find new schemas—I can borrow them from others. Whatever I see anyone else do will work in my catalogue—perhaps I use identities again to get new rules and schemas as I did for the Villa Barbaro. But whatever I do, the way it works isn't rote copying. No one confuses ice-rays and Glarner's paintings or imagines they're the same. There are different algebras, assignments, and transformations for the schemas I have. That's the beauty of it. Because of the way shapes are defined in terms of embedding, schemas and the rules they define are readily transferable and can be used in many creative ways. Being original isn't something you have to do all on your own. In fact in many ways, creativity implies community—both to make new things and to recognize their originality—and it's something that follows automatically when you calculate with shapes and rules.

I haven't paid very much attention to descriptions—despite this book, I really prefer seeing and doing more than saying what this is about. Nonetheless, it's easy to include schemas for descriptions in my catalogue, so that shapes and words interact usefully in design. I already have a number of schemas for counting and topologies of different kinds from part II, and surely there are schemas for many other things, as well. I can always find something else to say.

Latin and Greek, and Mathematics

I started this book with a question and an answer. I wanted to know how to draw lines on a blank sheet of paper. My question seemed easy enough, yet Miss H——'s response implied that I should look elsewhere—

If you don't know that, you'll never be an artist.

School wasn't the place for an answer. There wasn't anything to teach in the classroom. Explicit instruction didn't work—in fact, Miss H—— proved it in a neat reductio ad absurdum when she asked the kids in my class to figure out the possibilities in a drawing exercise. Drawing wasn't like the three R's—arithmetic and spelling were pointless without definite results. Everyone had a different way to draw—the results were your own and could vary in many ways. You had to look around to make sense of what was going on—to understand what you were doing and what others were trying. All of this was a surprise and something to get used to. Learning to draw meant learning to see and do—but seeing and doing what? It seemed that seeing was never really finished. Drawings were filled with ambiguity and could change freely at any time. There was more to see whenever you looked again and another way to go on. These were problems to solve. Yet everyone looked askance—nothing seemed to work. What good were problems that no one knew how to handle or wanted to try? Miss H—— was a conscientious teacher—why couldn't she help? There had to be something to learn that was definite and useful. You could start out with the basics in other subjects—so what about drawing? Education and training were important, but how? Did anyone know? What did the experts recommend?

Walter Smith pioneered art education in Boston public schools when Massachusetts made drawing a required subject. The law for this was passed in 1870 to gain a competitive edge for the state in world trade markets. And today, there's evident progress. Seeing doesn't matter anymore, but the goal hasn't changed. Instead of drawing, kids are required to take rigorous tests in reading, writing, and arithmetic to show they're worth hiring. There's a single standard for everyone that measures what's taught and what's learned. The idea is to "teach to the test" in each subject, so that everything is clear to teachers and students alike. There's no guesswork, only certainty and permanent results. All of this seems right, and it's easy to join in when everyone is saying exactly the same thing. No one ever disagrees. Nonetheless, it may be wrong, and saying why may not be what you want to hear. No one likes to talk about it in public—the reason is usually an embarrassment that's better to whisper and hide. What Søren Kierkegaard said about results also goes for tests—they're impossible without cheating.

While objective thought translates everything into results and helps all mankind to cheat, by copying these off and reciting them by rote, subjective thought puts everything in process and omits the results.

It's the same problem for everyone when what's taught and what's learned are translated into objective results that can be recited by rote. What are schools for and why bother to go if teachers cheat and kids follow their example? Without subjective thought, everything in process is another arrangement of given units—the only task is to combine them and count the results. It's the same both to teach and to learn. Schooling is senseless—there's little to say when there's nothing new to see and do. But what does Kierkegaard know about education today? He lived in nineteenth-century Denmark and was mostly ignored. Miss H—— didn't think drawing (subjective thought) belonged in the classroom and neither do the citizens of twenty-first-century Massachusetts. It's the law—good schools mean hard work and the chance to fail on objective tests. It's tough, it's fair, and it's a huge success. Everyone is asked the same questions and trained to give the same answers. There's no ambiguity. Everyone is prepared for the same future that's been decided in advance by someone else, and everyone is held accountable in the same way. It's simple enough: everyone is the same and sees the same things. Of course, 1870 was different—it was another time and another law. The decision was easy. Massachusetts hired Smith. He had a plan, he put it in place, and he made it work.

I find that not only does every person when he is taught rationally, and intelligently in the same way that he is taught Latin, and Greek, and mathematics, learn to draw well, but also to paint well, and to design well.

Then, as it does now, design mattered. It was drawing, and Smith wanted to teach drawing in the classroom along with language and mathematics. His teaching methods relied heavily on copying figures drawn on the blackboard, memorizing forms of objects and arrangements of them—was this vocabulary and syntax?—and repetition and practice. It was drill, drill, drill. Smith justified this in two ways: (1) copying was the only rational way to learn because drawing was essentially copying, and (2) it was the only practical way to teach to large classes that met just for short periods. This sounds pretty grim and horrible, and it goes hard against the emphasis on creative activity and open-ended experiment that's standard today in most design education. That's why there are studios instead of classrooms. And that's why students want them. But perhaps there's something to Smith's pedagogy. Copying needn't be as empty as it seems at first nor always produce rote results—combining predefined units in the way Kierkegaard scorns. Look again. Copying may hold something creative and original.

With shapes and rules, things change. That's been an important lesson throughout this book, and it's still the same. So it should come as no surprise that copying is in many ways at the root of calculating. When I apply a rule $A \to B$, I find a copy of A and replace it with a copy of B. An identity in the schema

$x \rightarrow x$

is a good example. I first erase the shape assigned to x and then draw it again exactly as it was. This is copying according to the formula

$(x - x) + x$

But there's more to rules than identities that keep shapes the same—even if this changes the way shapes look. Rules in the schema

$x \rightarrow t(x)$

copy a shape or any part of one, erasing it and drawing it someplace else. The schema shows again why embedding—fusing shapes and then dividing to pick out parts—is so important. What you copy depends on reciprocal tests—what you can see with your eyes or trace out with your hands. And there's nothing rote about the results when there aren't any units to keep you from going on in your own way. Copying triangles with the rule

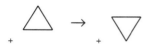

to turn the shape

upside down

proves it beyond doubt. Copying three triangles gives two new ones to copy, and then this goes in reverse from two triangles to three. There's magic in the scribe's hand when there's always something new to see. (This may not be scholarship, but it does seem to be art.) Or perhaps boundaries are better as copies to delineate regions and mark endpoints. This is one way drawing works to copy what's there. Then the rules in the schema

$x \rightarrow b(x)$

are perfect. The schema shows even more how copying changes according to what you see and what you draw, as boundaries are decided in different ways—here in a collage of points, lines, and planes

that's made first by outlining four triangles that are "embedded" in a square plane and then by highlighting the vertices in one of the squares that these triangles contain. Going from one part to the next skips all over the place, but it's still copying. And in addition, there's the more elaborate schema

$$x \rightarrow x + b(x)$$

that's much the same, and its counterpart

$$b(x) \rightarrow x + b(x)$$

to connect points and fill in areas in coloring-book exercises. Rules in these schemas produce copies without erasing as copies alternate between parts and their boundaries. Copying without erasing is also the case for rules in the schema

$$x \rightarrow x + t(x)$$

Now, parts can be copied more than once in different ways. This already leads to a host of creative possibilities. At least there are symmetrical patterns of all sorts—here's one I considered earlier

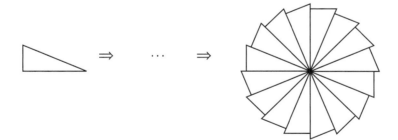

And, of course, there are fractals. But this kind of repetition isn't very exciting, when the same thing is copied over and over again in the same way. Klee wanted more freedom within the law—to see in different ways and to vary what he copied. With rules in the schema

$$x \rightarrow x'$$

and ones in the schema

$$x \rightarrow x + x'$$

copies may vary freely with parametric abandon. It's easy to be surprised—it's really almost effortless as long as you're ready and willing to calculate with shapes and rules

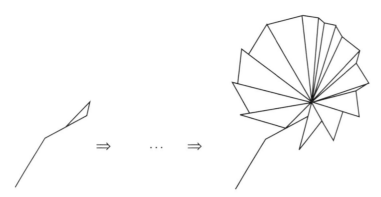

It's going on, seeing and doing in whatever way you like.

And there are other ways to copy shapes, too. In particular, I can combine algebras in products and copy across their components. This uses rules in the erasing schema

$x \rightarrow$

rules in its inverse

$\rightarrow x$

and identities $x \rightarrow x$ to calculate in parallel. For example, two new schemas can be defined—something more to put in my catalogue—that look like this

$x, - \rightarrow -, x$

$x, - \rightarrow x, x$

where the dash (−) indicates the empty shape. The first schema has a neat symmetry— it combines $x \rightarrow$ and $\rightarrow x$, so that the component or the part of it that's copied is erased. But in the second schema, $x \rightarrow x$ and $\rightarrow x$ are combined to preserve what's copied in its original place without changing anything. A slightly different example is in part II on pages 287–290. The schema

$x, - \rightarrow -, y$

is used to decompose the shape

into squares and triangles in five distinct ways. Simply put, these polygons in x are copied with the lines or the plane given in y. And this kind of copying is easy to elaborate in lots of ways—with added transformations, the boundary operator, parametric variation, etc. I can even use weights to get colors or other properties that interact as I draw, perhaps as in the example on pages 290–291, or in my design with Hilbert's curve and in the similar ones in figure 1. The conclusion is evident—once I can copy, I can calculate. (In fact this follows the letter of the law when triangles are copied in rules for Turing machines.) And once I can calculate, there's drawing and design, and the many delightful things that shapes and rules imply.

Smith really got it right—copying works, even if shapes, schemas, and rules may be a little more than he had in mind. It makes sense to go on from what others say and do. But perhaps there's more to this than blind luck and empty coincidence—there's also Smith's marvelous idea that drawing can be taught like language and mathematics in the classroom with worked examples and explicit instruction. And it's no surprise that this goes for what I've been showing for shapes, schemas, and rules. Does this mean I've changed my mind? I've spent a good portion of this book arguing that drawing isn't language. What can I possibly teach without vocabulary and syntax? Something is wrong. Well maybe not, vocabulary and syntax aren't at stake. Teaching drawing like language doesn't prove that

drawing is language

It's still a metaphor, although many accept it today as a heuristic or assume there's equivalence. And that's where the problem lies—not with teaching but with heuristics and equivalence. Certainly, all of the schemas I've described are things to teach in the classroom and to explain at the blackboard. There's a lot of copying to do to write schemas down and to try them out in exercises. And there's also showing why drawing isn't a language, how mathematics describes shapes and rules, and how shapes and words are connected when I calculate—it's Latin and Greek, and mathematics in another way. Many useful lessons are worth teaching in the classroom—there's everything in this book—before the vital transition into the studio to experiment freely with schemas. The opportunities for creativity and originality seem to be unlimited once you've learned to copy.

Of course, the idea of open-ended experiment in art and design is key in American art education after Smith—in particular, with Denman Ross at Harvard and Arthur Dow at Columbia University. Mine Ozkar traces the history of this—learning to draw wasn't rote copying, that is to say, blankly following instructions and blindly doing what you're told in the normal way you're trained to calculate. There was seeing, too.

For a great while we have been teaching art through imitation—of nature and the "historic styles"—leaving structure to take care of itself . . . so much modern painting is but picture-writing; only story-telling, not art; and so much architecture and decoration only dead copies of conventional motives.

For Ross and Dow, "picture-writing"—what a felicitous compound given what I've been saying about drawing and why it isn't language with letters and words—wasn't near enough for art. And "dead copies" of familiar devices—correct spelling—didn't work in design. Never mind that words are easy to mix up—imitation and copying take care of structure automatically; the latter is included in the former. But it's the intention that counts. Ross and Dow were good guys—you get what they mean in spite of their words:

Their pedagogies show how to set up temporary frameworks, instead of submitting to any predetermined structures. Frameworks develop based on variance in sense perception.

Sense perception lets me calculate my way—this depends on shapes and how rules are tried to pick out parts. And in keeping with this, work in the studio is trying what you've been taught in the classroom to go on to new things. It's also defining new schemas in terms of what you've done, and seeing what others are doing. It's learning from experience. It's another valuable way to add to your catalogue of schemas and to the rules you have to use in practice. It's becoming a creative designer. In the studio and in practice, designs (intellectual property) are free and only to share. This is copying to be original in the way schemas allow when they're used to define rules and calculate with shapes. Copying, community, and creativity run throughout design practice and education, and shapes and rules tie the three of them together. Both practice and teaching are seeing what to do in an open-ended process that involves us all. There's lasting community in the things we make—drawings, designs, etc.—not because we see them in the same way but because we don't have to. There's no common pool of assumptions or knowledge—tacit or not—that everyone has to accept in order to join in and take part. It's unnecessary to have shared anything ahead of time to go on. Otherwise, it would be enough to work alone—what's gained by working together is the other guy's point of view. Each of us is free to see and do in his or her own way without prior training or outside coercion. That's why shapes and rules and calculating with them are so crucially important—they let all of this happen. Design is never working alone, even if it seems that way. It isn't a solitary pursuit—there are just too many things to see.

When I calculate with shapes and rules, I get the easy corollary

design is copying

I really like this a lot because it's so practical—I know where I can look to see what to do—and it seems to reassure most people when they wonder where new designs come from. This is probably because it's an unremarkable answer, and copying is something everyone does—it works and it works well. The corollary allows for effective practice in design and shows how design can be taught without giving up any creativity. There's as much creativity in copying as there is in anything else. There are sources and precedents for just about everything. Almost nothing is aboriginal. But copying is PLAGIARISM—perhaps it is, but teaching and learning are more important. Plagiarism doesn't matter when there are no rote results. Then it isn't cheating. What you see and do belongs only to you—it's always your own work. There's something new and original every time you look, and who knows, the results may be spectacular. It's hard to imagine how to teach design without any plagiarism, much less how to design anything novel in practice. (Is it any surprise that design seems incongruous in great universities with their single-minded focus on academic integrity? The irony is that honor codes, student and faculty handbooks, and standards for research overlap from school to school, so that the "rules" to stop copying seem to be copied. Nonetheless, design studios are out. They rely on seeing what your classmates are doing and putting it to use as your own. This condones copying and encourages student work that looks the same—it's uncanny how often studio projects are alike and how no one ever seems to notice. But copying is no way to show what you can do in research—so much for reverse engineering and repeatable results in science—and in super-tough university classes where you can earn an F. Copying isn't allowed. It's a question of ownership—everyone has to do "original" work to guarantee that it's his or hers. That's how teaching and learning are measured—by the work you do on your own—and it's what it means to be creative. There's just no place for design!) As long as I don't assume there are units in a combinatorial process—that's been the big problem all along: how to calculate without symbols—it's easy to go on in new ways and to encourage others to do the same. Design needn't be a mystery. You can teach it and foster mastery instead. Design and teaching how to do it show meaningful results when there's copying. It's best practice, and it's always in process so that nothing is ever final. Results aren't set in advance and can't be repeated (recited) by rote. It may be that there are some useful alternatives to copying—anything can happen—but I wouldn't bank on it. I'll put my money on shapes and rules. Calculating—yes, copying—provides a competitive advantage that's hard to beat.

One of the things I've been trying to show throughout this book is that it's always possible to go on in new ways when you calculate with shapes and rules. It's about seeing for the first time again and again without ever having to start over. Going on, to be sure, is the way to design, but it's hardly the way to end a book. That calls for a conclusion. I started out in the introduction talking about seeing and doing in this way:

[Calculating with shapes and rules] is subjective and variable—the shape grammarist's voice is ineluctably personal.

And this seems to be the right ending, too. In many ways, it's just what this part of my book has shown. I've taken you through many examples of what I do when I use rules to calculate with shapes. Seeing and saying what I see are always personal. There are no rote results, whether I copy what I see or call this something else—descriptions don't count. My eyes have only their own way of knowing. That's a good reason to calculate, and it's why calculating works in design.

Background

The background to this part is pretty straightforward, especially if I stick to what I've said in the order I've said it. The quotation I start off with is from Walter Smith's testimony to the Royal Commission on Technical Instruction of 1883.[1] Smith sets the tone for what I go on to say. There are three points of interest. First, he equates drawing with painting and design. Second, he's sure that drawing can be taught rationally and intelligently in school like language and mathematics. And third, he turns to "a great wealth of illustration" to prove it. That design is drawing is where I begin, and that design can be taught in the classroom is where I end, but probably not with the kind of rationality and intelligence—copying—Smith has in mind. Within this locus, there's plenty of illustration. And, in fact, that's what really matters—what I can calculate with shapes and rules, and what you can see with your eyes.

Painting is how I started with shapes and rules, although this is recast here in terms of the algebras and rules I use now.[2] I first used schemas to produce Chinese lattice designs.[3] My discussion of these traditional window grilles—ice-rays included—hasn't changed much, except for the key addition of identities, etc., to handle descriptive aspects of style over and above what it takes to produce designs. This is easy with schemas as they're currently defined using twin variables.[4] The material on Palladio is from three early papers, but my discussion of the Villa Barbaro hasn't been seen before.[5] I tried description rules a little after Palladio, only not for his villa plans.[6] Their use in this way is new. The idea of calculating with rules in parallel, however, is already clear in *Pictorial and Formal Aspects of Shape and Shape Grammars*.[7] My original discussion of design synthesis and stylistic analysis is in "Two Exercises in Formal Composition," with a lot more in "Kindergarten Grammars" on design synthesis, spatial relations, and the schema $x \to A + B$ and its inverse.[8]

Of course, I owe much to many others in all of my examples. Paul Klee's drawings—in particular, the "palm-leaf umbrella"—are in *The Thinking Eye*, together with the quote on irregularity and the law.[9] Then there's Daniel Sheets Dye's *A Grammar of Chinese Lattice Designs*, which is valuable for both the drawings and the words it contains.[10] The plans for the Villa Foscari, the Villa Rotonda, and the Villa Barbaro are from Andrea Palladio's *The Four Books of Architecture*, and there's the quotation on page 343.[11] I've also relied on James Ackerman's book *Palladio* for useful commentary in four places—pages 341, 344, 346, and 347.[12] I don't discuss Palladio's system of building proportions, but Lionel March provides a pathbreaking analysis that the shape grammarist can't help but admire.[13] Terry Knight gives a comprehensive and critical account of different approaches to style and stylistic analysis that concludes with shapes and rules.[14] She goes on to investigate stylistic change in an original and effective way using a generalization of the schema $x \to A + B$ and its inverse. This includes her analysis of Greek meander designs, and a detailed discussion of the paintings of Georges Vantongerloo and Fritz Glarner—I borrow from her examples for all three. Alvaro Siza's ground plan at Malagueira is adapted from José Duarte's discursive survey of the project.[15] Also of interest, Andrew Li provides an elegant application of description rules to elaborate the building principles in the *Yingzao Fashi*.[16] Perhaps this isn't that surprising for a notoriously rigorous building manual. Nonetheless, to see the rules actually work is pretty impressive. And notice, too, that the relationship between rules and description rules mimics Gottlob Frege's principle of compositionality that links syntax and semantics—the meaning of a logical expression or a sentence in English is a function of the meanings of its parts and how they're combined. Of course, this fails for shapes because their parts aren't set in advance. There are options in retrospect—perhaps using topologies—but these probably wouldn't satisfy Frege and his current followers. They relish hard problems where things stay the same, yet sometimes problems are hard only because of the way they're set up to start. It's easier not to worry about this and to let things alter freely, as they do calculating with shapes or copying Wittgenstein's "figures on paper." An account of George Birkhoff's aesthetic measure and its information-theoretic counterpart E_Z is in *Algorithmic Aesthetics*.[17] For an incisive discussion of value in design, see March's classic essay "The Logic of Design and the Question of Value."[18] March goes on to consider C. S. Peirce's famous trio of inferential categories in design—these are deduction and induction, as expected, and then, in addition, abduction. Roughly speaking, going from shapes to their descriptions corresponds to deduction, going from descriptions to shapes to abduction, and figuring out schemas and rules in the first place to induction. March puts this together in a cyclic model of design that applies in some telling ways. Peirce is keen on clarity, albeit each kind of inference holds alternative choices with a combinatorial (syntactic) uncertainty or ambiguity of its own. The lines I've quoted form Søren Kierkegaard are copied from my introduction. Mine Ozkar chronicles the artistic adventures of Denman Ross and Arthur Dow, and the incidental interactions of the former with William James at Harvard and the noteworthy relationship of the latter with John Dewey at Columbia.[19] More important, though, shapes and rules are compatible with open-ended experiment in the design studio.

All this prevails in the distinctive pedagogical standpoint shared by Ross and Dow.... Individuals are encouraged in their unique ways, which can only be represented in temporary and discardable conceptual structures.[20]

Better still, every rule—even an identity—implies a new (original) conceptual structure every time it's applied to a shape. The way topologies are redefined on the fly is a good example of how this works, but there are many other examples throughout this book. Ordinarily, design and calculating are worlds apart. Sometimes, a brief alliance is formed when calculating produces things designers want to use and can't make on their own. Then it's one way calculating and another way when design works its magic—there's a discrepancy between what the computer does and what the designer sees. This exposes shortcomings in both calculating and design, and the divide between them. Yet now, the "two cultures" fuse. My initial metaphor is equality—

design = calculating

—not because design is calculating in the usual way, but because calculating is more than it's supposed to be. Design is calculating with shapes and rules. It's seeing and doing, and all that follows as I go on.

Today, there are far too many examples of shape grammars in design—including architecture and engineering—to be cited item by item. Most of this material is in *Environment and Planning B: Planning and Design* from 1976. Nonetheless, there are two pioneers of the subject whose work has been widely influential—Ulrich Flemming and Terry Knight.[21]

Notes

Introduction

1. S. Pinker, *The Blank Slate* (New York: Viking, 2002), 79.

2. Plato, *The Republic*, trans. B. Jowett (Cleveland: World Publishing Co., 1946), 211. Later on, Plato touts mathematics in secondary education as a prelude to reasoning. Five parts divide the curriculum, only to "reach the point of inter-communion and connection with one another." First, arithmetic, including counting and calculating—"The little matter of distinguishing one, two, and three—in a word, number and calculation:—do not all arts and sciences necessarily partake of them?" But this isn't all when arithmetic is "pursued in the spirit of a philosopher, and not of a shopkeeper! . . . [Then] arithmetic has a very great and elevating effect, compelling the soul to reason about abstract number, and rebelling against the introduction of visible or tangible objects into the argument." Plane geometry is next, followed by solid geometry, astronomy, and harmony. Plato's mathematics ties to visual calculating in some neat ways, for example, in the anthyphairetic ratio of the diagonal and the side of a square ($\sqrt{2}$:1). Once, in conversation, Lionel March told me the diagram

as a geometrical figure and as a proof that $\sqrt{2}$:1 repeats without end reminded him of the shape

because squares recur in the same way. In fact, the diagonal of the large square in the diagram shows the string *aba* when the side of the little square is *a* and the diagonal *b*. As Plato would have it, there's more to this than meets the eye. The ratio $\sqrt{2}$:1 and its successors in reciprocal subtraction fix segments in palindromes for sides of squares in my shape, as these segments are refined in differences. For an account of the diagram, see D. H. Fowler, *The Mathematics of Plato's Academy: A New Reconstruction* (New York: Oxford University Press, 1990), 33–35, and D. H. Fowler, "The Story of the Discovery of Incommensurability, Revisited," in *Trends in the Historiography of Science*, ed. K. Gavroglu, J. Christianidis, and E. Nicolaidis (Boston: Kluwer,

1994), 221–235. Of additional interest, see L. March, "Architectonics of Proportion: A Shape Grammatical Depiction of Classical Theory," *Environment and Planning B: Planning and Design* 26 (1999): 91–100, L. March, "Architectonics of Proportion: Historical and Mathematical Grounds," *Environment and Planning B: Planning and Design* 26 (1999): 447–454, and L. March, "Proportional Design in L. B. Alberti's Tempio Malatestiano, Rimini," *arq* 3 (1999): 259–269. March argues for geometry in design and against making it digital in computer models, echoing Fowler that Greek geometry wasn't arithmetized. This fits nicely with shapes and rules.

3. Christopher Alexander's "pattern language" is meant for a Platonic world that's divided once and for all. C. Alexander, *The Timeless Way of Building* (New York: Oxford University Press, 1979), and see also note 6 below. Still, change is a staple of studio teaching in architecture, especially for digital architects who use parametric models and other computer tools in nonstandard praxis. This is about being poetic—

[The] poetic act has no past, at least no recent past, in which its preparation and appearance [can] be followed.... [The] poetic image is essentially *variational*, and not, as in the case of the concept, *constitutive*.

G. Bachelard, *The Poetics of Space*, trans. M. Jolas (Boston: Beacon Press, 1969), xi, xv. It's hard to imagine a respectable design instructor who doesn't know Bachelard's phenomenology and rely on it in some way. But is the poetic image something to calculate? Variation is the business of parametric models. Nonetheless, they're constitutive and imply a Platonic world—finite elements, etc. (constituents) are set in advance, that is to say, entirely in the past. This gives objective (combinatorial) results that block subjective experience. A lot is left out. I'm free to see and do more than my prior decisions allow. Constituents change—once shapes fuse, their immediate past is lost and I can divide them in any way I choose. The whole reason for shapes and rules is to make this kind of variation possible, so that calculating and seeing coincide. When I calculate with shapes, what happens now isn't decided by the rules I've used (preparation), but depends on the rules I try (appearance). I can keep track of how shapes change in this process to define retrospective links between what I draw and what I see, but these relationships are never fixed. They're reestablished afresh every time I apply a rule. There's no concept for what I see and do, or anything permanent. What comes next doesn't follow a definite sequence. The poetic act has no past—it's always in the present. The poetic image is always something new.

4. G. Stiny and J. Gips, "Shape Grammars and the Generative Specification of Painting and Sculpture," in *Information Processing '71*, ed. C. V. Frieman (Amsterdam: North-Holland, 1972), 1460–1465. An early description of grammars for shapes (triangles) is in R. A. Kirsch, "Computer Implementation of English Text and Picture Patterns," *IEEE Transactions on Electronic Computers* EC-13, 4 (1964): 363–376. Kirsch's approach is unabashedly syntactic.

5. J. Gips, *Shape Grammars and Their Uses* (Basel: Birkhauser, 1975).

6. G. Stiny, *Pictorial and Formal Aspects of Shape and Shape Grammars* (Basel: Birkhauser, 1975). Here and also in G. Stiny, "Kindergarten Grammars: Designing with Froebel's Building Gifts," *Environment and Planning B* 7 (1980): 409–462, I rely on vocabularies (alphabets) of shapes to define shape grammars and spatial relations, but not without showing that vocabularies fail when you calculate with what you see. The use of vocabularies of constituents or units to link calculating and design may seem contrived. Yet history proves otherwise, for example, for logic and architecture—"Both enterprises sought to instantiate a modernism emphasizing what I will call 'transparent construction,' a manifest building up from simple elements to all higher forms," P. Galison, "Aufbau/Bauhaus: Logical Positivism and Architectural Modernism," *Critical Inquiry* 16 (1990): 709–752. Ludwig Wittgenstein's *Tractatus* is crucial to this, and it's the model for Susanne

Langer's discursive forms of symbolism. There's combinatorial play with "simple, accessible units," and in fact, Galison's story concludes neatly at the University of Chicago and New Bauhaus with Charles Morris—"We are now discussing the question as to how far art can be regarded as a language." And the same discussion continues today. Morris helped to get Rudolf Carnap from Vienna to Chicago, and this leads to Herbert Simon and his "sciences of the artificial" with their "logic of design." Then, tangled offshoots connect in sundry ways to others engaged in today's round of "transparent construction" using constituents and units of different kinds. Notably, from the Centre for Land Use and Built Form Studies at Cambridge, see L. March, "The Logic of Design and the Question of Value," in *The Architecture of Form*, ed. L. March (Cambridge: Cambridge University Press, 1976), 1–40, for a telling account of Alexander's pattern language, followed by L. March, "A Boolean Description of a Class of Built Forms," 41–73. The combinatorial approach is pretty much the same for both Alexander and March, although the emphasis shifts. On the one hand, there are permanent "atoms" of space to make what's right, and on the other, arbitrary units of geometry and form to explore what's possible. L. March and C. F. Earl, "On Counting Architectural Plans," *Environment and Planning B* 4 (1977): 57–80, show the kind of configurational enumeration that March recommends and that many try with important results. W. J. Mitchell, *The Logic of Architecture: Design, Computation, and Cognition* (Cambridge, Mass.: MIT Press, 1990), is overtly linguistic with vocabulary and syntax, and there are intersections wherever computers are used in design. I guess I'm involved, as well, yet this hardly seems to matter with embedding. I've had an out from the start, and I use it freely as my eyes wander promiscuously. You don't have to make up your mind once and for all to go on—you can see and do anything you like—unless foundational units, and from them, the "manifest building up" of guaranteed results, set the way in advance. There is no vocabulary. Design is more than combining units no matter what they are. Shapes and rules allow for calculating in another way in which seeing is key.

7. G. Stiny and W. J. Mitchell, "The Palladian Grammar," *Environment and Planning B* 5 (1978): 5–18. Even though the grammar has no vocabulary and isn't syntax, it works for configurational enumeration. The details are in G. Stiny and W. J. Mitchell, "Counting Palladian Plans," *Environment and Planning B* 5 (1978): 189–198.

8. *The Flip Wilson Show*, NBC, 1970–1974.

9. *Kierkegaard's Concluding Unscientific Postscript*, trans. D. F. Swenson and W. Lowrie (Princeton, N.J.: Princeton University Press, 1968), 68.

10. D. A. Schon, *The Reflective Practitioner* (New York: Basic Books, 1983).

11. J. Dewey, *Logic: The Theory of Inquiry*, vol. 12 of *John Dewey: The Later Works, 1925–1953* (Carbondale: Southern Illinois University Press, 1986), 108.

12. P. Klee, *Pedagogical Sketchbook*, trans. S. Moholy-Nagy (New York: F. A. Praeger, 1953), 18. For a lively reprise of Klee's medial lines, see T. W. Knight, "Computing with Ambiguity," *Environment and Planning B: Planning and Design* 30 (2003): 165–180. I use Knight's bivalent description of the shape

to begin the dialogue on page 12. This contrasts my "part ambiguity" that embedding entails—what triangles are there?—with the "representational ambiguity" that medial lines imply—what planes are shown? There's seeing and making something out of it, although the two may look the same—try polygons, but also letters or words or Chinese ideograms, or other familiar things. Part ambiguity is "special and consequential" in Knight's synoptic taxonomy, and representational ambiguity is "pervasive." Yet my dialogue proves there's dependence, too—the pervasive is a consequence of the special. Klee draws lines to get planes, and surely he relies on the lines he draws and the shapes he sees to decide what he's shown. That's why lines are medial, even if this works in reverse drawing planes to get lines (boundaries). I guess all basic elements—points, lines, planes, and solids—are medial in one way, while lines and planes are medial in two—this despite the evident sequence in Wassily Kandinsky's *Point and Line to Plane*. (At the time, the problem in logic was to go from solids to points. Alfred North Whitehead's method of extensive abstraction did the trick, but for an inclusive review see A. Tarski, "Foundations of the Geometry of Solids," in *Logic, Semantics, Metamathematics*, trans. J. H. Woodger [Indianapolis, Ill.: Hackett, 1983], 24–29. This is all pretty neat, only it isn't about shapes. Basic elements of different kinds combine finitely and not as members of sets. They're independent and equal, and aren't defined one kind from another.) Then perhaps there are more types of ambiguity, for example, functional ambiguity where the question is about behavior or patterns of events. But part ambiguity may be implicated here, too. Also on page 13, I said that the above square-and-diagonals with small triangles is a pyramid in Chinese or Renaissance perspective, and with large triangles, a Necker-cube-like tetrahedron. On the pyramid, see El Lissitzky, "A. and Pangeometry," in *El Lissitzky: Life, Letters, Texts*, ed. S. Lissitzky-Küppers (London: Thames and Hudson, 1968), 349.

13. "Transparent construction" was rife at the Bauhaus—in particular, "Kandinsky ... was one of the leaders of the constructivist curriculum ... [and] shared the basic faith in a building up from the elementary." Galison, "Aufbau/Bauhaus," 738.

14. G. D. Birkhoff, *Aesthetic Measure* (Cambridge, Mass.: Harvard University Press, 1933).

15. G. Stiny and J. Gips, *Algorithmic Aesthetics* (Berkeley: University of California Press, 1978). A worked example of E_Z is given in G. Stiny and J. Gips, "An Evaluation of Palladian Plans," *Environment and Planning B* 5 (1978): 199–206.

16. O. Neurath, "Visual Education: Humanisation Versus Popularisation," in *Encyclopedia and Utopia: The Life and Work of Otto Neurath (1882–1945)*, ed. E. Nemeth and F. Stadler (Dordrecht: Kluwer, 1996), 330. Galison, 709–752, discusses Neurath's role in the Vienna Circle and his relationship to the Bauhaus. Moreover, "Neurath's pictures were intended as clear, universal building blocks on which all else could be built.... [They were] essentially a linguistic [syntactic] and pictorial form of transparent construction." (Galison's phrase "pictorial form of transparent construction" is ironic in the same way the term "shape grammar" is, but nonetheless it's consistent with Neurath's idea of a picture—and Wittgenstein's, for that matter. This isn't the case for the title of my book *Pictorial and Formal Aspects of Shape and Shape Grammars*, where "pictorial" and "formal" anticipate the scheme for visual and verbal expression I outline on pages 7 and 8, and develop in part II. *Aspects of a Theory of Syntax* is one of Noam Chomsky's famous titles. Yet, even so, shape grammars were never syntax—it's always been shapes to shapes rather than symbols to strings. The distinction is explicit in my *Aspects*, 28. The difference is huge when shapes aren't symbols, that is to say, when predefined units aren't distinguished in shapes to add up to whatever there is.)

17. E. Pound, *ABC of Reading* (New York: New Directions, 1960), 21–22.

18. M. L. Minsky, *Computation: Finite and Infinite Machines* (Englewood Cliffs, N.J.: Prentice-Hall, 1968).

19. H. L. Dreyfus, "Alchemy and Artificial Intelligence" (Paper P-3244, RAND Corporation, Santa Monica, Calif., 1965). H. L. Dreyfus, *What Computers Can't Do* (New York: Harper and Row, 1972). H. L. Dreyfus and S. E. Dreyfus, *Mind Over Machine* (New York: Free Press, 1986).

20. See, for example, S. Papert, "The Artificial Intelligence of Hubert L. Dreyfus: a Budget of Fallacies" (AI Memo 154, MIT Project MAC, Cambridge, Mass., 1968).

21. A. Newell, "Intellectual Issues in the History of Artificial Intelligence," in *The Study of Information: Interdisciplinary Messages*, ed. F. Machlup and U. Mansfield (New York: John Wiley and Sons, 1983), 222–223.

22. J. Holland, *Hidden Order: How Adaptation Builds Complexity* (Reading, Mass.: Addison-Wesley, 1995). S. Wolfram, *A New Kind of Science* (Champaign, Ill.: Wolfram Media, 2002).

23. N. Chomsky, *Syntactic Structures* (The Hague: Mouton, 1957).

24. Numerous entries in *The MIT Encyclopedia of the Cognitive Sciences*, ed. R. A. Wilson and F. C. Keil (Cambridge, Mass.: MIT Press, 1999). For a popular account with an aptly combinatorial title that multiplies the right sides of analogies 1 and 2 on page 18 and flips the result in a two-term conjunction, see S. Pinker, *Words and Rules: The Ingredients of Language* (New York: Perennial, 2000). And also try the left sides of analogies 1 and 2 to get x and rules. But if x is undefined, then how do rules work? Surely, this can't be calculating.

25. A. L. Benton and O. Spreen, *Embedded Figures Test: Manual of Instructions and Norms* (Victoria, British Columbia: Department of Psychology, University of Victoria, 1969).

26. After Pinker, *Words and Rules*, 6.

27. G. Stein, "Sacred Emily," in *Gertrude Stein: Writings 1903–1932* (New York: Library of America, 1998), 395.

28. S. K. Langer, *Philosophy in a New Key* (Cambridge, Mass.: Harvard University Press, 1957), 95.

29. G. Stiny, "Spatial Relations and Grammars," *Environment and Planning B* 9 (1982): 113–114.

30. I first looked at ways to segment this shape in terms of rotating squares twenty years ago: G. Stiny, "A New Line on Drafting Systems," *Design Computing* 1 (1986): 5–19. Then, I didn't give the exact solution. I relied on units of equal length instead, as I must for all of the other shapes in the series on page 28.

31. H. A. Simon, *The Sciences of the Artificial*, 1st, 2nd, and 3rd eds. (Cambridge, Mass.: MIT Press, 1969, 1981, 1996).

32. *Letters of Euler to a German Princess*, vol. II, ed. H. Hunter (London: H. Murray, 1795), 64.

33. For details, see P. J. Federico, *Descartes on Polyhedra* (New York: Springer, 1982), 65–71.

34. P. Cromwell, 1997, *Polyhedra* (Cambridge: Cambridge University Press, 1997), 191.

35. E. Panofsky, *Albrecht Dürer*, vol. 1 (Princeton, N.J.: Princeton University Press, 1948), 259–260.

36. W. Blake, "To George Cumberland 12 April 1827," in *Blake: Complete Writings*, ed. G. Keynes (London: Oxford University Press, 1974), 878.

37. C. S. Peirce, "How to Make Our Ideas Clear," in *Charles S. Peirce: Selected Writings (Values in a Universe of Chance)*, ed. P. P. Wiener (New York: Dover, 1966), 121–122.

38. Peirce, 123.

39. W. James, *The Principles of Psychology* (Cambridge, Mass.: Harvard University Press, 1981), 956–958.

40. W. James, *Talks to Teachers on Psychology* (Cambridge, Mass.: Harvard University Press, 1983), 27.

41. W. Blake, "Auguries of Innocence," 431.

42. The reference I have in mind is in James's *Pragmatism*. The quotation is recorded in full in part I, page 152.

43. M. Levine, *A Mind at a Time* (New York: Simon and Schuster, 2002), 162.

44. E. J. Langer, *The Power of Mindful Learning* (Reading, Mass.: Addison-Wesley, 1997), 22–28. See also note 20 in part III, and my descriptions of situated learning in part I on pages 133 and 157. Mindful learning and situated learning are easy to confuse when it comes to calculating with shapes and rules—then they're likely different names for the same thing.

45. M. Warnock, *Imagination* (London: Faber and Faber, 1976), 187.

46. W. V. Quine, "Atoms," in *Quiddities: An Intermittently Philosophical Dictionary* (Cambridge, Mass.: Harvard University Press, 1987), 12–16.

47. Quine, 15.

48. Quine, 13–14.

49. For some details, see R. J. Sternberg, *Successful Intelligence: How Practical and Creative Intelligence Determine Success in Life* (New York: Plume, 1997), 53–56. Francis Galton's motto, "Whenever you can, count," is quoted in P. Sacks, *Standardized Minds* (Cambridge, Mass.: Perseus Books, 1999), 18.

50. M. Batty, editorial, *Environment and Planning B: Planning and Design* 26 (1999): 475–476.

51. M. Batty and P. Longley, *Fractal Cities: A Geometry of Form and Function* (London: Academic Press, 1994). B. Hillier and J. Hanson, *The Social Logic of Space* (Cambridge: Cambridge University Press, 1984).

Part I

1. W. James, *The Principles of Psychology* (Cambridge, Mass.: Harvard University Press, 1981), 956–966.

2. James, *Principles*, 754.

3. James, *Principles*, 1250.

4. W. James, *Some Problems of Philosophy* (Cambridge, Mass.: Harvard University Press, 1979), 94.

5. W. James, *Essays in Radical Empiricism* (Cambridge, Mass.: Harvard University Press, 1976), 121.

6. W. James, *Pragmatism* (Cambridge, Mass.: Harvard University Press, 1975), 121.

7. W. James, *Talks to Teachers on Psychology* (Cambridge, Mass.: Harvard University Press, 1983), 97, 107.

8. R. Narasimhan, "Picture Languages," in *Picture Language Machines*, ed. S. Kaneff (London: Academic Press, 1970), 9–10.

9. C. Alexander, *The Timeless Way of Building* (New York: Oxford University Press, 1979). "Timeless" is Platonic in matching ways—first in terms of Alexander's aims, and then in terms of the syntactic devices he recommends to achieve them.

10. I. Sutherland, "Structure in Drawings and the Hidden-Surface Problem," in *Reflections on Computer Aids to Design and Architecture*, ed. N. Negroponte (New York: Petrocelli/Charter, 1975), 75.

11. H. A. Simon, *The Sciences of the Artificial*, 2nd ed. (Cambridge, Mass.: MIT Press, 1981), 92, 153–154, 186–187, 189–190, 217–219.

12. J. McCarthy, "Circumscription: A Form of Non-monotonic Reasoning," *Artificial Intelligence* 13 (1980): 29–30.

13. McCarthy, 32.

14. M. Minsky, *The Society of Mind* (New York: Simon and Schuster, 1985), 134. Chapter 13—"Seeing and Believing"—contains more, notably in 13.3 and 13.4 in Minsky's *Tractatus*-like numbering scheme. Children are apt to use a single shape in multiple ways, for example, the circle in the drawing

is the head and torso of a person. The ability to count parts properly that blocks this kind of ambiguity matures later. R. Arnheim, *Art and Visual Perception* (Berkeley: University of California Press, 1971), 188–190, notes that these "tadpole" figures of our early years are "misnamed," although not as *"hommes têtards"* in French and *"Kopffüssler"* in German. It's good to be clear, and to say what you mean when you can. But whatever they're called, tadpoles look like tadpoles, and all sorts of other creepy-crawlies. (Tadpoles work like stars—my tadpole includes four bugs and maybe more.) Putting heads and torsos in circles and making mistakes with names use embedding in pretty much the same way. Minsky's moral rings true—cognitive development (counting) circumscribes seeing, so that what's left out looks wrong. Is it any wonder "old fogyism" is hard to avoid? (Education is important, too. For Ludwig Wittgenstein, training is why we read figures correctly when we calculate, and for Herbert Simon, children's drawings lack the hierarchic order in the pictures of trained artists.)

15. M. Minsky, "A Framework for Representing Knowledge," in *The Psychology of Computer Vision*, ed. P. H. Winston (New York: McGraw-Hill, 1975), 256, 258, 275.

16. T. Winograd and F. Flores, *Understanding Computers and Cognition* (Norwood, N.J.: Ablex, 1986), 97–98.

17. H.-G. Gadamer, *Truth and Method* (New York: Seabury Press, 1975), 236.

18. R. Sokolowski, *Husserlian Meditations* (Evanston, Ill.: Northwestern University Press, 1974), 163.

19. G.-C. Rota, *Indiscrete Thoughts* (Boston: Birkhauser, 1997), 180, 285.

20. M. Merleau-Ponty, *Phenomenology of Perception* (London: Routledge and Kegan Paul, 1962), xix.

21. R. W. Emerson, "Self-Reliance," in *The Essential Writings of Ralph Waldo Emerson*, ed. B. Atkinson (New York: Modern Library, 2000), 138.

22. J. Barzun, *A Stroll with William James* (New York: Harper and Row, 1983), 54.

23. N. Goodman, *Languages of Art* (Indianapolis: Hackett, 1976 [1985]), 142–143.

24. J. Dewey, *How We Think*, vol. 6 of *John Dewey: The Middle Works, 1899–1924* (Carbondale: Southern Illinois University Press, 1978), 267.

25. Barzun, 282–283.

26. Barzun, 282.

27. L. Wittgenstein, *Remarks on the Foundations of Mathematics* (Cambridge, Mass.: MIT Press, 1967), 189e.

28. W. F. Hanks, foreword to *Situated Learning: Legitimate Peripheral Participation*, by J. Lave and E. Wenger (Cambridge: Cambridge University Press, 1991), 17. In the same vein, there's mindful learning in the introduction, page 56, and note 20 in part III.

29. H. Putnam, *The Many Faces of Realism* (LaSalle, Ill.: Open Court, 1987), 19, 20, 29–30.

30. R. Rorty, *Contingency, Irony, and Solidarity* (Cambridge: Cambridge University Press, 1989), 78.

Part II

1. G. Stiny and J. Gips, "Shape Grammars and the Generative Specification of Painting and Sculpture," in *Information Processing '71*, ed. C. V. Frieman (Amsterdam: North-Holland, 1972), 1460–1465.

2. G. Stiny, *Pictorial and Formal Aspects of Shape and Shape Grammars* (Basel: Birkhauser, 1975).

3. P. Klee, *Pedagogical Sketchbook*, trans. S. Moholy-Nagy (New York: F. A. Praeger, 1953), 16–17.

4. G. Stiny, "Two Exercises in Formal Composition," *Environment and Planning B* 3 (1976): 187–210.

5. G. Stiny, "Ice Ray: A Note on the Generation of Chinese Lattice Designs," *Environment and Planning B* 4 (1977): 89–98. Schemas as I frame them now with twin variables and predicates were first in G. Stiny, "How to Calculate with Shapes," in *Formal Engineering Design Synthesis*, ed. E. K. Antonsson and J. Cagan (Cambridge: Cambridge University Press, 2001), 48–50.

6. J. Tchérnikhov, *Construction des formes d'architecture et de machines* (Leningrad: Société des Architectes, 1931), 46, 47.

7. G. Stiny, "Kindergarten Grammars: Designing with Froebel's Building Gifts," *Environment and Planning B* 7 (1980): 409–462.

8. T. W. Knight, *Transformations in Design* (Cambridge: Cambridge University Press, 1994).

9. T. W. Knight, "Shape Grammars," *Environment and Planning B: Planning and Design*, 25th Anniversary Issue (1998): 86–91. The poverty of syntax in music, that is to say, segmentation in terms

of lowest-level constituents from a given vocabulary, is noted elsewhere without doing anything about it in a noncombinatorial way. This seems to be outside of what's allowed—embedding with dimension greater than zero is never an option. Moreover, lowest-level constituents are a problem for education in music and design.

It is not surprising, then, that students, often those who are best at improvising and playing by ear (as well as those who are best at improvising when making and fixing mechanical gadgets), are sometimes baffled and discouraged when we ask them to start out by listening for, looking at, and identifying the smallest, isolated objects. For in stressing isolated, decontextualized objects to which our units of description refer—to measure and name objects in spite of where they happen and their changing structural function—we are asking students to put aside their most intimate ways of knowing.

This sounds pretty good. Seeing and hearing are personal and idiosyncratic, especially in creative activity. Only it's just a dodge that ends with "tuneblocks"—computer icons to click and play melodic motives that "function for beginning students in their initial composing projects as both units of perception and units of work." It's musical Lego with thematic units like walls, windows, and doors, something less than spatial relations and set grammars—ugh! (The shape

and its successors illustrate the inverse problem when squares are "pictureblocks," and I try to divide their sides into segments or "notes" in terms of what I see and do. This can be hard—it seems notes are wrong whichever way you go. Then there's another kind of inverse that's difficult, too. After pictureblocks combine, or notes, for that matter, they may not be uniquely retrievable. I showed this in part I for given vocabularies of shapes.) These comments on music are based on two references I copied from Knight's class handouts. For the quotations and an upbeat approach to teaching, see J. S. Bamberger, "Developing Musical Structures: A Reflective Practicum," *MIT Faculty Newsletter*, 17, 1 (2004): 8–9. And for the sad relationship between language and computer music from an aficionado of the latter, see D. Cope, *Virtual Music* (Cambridge, Mass.: MIT Press, 2001), 323–324. Cope gives a musical rendition of Benjamin Whorf's linguistic segmentation. But this is a vain standard in an extensive repertoire once basic elements have dimension greater than zero. There's neither vocabulary nor syntax for shapes and rules. Units of perception and work are automatically the same when I calculate with shapes. What you see is what you get without finer divisions as rules are tried. Size doesn't matter when there's nothing independent of what I see and do now to measure and name, or even better, to count. Units are always in context. They're big and small and anything in between, fusing and dividing anywhere. Units are whatever I want them to be whenever I go on. I can see and do more than words allow. Language doesn't begin to exhaust seeing, or calculating with shapes and rules. (And note, too, that finding rules to calculate with shapes—learning as William James puts it—isn't like computer programming. Writing code may depend on instructions that are individually too small to convey meaningful actions.)

10. G. Stiny, "The Algebras of Design," *Research in Engineering Design* 2 (1991): 171–181.

11. G. Stiny, "Spatial Relations and Grammars," *Environment and Planning B* 9 (1982): 113–114.

12. G. Stiny, "Weights," *Environment and Planning B: Planning and Design* 19 (1992): 413–430.

13. T. W. Knight, "Color Grammars: Designing with Lines and Colors," *Environment and Planning B: Planning and Design* 16 (1989): 417–449. See also N. Goodman, *The Structure of Appearance* (Indianapolis: Bobbs-Merrill, 1966).

14. G. Stiny, "A Note on the Description of Designs," *Environment and Planning B* 8 (1981): 257–267. G. Stiny, "What is a Design?" *Environment and Planning B: Planning and Design* 17 (1990): 97–103.

15. G. Stiny, "Shape Rules: Closure, Continuity, and Emergence," *Environment and Planning B: Planning and Design* 21 (1994): s49–s78. G. Stiny, "Useless Rules," *Environment and Planning B: Planning and Design* 23 (1996): 235–237. G. Stiny, "How to Calculate with Shapes," 50–61.

16. S. C. Chase, "Modeling Designs with Shape Algebras and Formal Logic" (PhD dissertation, University of California, Los Angeles, 1996). S. C. Chase, "Shape Grammars: From Mathematical Model to Computer Implementation," *Environment and Planning B: Planning and Design* 16 (1989): 215–242.

17. C. F. Earl, "Shape Boundaries," *Environment and Planning B: Planning and Design* 24 (1997): 668–687. R. Krishnamurti and C. F. Earl, "Shape Recognition in Three Dimensions," *Environment and Planning B: Planning and Design* 19 (1992): 585–603. I. Jowers and C. F. Earl, "Classifying Shape Algebras by Types of Elements and Space" (paper, The Open University, Milton Keynes, U.K., 2005).

18. T. W. Knight, "Computing with Emergence," *Environment and Planning B: Planning and Design* 30 (2003): 125–155. T. W. Knight, "Computing with Ambiguity," *Environment and Planning B: Planning and Design* 30 (2003): 165–180. For some history, see T. W. Knight, "either/or → and," *Environment and Planning B: Planning and Design* 30 (2003): 327–338, but also, with a complementary slant, P. Galison, "Aufbau/Bauhaus: Logical Positivism and Architectural Modernism," *Critical Inquiry* 16 (1990): 709–752. Novel algebras and ways of calculating are always welcome, yet an open invitation needn't mean familiar algebras and ways of calculating are incomplete. I believe many of Knight's speculative proposals are also covered in the schemas I show in part III. Different ways of doing the same thing are appealing in different ways. At least, there's a chance for an algebraic type of ambiguity.

19. R. Krishnamurti, "The Arithmetic of Shapes," *Environment and Planning B* 7 (1980): 463–484. R. Krishnamurti, "The Construction of Shapes," *Environment and Planning B* 8 (1981): 5–40. R. Krishnamurti, "The Maximal Representation of a Shape," *Environment and Planning B: Planning and Design* 19 (1992): 267–288. R. Krishnamurti, "The Arithmetic of Maximal Planes," *Environment and Planning B: Planning and Design* 19 (1992): 431–464.

20. D. Krstic, "Algebras and Grammars for Shapes and Their Boundaries," *Environment and Planning B: Planning and Design* 28 (2001): 151–162. D. Krstic, "Computing with Analyzed Shapes," in *Design Computing and Cognition '04*, ed. J. Gero (Dordrecht: Kluwer Academic, 2004), 397–416.

21. L. March, "Babbage's Miraculous Computation Revisited," *Environment and Planning B: Planning and Design* 23 (1996): 369–376.

22. M. A. Tapia, "From Shape to Style" (PhD dissertation, University of Toronto, 1996).

23. G. A. Miller, "Information Theory in Psychology," in *The Study of Information: Interdisciplinary Messages*, ed. F. Machlup and U. Mansfield (New York: John Wiley and Sons, 1983), 495–496.

24. The "no ambiguity" sign was sent to faculty and PhD students in the Computer Science and Artificial Intelligence Laboratory (CSAIL) at MIT. According to one of the students, "I got the sign from a guy who claimed to have 'solved AI' thus removing all the ambiguity in the field/world.... I found the no ambiguity sign to be silly/fun and reusable at the same time, because a great chunk of our research is about getting rid of ambiguity that crops up during sketch recognition." The sketch recognition language is described in T. Hammond and R. Davis, "LADDER: A Language to Describe Drawing, Display, and Editing in Sketch Recognition," in *IJCAI–03: Proceedings of the Eighteenth International Joint Conference on Artificial Intelligence, Acapulco, Mexico, August 9–15, 2003*, ed. G. Gottlob and T. Walsh (San Francisco: Morgan Kaufmann, 2003), 461–467. The authors mention shape grammars, albeit in their aboriginal form, as "shape description languages." Scholarship can have some funny results. The gap between what you think you're doing and saying about it, and how others understand and use this, can be huge—and who's to say who's right? It's easy to be wrong about meaning, whether or not you're the source. The only thing to do is to keep on talking, and seeing and drawing, so that meaning can change. Change, of course, is what CSAIL is about. It's proud of its accomplishments and sure that it can do more— "[We] have a history of daring innovation and visionary research which change the way the rest of the world works. We think this is how it ought to be, and are organizing [the *Dangerous Ideas Seminar Series*] to help stimulate people to think big." Gerald Jay Sussman was one of the "instigators." He enlarged on this theme in the title of his seminar on March 17, 2005: "Engineering as an Intellectual Revolution." And what he proposed was indeed "intellectual"—

The key idea is the development of engineering "languages" that allow us to separate concerns in design. Such languages provide ways of expressing modularity and isolation between modules. They provide means of composition that allow the construction of compound systems from independently-specified and implemented parts. They allow characterization of both structure and function, and how function is determined by and implemented in terms of structure. They provide black-box abstractions that allow one to specify the behavior of a composition independently of the implementation.

Computer scientists like to divide things into independent units to make problems combinatorial. Language is vocabulary and syntax, and an engineering language uses both to fix structure and function. Compositionality precedes design—what a compound system does depends on its constituent modules (parts), what they do separately, and how they're put together. The shape grammarist agrees that this is a dangerous idea—before you know it, design is impossible. Sussman, to be sure, has other hazards in mind. Once-novel ideas may be dangerous because they're revolutionary when they're tried in new places. Today, compositionality is key in biological engineering—MIT's "Registry of Standard Biological Parts" holds an amazing future. And compositionality works elsewhere outside of engineering—for example, there's "the timeless way of building" in Christopher Alexander's pattern language. But what does any of this add to Franz Reuleaux or Herbert Simon? What is it about how we're trained to think that makes both design and calculating combinatorial? Neither has to be. Still, there's no telling where a big idea might go, and Sussman's big idea is no exception. Computers are used everywhere, so perhaps CSAIL will "change the way the rest of the world works" in art and design—but only if there's nothing to see.

25. There are other options in computer science, for example, R. A. Brooks, "Intelligence without Representation," *Artificial Intelligence* 47 (1991): 139–159. Brooks shares the shape grammarist's distaste for representation—"explicit representations and models of the world simply get in the way. It turns out to be better to use the world as its own model." This is true for shapes, and is the reason for embedding and maximal elements. But the focus is elsewhere in AI—"[To segment

the world into meaningful units] is the essence of intelligence and the hard part of the problems being solved. Under the current scheme the abstraction is done by the researchers leaving little for the AI programs to do but search. A truly intelligent program would study the photograph, perform the abstraction and solve the problem." Is it any wonder that Brooks gives up on the current scheme and search, when parts of shapes—what's in the photograph—are resolved only in some sort of precalculating? "[This abstraction] is the essence of intelligence" and of calculating with shapes and rules, too. (Visual experience—in fact, photography—was also decisive for Susanne Langer when she abandoned vocabulary and syntax for presentational forms of symbolism.) Brooks appeals to perception and action (seeing and doing) to make autonomous mobile agents or "Creatures." They segment the world and change it. The analogy goes like this

Creatures : world(s) :: rules : shape(s)

although the idea was clear to C. S. Peirce (page 55) 125 years ago. He thought Creatures were creatures of habit. Yet something is amiss. Creatures act like cellular automata in that "there emerges, [only] in the eye of an [outside] observer, a coherent pattern of behavior." Embedding and transformations, and the ensuing ambiguity, aren't part of perception for Creatures. Intelligence caps a recursive ascent, but what kind of intelligence is unaware of itself and what it does? It's pretty much the same drawing the three lines on page 2 and not seeing the triangle, or rotating three triangles in the series on page 296 and not trying two. Why should perception stop? Then everything adds up without making anything new. Action is senseless when there's no way to see what's going on. (In fact, this is the same kind of problem I had earlier in note 9 with music and Bamberger's units of perception and units of work. The distinction is a hobbling artifact of representation and another reason to try something new. Units fail for perception whether seeing or hearing, and when there's creative work to do. But this is never a problem with shapes and rules—then one "size" fits all.)

26. A. N. Whitehead, *Process and Reality* (New York: Free Press, 1978), 294–297.

27. H. Leonard and N. Goodman, "The Calculus of Individuals and Its Uses," *Journal of Symbolic Logic* 5 (1940): 45. See also N. Goodman, *The Structure of Appearance*, 46–56.

28. A. Tarski, "Foundations of the Geometry of Solids," in *Logic, Semantics, Metamathematics*, trans. J. H. Woodger (Indianapolis: Hackett, 1983), 24–29.

29. P. Simons, *Parts: A Study in Ontology* (Oxford: Clarendon Press, 1987).

30. N. Goodman and W. V. Quine, "Steps toward a Constructive Nominalism," in *Problems and Projects,* ed. N. Goodman (Indianapolis: Bobbs-Merrill, 1972), 173–198.

31. A. Tarski, "On the Foundations of Boolean Algebra," in *Logic, Semantics, Metamathematics*, 333, fn. 1.

32. A. A. G. Requicha, "Representations of Rigid Solids: Theory, Methods, and Systems," *ACM Computer Surveys* 12 (1980): 437–464.

33. M. H. Stone, "The Theory of Representations for Boolean Algebras," *Transactions of the American Mathematical Society* 40 (1936): 37–111.

34. Earl, "Shape Boundaries." For a scattered but more detailed account of the same material, see H. Rasiowa and R. Sikorski, *The Mathematics of Metamathematics*, 3rd ed. (Warsaw: Panstwowe Wydawnictwo Naukowe, 1970).

35. G. Stiny, "Boolean Algebras for Shapes and Individuals," *Environment and Planning B: Planning and Design* 20 (1993): 359–362.

36. M. Gross and A. Lentin, *Introduction to Formal Grammars* (New York: Springer-Verlag, 1970).

37. J. Gips and G. Stiny, "Production Systems and Grammars: A Uniform Characterization," *Environment and Planning B* 7 (1980): 399–408.

38. N. Chomsky, "Formal Properties of Grammars," in *Handbook of Mathematical Psychology*, vol. 2, ed. R. D. Luce, R. R. Bush, and E. Galanter (New York: John Wiley and Sons, 1963), 323–418.

39. S. Wolfram, *A New Kind of Science* (Champaign, Ill.: Wolfram Media, 2002). In particular, see pp. 25–26 for a preliminary discussion of the fractal pattern shown on my page 274.

40. Wolfram, 880.

41. L. B. Alberti, *On the Art of Building in Ten Books*, trans. J. Rykwert, N. Leach, and R. Tavernor (Cambridge, Mass.: MIT Press, 1988), 7.

42. Alberti, 23.

43. W. James, *The Principles of Psychology* (Cambridge, Mass.: Harvard University Press, 1981), 957–958.

44. F. Reuleaux, *The Kinematics of Machinery*, trans. and ed. A. B. W. Kennedy (New York: Dover, 1963), 3, 20.

45. Reuleaux, 531–532. Spatial relations and rules in my "Kindergarten Grammars" work in much the same way as pairs and chains do in indirect synthesis.

46. S. Pinker, *The Blank Slate* (New York: Viking, 2002), 78–83.

47. Anyone—visual or not—can generate new things. Perhaps that's why artists and designers avoid "rules"—combining units recursively isn't enough. It takes embedding to be creative. Recursion and embedding—as technical devices—define creativity when they're used to calculate. Then rules let you see what you're doing and use what you see.

Part III

1. "Seventeenth Day, Friday 27th April 1883, Mr. Bernhard Samuelson, M. P., F. R. S., in the Chair," in *Second Report of the Royal Commissioners on Technical Instruction* (London: Royal Commission on Technical Instruction, 1884), 502. For a little more on Walter Smith's founding role in American art education and later changes in the subject, see H. Green, "Walter Smith: The Forgotten Man," *Art Education*, 19, 1 (1966): 3–9, and C. D. Gaitskell, A. Hurwitz, and M. Day, *Children and Their Art: Methods for the Elementary School*, 4th ed. (New York: Harcourt Brace Jovanovich, 1982), 33–44. (Copying was routine in nineteenth-century art education—famously, in Charles Bargue's *Cours de dessin* followed by van Gogh and Picasso. For a fresh take on Bargue's pedagogy, see E. J. Langer, *On Becoming an Artist* [New York: Ballantine Books, 2005], 239. Shapes and rules may include the twenty-first-century drawing lessons Langer wants, "based on mastering rendering the ineffable through subtle distortions rather than through exact replication." In fact, her painting on the book jacket shows what shapes and rules do—two figures occlude a third, or are they another way? Look for yourself. And Langer, 191, puts this in words, too. "Can you draw a

reasonably straight line? . . . Can you recognize different colors? If so, all that is left to be able to draw or paint is to learn how to see." This implies an algebra of shapes—basic elements and weights, embedding, transformations, etc.—and rules to calculate.) The flip side of Smith's kind of copying was tried in twentieth-century art, when copying was copying what's new and not what's really there. Of course, the two are likely the same, so long as ambiguity is something to use. (What's what in art tallies with the phenomenal what on pages 142–143.) It's easy to see that Richard Mutt's *Fountain* of 1917 is copying—"plagiarism, a plain piece of plumbing." But as soon as Marcel Duchamp saw his urinal, it was a readymade. (This kind of change is universal, yet it's easy to miss and thereby creative—perhaps also in Gertrude Stein's line " . . . a rose . . . ." Langer, 174–175, may not hear it when she explains how rote knowing makes us blind.) Alfred Stieglitz's documentary photograph of *Fountain* opened the second and final issue of *The Blind Man* (New York: May 1917), edited by Duchamp, Beatrice Wood, and Henri-Pierre Roché. (Smith would have approved of this picture as a frontispiece for one of his instructional-drawing books— an exact copy of an industrial object!) And the unsigned editorial on the facing page was just as clear.

Whether Mr. Mutt with his own hands made the fountain or not has no importance. He CHOSE it. He took an ordinary article of life, placed it so that its useful significance disappeared under the new title and point of view—created a new thought for that object.

In one way or another, "CHOOSING" has been standard in art, including the avant-garde, and art education for years. It's about seeing again, now and as I go on. What's changed is that this is what happens with shapes and rules. They show how art is calculating, and offer an effective pedagogy. (We were too young for Miss H—— to tell us about Mutt, although I read about Duchamp's antics on my own and saw *Nude Descending a Staircase (No. 2)*. Duchamp never tired of making copies. In fact, he authorized a number of different versions of *Fountain*, and colored in a full-scale photograph of his painting for the collector Walter Arensberg. A schema $b(x) \to x$ or $b(x) \to x + b(x)$, or something close applies to a photograph to add colors. But better yet, there's plenty of copying in Duchamp's nude(s) using rules in the schema $x \to x + x'$. This makes it easy to explore movement or any series of alternative views in a sum. Paul Klee's palm-leaf umbrella suggests as much with less fanfare, and so does Jacob Tchérnikhov's drawing on page 278 in which quadrilaterals are copied vertex to edge one either outside or inside another—triangles optional. There's always more to see and do, both copying and not.)

2. G. Stiny and J. Gips, "Shape Grammars and the Generative Specification of Painting and Sculpture," in *Information Processing '71*, ed. C. V. Frieman (Amsterdam: North-Holland, 1972), 1460–1465. G. Stiny, *Pictorial and Formal Aspects of Shape and Shape Grammars* (Basel: Birkhauser, 1975).

3. G. Stiny, "Ice Ray: A Note on the Generation of Chinese Lattice Designs," *Environment and Planning B* 4 (1977): 89–98. What others say about shapes and rules when they're used to produce designs is likely to take the linguistic turn that the term "shape grammar" implies—

Architects and environmental planners, for instance, have used "[shape] grammars" to generate new "sentences," novel spatial structures that are intuitively acceptable instances of the genre concerned. . . . The decorative arts have received similar attention: traditional Chinese lattice designs have been described by a computer algorithm, which generates the seemingly irregular patterns called "ice-rays" as well as the more obviously regular forms.

The ice ray example shows that a rigorous analysis of a conceptual space can uncover hidden regularities, and so increase—not merely codify—our aesthetic understanding of the style. . . . It shows which aspects are relatively fundamental (like Euclid's axioms in geometry, or *NP* and *VP* in syntax), and how certain features are constrained by others.

M. A. Boden, *Dimensions of Creativity* (Cambridge, Mass.: MIT Press, 1994), 86–87. This can be harmless, perhaps as above, but usually ends with a closed definition of style that stops what shapes and rules do.

4. Schemas were first defined in terms of a pair of variables in G. Stiny, "How to Calculate with Shapes," in *Formal Engineering Design Synthesis*, ed. E. K. Antonsson and J. Cagan (Cambridge: Cambridge University Press, 2001), 48–50.

5. G. Stiny and W. J. Mitchell, "The Palladian Grammar," *Environment and Planning B* 5 (1978): 5–18. G. Stiny and W. J. Mitchell, "Counting Palladian Plans," *Environment and Planning B* 5 (1978): 189–198. G. Stiny and J. Gips, "An Evaluation of Palladian Plans," *Environment and Planning B* 5 (1978): 199–206.

6. G. Stiny, "A Note on the Description of Designs," *Environment and Planning B* 8 (1981): 257–267.

7. G. Stiny, *Pictorial and Formal Aspects of Shape and Shape Grammars*.

8. G. Stiny, "Two Exercises in Formal Composition," *Environment and Planning B* 3 (1976): 187–210. G. Stiny, "Kindergarten Grammars: Designing with Froebel's Building Gifts," *Environment and Planning B* 7 (1980): 409–462.

9. P. Klee, *The Thinking Eye*, ed. J. Spiller (New York: George Wittenborn, 1961), 71, 98.

10. D. S. Dye, *A Grammar of Chinese Lattice* (Cambridge, Mass.: Harvard University Press, 1949), 17, 56, 186, 298–300, 303–304, 308, 340, 424.

11. A. Palladio, *The Four Books of Architecture* (New York: Dover, 1965).

12. J. S. Ackerman, *Palladio* (New York: Penguin Books, 1966), 36, 65, 160.

13. L. March, *Architectonics of Humanism: Essays on Number in Architecture* (New York: Academy Editions, 1998).

14. T. W. Knight, *Transformations in Design* (Cambridge: Cambridge University Press, 1994).

15. J. P. Duarte, "Customizing Mass Housing: A Discursive Grammar for Siza's Malagueira Houses" (PhD dissertation, Massachusetts Institute of Technology, 2001).

16. A. Li, "A Shape Grammar for Teaching the Architectural Style of the Yingzao Fashi" (PhD dissertation, Massachusetts Institute of Technology, 2001).

17. G. Stiny and J. Gips, *Algorithmic Aesthetics* (Berkeley: University of California Press, 1978).

18. L. March, "The Logic of Design and the Question of Value," in *The Architecture of Form*, ed. L. March (Cambridge: Cambridge University Press, 1976), 1–40.

19. M. Ozkar, "Uncertainties of Reason: Pragmatist Plurality in Basic Design Education" (PhD dissertation, Massachusetts Institute of Technology, 2004), 65.

20. Ozkar, 70. This takes "mindful learning"—I mentioned it in the introduction on page 56: E. J. Langer, *The Power of Mindful Learning* (Reading, Mass.: Addison-Wesley, 1997), 23, 108, 114. And flipping Langer does more. In spite of her jaundiced view of calculating—"In a [mindful state], basic skills and information guide our behavior in the present, rather than run it like a computer program."—her five-point description of mindfulness is another way to talk about shapes and rules. Ambiguity is the reason why. It implies mindfulness, even when design is copying and the

artist's hand is lost in impersonal line drawings on a computer. These are the things Langer considers:

(1) openness to novelty; (2) alertness to distinction; (3) sensitivity to different contexts; (4) implicit, if not explicit, awareness of multiple perspectives; and (5) orientation in the present.

My twin formulas for rule application guarantee number 5—"orientation in the present." Shapes divide and fuse every time a rule is tried, so that all past distinctions are lost in the present. What I see and do is what I see and do now, independent of anything that may have happened before. Parts vanish without a trace—they're gone and forgotten. Identities in the schema $x \rightarrow x$ are nice examples of this—try them as often as you like and see. But why stop when Langer's four preceding points describe shapes and rules, too? And maybe there's more in my copies of Langer's copies of a few lines from the concluding part of William James's third essay in *The Meaning of Truth*. Nit-picking here isn't idle. Langer first quotes James so—

Owing to the fact that all experience is a process, no point of view can ever be *the* last one. Every one is insufficient and off its balance, and responsible to later points of view than itself.

—and then she quotes another passage to start a creative (design) process with rules in schemas like $x \rightarrow t(x)$ and $x \rightarrow x'$. There's James, then Langer's copy in her book that distorts this in a subtle way, and then my own copy of her copy that changes it

The standard [for what's right] perpetually grows up endogenously inside the web of experience.

and also a third copy ends my second paragraph on page 58. What James says may seem more important than how it's copied, although copying what he says shows how it works. James sets the original standard with his own words, but this isn't rigid. Its structure varies as it's copied. The standard evolves and shifts—refined and distilled or changed entirely. And the preceding sentence is a new copy of James in the same ongoing process. (It's funny how copying is used, and not just to design. In the Turing test for artificial intelligence, calculating machines are supposed to imitate you and me. But my way of copying with shapes and rules, and a shifting standard may alter this. At least copying—again in my way—allows for novelty and the reasoning it implies. All of this turns on the question I asked in the early pages of this book—what would calculating be like if Turing were a painter?) A permanent structure is an unproductive stricture. That's because the letters u and i are side by side—inverse translations on my computer keyboard. Taking orthography too seriously only brakes/breaks the free flow of experience. I can derive the palindrome *ababaababa* or spell it from memory to rotate the three squares in the shape

but does anyone really believe this happens before I erase and copy the squares, and what about other parts of the shape and its successors with five squares, seven, etc. if everything is spelled out ahead of time? Perhaps I can compile and use a dictionary of shapes with variants that are spelled differently. But then are some parts of shapes missing? How do shapes look? What an awful mess without embedding and mindful (visual) calculating! It's lucky spelling is so easy to ignore, at least for scofflaws like James. (On James's distaste for "the authority of prior use" and "obsolete verbal ritual," namely, spelling—"he didn't even like the fact that everyone was expected to spell the same way"—see L. Menand, *The Metaphysical Club* [New York: Farrar, Straus, and Giroux, 2001], 88–89.) In fact, James tries copying, and our separate versions of it match exactly where they should. Langer's two quotations follow a few pages after this:

The essence in any case would not be the copying, but the enrichment of the previous world.

James and Mr. Mutt agree—they opt for novelty and what's new to add to what's real. There's more to copying than correct spelling and rote recitation. Structure isn't fixed—what you see is what you get. (Copying may also reinforce Langer's observation that many of us miss letters and words when we read. It seems that familiar ways of looking temper the results on embedded figures given on page 52. Keeping your eyes wide open for surprising possibilities may not be that easy—novelty takes work and for shapes, this means calculating.) The coincidence with James is rich indeed, as my topologies show when they're defined retrospectively. Langer's first quotation—"Owing to the fact that . . ."—and mine on copying are perfect in this regard. Rules aren't locked in a definite past. They're tested in a vague and ambiguous future that goes on in a new way. The past is different in response. A series of topologies is merely what works in the present—it's history ready to change. Computer programs are like shapes. They're worth a second look. Mindful calculating makes pretty good sense.

21. U. Flemming, "The Secret of the Casa Guiliani Frigerio," *Environment and Planning B* 8 (1981): 87–96. U. Flemming, "More than the Sum of Parts: The Grammar of Queen Anne Houses," *Environment and Planning B: Planning and Design* 14 (1987): 323–350. U. Flemming, "A Pattern Book for Shadyside" (technical report, Department of Architecture, Carnegie Mellon University, Pittsburgh, 1987). T. W. Knight, "The Generation of Hepplewhite-style Chair Back Designs," *Environment and Planning B* 7 (1980): 227–238. T. W. Knight, "The Forty-one Steps," *Environment and Planning B* 8 (1981): 97–114. T. W. Knight, *Transformations in Design*.

Index

A + E = AE, 93

ababaababa, 25–28, 391n2, 398–399n9, 405–406n20

Abbatt building bricks, 304

ABC's, 41

abduction, 389

abstract symbol systems, 274, 308

academicism, 354

accountability, 57–58, 132, 381

Ackerman, J. S., 388, 405n12

addition: shapes versus symbols, 33–35

aesthetic measure, 10–11, 19, 39, 50, 364, 389, 394n14

aesthetics, 50, 157, 341, 354, 368, 394n15, 404–405n3

Alberti, L. B., 214, 215, 251, 308, 391–392n2, 403n41

Alexander, C., 65, 156, 392n3, 392–393n6, 397n9, 401n24

Alexandra, 42–44, 50

algebra of shapes

  composite, 224–225, 288–291

  U_{ij}, 180–196

  V_{ij}, 217–219

  W_{ij}, 219–224

algebraic ambiguity, 400n18

algebraic operations

  complement, 205–206

  difference, 188

  product, 192

  sum, 185

  symmetric difference, 192

  transformations, 194–195

algorithm for

  difference, 191–192, 276

  maximal lines, 186–188, 276

  parts, 184, 276

  rule application, 276

  symmetry, 262

  sum, 186–188, 276

  transformations, 260–265, 276

Alice, 50

ambiguity, 2, 47, 65, 161–163, and anywhere else you look

ambiguity = noise, 161, 305

analogy for

  basic elements and regions, 211

  designs and sentences, 18

  discursive and presentational forms of symbolism, 18

  intellectual and physical analysis, 125

  mappings of shapes and sets, 285

  shape grammar and generative grammar, 18

  shapes and sentences, 21

  $t(A)$ and A, 233

  $t(A)$ and sagacity, 233

  $t(A) \leq C$ and sagacity, 233

  visual expression and verbal expression, 7

  visual reasoning and visual calculating, 62

  x and member, 285

analysis, 6, 21–30, 47, 144, 163

analysis and rules, 84–88, 106–112, 282–301

anatomical and morphological method, 125

animation, 4

architects, 159, 341–342, 354, 392n3, 404n3

architecture, 54, 58, 134, 214, 275, 340–341, 341–168, 389, 392n3, 392–393n6

Arensberg, W., 403–404n1

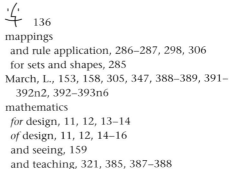